C000051335

HARDPRESS.NET
HOME OF HARD-TO-FIND BOOKS

The Works of the Late Edgar Allan Poe:
Poems and Tales
by Edgar Allan Poe

Address:
HardPress
8345 NW 66TH ST #2561
MIAMI FL 33166-2626
USA
Email: info@hardpress.net

THE WORKS

OF THE LATE

EDGAR ALLAN POE

WITH

A Memoir
BY RUFUS WILMOT GRISWOLD

AND

NOTICES OF HIS LIFE AND GENIUS
BY N. P. WILLIS AND J. R. LOWELL

IN FOUR VOLUMES

II.
POEMS AND TALES

NEW YORK:
BLAKEMAN & MASON
1859

PREFACE TO THE POEMS.

~~~~~~~~~~~~~~~~~~~~~~~~

These trifles are collected and republished chiefly with a view to their redemption from the many improvements to which they have been subjected while going at random " the rounds of the press." I am naturally anxious that what I have written should circulate as I wrote it, if it circulate at all. In defence of my own taste, nevertheless, it is incumbent upon me to say that I think nothing in this volume of much value to the public, or very creditable to myself. Events not to be controlled have prevented me from making, at any time, any serious effort in what, under happier circumstances, would have been the field of my choice. With me poetry has been not a purpose, but a passion; and the passions should be held in reverence; they must not—they cannot at will be excited, with an eye to the paltry compensations, or the more paltry commendations of mankind.

<div align="right">

E. A. P.

</div>

CONTENTS OF VOL. II.

THE POETIC PRINCIPLE.

In speaking of the Poetic Principle, I have no design to be either thorough or profound. While discussing, very much at random, the essentiality of what we call Poetry, my principal purpose will be to cite for consideration, some few of those minor English or American poems which best suit my own taste, or which, upon my own fancy, have left the most definite impression. By "minor poems" I mean, of course, poems of little length. And here, in the beginning, permit me to say a few words in regard to a somewhat peculiar principle, which, whether rightfully or wrongfully, has always had its influence in my own critical estimate of the poem. I hold that a long poem does not exist. I maintain that the phrase, "a long poem," is simply a flat contradiction in terms.

I need scarcely observe that a poem deserves its title only inasmuch as it excites, by elevating the soul. The value of the poem is in the ratio of this elevating excitement. But all excitements are, through a psychal necessity, transient. That degree of excitement which would entitle a poem to be so called at all, cannot be sustained throughout a composition of any great length. After the lapse of half an hour, at the very utmost, it flags—fails—a revulsion ensues—and then the poem is, in effect, and in fact, no longer such.

There are, no doubt, many who have found difficulty in reconciling the critical dictum that the "Paradise Lost" is to be devoutly admired throughout, with the absolute impossibility of maintaining for it, during perusal, the amount of enthusiasm which that critical dictum would demand. This great work, in fact, is to be regarded as poetical, only when, losing sight of that vital requisite in all works of Art, Unity, we view it merely as a series of minor poems. If, to preserve its Unity—its totality of effect or impression—we read it (as would be necessary) at a single sitting, the result is but a constant alternation of excitement and depression. After a passage of what we feel to be true poetry, there follows, inevitably, a passage of platitude which no critical pre-judgment can force us to admire; but if, upon completing the work, we read it again; omitting the first book—that is to say, commencing with the second—we shall be surprised at now finding that admirable which we before condemned—that damnable which we had previously so much admired. It follows from all this that the ultimate, aggregate, or absolute effect of even the best epic under the sun, is a nullity :—and this is precisely the fact.

In regard to the Iliad, we have, if not positive proof, at least very good reason, for believing it intended as a series of lyrics; but, granting the epic intention, I can say only that the work is based in an imperfect sense of Art. The modern epic is, of the suppositious ancient model, but an inconsiderate and blindfold imitation. But the day of these artistic anomalies is over. If, at any time, any very long poem *were* popular in reality—which I doubt—it is at least clear that no very long poem will ever be popular again.

That the extent of a poetical work is, *ceteris paribus*, the measure of its merit, seems undoubtedly, when we thus state it, a proposition sufficiently absurd—yet we are indebted for it to the quarterly Reviews. Surely there can be nothing in mere *size*, abstractly considered—there can be nothing in mere *bulk*, so far as a volume is concerned, which has so continuously elicited admiration from these saturnine pamphlets! A mountain, to be sure, by the mere sentiment of physical magnitude which it conveys, *does* impress us with a sense of the sublime—but no man is impressed after *this* fashion by the material grandeur of even "The Columbiad." Even the Quarterlies have not instructed us to be so impressed by it. *As yet*, they have not *insisted* on our estimating Lamartine by the cubic foot, or Pollock by the pound—

but what else are we to *infer* from their continual prating about "sustained effort?" If, by "sustained effort," any little gentleman has accomplished an epic, let us frankly commend him for the effort—if this indeed be a thing commendable—but let us forbear praising the epic on the effort's account. It is to be hoped that common sense, in the time to come, will prefer deciding upon a work of Art, rather by the impression it makes—by the effect it produces—than by the time it took to impress the effect, or by the amount of "sustained effort" which had been found necessary in effecting the impression. The fact is, that perseverance is one thing and genius quite another—nor can all the Quarterlies in Christendom confound them. By-and-by, this proposition, with many which I have been just urging, will be received as self-evident. In the meantime, by being generally condemned as falsities, they will not be essentially damaged as truths.

On the other hand, it is clear that a poem may be improperly brief. Undue brevity degenerates into mere epigrammatism. A *very* short poem, while now and then producing a brilliant or vivid, never produces a profound or enduring effect. There must be the steady pressing down of the stamp upon the wax. De Béranger has wrought innumerable things, pungent and spirit-stirring; but, in general, they have been too imponderous to stamp themselves deeply into the public attention; and thus, as so many feathers of fancy, have been blown aloft only to be whistled down the wind.

A remarkable instance of the effect of undue brevity in depressing a poem—in keeping it out of the popular view—is afforded by the following exquisite little Serenade :

I arise from dreams of thee
  In the first sweet sleep of night
When the winds are breathing low,
  And the stars are shining bright.
I arise from dreams of thee,
  And a spirit in my feet
Has led me—who knows how?—
  To thy chamber-window, sweet!

The wandering airs they faint
  On the dark, the silent stream—
The champak odors fail
  Like sweet thoughts in a dream;
1*

The nightingale's complaint,
  It dies upon her heart,
As I must die on thine,
  O, beloved as thou art !

O, lift me from the grass !
  I die, I faint, I fail !
Let thy love in kisses rain
  On my lips and eyelids pale.
My cheek is cold and white, alas !
  My heart beats loud and fast :
Oh ! press it close to thine again,
  Where it will break at last !

Very few, perhaps, are familiar with these lines—yet no
less a poet than Shelley is their author. Their warm, yet
delicate and ethereal imagination will be appreciated by all—
but by none so thoroughly as by him who has himself arisen from
sweet dreams of one beloved, to bathe in the aromatic air of a
southern midsummer night.

One of the finest poems by Willis—the very best, in my
opinion, which he has ever written—has, no doubt, through this
same defect of undue brevity, been kept back from its proper position, not less in the critical than in the popular view.

The shadows lay along Broadway,
  'Twas near the twilight-tide—
And slowly there a lady fair
  Was walking in her pride.
Alone walk'd she ; but, viewlessly,
  Walk'd spirits at her side.

Peace charm'd the street beneath her feet,
  And Honor charm'd the air ;
And all astir looked kind on her,
  And call'd her good as fair—
For all God ever gave to her
  She kept with chary care.

She kept with care her beauties rare
  From lovers warm and true—
For her heart was cold to all but gold,
  And the rich came not to woo—
But honor'd well are charms to sel
  If priests the selling do.

Now walking there was one more fair—
  A slight girl, lily-pale ;
And she had unseen company
  To make the spirit quail—

'Twixt Want and Scorn she walk'd forlorn,
And nothing could avail.

No mercy now can clear her brow
For this world's peace to pray ;
For, as love's wild prayer dissolved in air,
Her woman's heart gave way !—
But the sin forgiven by Christ in Heaven
By man is cursed alway !

In this composition we find it difficult to recognise the Willis who has written so many mere " verses of society." The lines are not only richly ideal, but full of energy ; while they breathe an earnestness—an evident sincerity of sentiment—for which we look in vain throughout all the other works of this author.

While the epic mania—while the idea that, to merit in poetry, prolixity is indispensable—has, for some years past, been gradually dying out of the public mind, by mere dint of its own absurdity—we find it succeeded by a heresy too palpably false to be long tolerated, but one which, in the brief period it has already endured, may be said to have accomplished more in the corruption of our Poetical Literature than all its other enemies combined. I allude to the heresy of *The Didactic*. It has been assumed, tacitly and avowedly, directly and indirectly, that the ultimate object of all Poetry is Truth. Every poem, it is said, should inculcate a moral ; and by this moral is the poetical merit of the work to be adjudged. We Americans especially have patronized this happy idea ; and we Bostonians, very especially, have developed it in full. We have taken it into our heads that to write a poem simply for the poem's sake, and to acknowledge such to have been our design, would be to confess ourselves radically wanting in the true Poetic dignity and force :—but the simple fact is, that, would we but permit ourselves to look into our own souls, we should immediately there discover that under the sun there neither exists nor *can* exist any work more thoroughly dignified— more supremely noble than this very poem—this poem *per se*— this poem which is a poem and nothing more—this poem written solely for the poem's sake.

With as deep a reverence for the True as ever inspired the bosom of man, I would, nevertheless, limit, in some measure, its modes of inculcation. I would limit to enforce them. I would not enfeeble them by dissipation. The demands of Truth are severe. She has no sympathy with the myrtles. All *that* which is so indispensable in Song, is precisely all *that* with which *she* has nothing whatever to do. It is but making her a flaunting paradox, to wreathe her in gems and flowers. In enforcing a truth, we need severity rather than efflorescence of language. We must be simple, precise, terse. We must be cool, calm, unimpassioned. In a word, we must be in that mood which, as nearly as possible, is the exact converse of the poetical. *He* must be blind indeed who does not perceive the radical and chasmal differences between the truthful and the poetical modes of inculcation. He must be theory-mad beyond redemption who, in spite of these differences, shall still persist in attempting to reconcile the obstinate oils and waters of Poetry and Truth.

Dividing the world of mind into its three most immediately obvious distinctions, we have the Pure Intellect, Taste, and the Moral Sense. I place Taste in the middle, because it is just this position which, in the mind, it occupies. It holds intimate relations with either extreme; but from the Moral Sense is separated by so faint a difference that Aristotle has not hesitated to place some of its operations among the virtues themselves. Nevertheless, we find the *offices* of the trio marked with a sufficient distinction. Just as the Intellect concerns itself with Truth, so Taste informs us of the Beautiful while the Moral Sense is regardful of Duty. Of this latter, while Conscience teaches the obligation, and Reason the expediency, Taste contents herself with displaying the charms :—waging war upon Vice solely on the ground of her deformity—her disproportion—her animosity to the fitting, to the appropriate, to the harmonious—in a word, to Beauty.

An immortal instinct, deep within the spirit of man, is thus, plainly, a sense of the Beautiful. This it is which administers to his delight in the manifold forms, and sounds, and odors, and sentiments amid which he exists. And just as the lily is repeated in the lake, or the eyes of Amaryllis in the mirror, so is the mere oral or written repetition of these forms, and sounds, and colors, and odors, and sentiments, a duplicate source of delight. But this mere repetition is not poetry. He who shall simply sing, with however glowing enthusiasm, or with however vivid a truth of description, of the sights, and sounds, and odors, and colors, and sentiments, which greet *him* in common with all mankind — he, I say, has yet failed to prove his divine title. There is still a something in the distance which he has been unable to attain. We have still a thirst unquenchable, to allay which he has not shown us the crystal springs. This thirst belongs to the immortality of Man. It is at once a consequence and an indication of his perennial existence. It is the desire of the moth for the star. It is no mere appreciation of the Beauty before us—but a wild effort to reach the Beauty above. Inspired by an ecstatic prescience of the glories beyond the grave, we struggle, by multiform combinations among the things and thoughts of Time, to attain a portion of that Loveliness whose very elements, perhaps, appertain to eternity alone. And thus when by Poetry—or when by Music, the most entrancing of the Poetic moods—we find ourselves melted into tears—we weep then—not as the Abbaté Gravina supposes—through excess of pleasure, but through a certain, petulant, impatient sorrow at our inability to grasp *now*, wholly, here on earth, at once and forever, those divine and rapturous joys, of which *through* the poem, or *through* the music, we attain to but brief and indeterminate glimpses.

The struggle to apprehend the supernal Loveliness—this struggle, on the part of souls fittingly constituted—has given to the world all *that* which it (the world) has ever been enabled at once to understand and *to feel* as poetic.

The Poetic Sentiment, of course, may develope itself in various modes—in Painting, in Sculpture, in Architecture, in the Dance—very especially in Music—and very peculiarly, and with a wide field, in the composition of the Landscape Garden. Our present theme, however, has regard only to its manifestation in words. And here let me speak briefly on the topic of rhythm. Contenting myself with the certainty that Music, in its various modes of metre, rhythm, and rhyme, is of so vast a moment in Poetry as never to be wisely rejected—is so vitally important an adjunct, that he is simply silly who declines its assistance, I will not now pause to maintain its absolute essentiality. It is in Music, perhaps, that the soul most nearly attains the great end for which, when inspired by the Poetic Sentiment, it struggles—the creation

of supernal Beauty.   It *may* be, indeed, that here this sublime end
is, now and then, attained *in fact.*   We are often made to feel,
with a shivering delight, that from an earthly harp are stricken
notes which *cannot* have been unfamiliar to the angels.   And thus
there can be little doubt that in the union of Poetry with Music
in its popular sense, we shall find the widest field for the Poetic
development.   The old Bards and Minnesingers had advantages
which we do not possess—and Thomas Moore, singing his own
songs, was, in the most legitimate manner, perfecting them as poems.

To recapitulate, then :—I would define, in brief, the Poetry of
words as *The Rythmical Creation of Beauty.*   Its sole arbiter is
Taste.   With the Intellect or with the Conscience, it has only
collateral relations.   Unless incidentally, it has no concern whatever either with Duty or with Truth.

A few words, however, in explanation.   *That* pleasure which
is at once the most pure, the most elevating, and the most intense,
is derived, I maintain, from the contemplation of the Beautiful.
In the contemplation of Beauty we alone find it possible to attain
that pleasurable elevation, or excitement, *of the soul,* which we
recognise as the Poetic Sentiment, and which is so easily distinguished from Truth, which is the satisfaction of the Reason, or
from Passion, which is the excitement of the heart.   I make
Beauty, therefore—using the word as inclusive of the sublime—I
make Beauty the province of the poem, simply because it is an
obvious rule of Art that effects should be made to spring as directly as possible from their causes :—no one as yet having been
weak enough to deny that the peculiar elevation in question is at
least *most readily* attainable in the poem.   It by no means follows, however, that the incitements of Passion, or the precepts of
Duty, or even the lessons of Truth, may not be introduced into a
poem, and with advantage ; for they may subserve, incidentally,
in various ways, the general purposes of the work :—but the true
artist will always contrive to tone them down in proper subjection
to that *Beauty* which is the atmosphere and the real essence of
the poem.

I cannot better introduce the few poems which I shall present
for your consideration than by the citation of the Pröem to Mr.
Longfellow's " Waif "

The day is done, and the darkness
  Falls from the wings of Night,
As a feather is wafted downward
  From an Eagle in his flight.

I see the lights of the village
  Gleam through the rain and the mist,
And a feeling of sadness comes o'er me,
  That my soul cannot resist;

A feeling of sadness and longing,
  That is not akin to pain,
And resembles sorrow only
  As the mist resembles the rain.

Come, read to me some poem,
  Some simple and heartfelt lay,
That shall soothe this restless feeling,
  And banish the thoughts of day.

Not from the grand old masters,
  Not from the bards sublime,
Whose distant footsteps echo
  Through the corridors of time.

For, like strains of martial music,
  Their mighty thoughts suggest
Life's endless toil and endeavor;
  And to-night I long for rest.

Read from some humbler poet,
  Whose songs gushed from his heart,
As showers from the clouds of summer,
  Or tears from the eyelids start;

Who through long days of labor,
  And nights devoid of ease,
Still heard in his soul the music
  Of wonderful melodies.

Such songs have power to quiet
  The restless pulse of care,
And come like the benediction
  That follows after prayer.

Then read from the treasured volume
  The poem of thy choice,
And lend to the rhyme of the poet
  The beauty of thy voice.

And the night shall be filled with music,
  And the cares, that infest the day,
Shall fold their tents, like the Arabs,
  And as silently steal away.

With no great range of imagination, these lines have been justly admired for their delicacy of expression. Some of the images are very effective. Nothing can be better than—

> ——————The bards sublime,
> Whose distant footsteps echo
> Down the corridors of Time.

The idea of the last quartrain is also very effective. The poem, on the whole, however, is chiefly to be admired for the graceful *insouciance* of its metre, so well in accordance with the character of the sentiments, and especially for the *ease* of the general manner. This "ease," or naturalness, in a literary style, it has long been the fashion to regard as ease in appearance alone—as a point of really difficult attainment. But not so :—a natural manner is difficult only to him who should never meddle with it—to the unnatural. It is but the result of writing with the understanding, or with the instinct, that *the tone*, in composition, should always be that which the mass of mankind would adopt—and must perpetually vary, of course, with the occasion. The author who, after the fashion of "The North American Review," should be, upon *all* occasions, merely "quiet," must necessarily upon *many* occasions, be simply silly, or stupid ; and has no more right to be considered "easy," or "natural," than a Cockney exquisite, or than the sleeping Beauty in the wax-works.

Among the minor poems of Bryant, none has so much impressed me as the one which he entitles "June." I quote only a portion of it :

> There, through the long, long summer hours,
>   The golden light should lie,
> And thick, young herbs and groups of flowers
>   Stand in their beauty by.
> The oriole should build and tell
> His love-tale, close beside my cell;
>   The idle butterfly
> Should rest him there, and there be heard
> The housewife-bee and humming bird.
>
> And what, if cheerful shouts, at noon,
>   Come, from the village sent,
> Or songs of maids, beneath the moon,
>   With fairy laughter blent ?
> And what if, in the evening light,
> Betrothed lovers walk in sight
>   Of my low monument ?
> I would the lovely scene around
> Might know no sadder sight nor sound
>
> I know, I know I should not see
>   The season's glorious show,

Nor would its brightness shine for me,
  Nor its wild music flow ;
But if, around my place of sleep,
  The friends I love should come to weep,
    They might not haste to go.
Soft airs, and song, and light, and bloom
Should keep them lingering by my tomb.

These to their soften'd hearts should bear
  The thought of what has been,
And speak of one who cannot share
  The gladness of the scene ;
Whose part in all the pomp that fills
The circuit of the summer hills,
  Is—that his grave is green ;
And deeply would their hearts rejoice
To hear again his living voice.

The rythmical flow, here, is even voluptuous—nothing could
be more melodious. The poem has always affected me in a remarkable manner. The intense melancholy which seems to well
up, perforce, to the surface of all the poet's cheerful sayings about
his grave, we find thrilling us to the soul—while there is the truest poetic elevation in the thrill. The impression left is one of a
pleasurable sadness. And if, in the remaining compositions which
I shall introduce to you, there be more or less of a similar tone
always apparent, let me remind you that (how or why we know
not) this certain taint of sadness is inseparably connected with all
the higher manifestations of true Beauty. It is, nevertheless,

A feeling of sadness and longing
  That is not akin to pain,
And resembles sorrow only
  As the mist resembles the rain.

The taint of which I speak is clearly perceptible even in a poem
so full of brilliancy and spirit as the "Health" of Edward Coote
Pinkney :

I fill this cup to one made up
  Of loveliness alone,
A woman, of her gentle sex
  The seeming paragon ;
To whom the better elements
  And kindly stars have given
A form so fair, that, like the air,
  'Tis less of earth than heaven.

Her every tone is music's own,
  Like those of morning birds,
And something more than melody
  Dwells ever in her words ;

> The coinage of her heart are they,
>   And from her lips each flows
> As one may see the burden'd bee
>   Forth issue from the rose.
>
> Affections are as thoughts to her,
>   The measures of her hours;
> Her feelings have the fragrancy,
>   The freshness of young flowers;
> And lovely passions, changing oft,
>   So fill her, she appears
> The image of themselves by turns,—
>   The idol of past years!
>
> Of her bright face one glance will trace
>   A picture on the brain,
> And of her voice in echoing hearts
>   A sound must long remain;
> But memory, such as mine of her,
>   So very much endears.
> When death is nigh my latest sigh
>   Will not be life's, but hers.
>
> I fill'd this cup to one made up
>   Of loveliness alone,
> A woman, of her gentle sex
>   The seeming paragon—
> Her health! and would on earth there stood,
>   Some more of such a frame,
> That life might be all poetry,
>   And weariness a name.

It was the misfortune of Mr. Pinkney to have been born too far south. Had he been a New Englander, it is probable that he would have been ranked as the first of American lyrists, by that magnanimous cabal which has so long controlled the destinies of American Letters, in conducting the thing called "The North American Review." The poem just cited is especially beautiful; but the poetic elevation which it induces, we must refer chiefly to our sympathy in the poet's enthusiasm. We pardon his hyperboles for the evident earnestness with which they are uttered.

It was by no means my design, however, to expatiate upon the *merits* of what I should read you. These will necessarily speak for themselves. Boccalini, in his "Advertisements from Parnassus," tells us that Zoilus once presented Apollo a very caustic criticism upon a very admirable book:—whereupon the god asked him for the beauties of the work. He replied that he only busied himself about the errors. On hearing this, Apollo, hand-ing him a sack of unwinnowed wheat, bade him pick out *all the chaff* for his reward.

Now this fable answers very well as a hit at the critics—but I am by no means sure that the god was in the right. I am by no means certain that the true limits of the critical duty are not grossly misunderstood. Excellence, in a poem especially, may be considered in the light of an axiom, which need only be properly *put*, to become self-evident. It is *not* excellence if it require to be demonstrated as such :—and thus, to point out too particularly the merits of a work of Art, is to admit that they are *not* merits altogether.

Among the "Melodies" of Thomas Moore, is one whose distinguished character as a poem proper, seems to have been singularly left out of view. I allude to his lines beginning—"Come rest in this bosom." The intense energy of their expression is not surpassed by anything in Byron. There are two of the lines in which a sentiment is conveyed that embodies the *all in all* of the divine passion of Love—a sentiment which, perhaps, has found its echo in more, and in more passionate, human hearts than any other single sentiment ever embodied in words :

> Come, rest in this bosom, my own stricken deer,
> Though the herd have fled from thee, thy home is still here ;
> Here still is the smile, that no cloud can o'ercast,
> And a heart and a hand all thy own to the last.
>
> Oh ! what was love made for, if 't is not the same
> Through joy and through torment, through glory and shame !
> I know not, I ask not, if guilt 's in that heart,
> I but know that I love thee, whatever thou art.
>
> Thou hast call'd me thy Angel in moments of bliss,
> And thy Angel I'll be, 'mid the horrors of this,—
> Through the furnace, unshrinking, thy steps to pursue,
> And shield thee, and save thee,—or perish there too !

It has been the fashion, of late days, to deny Moore Imagination, while granting him Fancy—a distinction originating with Coleridge—than whom no man more fully comprehended the great powers of Moore. The fact is, that the fancy of this poet so far predominates over all his other faculties, and over the fancy of all other men, as to have induced, very naturally, the idea that he is fanciful *only*. But never was there a greater mistake. Never was a grosser wrong done the fame of a true poet. In the compass of

the English language I can call to mind no poem more profoundly—more wierdly *imaginative*, in the best sense, than the lines
commencing—"I would I were by that dim lake"—which are the
composition of Thomas Moore. I regret that I am unable to
remember them.

One of the noblest—and, speaking of Fancy, one of the most
singularly fanciful of modern poets, was Thomas Hood. His " Fair
Ines" had always, for me, an inexpressible charm :

O saw ye not fair Ines !
  She's gone into the West,
To dazzle when the sun is down,
  And rob the world of rest :
She took our daylight with her,
  The smiles that we love best,
With morning blushes on her cheek,
  And pearls upon her breast.

O turn again, fair Ines,
  Before the fall of night,
For fear the moon should shine alone,
  And stars unrivall'd bright ;
And blessed will the lover be
  That walks beneath their light,
And breathes the love against thy cheek
  I dare not even write !

Would I had been, fair Ines,
  That gallant cavalier,
Who rode so gaily by thy side,
  And whisper'd thee so near !
Were there no bonny dames at home,
  Or no true lovers here,
That he should cross the seas to win
  The dearest of the dear !

I saw thee, lovely Ines,
  Descend along the shore,
With bands of noble gentlemen,
  And banners wav'd before ;
And gentle youth and maidens gay,
  And snowy plumes they wore ;
It would have been a beauteous dream,
  —If it had been no more !

Alas, alas, fair Ines,
  She went away with song,
With Music waiting on her steps,
  And shoutings of the throng ;
But some were sad and felt no mirth,
  But only Music's wrong,
In sounds that sang Farewell, Farewell,
  To her you've loved so long.

Farewell, farewell, fair Ines,
  That vessel never bore
So fair a lady on its deck,
  Nor danced so light before.—
Alas for pleasure on the sea,
  And sorrow on the shore!
The smile that blest one lover's heart
  Has broken many more!

"The Haunted House," by the same author, is one of the truest poems ever written—one of the *truest*—one of the most unexceptionable—one of the most thoroughly artistic, both in its theme and in its execution. It is, moreover, powerfully ideal—imaginative. I regret that its length renders it unsuitable for the purposes of this Lecture. In place of it, permit me to offer the universally appreciated "Bridge of Sighs."

One more Unfortunate,
Weary of breath,
Rashly importunate,
Gone to her death!

Take her up tenderly,
Lift her with care;——
Fashion'd so slenderly,
Young, and so fair!

Look at her garments
Clinging like cerements;
Whilst the wave constantly
Drips from her clothing;
Take her up instantly,
Loving, not loathing.—

Touch her not scornfully;
Think of her mournfully,
Gently and humanly;
Not of the stains of her,
All that remains of her
Now, is pure womanly.

Make no deep scrutiny
Into her mutiny
Rash and undutiful;
Past all dishonor,
Death has left on her
Only the beautiful.

Still, for all slips of hers,
One of Eve's family—
Wipe those poor lips of hers
Oozing so clammily

Loop up her tresses
Escaped from the comb,
Her fair auburn tresses;
Whilst wonderment guesses
Where was her home?

Who was her father?
Who was her mother?
Had she a sister?
Had she a brother?
Or was there a dearer one
Still, and a nearer one
Yet, than all other?

Alas! for the rarity
Of Christian charity
Under the sun!
Oh! it was pitiful!
Near a whole city full,
Home she had none.

Sisterly, brotherly,
Fatherly, motherly,
Feelings had changed:
Love, by harsh evidence,
Thrown from its eminence;
Even God's providence
Seeming estranged.

Where the lamps quiver
So far in the river,
With many a light
From window and casement,
From garret to basement,
She stood, with amazement,
Houseless by night.

The bleak wind of March
Made her tremble and shiver;
But not the dark arch,
Or the black flowing river:
Mad from life's history,
Glad to death's mystery,
Swift to be hurl'd—
Anywhere, anywhere
Out of the world!

In she plunged boldly,
No matter how coldly
The rough river ran,—
Over the brink of it,
Picture it,—think of it,
Dissolute Man!
Lave in it, drink of it
Then, if you can!

Take her up tenderly,
Lift her with care;
Fashion'd so slenderly,
Young, and so fair!

Ere her limbs frigidly
Stiffen too rigidly,
Decently,—kindly,—
Smooth, and compose them;
And her eyes, close them,
Staring so blindly!

Dreadfully staring
Through muddy impurity,
As when with the daring
Last look of despairing
Fixed on futurity.

Perishing gloomily,
Spurred by contumely,
Cold inhumanity,
Burning insanity,
Into her rest,—
Cross her hands humbly,
As if praying dumbly,
Over her breast!
Owning her weakness,
Her evil behavior,
And leaving, with meekness,
Her sins to her Savior!

The vigor of this poem is no less remarkable than its pathos. The versification, although carrying the fanciful to the very verge of the fantastic, is nevertheless admirably adapted to the wild insanity which is the thesis of the poem.

Among the minor poems of Lord Byron, is one which has never received from the critics the praise which it undoubtedly deserves:

Though the day of my destiny's over,
    And the star of my fate hath declined,
Thy soft heart refused to discover
    The faults which so many could find;
Though thy soul with my grief was acquainted,
    It shrunk not to share it with me,
And the love which my spirit hath painted
    It never hath found but in *thee*.

Then when nature around me is smiling,
    The last smile which answers to mine,
I do not believe it beguiling,
    Because it reminds me of thine;
And when winds are at war with the ocean,
    As the breasts I believed in with me,
If their billows excite an emotion,
    It is that they bear me from *thee*.

Though the rock of my last hope is shivered,
    And its fragments are sunk in the wave,
Though I feel that my soul is delivered
    To pain—it shall not be its slave.
There is many a pang to pursue me:
    They may crush, but they shall not contemn—
They may torture, but shall not subdue me—
    'Tis of *thee* that I think—not of them.

Though human, thou didst not deceive me,
    Though woman, thou didst not forsake,
Though loved, thou forborest to grieve me,
    Though slandered, thou never couldst shake,—
Though trusted, thou didst not disclaim me,
    Though parted, it was not to fly,
Though watchful, 't was not to defame me,
    Nor mute, that the world might belie.

Yet I blame not the world, nor despise it,
    Nor the war of the many with one—
If my soul was not fitted to prize it,
    'T was folly not sooner to shun:
And if dearly that error hath cost me,
    And more than I once could foresee,
I have found that whatever it lost me,
    It could not deprive me of *thee*.

From the wreck of the past, which hath perished,
    Thus much I at least may recall,
It hath taught me that which I most cherished
    Deserved to be dearest of all:
In the desert a fountain is springing,
    In the wide waste there still is a tree,
And a bird in the solitude singing,
    Which speaks to my spirit of *thee*.

Although the rhythm, here, is one of the most difficult, the versification could scarcely be improved. No nobler *theme* ever engaged the pen of poet. It is the soul-elevating idea, that no man can consider himself entitled to complain of Fate while, in his adversity, he still retains the unwavering love of woman.

From Alfred Tennyson—although in perfect sincerity I regard him as the noblest poet that ever lived—I have left myself time to cite only a very brief specimen. I call him, and *think* him the noblest of poets—*not* because the impressions he produces are, at *all* times, the most profound—*not* because the poetical excitement which he induces is, at *all* times, the most intense—but because it *is*, at all times, the most ethereal—in other words, the most elevating and the most pure. No poet is so little of the earth, earthy. What I am about to read is from his last long poem, "The Princess:"

> Tears, idle tears, I know not what they mean,
> Tears from the depth of some divine despair
> Rise in the heart, and gather to the eyes,
> In looking on the happy Autumn-fields,
> And thinking of the days that are no more.
>
> Fresh as the first beam glittering on a sail,
> That brings our friends up from the underworld,
> Sad as the last which reddens over one
> That sinks with all we love below the verge;
> So sad, so fresh, the days that are no more.
>
> Ah, sad and strange as in dark summer dawns
> The earliest pipe of half-awaken'd birds
> To dying ears, when unto dying eyes
> The casement slowly grows a glimmering square;
> So sad, so strange, the days that are no more.
>
> Dear as remember'd kisses after death,
> And sweet as those by hopeless fancy feign'd
> On lips that are for others; deep as love,
> Deep as first love, and wild with all regret;
> O Death in Life, the days that are no more.

Thus, although in a very cursory and imperfect manner, I have endeavored to convey to you my conception of the Poetic Principle. It has been my purpose to suggest that, while this Principle itself is, strictly and simply, the Human Aspiration for Supernal Beauty, the manifestation of the Principle is always found in *an elevating excitement of the Soul*—quite independent of that passion which is the intoxication of the Heart—or of that Truth which is the satisfaction of the Reason. For, in regard to Passion, alas! its tendency is to degrade, rather than to elevate the Soul. Love, on the contrary—Love—the true, the divine Eros—the Uranian, as distinguished from the Dionæan Venus—is unquestionably the purest and truest of all poetical themes. And in regard to Truth—if, to be sure, through the attainment of a truth, we are led to perceive a harmony where none was apparent before, we experience, at once, the true poetical effect—but this effect is referable to the harmony alone, and not in the least degree to the truth which merely served to render the harmony manifest.

We shall reach, however, more immediately a distinct concep-

tion of what the true Poetry is, by mere reference to a few of the
simple elements which induce in the Poet himself the true poetical effect   He recognises the ambrosia which nourishes his soul,
in the bright orbs that shine in Heaven—in the volutes of the
flower—in the clustering of low shrubberies—in the waving of the
grain-fields—in the slanting of tall, Eastern trees—in the blue distance of mountains—in the grouping of clouds—in the twinkling
of half-hidden brooks—in the gleaming of silver rivers—in the
repose of sequestered lakes—in the star-mirroring depths of lonely
wells.   He perceives it in the songs of birds—in the harp of
Æolus—in the sighing of the night-wind—in the repining voice
of the forest—in the surf that complains to the shore—in the fresh
breath of the woods—in the scent of the violet—in the voluptuous
perfume of the hyacinth—in the suggestive odor that comes to
him, at eventide, from far-distant, undiscovered islands, over dim
oceans, illimitable and unexplored.   He owns it in all noble
thoughts—in all unworldly motives—in all holy impulses—in all
chivalrous, generous, and self-sacrificing deeds.   He feels it in the
beauty of woman—in the grace of her step—in the lustre of her
eye—in the melody of her voice—in her soft laughter—in her
sigh—in the harmony of the rustling of her robes.   He deeply
feels it in her winning endearments—in her burning enthusiasms
—in her gentle charities—in her meek and devotional endurances
—but above all—ah, far above all—he kneels to it—he worships
it in the faith, in the purity, in the strength, in the altogether
divine majesty—of her *love*.

Let me conclude—by the recitation of yet another brief poem—
one very different in character from any that I have before
quoted.   It is by Motherwell, and is called "The Song of the Cavalier."   With our modern and altogether rational ideas of the
absurdity and impiety of warfare, we are not precisely in that
frame of mind best adapted to sympathize with the sentiments,
and thus to appreciate the real excellence of the poem.   To do
this fully, we must identify ourselves, in fancy, with the soul of the
old cavalier.

> Then mounte! then mounte, brave gallants, all;
>   And don your helmes amaine:
> Deathe's couriers, Fame and Honor, call
>   Us to the field againe.

VOL. II.—2.

No shrewish teares shall fill our eye
  When the sword-hilt 's in our hand,—
Heart-whole we'll part, and no whit sighe
  For the fayrest of the land ;
Let piping swaine, and craven wight,
  Thus weepe and puling crye,
Our business is like men to fight,
  And hero-like to die !

MISCELLANEOUS POEMS

THE RAVEN.

Once upon a midnight dreary, while I pondered, weak and weary,
Over many a quaint and curious volume of forgotten lore—
While I nodded, nearly napping, suddenly there came a tapping,
As of some one gently rapping, rapping at my chamber door.
" 'Tis some visiter," I muttered, " tapping at my chamber door—
                Only this and nothing more."

Ah, distinctly I remember it was in the bleak December,
And each separate dying ember wrought its ghost upon the floor.
Eagerly I wished the morrow ;—vainly I had sought to borrow
From my books surcease of sorrow—sorrow for the lost Lenore—
For the rare and radiant maiden whom the angels name Lenore—
                Nameless here for evermore.

And the silken sad uncertain rustling of each purple curtain
Thrilled me—filled me with fantastic terrors never felt before ;
So that now, to still the beating of my heart, I stood repeating
" 'Tis some visiter entreating entrance at my chamber door—
Some late visiter entreating entrance at my chamber door ;
                This it is and nothing more."

Presently my soul grew stronger ; hesitating then no longer,
"Sir," said I, " or Madam, truly your forgiveness I implore ;
But the fact is I was napping, and so gently you came rapping,
And so faintly you came tapping, tapping at my chamber door,
That I scarce was sure I heard you"—here I opened wide the
   door :——
        Darkness there and nothing more.

Deep into that darkness peering, long I stood there wondering,
   fearing,
Doubting, dreaming dreams no mortals ever dared to dream
   before ;
But the silence was unbroken, and the stillness gave no token,
And the only word there spoken was the whispered word, " Lenore ?"
This I whispered, and an echo murmured back the word, " Lenore !"—
        Merely this and nothing more.

Back into the chamber turning, all my soul within me burning,
Soon again I heard a tapping something louder than before.
"Surely," said I, " surely that is something at my window
   lattice ;
Let me see, then, what thereat is and this mystery explore—
Let my heart be still a moment and this mystery explore ;—
       'Tis the wind and nothing more."

Open here I flung the shutter, when, with many a flirt and flutter,
In there stepped a stately Raven of the saintly days of yore.
Not the least obeisance made he ; not a minute stopped or stayed he ;
But, with mien of lord or lady, perched above my chamber door—
Perched upon a bust of Pallas just above my chamber door—
       Perched, and sat, and nothing more.

Then this ebony bird beguiling my sad fancy into smiling,
By the grave and stern decorum of the countenance it wore,

"Though thy crest be shorn and shaven, thou," I said, "art sure
no craven,
Ghastly grim and ancient Raven wandering from the Nightly
shore—
Tell me what thy lordly name is on the Night's Plutonian shore!"
Quoth the Raven, "Nevermore."

Much I marvelled this ungainly fowl to hear discourse so plainly,
Though its answer little meaning—little relevancy bore;
For we cannot help agreeing that no living human being
Ever yet was blessed with seeing bird above his chamber door—
Bird or beast upon the sculptured bust above his chamber
door,
With such name as "Nevermore."

But the Raven, sitting lonely on that placid bust, spoke only
That one word, as if his soul in that one word he did outpour.
Nothing farther then he uttered; not a feather then he fluttered—
Till I scarcely more than muttered "Other friends have flown
before—
On the morrow *he* will leave me, as my Hopes have flown
before."
Then the bird said "Nevermore."

Startled at the stillness broken by reply so aptly spoken,
"Doubtless," said I, "what it utters is its only stock and store
Caught from some unhappy master whom unmerciful Disaster
Followed fast and followed faster till his songs one burden bore—
Till the dirges of his Hope that melancholy burden bore
Of 'Never—nevermore.' "

But the Raven still beguiling all my sad soul into smiling,
Straight I wheeled a cushioned seat in front of bird and bust and
door;
Then, upon the velvet sinking, I betook myself to linking

Fancy unto fancy, thinking what this ominous bird of yore—
What this grim, ungainly, ghastly, gaunt, and ominous bird of
        yore
                        Meant in croaking " Nevermore."

This I sat engaged in guessing, but no syllable expressing
To the fowl whose fiery eyes now burned into my bosom's core ;
This and more I sat divining, with my head at ease reclining
On the cushion's velvet lining that the lamp-light gloated o'er,
But whose velvet violet lining with the lamp-light gloating o'er
                        She shall press, ah, nevermore !

Then, methought, the air grew denser, perfumed from an unseen
        censer
Swung by Seraphim whose foot-falls tinkled on the tufted floor.
" Wretch," I cried, " thy God hath lent thee—by these angels
        he hath sent thee
Respite—respite and nepenthe from thy memories of Lenore !
Quaff, oh quaff this kind nepenthe and forget this lost Lenore !"
                        Quoth the Raven, " Nevermore."

" Prophet !" said I, " thing of evil !—prophet still, if bird or devil !—
Whether Tempter sent, or whether tempest tossed thee here ashore,
Desolate yet all undaunted, on this desert land enchanted—
On this home by Horror haunted—tell me truly, I implore—
Is there—*is* there balm in Gilead ?—tell me—tell me, I implore !"
                        Quoth the Raven, " Nevermore."

" Prophet !" said I, " thing of evil—prophet still, if bird or devil !
By that Heaven that bends above us—by that God we both
        adore—
Tell this soul with sorrow laden if, within the distant Aidenn,
It shall clasp a sainted maiden whom the angels name Lenore—
Clasp a rare and radiant maiden whom the angels name Lenore.'
                        Quoth the Raven, " Nevermore."

"Be that word our sign of parting, bird or fiend !" I shrieked,
    upstarting—
"Get thee back into the tempest and the Night's Plutonian
    shore !
Leave no black plume as a token of that lie thy soul hath
    spoken !
Leave my loneliness unbroken !—quit the bust above my door !
Take thy beak from out my heart, and take thy form from off
    my door !"
                Quoth the Raven, " Nevermore."

And the Raven, never flitting, still is sitting, still is sitting
On the pallid bust of Pallas just above my chamber door ;
And his eyes have all the seeming of a demon's that is dreaming
And the lamp-light o'er him streaming throws his shadow on the
    floor ;
And my soul from out that shadow that lies floating on the floor
              Shall be lifted—nevermore !

LENORE.

AH, broken is the golden bowl! the spirit flown forever!
Let the bell toll!—a saintly soul floats on the Stygian river;
And, Guy De Vere, hast *thou* no tear?—weep now or never
     more!
See! on yon drear and rigid bier low lies thy love, Lenore!
Come! let the burial rite be read—the funeral song be sung!—
An anthem for the queenliest dead that ever died so young—
A dirge for her the doubly dead in that she died so young.

" Wretches! ye loved her for her wealth and hated her for her
     pride,
" And when she fell in feeble health, ye blessed her—that she
     died!
" How *shall* the ritual, then, be read?—the requiem how be sung
" By you—by yours, the evil eye,—by yours, the slanderous
     tongue
" That did to death the innocence that died, and died so young?"

Peccavimus ; but rave not thus! and let a Sabbath song
Go up to God so solemnly the dead may feel no wrong!
The sweet Lenore hath " gone before," with Hope, that flew
     beside,
Leaving thee wild for the dear child that should have been thy
     bride—

For her, the fair and *debonair*, that now so lowly lies,
The life upon her yellow hair but not within her eyes—
The life still there, upon her hair—the death upon her eyes.

" Avaunt! to-night my heart is light.   No dirge will I upraise,
" But waft the angel on her flight with a Pœan of old days!
" Let *no* bell toll!—lest her sweet soul, amid its hallowed mirth,
" Should catch the note, as it doth float up from the damnéd
    Earth.
" To friends above, from fiends below, the indignant ghost is
    riven—
" From Hell unto a high estate far up within the Heaven—
" From grief and groan, to a golden throne, beside the King of
    Heaven."

HYMN.

At morn—at noon—at twilight dim—
Maria! thou hast heard my hymn!
In joy and wo—in good and ill—
Mother of God, be with me still!
When the Hours flew brightly by,
And not a cloud obscured the sky,
My soul, lest it should truant be,
Thy grace did guide to thine and thee;
Now, when storms of Fate o'ercast
Darkly my Present and my Past,
Let my Future radiant shine
With sweet hopes of thee and thine!
2*

A VALENTINE.

For her this rhyme is penned, whose luminous eyes,
    Brightly expressive as the twins of Lœda,
Shall find her own sweet name, that, nestling lies
    Upon the page, enwrapped from every reader.
Search narrowly the lines!—they hold a treasure
    Divine—a talisman—an amulet
That must be worn *at heart*.   Search well the measure—
    The words—the syllables!   Do not forget
The trivialest point, or you may lose your labor!
    And yet there is in this no Gordian knot
Which one might not undo without a sabre,
    If one could merely comprehend the plot.
Enwritten upon the leaf where now are peering
    Eyes scintillating soul, there lie *perdus*
Three eloquent words oft uttered in the hearing
    Of poets, by poets—as the name is a poet's, too.
Its letters, although naturally lying
    Like the knight Pinto—Mendez Ferdinando—
Still form a synonym for Truth.—Cease trying!
    You will not read the riddle, though you do the best you *can do.*

[To translate the address, read the first letter of the first line
in connection with the second letter of the second line, the third
letter of the third line, the fourth of the fourth, and so on to the
end.   The name will thus appear.]

THE COLISEUM.

TYPE of the antique Rome!   Rich reliquary
Of lofty contemplation left to Time|
By buried centuries of pomp and power!
At length—at length—after so many days
Of weary pilgrimage and burning thirst,
(Thirst for the springs of lore that in thee lie,)
I kneel, an altered and an humble man,
Amid thy shadows, and so drink within
My very soul thy grandeur, gloom, and glory!

Vastness! and Age! and Memories of Eld!
Silence! and Desolation! and dim Night!
I feel ye now—I feel ye in your strength—
O spells more sure than e'er Judæan king
Taught in the gardens of Gethsemane!
O charms more potent than the rapt Chaldee
Ever drew down from out the quiet stars!

Here, where a hero fell, a column falls!
Here, where the mimic eagle glared in gold,
A midnight vigil holds the swarthy bat!
Here, where the dames of Rome their gilded hair
Waved to the wind, now wave the reed and thistle!
Here, where on golden throne the monarch lolled,
Glides, spectre-like, unto his marble home,

Lit by the wan light of the hornéd moon,
The swift and silent lizard of the stones!

But stay! these walls—these ivy-clad arcades—
These mouldering plinths—these sad and blackened shafts—
These vague entablatures—this crumbling frieze—
These shattered cornices—this wreck—this ruin—
These stones—alas! these gray stones—are they all—
All of the famed, and the colossal left
By the corrosive Hours to Fate and me?

" Not all"—the Echoes answer me—" not all!
" Prophetic sounds and loud, arise forever
" From us, and from all Ruin, unto the wise,
" As melody from Memnon to the Sun.
" We rule the hearts of mightiest men—we rule
" With a despotic sway all giant minds.
" We are not impotent—we pallid stones.
" Not all our power is gone—not all our fame—
" Not all the magic of our high renown—
" Not all the wonder that encircles us—
" Not all the mysteries that in us lie—
" Not all the memories that hang upon
" And cling around about us as a garment,
" Clothing us in a robe of more than glory."

TO HELEN.

I saw thee once—once only—years ago :
I must not say *how* many—but *not* many.
It was a July midnight ; and from out
A full-orbed moon, that, like thine own soul, soaring,
Sought a precipitate pathway up through heaven,
There fell a silvery-silken veil of light,
With quietude, and sultriness, and slumber,
Upon the upturn'd faces of a thousand
Roses that grew in an enchanted garden,
Where no wind dared to stir, unless on tiptoe—
Fell on the upturn'd faces of these roses
That gave out, in return for the love-light,
Their odorous souls in an ecstatic death—
Fell on the upturn'd faces of these roses
That smiled and died in this parterre, enchanted
By thee, and by the poetry of thy presence.

Clad all in white, upon a violet bank
I saw thee half reclining ; while the moon
Fell on the upturn'd faces of the roses,
And on thine own, upturn'd—alas, in sorrow !

Was it not Fate, that, on this July midnight—
Was it not Fate, (whose name is also Sorrow,)
That bade me pause before that garden-gate,
To breathe the incense of those slumbering roses ?
No footstep stirred : the hated world all slept,
Save only thee and me.   (Oh, Heaven !—oh, God !
How my heart beats in coupling those two words !)
Save only thee and me.   I paused—I looked—
And in an instant all things disappeared.
(Ah, bear in mind this garden was enchanted !)

The pearly lustre of the moon went out :
The mossy banks and the meandering paths,
The happy flowers and the repining trees,
Were seen no more : the very roses' odors
Died in the arms of the adoring airs.
All—all expired save thee—save less than thou :
Save only the divine light in thine eyes—
Save but the soul in thine uplifted eyes.
I saw but them—they were the world to me.
I saw but them—saw only them for hours—
Saw only them until the moon went down.
What wild heart-histories seemed to lie enwritten
Upon those crystalline, celestial spheres !
How dark a wo ! yet how sublime a hope !
How silently serene a sea of pride !
How daring an ambition ! yet how deep—
How fathomless a capacity for love !

But now, at length, dear Dian sank from sight,
Into a western couch of thunder-cloud ;
And thou, a ghost, amid the entombing trees
Didst glide way.   *Only thine eyes remained.*
They *would not* go—they never yet have gone.
Lighting my lonely pathway home that night,
They have not left me (as my hopes have) since.
They follow me—they lead me through the years.
They are my ministers—yet I their slave.
Their office is to illumine and enkindle—
My duty, *to be saved* by their bright light,
And purified in their electric fire,
And sanctified in their elysian fire.
They fill my soul with Beauty (which is Hope,)
And are far up in Heaven—the stars I kneel to
In the sad, silent watches of my night ;
While even in the meridian glare of day
I see them still—two sweetly scintillant
Venuses, unextinguished by the sun !

TO —— ——.

Nor long ago, the writer of these lines,
In the mad pride of intellectuality,
Maintained "the power of words"—denied that ever
A thought arose within the human brain
Beyond the utterance of the human tongue:
And now, as if in mockery of that boast,
Two words—two foreign soft dissyllables—
Italian tones, made only to be murmured
By angels dreaming in the moonlit "dew
That hangs like chains of pearl on Hermon hill,"—
Have stirred from out the abysses of his heart,
Unthought-like thoughts that are the souls of thought,
Richer, far wilder, far diviner visions
Than even the seraph harper, Israfel,
(Who has "the sweetest voice of all God's creatures,")
Could hope to utter.   And I ! my spells are broken.
The pen falls powerless from my shivering hand.
With thy dear name as text, though bidden by thee,
I cannot write—I cannot speak or think—
Alas, I cannot feel ; for 'tis not feeling,
This standing motionless upon the golden
Threshold of the wide-open gate of dreams,
Gazing, entranced, adown the gorgeous vista,
And thrilling as I see, upon the right,
Upon the left, and all the way along,
Amid unpurpled vapors, far away
To where the prospect terminates—*thee only*.

ULALUME.

THE skies they were ashen and sober;
    The leaves they were crisped and sere—
    The leaves they were withering and sere;
It was night in the lonesome October
    Of my most immemorial year;
It was hard by the dim lake of Auber,
    In the misty mid region of Weir—
It was down by the dank tarn of Auber,
    In the ghoul-haunted woodland of Weir.

Here once, through an alley Titantic,
    Of cypress, I roamed with my Soul—
    Of cypress, with Psyche, my Soul.
These were days when my heart was volcanic
    As the scoriac rivers that roll—
    As the lavas that restlessly roll
Their sulphurous currents down Yaanek
    In the ultimate climes of the pole—
That groan as they roll down Mount Yaanek
    In the realms of the boreal pole.

Our talk had been serious and sober,
    But our thoughts they were palsied and sere—
    Our memories were treacherous and sere—
For we knew not the month was October,
    And we markēd not the night of the year—
    (Ah, night of all nights in the year!)
We noted not the dim lake of Auber—
    (Though once we had journeyed down here)—
Remembered not the dank tarn of Auber,
    Nor the ghoul-haunted woodland of Weir.

And now, as the night was senescent
　　And star-dials pointed to morn—
　　As the star-dials hinted of morn—
At the end of our path a liquescent
　　And nebulous lustre was born,
Out of which a miraculous crescent
　　Arose with a duplicate horn—
Astarte's bediamonded crescent
　　Distinct with its duplicate hern.

And I said—"She is warmer than Dian:
　　She rolls through an ether of sighs—
　　She revels in a region of sighs:
She has seen that the tears are not dry on
　　These checks, where the worm never dies,
And has come past the stars of the Lion
　　To point us the path to the skies—
　　To the Lethean peace of the skies—
Come up, in despite of the Lion,
　　To shine on us with her bright eyes—
Come up through the lair of the Lion,
　　With love in her luminous eyes."

But Psyche, uplifting her finger,
　　Said—"Sadly this star I mistrust—
　　Her pallor I strangely mistrust:—
Oh, hasten!—oh, let us not linger!
　　Oh, fly!—let us fly!—for we must."
In terror she spoke, letting sink her
　　Wings until they trailed in the dust—
In agony sobbed, letting sink her
　　Plumes till they trailed in the dust—
　　Till they sorrowfully trailed in the dust.

I replied—"This is nothing but dreaming:
　　Let us on by this tremulous light!
　　Let us bathe in this crystalline light!

Its Sybilic splendor is beaming
    With Hope and in Beauty to-night :—
    See !—it flickers up the sky through the night !
Ah, we safely may trust to its gleaming,
    And be sure it will lead us aright—
We safely may trust to a gleaming
    That cannot but guide us aright,
    Since it flickers up to Heaven through the night."

Thus I pacified Psyche and kissed her,
    And tempted her out of her gloom—
    And conquered her scruples and gloom ;
And we passed to the end of the vista,
    But were stopped by the door of a tomb—
    By the door of a legended tomb ;
And I said—" What is written, sweet sister,
    On the door of this legended tomb ?"
    She replied—" Ulalume—Ulalume—
    'Tis the vault of thy lost Ulalume !"

Then my heart it grew ashen and sober
    As the leaves that were crisped and sere—
    As the leaves that were withering and sere,
And I cried—" It was surely October
    On *this* very night of last year
    That I journeyed—I journeyed down here—
    That I brought a dread burden down here—
    On this night of all nights in the year,
    Ah, what demon has tempted me here !
Well I know, now, this dim lake of Auber—
    This misty mid region of Weir—
Well I know, now, this dank tarn of Auber,
    This ghoul-haunted woodland of Weir."

THE BELLS.

I.

HEAR the sledges with the bells—
Silver bells !
What a world of merriment their melody foretells !
How they tinkle, tinkle, tinkle,
In the icy air of night !
While the stars that oversprinkle
All the heavens, seem to twinkle
With a crystalline delight ;
Keeping time, time, time,
In a sort of Runic rhyme,
To the tintinabulation that so musically wells
From the bells, bells, bells, bells,
Bells, bells, bells—
From the jingling and the tinkling of the bells.

II.

Hear the mellow wedding bells,
Golden bells !
What a world of happiness their harmony foretells !
Through the balmy air of night
How they ring out their delight !
From the molten-golden notes,
And all in tune,
What a liquid ditty floats
To the turtle-dove that listens, while she gloats
On the moon !
Oh, from out the sounding cells,
What a gush of euphony voluminously wells !
How it swells !
How it dwells

On the Future! how it tells
Of the rapture that impels
To the swinging and the ringing
Of the bells, bells, bells,
Of the bells, bells, bells, bells,
Bells, bells, bells—
To the rhyming and the chiming of the bells!

III.

Hear the loud alarum bells—
Brazen bells!
What a tale of terror, now, their turbulency tells!
In the startled ear of night
How they scream out their affright!
Too much horrified to speak,
They can only shriek, shriek,
Out of tune,
In a clamorous appealing to the mercy of the fire,
In a mad expostulation with the deaf and frantic fire
Leaping higher, higher, higher,
With a desperate desire,
And a resolute endeavor
Now—now to sit or never,
By the side of the pale-faced moon.
Oh, the bells, bells, bells!
What a tale their terror tells
Of Despair!
How they clang, and clash, and roar!
What a horror they outpour
On the bosom of the palpitating air!
Yet the ear it fully knows,
By the twanging,
And the clanging,
How the danger ebbs and flows;
Yet the ear distinctly tells,
In the jangling,
And the wrangling,
How the danger sinks and swells,
By the sinking or the swelling in the anger of the bells—

Of the bells—
Of the bells, bells, bells, bells,
Bells, bells, bells—
In the clamor and the clangor of the bells !

IV.

Hear the tolling of the bells—
Iron bells !
What a world of solemn thought their monody compels !
In the silence of the night,
How we shiver with affright
At the melancholy menace of their tone !
For every sound that floats
From the rust within their throats
Is a groan.
And the people—ah, the people—
They that dwell up in the steeple,
All alone,
And who tolling, tolling, tolling,
In that muffled monotone,
Feel a glory in so rolling
On the human heart a stone—
They are neither man nor woman—
They are neither brute nor human—
They are Ghouls :
And their king it is who tolls ;
And he rolls, rolls, rolls,
Rolls
A pæan from the bells !
And his merry bosom swells
With the pæan of the bells !
And he dances, and he yells ;
Keeping time, time, time,
In a sort of Runic rhyme,
To the pæan of the bells—
Of the bells :
Keeping time, time, time,
In a sort of Runic rhyme,
To the throbbing of the bells—

Of the bells, bells, bells—
    To the sobbing of the bells ;
Keeping time, time, time,
    As he knells, knells, knells,
In a happy Runic rhyme,
    To the rolling of the bells—
Of the bells, bells, bells—
    To the tolling of the bells,
Of the bells, bells, bells, bells—
    Bells, bells, bells—
To the moaning and the groaning of the bells.

AN ENIGMA.

" SELDOM we find," says Solomon Don Dunce,
    Half an idea in the profoundest sonnet.
Through all the flimsy things we see at once
    As easily as through a Naples bonnet—
    Trash of all trash !—how *can* a lady don it ?
Yet heavier far than your Petrarchan stuff—
Owl-downy nonsense that the faintest puff
    Twirls into trunk-paper the while you con it."
And, veritably, Sol is right enough.
The general tuckermanities are arrant
Bubbles—ephemeral and *so* transparent—
    But *this* is, now,—you may depend upon it—
Stable, opaque, immortal—all by dint
Of the dear names that lie concealed within 't.

ANNABEL LEE.

It was many and many a year ago,
    In a kingdom by the sea,
That a maiden there lived whom you may know
    By the name of Annabel Lee;
And this maiden she lived with no other thought
    Than to love and be loved by me.

I was a child and *she* was a child,
    In this kingdom by the sea:
But we loved with a love that was more than love—
    I and my Annabel Lee;
With a love that the winged seraphs of heaven
    Coveted her and me.

And this was the reason that, long ago,
    In this kingdom by the sea,
A wind blew out of a cloud, chilling
    My beautiful Annabel Lee;
So that her highborn kinsman came
    And bore her away from me,
To shut her up in a sepulchre
    In this kingdom by the sea.

The angels, not half so happy in heaven,
    Went envying her and me—
Yes!—that was the reason (as all men know,
    In this kingdom by the sea)
That the wind came out of the cloud by night,
    Chilling and killing my Annabel Lee.

But our love it was stronger by far than the love
    Of those who were older than we—
    Of many far wiser than we—
And neither the angels in heaven above,
    Nor the demons down under the sea,
Can ever dissever my soul from the soul
    Of the beautiful ANNABEL LEE :

For the moon never beams, without bringing me dreams
    Of the beautiful ANNABEL LEE ;
And the stars never rise, but I feel the bright eyes
    Of the beautiful ANNABEL LEE ;
And so, all the night-tide, I lie down by the side
Of my darling—my darling—my life and my bride,
    In the sepulchre there by the sea,
    In her tomb by the sounding sea.

TO MY MOTHER.

BECAUSE I feel that, in the Heavens above,
    The angels, whispering to one another,
Can find, among their burning terms of love,
    None so devotional as that of " Mother,"
Therefore by that dear name I long have called you—
    You who are more than mother unto me,
And fill my heart of hearts, where Death installed you
    In setting my Virginia's spirit free.
My mother—my own mother, who died early,
    Was but the mother of myself; but you
Are mother to the one I loved so dearly,
    And thus are dearer than the mother I knew
By that infinity with which my wife
    Was dearer to my soul than its soul-life.

THE HAUNTED PALACE.

In the greenest of our valleys
   By good angels tenanted,
Once a fair and stately palace—
   Radiant palace—reared its head.
In the monarch Thought's dominion—
   It stood there !
Never seraph spread a pinion
   Over fabric half so fair !

Banners yellow, glorious, golden,
   On its roof did float and flow,
(This—all this—was in the olden
   Time long ago,)
And every gentle air that dallied,
   In that sweet day,
Along the ramparts plumed and pallid,
   A wingéd odour went away.

Wanderers in that happy valley,
   Through two luminous windows, saw
Spirits moving musically,
   To a lute's well-tunéd law,
Round about a throne where, sitting
   (Porphyrogene !)
In stute his glory well befitting,
   The ruler of the realm was seen.

And all with pearl and ruby glowing
   Was the fair palace door,
Through which came flowing, flowing, flowing,
   And sparkling evermore,
A troop of Echoes, whose sweet duty
   Was but to sing,
In voices of surpassing beauty,
   The wit and wisdom of their king.

But evil things, in robes of sorrow,
   Assailed the monarch's high estate.
(Ah, let us mourn !—for never morrow
   Shall dawn upon him desolate !)
And round about his home the glory
   That blushed and bloomed,
Is but a dim-remembered story
   Of the old time entombed.

And travellers, now, within that valley,
   Through the red-litten windows see
Vast forms, that move fantastically
   To a discordant melody,
While, like a ghastly rapid river,
   Through the pale door
A hideous throng rush out forever
   And laugh—but smile no more.

THE CONQUEROR WORM.

Lo ! 'tis a gala night
  Within the lonesome latter years !
An angel throng, bewinged, bedight
  In veils, and drowned in tears,
Sit in a theatre, to see
  A play of hopes and fears,
While the orchestra breathes fitfully
  The music of the spheres.

Mimes, in the form of God on high,
  Mutter and mumble low,
And hither and thither fly—
  Mere puppets they, who come and go
At bidding of vast formless things
  That shift the scenery to and fro,
Flapping from out their Condor wings
  Invisible Wo !

That motley drama—oh, be sure
  It shall not be forgot !
With its Phantom chased for evermore,
  By a crowd that seize it not,
Through a circle that ever returneth in
  To the self-same spot,
And much of Madness, and more of Sin,
  And Horror the soul of the plot.

But see, amid the mimic rout
   A crawling shape intrude !
A blood-red thing that writhes from out
   The scenic solitude !
It writhes !—it writhes !—with mortal pangs
   The mimes become its food,
And the angels sob at vermin fangs
   In human gore imbued.

Out—out are the lights—out all !
   And, over each quivering form,
The curtain, a funeral pall,
   Comes down with the rush of a storm,
And the angels, all pallid and wan,
   Uprising, unveiling, affirm
That the play is the tragedy, " Man,"
   And its hero the Conqueror Worm.

TO F——s S. O——d.

Thou wouldst be loved ?—then let thy heart
   From its present pathway part not !
Being everything which now thou art,
   Be nothing which thou art not.
So with the world thy gentle ways,
   Thy grace, thy more than beauty,
Shall be an endless theme of praise,
   And love—a simple duty.

TO ONE IN PARADISE.

THOU wast that all to me, love,
  For which my soul did pine—
A green isle in the sea, love,
  A fountain and a shrine,
All wreathed with fairy fruits and flowers,
  And all the flowers were mine.

Ah, dream too bright to last !
  Ah, starry Hope ! that didst arise
But to be overcast !
  A voice from out the Future cries,
" On ! on !"—but o'er the Past
  (Dim gulf !) my spirit hovering lies
Mute, motionless, aghast !

For, alas ! alas ! with me
  The light of Life is o'er !
  "No more—no more—no more—"
(Such language holds the solemn sea
  To the sands upon the shore)
Shall bloom the thunder-blasted tree,
  Or the stricken eagle soar !

And all my days are trances,
  And all my nightly dreams
Are where thy dark eye glances,
  And where thy footstep gleams—
In what ethereal dances,
  By what eternal streams

THE VALLEY OF UNREST.

Once it smiled a silent dell
Where the people did not dwell ;
They had gone unto the wars,
Trusting to the mild-eyed stars,
Nightly, from their azure towers,
To keep watch above the flowers,
In the midst of which all day
The red sun-light lazily lay.
Now each visiter shall confess
The sad valley's restlessness.
Nothing there is motionless—
Nothing save the airs that brood
Over the magic solitude.
Ah, by no wind are stirred those trees
That palpitate like the chill seas
Around the misty Hebrides !
Ah, by no wind those clouds are driven
That rustle through the unquiet Heaven
Uneasily, from morn till even,
Over the violets there that lie
In myriad types of the human eye—
Over the lilies there that wave
And weep above a nameless grave !
They wave :—from out their fragrant tops
Eternal dews come down in drops.
They weep :—from off their delicate stems
Perennial tears descend in gems.

THE CITY IN THE SEA.

Lo! Death has reared himself a throne
In a strange city lying alone
Far down within the dim West,
Where the good and the bad and the worst and the best
Have gone to their eternal rest.
There shrines and palaces and towers
(Time-eaten towers that tremble not!)
Resemble nothing that is ours.
Around, by lifting winds forgot,
Resignedly beneath the sky
The melancholy waters lie.

No rays from the holy heaven come down
On the long night-time of that town;
But light from out the lurid sea
Streams up the turrets silently—
Gleams up the pinnacles far and free—
Up domes—up spires—up kingly halls—
Up fanes—up Babylon-like walls—
Up shadowy long-forgotten bowers
Of sculptured ivy and stone flowers—
Up many and many a marvellous shrine
Whose wreathéd friezes intertwine
The v ol, the violet, and the vine.

Resignedly beneath the sky
The melancholy waters lie.
So blend the turrets and shadows there
That all seem pendulous in air,
While from a proud tower in the town
Death looks gigantically down.

There open fanes and gaping graves
Yawn level with the luminous waves;
But not the riches there that lie
In each idol's diamond eye—
Not the gaily-jewelled dead
Tempt the waters from their bed;
For no ripples curl, alas!
Along that wilderness of glass—
No swellings tell that winds may be
Upon some far-off happier sea—
No heavings hint that winds have been
On seas less hideously serene.

But lo, a stir is in the air!
The wave—there is a movement there!
As if the towers had thrust aside,
In slightly sinking, the dull tide—
As if their tops had feebly given
A void within the filmy Heaven.
The waves have now a redder glow—
The hours are breathing faint and low—
And when, amid no earthly moans,
Down, down that town shall settle hence,
Hell, rising from a thousand thrones,
Shall do it reverence.

THE SLEEPER.

At midnight, in the month of June,
I stand beneath the mystic moon.
An opiate vapour, dewy, dim,
Exhales from out her golden rim,
And, softly dripping, drop by drop,
Upon the quiet mountain top,
Steals drowsily and musically
Into the universal valley.
The rosemary nods upon the grave ;
The lily lolls upon the wave ;
Wrapping the fog about its breast,
The ruin moulders into rest ;
Looking like Lethe, see ! the lake
A conscious slumber seems to take,
And would not, for the world, awake.
All Beauty sleeps !—and lo ! where lies
(Her casement open to the skies)
Irene, with her Destinies !

Oh, lady bright ! can it be right—
This window open to the night ?
The wanton airs, from the tree-top,
Laughingly through the lattice drop—
The bodiless airs, a wizard rout,
Flit through thy chamber in and out,

3*

And wave the curtain canopy
So fitfully—so fearfully—
Above the closed and fringed lid
'Neath which thy slumb'ring soul lies hid,
That, o'er the floor and down the wall,
Like ghosts the shadows rise and fall !
Oh, lady dear, hast thou no fear ?
Why and what art thou dreaming here ?
Sure thou art come o'er far-off seas,
A wonder to these garden trees !
Strange is thy pallor ! strange thy dress !
Strange, above all, thy length of tress,
And this all solemn silentness !

The lady sleeps ! Oh, may her sleep,
Which is enduring, so be deep !
Heaven have her in its sacred keep !
This chamber changed for one more holy,
This bed for one more melancholy,
I pray to God that she may lie
Forever with unopened eye,
While the dim sheeted ghosts go by !

My love, she sleeps ! Oh, may her sleep
As it is lasting, so be deep !
Soft may the worms about her creep !
Far in the forest, dim and old,
For her may some tall vault unfold—
Some vault that oft hath flung its black
And winged pannels fluttering back,
Triumphant, o'er the crested palls,
Of her grand family funerals—
Some sepulchre, remote, alone,

Against whose portal she hath thrown,
In childhood, many an idle stone —
Some tomb from out whose sounding door
She ne'er shall force an echo more,
Thrilling to think, poor child of sin !
It was the dead who groaned within.

SILENCE.

THERE are some qualities—some incorporate things,
  That have a double life, which thus is made
A type of that twin entity which springs
  From matter and light, evinced in solid and shade.
There is a two-fold *Silence*—sea and shore—
  Body and soul. One dwells in lonely places,
  Newly with grass o'ergrown ; some solemn graces,
Some human memories and tearful lore,
Render him terrorless : his name's " No More."
He is the corporate Silence : dread him not !
  No power hath he of evil in himself ;
But should some urgent fate (untimely lot !)
  Bring thee to meet his shadow (nameless elf,
That haunteth the lone regions where hath trod
No foot of man,) commend thyself to God !

A DREAM WITHIN A DREAM.

TAKE this kiss upon the brow !
And, in parting from you now,
Thus much let me avow—
You are not wrong, who deem
That my days have been a dream ;
Yet if hope has flown away
In a night, or in a day,
In a vision, or in none,
Is it therefore the less *gone ?*
All that we see or seem
Is but a dream within a dream.

I stand amid the roar
Of a surf-tormented shore,
And I hold within my hand
Grains of the golden sand—
How few ! yet how they creep
Through my fingers to the deep,
While I weep—while I weep !
O God ! can I not grasp
Them with a tighter clasp ?
O God ! can I not save
One from the pitiless wave ?
Is *all* that we see or seem
But a dream within a dream !

DREAM-LAND

By a route obscure and lonely,
Haunted by ill angels only,
Where an Eidolon, named NIGHT,
On a black throne reigns upright,
I have reached these lands but newly
From an ultimate dim Thule—
From a wild weird clime that lieth, sublime,
    Out of SPACE—out of TIME.

Bottomless vales and boundless floods,
And chasms, and caves, and Titan woods,
With forms that no man can discover
For the dews that drip all over ;
Mountains toppling evermore
Into seas without a shore ;
Seas that restlessly aspire,
Surging, unto skies of fire ;
Lakes that endlessly outspread
Their lone waters—lone and dead .—
Their still waters—still and chilly
With the snows of the lolling lily.

By the lakes that thus outspread
Their lone waters, lone and dead,—

Their sad waters, sad and chilly
With the snows of the lolling lily,—
By the mountains—near the river
Murmuring lowly, murmuring ever,—
By the grey woods,—by the swamp
Where the toad and the newt encamp,—
By the dismal tarns and pools
    Where dwell the Ghouls,—
By each spot the most unholy—
In each nook most melancholy,—
There the traveller meets aghast
Sheeted Memories of the Past—
Shrouded forms that start and sigh
As they pass the wanderer by—
White-robed forms of friends long given,
In agony, to the Earth—and Heaven.

For the heart whose woes are legion
'Tis a peaceful, soothing region—
For the spirit that walks in shadow
'Tis—oh 'tis an Eldorado !
But the traveller, travelling through it,
May not—dare not openly view it ;
Never its mysteries are exposed
To the weak human eye unclosed ;
So wills its King, who hath forbid
The uplifting of the fringed lid ;
And thus the sad Soul that here passes
Beholds it but through darkened glasses.

By a route obscure and lonely,
Haunted by ill angels only,

Where an Eidolon, named NIGHT,
On a black throne reigns upright,
I have wandered home but newly
From this ultimate dim Thule.

TO ZANTE.

Fair isle, that from the fairest of all flowers,
  Thy gentlest of all gentle names dost take !
How many memories of what radiant hours
  At sight of thee and thine at once awake !
How many scenes of what departed bliss !
  How many thoughts of what entombéd hopes !
How many visions of a maiden that is
  No more—no more upon thy verdant slopes !
No more ! alas, that magical sad sound
  Transforming all !   Thy charms shall please *no more*—
Thy memory *no more !*   Accurséd ground
  Henceforth I hold thy flower-enamelled shore,
O hyacinthine isle !   O purple Zante !
  "Isola d' oro !   Fior di Levante !"

EULALIE.

I DWELT alone
In a world of moan,
And my soul was a stagnant tide,
Till the fair and gentle Eulalie became my blushing bride—
Till the yellow-haired young Eulalie became my smiling bride.

Ah, less—less bright
The stars of the night
Than the eyes of the radiant girl !
And never a flake
That the vapour can make
With the moon-tints of purple and pearl,
Can vie with the modest Eulalie's most unregarded curl—
Can compare with the bright-eyed Eulalie's most humble and
careless curl.

Now Doubt—now Pain
Come never again,
For her soul gives me sigh for sigh,
And all day long
Shines, bright and strong,
Astarté within the sky,
While ever to her dear Eulalie upturns her matron eye—
While ever to her young Eulalie upturns her violet eye.

ELDORADO.

GAILY bedight,
A gallant knight,
In sunshine and in shadow,
Had journeyed long,
Singing a song,
In search of Eldorado.

But he grew old——
This knight so bold——
And o'er his heart a shadow
Fell as he found
No spot of ground
That looked like Eldorado.

And, as his strength
Failed him at length,
He met a pilgrim shadow——
"Shadow," said he,
"Where can it be——
This land of Eldorado?"

"Over the Mountains
Of the Moon,
Down the Valley of the Shadow,
Ride, boldly ride,"
The shade replied,——
"If you seek for Eldorado!"

ISRAFEL.[*]

In Heaven a spirit doth dwell
  " Whose heart-strings are a lute ;"
None sing so wildly well
As the angel Israfel,
And the giddy stars (so legends tell)
Ceasing their hymns, attend the spell
  Of his voice, all mute.

Tottering above
  In her highest noon,
  The enamoured moon
Blushes with love,
  While, to listen, the red levin
  (With the rapid Pleiads, even,
  Which were seven,)
  Pauses in Heaven.

And they say (the starry choir
  And the other listening things)
That Israfeli's fire
Is owing to that lyre
  By which he sits and sings—
The trembling living wire
Of those unusual strings.

[*] And the angel Israfel, whose heart-strings are a lute, and who has the
sweetest voice of all God's creatures.—KORAN.

But the skies that angel trod,
  Where deep thoughts are a duty—
Where Love's a grown up God—
  Where the Houri glances áre
Imbued with all the beauty
  Which we worship in a star.

Therefore, thou art not wrong,
  Israfeli, who despisest
An unimpassioned song ;
To thee the laurels belong,
  Best bard, because the wisest !
Merrily live, and long !

The ecstasies above
  With thy burning measures suit—
Thy grief, thy joy, thy hate, thy love,
  With the fervour of thy lute—
  Well may the stars be mute !

Yes, Heaven is thine ; but this
  Is a world of sweets and sours ;
  Our flowers are merely—flowers,
And the shadow of thy perfect bliss
  Is the sunshine of ours.

If I could dwell
Where Israfel
  Hath dwelt, and he where I,
He might not sing so wildly well
  A mortal melody,
While a bolder note than this might swell
  From my lyre within the sky.

FOR ANNIE.

THANK Heaven! the crisis—
  The danger is past,
And the lingering illness
  Is over at last—
And the fever called "Living"
  Is conquered at last.

Sadly, I know
  I am shorn of my strength,
And no muscle I move
  As I lie at full length—
But no matter!—I feel
  I am better at length.

And I rest so composedly,
  Now, in my bed,
That any beholder
  Might fancy me dead—
Might start at beholding me,
  Thinking me dead.

The moaning and groaning,
  The sighing and sobbing,
Are quieted now,
  With that horrible throbbing
At heart :—ah, that horrible,
  Horrible throbbing!

The sickness—the nausea—
　The pitiless pain—
Have ceased, with the fever
　That maddened my brain—
With the fever called "Living"
　That burned in my brain.

And oh ! of all tortures
　That torture the worst
Has abated—the terrible
　Torture of thirst
For the napthaline river
　Of Passion accurst :—
I have drank of a water
　That quenches all thirst :—

Of a water that flows,
　With a lullaby sound,
From a spring but a very few
　Feet under ground—
From a cavern not very far
　Down under ground.

And ah ! let it never
　Be foolishly said
That my room it is gloomy
　And narrow my bed ;
For man never slept
　In a different bed—
And, to *sleep*, you must slumber
　In just such a bed.

My tantalized spirit
　Here blandly reposes,
Forgetting, or never
　Regretting its roses—
Its old agitations
　Of myrtles and roses :

For now, while so quietly
   Lying, it fancies
A holier odor
   About it, of pansies—
A rosemary odor,
   Commingled with pansies—
With rue and the beautiful
   Puritan pansies.

And so it lies happily,
   Bathing in many
A dream of the truth
   And the beauty of Annie—
Drowned in a bath
   Of the tresses of Annie.

She tenderly kissed me,
   She fondly caressed,
And then I fell gently
   To sleep on her breast—
Deeply to sleep
   From the heaven of her breast.

When the light was extinguished,
   She covered me warm,
And she prayed to the angels
   To keep me from harm—
To the queen of the angels
   To shield me from harm.

And I lie so composedly,
   Now, in my bed,
(Knowing her love)
   That you fancy me dead—
And I rest so contentedly,
   Now in my bed,
(With her love at my breast)
   That you fancy me dead—

That you shudder to look at me,
  Thinking me dead :——

But my heart it is brighter
  Than all of the many
Stars in the sky,
  For it sparkles with Annie——
It glows with the light
  Of the love of my Annie——
With the thought of the light
  Of the eyes of my Annie.

T O ———.

I HEED not that my earthly lot
  Hath——little of Earth in it——
That years of love have been forgot
  In the hatred of a minute :——
I mourn not that the desolate
  Are happier, sweet, than I,
But that *you* sorrow for *my* fate
  Who am a passer by.

BRIDAL BALLAD.

Tʜᴇ ring is on my hand,
   And the wreath is on my brow ;
Satins and jewels grand
Are all at my command,
   And I am happy now.

And my lord he loves me well ;
   But, when first he breathed his **vow**
I felt my bosom swell—
For the words rang as a knell,
And the voice seemed *his* who fell
In the battle down the dell,
   And who is happy now.

But he spoke to re-assure me,
   And he kissed my pallid brow
While a reverie came o'er me,
And to the church-yard bore me,
And I sighed to him before me,
Thinking him dead D'Elormie,
   " Oh, I am happy now !"

And thus the words were spoken,
   And this the plighted vow,
And, though my faith be broken,
And, though my heart be broken,

Behold the golden token
  That *proves* me happy now !

Would God I could awaken !
  For I dream I know not now,
And my soul is sorely shaken
Lest an evil step be taken,—
Lest the dead who is forsaken
  May not be happy now.

TO F———.

BELOVED ! amid the earnest woes
  That crowd around my earthly path—
(Drear path, alas ! where grows
Not even one lonely rose)—
  My soul at least a solace hath
In dreams of thee, and therein knows
An Eden of bland repose.

And thus thy memory is to me
  Like some enchanted far-off isle
In some tumultuous sea—
Some ocean throbbing.far and free
  With storms—but where meanwhile
Serenest skies continually
  Just o'er that one bright island smile.

SCENES from "POLITIAN;

AN UNPUBLISHED DRAMA.

I.

ROME.—A Hall in a Palace.   Alessandra and Castiglione

Alessandra. Thou art sad, Castiglione.
Castiglione. Sad !—not I.
Oh, I'm the happiest, happiest man in Rome !
A few days more, thou knowest, my Alessandra,
Will make thee mine.   Oh, I am very happy !
  Aless. Methinks thou hast a singular way of showing
Thy happiness '—what ails thee, cousin of mine ?
Why didst thou sigh so deeply ?
  Cas. Did I sigh ?
I was not conscious of it.   It is a fashion,
A sil'v—a most silly fashion I have
When I am *very* happy.   Did I sigh ?   (*sighing.*)
  Aless. Thou didst.   Thou art not well.   Thou hast indulged
Too much of late, and I am vexed to see it.
Late hours and wine, Castiglione,—these
Will ruin thee ! thou art already altered—
Thy looks are haggard—nothing so wears away
The constitution as late hours and wine.
  Cas. (*musing.*) Nothing, fair cousin, nothing—not even deep
    sorrow—·

Wears it away like evil hours and wine.
I will amend.

 Aless. Do it! I would have thee drop
Thy riotous company, too—fellows low born—
Ill suit the like with old Di Broglio's heir
And Alessandra's husband.

 Cas. I will drop them.

 Aless. Thou wilt—thou must. Attend thou also more
To thy dress and equipage—they are over plain
For thy lofty rank and fashion—much depends
Upon appearances.

 Cas. I'll see to it.

 Aless. Then see to it!—pay more attention, sir,
To a becoming carriage—much thou wantest
In dignity.

 Cas. Much, much, oh much I want
In proper dignity.

 Aless. (*haughtily.*) Thou mockest me, sir!

 Cas. (*abstractedly.*) Sweet, gentle Lalage!

 Aless. Heard I aright?
I speak to him—he speaks of Lalage!
Sir Count! (*places her hand on his shoulder*) what art thou
  dreaming? he's not well!
What ails thee, sir?

 Cas. (*starting.*) Cousin! fair cousin!—madam!
I crave thy pardon—indeed I am not well—
Your hand from off my shoulder, if you please.
This air is most oppressive!—Madam—the Duke!

Enter Di Broglio.

 Di Broglio. My son, I've news for thee!—hey?—what's the
  matter? (*observing Alessandra.*)
I' the pouts? Kiss her, Castiglione! kiss her,
You dog! and make it up, I say, this minute!

I've news for you both.   Politian is expected
Hourly in Rome—Politian, Earl of Leicester!
We'll have him at the wedding.   'Tis his first visit
To the imperial city.
    Aless. What! Politian
Of Britain, Earl of Leicester?
    Di Brog. The same, my love.
We'll have him at the wedding.   A man quite young
In years, but grey in fame.   I have not seen him, ·
But Rumour speaks of him as of a prodigy
Pre-eminent in arts and arms, and wealth,
And high descent.   We'll have him at the wedding.
    Aless. I have heard much of this Politian.
Gay, volatile and giddy—is he not?
And little given to thinking.
    Di Brog. Far from it, love.
No branch, they say, of all philosophy
So deep abstruse he has not mastered it.
Learned as few are learned.
    Aless. 'Tis very strange!
I have known men have seen Politian
And sought his company.   They speak of him
As of one who entered madly into life,
Drinking the cup of pleasure to the dregs.
    Cas. Ridiculous!   Now *I* have seen Politian
And know him well—nor learned nor mirthful he.
He is a dreamer and a man shut out
From common passions.
    Di Brog. Children, we disagree.
Let us go forth and taste the fragrant air
Of the garden.   Did I dream, or did I hear
Politian was a *melancholy* man?   *(exeunt.)*

II.

ROME. A Lady's apartment, with a window open and looking into a garden. Lalage, in deep mourning, reading at a table on which lie some books and a hand mirror. In the back ground Jacinta (a servant maid) leans carelessly upon a chair.

Lal. Jacinta! is it thou?

Jac. (*pertly.*) Yes, Ma'am, I'm here.

Lal. I did not know, Jacinta, you were in waiting.
Sit down!—let not my presence trouble you—
Sit down!—for I am humble, most humble.

Jac. (*aside.*) 'Tis time.

> (*Jacinta seats herself in a side-long manner upon the chair, resting her elbows upon the back, and regarding her mistress with a contemptuous look. Lalage continues to read.*)

Lal. " It in another climate, so he said,
" Bore a bright golden flower, but not i' this soil!"

> (*pauses—turns over some leaves, and resumes.*)

" No lingering winters there, nor snow, nor shower—
" But Ocean ever to refresh mankind
" Breathes the shrill spirit of the western wind."
Oh, beautiful!—most beautiful!—how like
To what my fevered soul doth dream of Heaven!
O happy land! (*pauses.*) She died!—the maiden died!
O still more happy maiden who couldst die!
Jacinta!

> (*Jacinta returns no answer, and Lalage presently resumes.*)

Again!—a similar tale
Told of a beauteous dame beyond the sea!

Thus speaketh one Ferdinand in the words of the play—
" She died full young"—one Bossola answers him—
" I think not so—her infelicity
" Seemed to have years too many"—Ah luckless lady !
Jacinta ! (*still no answer.*)

    Here's a far sterner story
But like—oh, very like in its despair—
Of that Egyptian queen, winning so easily
A thousand hearts—losing at length her own.
She died. Thus endeth the history—and her maids
Lean over her and weep—two gentle maids
With gentle names—Eiros and Charmion !
Rainbow and Dove !——Jacinta !

  Jac. (*pettishly.*) Madam, what *is* it ?

  Lal. Wilt thou, my good Jacinta, be so kind
As go down in the library and bring me
The Holy Evangelists.

  Jac. Pshaw ! (*exit.*)

  Lal. If there be balm
For the wounded spirit in Gilead it is there !
Dew in the night time of my bitter trouble
Will there be found—" dew sweeter far than that
Which hangs like chains of pearl on Hermon hill."

   (*re-enter Jacinta, and throws a volume on the table.*)
There, ma'am, 's the book. Indeed she is very troublesome.
             (*aside.*)

  Lal. (*astonished.*) What didst thou say, Jacinta ? Have I
   done aught
To grieve thee or to vex thee ?—I am sorry.
For thou hast served me long and ever been
Trust-worthy and respectful. (*resumes her reading.*)

  Jac. I can't believe
She has any more jewels—no—no—she gave me all. (*aside.*)

Lal. What didst thou say, Jacinta ? Now I bethink me
Thou hast not spoken lately of thy wedding.
How fares good Ugo ?—and when is it to be ?
Can I do aught ?—is there no farther aid
Thou needest, Jacinta ?

    Jac. Is there no *further* aid !
That's meant for me. (*aside*) I'm sure, Madam, you need not
Be always throwing those jewels in my teeth.

    Lal. Jewels ! Jacinta,—now indeed, Jacinta,
I thought not of the jewels.

    Jac. Oh ! perhaps not !
But then I might have sworn it. After all,
There's Ugo says the ring is only paste,
For he's sure the Count Castiglione never
Would have given a real diamond to such as you ;
And at the best I'm certain, Madam, you cannot
Have use for jewels *now*. But I might have sworn it. (*exit.*)
      (*Lalage bursts into tears and leans her head upon the
      table—after a short pause raises it.*)

    Lal. Poor Lalage !—and is it come to this ?
Thy servant maid !—but courage !—'tis but a viper
Whom thou hast cherished to sting thee to the soul !
        (*taking up the mirror.*)
Ha ! here at least's a friend—too much a friend
In earlier days—a friend will not deceive thee.
Fair mirror and true ! now tell me (for thou canst)
A tale—a pretty tale—and heed thou not
Though it be rife with woe. It answers me.
It speaks of sunken eyes, and wasted cheeks,
And Beauty long deceased—remembers me
Of Joy departed—Hope, the Seraph Hope,
Inurned and entombed !—now, in a tone
Low, sad, and solemn, but most audible,

Whispers of early grave untimely yawning
For ruined maid.   Fair mirror and true !—thou liest not !
Thou hast no end to gain—no heart to break—
Castiglione lied who said he loved——
Thou true—he false !—false !—false !

> (*while she speaks, a monk enters her apartment, and approaches unobserved.*)

Monk. Refuge thou hast,
Sweet daughter ! in Heaven.   Think of eternal things !
Give up thy soul to penitence, and pray !

Lal. (*arising hurriedly.*) I *cannot* pray !—My soul is at war
with God !
The frightful sounds of merriment below
Disturb my senses—go ! I cannot pray—
The sweet airs from the garden worry me !
Thy presence grieves me—go !—thy priestly raiment
Fills me with dread—thy ebony crucifix
With horror and awe !

Monk. Think of thy precious soul !

Lal. Think of my early days !—think of my father
And mother in Heaven ! think of our quiet home,
And the rivulet that ran before the door !
Think of my little sisters !—think of them !
And think of me !—think of my trusting love
And confidence—his vows—my ruin—think—think
Of my unspeakable misery !——begone !
Yet stay ! yet stay !—what was it thou saidst of prayer
And penitence ?   Didst thou not speak of faith
And vows before the throne ?

Monk. I did.

Lal. 'Tis well.   .
There *is* a vow were fitting should be made—

A sacred vow, imperative, and urgent,
A solemn vow!

   Monk. Daughter, this zeal is well!

   Lal. Father, this zeal is anything but well!
Hast thou a crucifix fit for this thing?
A crucifix whereon to register
This sacred vow?   (*he hands her his own.*)
Not that—Oh! no!—no!—no!   (*shuddering.*)
Not that! Not that!—I tell thee, holy man,
Thy raiments and thy ebony cross affright me!
Stand back! I have a crucifix myself,—
I have a crucifix! Methinks 'twere fitting
The deed—the vow—the symbol of the deed—
And the deed's register should tally, father!

      (*draws a cross-handled dagger and raises it on high.*)
Behold the cross wherewith a vow like mine
Is written in Heaven!

   Monk. Thy words are madness, daughter,
And speak a purpose unholy—thy lips are livid—
Thine eyes are wild—tempt not the wrath divine!
Pause ere too late!—oh be not—be not rash!
Swear not the oath—oh swear it not!

   Lal. 'Tis sworn!

*

III.

Baldazzar.————Arouse thee now, Politian !
Thou must not—nay indeed, indeed, thou shalt not
Give way unto these humours.   Be thyself !
Shake off the idle fancies that beset thee,
And live, for now thou diest !
   Politian. Not so, Baldazzar !
Surely I live.
   Bal. Politian, it doth grieve me
To see thee thus.
   Pol. Baldazzar, it doth grieve me
To give thee cause for grief, my honoured friend.
Command me, sir ! what wouldst thou have me do ?
At thy behest I will shake off that nature
Which from my forefathers I did inherit,
Which with my mother's milk I did imbibe,
And be no more Politian, but some other.
Command me, sir !
   Bal. To the field then—to the field—
To the senate or the field.
   Pol. Alas ! alas !
There is an imp would follow me even there !
There is an imp *hath* followed me even there !
There is——what voice was that ?
   Bal. I heard it not.
1 heard not any voice except thine own,
And the echo of thine own.

Pol. Then I but dreamed.

Bal. Give not thy soul to dreams : the camp—the court
Befit thee—Fame awaits thee—Glory calls—
And her the trumpet-tongued thou wilt not hear
In hearkening to imaginary sounds
And phantom voices.

Pol. It *is* a phantom voice !
Didst thou not hear it *then ?*

Bal. I heard it not.

Pol. Thou heardst it not !——Baldazzar, speak no more
To me, Politian, of thy camps and courts.
Oh ! I am sick, sick, sick, even unto death,
Of the hollow and high-sounding vanities
Of the populous Earth ! Bear with me yet awhile !
We have been boys together—school-fellows—
And now are friends—yet shall not be so long—
For in the eternal city thou shalt do me
A kind and gentle office, and a Power—
A Power august, benignant and supreme—
Shall then absolve thee of all farther duties
Unto thy friend.

Bal. Thou speakest a fearful riddle
I *will* not understand.

Pol. Yet now as Fate
Approaches, and the Hours are breathing low,
The sands of Time are changed to golden grains,
And dazzle me, Baldazzar. Alas ! alas !
I *cannot* die, having within my heart
So keen a relish for the beautiful
As hath been kindled within it. Methinks the air
Is balmier now than it was wont to be—
Rich melodies are floating in the winds—
A rarer loveliness bedecks the earth—

And with a holier lustre the quiet moon
Sitteth in Heaven.—Hist ! hist ! thou canst not say
Thou hearest not *now*, Baldazzar ?

. *Bal.* Indeed I hear not.

    Pol. Not hear it !—listen now—listen !—the faintest sound
And yet the sweetest that ear ever heard !
A lady's voice !—and sorrow in the tone !
Baldazzar, it oppresses me like a spell !
Again !—again !—how solemnly it falls
Into my heart of hearts ! that eloquent voice
Surely I never heard—yet it were well
Had I *but* heard it with its thrilling tones
In earlier days !

    Bal. I myself hear it now.
Be still !—the voice, if I mistake not greatly,
Proceeds from yonder lattice—which you may see
Very plainly through the window—it belongs,
Does it not ? unto this palace of the Duke.
The singer is undoubtedly beneath
The roof of his Excellency—and perhaps
Is even that Alessandra of whom he spoke
As the betrothed of Castiglione,
His son and heir.

    Pol. Be still !—it comes again !

    Voice   " And is thy heart so strong
(very faintly.) As for to leave me thus
              Who hath loved thee so long
              In wealth and wo among ?
              And is thy heart so strong
              As for to leave me thus ?
                    Say nay—say nay !"

    Bal. The song is English, and I oft have heard it
In merry England—never so plaintively—

Hist ! hist ! it comes again !

  Voice   " Is it so strong
(*more loudly.*) As for to leave me thus
     Who hath loved thee so long
     In wealth and wo among ?
     And is thy heart so strong
     As for to leave me thus ?

       Say nay—say nay !'"

Bal. 'Tis hushed and all is still !

Pol. All *is not* still.

Bal. Let us go down.

Pol. Go down, Baldazzar, go !

Bal. The hour is growing late—the Duke awaits us,—
Thy presence is expected in the hall
Below. What ails thee, Earl Politian ?

  Voice " Who hath loved thee so long,
(*distinctly.*) In wealth and wo among,
     And is thy heart so strong ?

      Say nay—say nay !'"

Bal. Let us descend !—'tis time. Politian, give
These fancies to the wind. Remember, pray,
Your bearing lately savoured much of rudeness
Unto the Duke. Arouse thee ! and remember !

 Pol. Remember ? I do. Lead on ! I *do* remember.

           (*going.*)

Let us descend. Believe me I would give,
Freely would give the broad lands of my earldom
To look upon the face hidden by yon lattice—
" To gaze upon that veiled face, and hear
Once more that silent tongue."

 Bal. Let me beg you, sir,
Descend with me—the Duke may be offended.
Let us go down, I pray you.

(*Voice loudly.*) *Say nay !—say nay !*

Pol. (*aside.*) 'Tis strange !—'tis very strange—methought the voice

Chimed in with my desires and bade me stay !

                             (*approaching the window.*) ·

Sweet voice ! I heed thee, and will surely stay.

Now be this Fancy, by Heaven, or be it Fate,

Still will I not descend. Baldazzar, make

Apology unto the Duke for me ;

I go not down to-night.

   Bal. Your lordship's pleasure

Shall be attended to. Good night, Politian.

   Pol. Good night, my friend, good night.

IV.

The gardens of a palace—Moonlight. Lalage and Politian.

Lalage. And dost thou speak of love
To *me*, Politian ?—dost thou speak of love
To Lalage ?—ah wo—ah wo is me !
This mockery is most cruel—most cruel indeed !
Politian. Weep not ! oh, sob not thus !—thy bitter tears
Will madden me.   Oh mourn not, Lalage—
Be comforted !   I know—I know it all,
And *still* I speak of love.   Look at me, brightest,
And beautiful Lalage !—turn here thine eyes !
Thou askest me if I could speak of love,
Knowing what I know, and seeing what I have seen.
Thou askest me that—and thus I answer thee—
Thus on my bended knee I answer thee.   (*kneeling.*)
Sweet Lalage, *I love thee—love thee—love thee ;*
Thro' good and ill—thro' weal and wo I *love thee.*
Not mother, with her first born on her knee,
Thrills with intenser love than I for thee.
Not on God's altar, in any time or clime,
Burned there a holier fire than burneth now
Within my spirit for *thee*.   And do I love ?   (*arising.*)
Even for thy woes I love thee—even for thy woes—
Thy beauty and thy woes.
Lal. Alas, proud Earl,
Thou dost forget thyself, remembering me !
How, in thy father's halls, among the maidens
Pure and reproachless of thy princely line,

Could the dishonoured Lalage abide ?
Thy wife, and with a tainted memory—
My seared and blighted name, how would it tally
With the ancestral honours of thy house,
And with thy glory ?

   Pol. Speak not to me of glory !
I hate—I loathe the name ; I do abhor
The unsatisfactory and ideal thing.
Art thou not Lalage and I Politian ?
Do I not love—art thou not beautiful—
What need we more ?   Ha ! glory !—now speak not of it
By all I hold most sacred and most solemn—
By all my wishes now—my fears hereafter—
By all I scorn on earth and hope in heaven—
There is no deed I would more glory in,
Than in thy cause to scoff at this same glory
And trample it under foot.   What matters it—
What matters it, my fairest, and my best,
That we go down unhonoured and forgotten
Into the dust—so we descend together.
Descend together—and then—and then perchance——

   Lal. Why dost thou pause, Politian ?

   Pol. And then perchance
Arise together, Lalage, and roam
The starry and quiet dwellings of the blest,
And still——

   Lal. Why dost thou pause, Politian ?

   Pol. And still *together—together*.

   Lal. Now Earl of Leicester !
Thou *lovest* me, and in my heart of hearts
I feel thou lovest me truly.

   Pol. Oh, Lalage ! (*throwing himself upon his knee.*)
And lovest thou *me* ?

Lal. Hist! hush! within the gloom
Of yonder trees methought a figure past—
A spectral figure, solemn, and slow, and noiseless—
Like the grim shadow Conscience, solemn and noiseless.

                                    (*walks across and returns.*)
I was mistaken—'twas but a giant bough
Stirred by the autumn wind.   Politian!

  Pol. My Lalage—my love! why art thou moved?
Why dost thou turn so pale?   Not Conscience' self,
Far less a shadow which thou likenest to it,
Should shake the firm spirit thus.   But the night wind
Is chilly—and these melancholy boughs
Throw over all things a gloom.

  Lal. Politian!
Thou speakest to me of love.   Knowest thou the land
With which all tongues are busy—a land new found—
Miraculously found by one of Genoa—
A thousand leagues within the golden west?
A fairy land of flowers, and fruit, and sunshine,
And crystal lakes, and over-arching forests,
And mountains, around whose towering summits the winds
Of Heaven untrammelled flow—which air to breathe
Is Happiness now, and will be Freedom hereafter
In days that are to come?

  Pol. O, wilt thou—wilt thou
Fly to that Paradise—my Lalage, wilt thou
Fly thither with me?   There Care shall be forgotten,
And Sorrow shall be no more, and Eros be all.
And life shall then be mine, for I will live
For thee, and in thine eyes—and thou shalt be
No more a mourner—but the radiant Joys
Shall wait upon thee, and the angel Hope
Attend thee ever; and I will kneel to thee

And worship thee, and call thee my beloved,
My own, my beautiful, my love, my wife,
My all ;—oh, wilt thou—wilt thou, Lalage,
Fly thither with me ?

   Lal. A deed is to be done—
Castiglione lives !

   Pol. And he shall die !   (*exit.*)

   Lal. (*after a pause.*) And—he—shall—die !———alas !
Castiglione die ?   Who spoke the words ?
Where am I ?—what was it he said ?—Politian !
Thou *art* not gone—thou art not *gone*, Politian !
I *feel* thou art not gone—yet dare not look,
Lest I behold thee not ; thou *couldst* not go
With those words upon thy lips—O, speak to me !
And let me hear thy voice—one word—one word,
To say thou art not gone,—one little sentence,
To say how thou dost scorn—how thou dost hate
My womanly weakness. Ha ! ha ! thou *art* not gone—
O speak to me ! I *knew* thou wouldst not go !
I knew thou wouldst not, couldst not, *durst* not go.
Villain, thou *art* not gone—thou mockest me !
And thus I clutch thee—thus !———He is gone, he is gone—
Gone—gone. Where am I ?———'tis well—'tis very well !
So that the blade be keen—the blow be sure,
'Tis well, 'tis *very* well—alas ! alas !

V.

The suburbs.   Politian alone.

Politian. This weakness grows upon me.   I am faint,
And much I fear me ill—it will not do
To die ere I have lived !—Stay—stay thy hand,
O Azrael, yet awhile !—Prince of the Powers
Of Darkness and the Tomb, O pity me !
O pity me ! let me not perish now,
In the budding of my Paradisal Hope !
Give me to live yet—yet a little while :
'Tis I who pray for life—I who so late
Demanded but to die !—what sayeth the Count ?
                    Enter Baldazzar.

Baldazzar. That knowing no cause of quarrel or of feud
Between the Earl Politian and himself,
He doth decline your cartel.

   Pol. What didst thou say ?
What answer was it you brought me, good Baldazzar ?
With what excessive fragrance the zephyr comes
Laden from yonder bowers !—a fairer day,
Or one more worthy Italy, methinks
No mortal eyes have seen !—*what* said the Count ?

   Bal. That he, Castiglione, not being aware
Of any feud existing, or any cause
Of quarrel between your lordship and himself
Cannot accept the challenge.

   Pol. It is most true—
All this is very true.   When saw you, sir,

When saw you now, Baldazzar, in the frigid
Ungenial Britain which we left so lately,
A heaven so calm as this—so utterly free
From the evil taint of clouds?—and he did *say?*

   Bal. No more, my lord, than I have told you, sir:
The Count Castiglione will not fight,
Having no cause for quarrel.

   Pol. Now this is true—
All very true. Thou art my friend, Baldazzar,
And I have not forgotten it—thou'lt do me
A piece of service; wilt thou go back and say
Unto this man, that I, the Earl of Leicester,
Hold him a villain?—thus much, I prythee, say
Unto the Count—it is exceeding just
He should have cause for quarrel.

   Bal. My lord!—my friend!———

   Pol. (*aside.*) 'Tis he—he comes himself! (*aloud.*) thou rea-
     sonest well.
I know what thou wouldst say—not send the message—
Well!—I will think of it—I will not send it.
Now prythee, leave me—hither doth come a person
With whom affairs of a most private nature
I would adjust.

   Bal. I go—to-morrow we meet,
Do we not?—at the Vatican.

   Pol. At the Vatican.   (*exit Bal.*)

Enter Castiglione.

   Cas. The Earl of Leicester here!

   Pol. I *am* the Earl of Leicester, and thou seest,
Dost thou not? that I am here.

   Cas. My lord, some strange,
Some singular mistake—misunderstanding—
Hath without doubt arisen: thou hast been urged

Thereby, in heat of anger, to address
Some words most unaccountable, in writing,
To me, Castiglione; the bearer being
Baldazzar, Duke of Surrey. I am aware
Of nothing which might warrant thee in this thing,
Having given thee no offence. Ha!—am I right?
'Twas a mistake?—undoubtedly—we all
Do err at times.

   Pol. Draw, villain, and prate no more!

   Cas. Ha!—draw?—and villain? have at thee then at once,
Proud Earl!   (*draws.*)

   Pol. (*drawing.*) Thus to the expiatory tomb,
Untimely sepulchre, I do devote thee
In the name of Lalage!

   Cas. (*letting fall his sword and recoiling to the extremity of
     the stage.*)
Of Lalage!
Hold off—thy sacred hand!—avaunt I say!
Avaunt—I will not fight thee—indeed I dare not.

   Pol. Thou wilt not fight with me didst say, Sir Count?
Shall I be baffled thus?—now this is well;
Didst say thou *darest* not? Ha!

   Cas. I dare not—dare not—
Hold off thy hand—with that beloved name
So fresh upon thy lips I will not fight thee—
I cannot—dare not.

   Pol. Now by my halidom
I do believe thee!—coward, I do believe thee!

   Cas. Ha!—coward!—this may not be!
     (*clutches his sword and staggers towards Politian, but his
      purpose is changed before reaching him, and he falls
      upon his knee at the feet of the Earl.*)
                Alas! my lord,

It is—it is—most true.   In such a cause
I am the veriest coward.   O pity me!

  Pol. (*greatly softened.*) Alas!—I do—indeed I pity thee

  Cas. And Lalage———

  Pol. Scoundrel!—arise and die!

  Cas. It needeth not be—thus—thus—O let me die
Thus on my bended knee.   It were most fitting
That in this deep humiliation I perish.
For in the fight I will not raise a hand
Against thee, Earl of Leicester.   Strike thou home—

                                   (*baring his bosom.*)

Here is no let or hindrance to thy weapon—
Strike home.   I *will not* fight thee.

  Pol. Now s'Death and Hell!
Am I not—am I not sorely—grievously tempted
To take thee at thy word?   But mark me, si.
Think not to fly me thus.   Do thou prepare
For public insult in the streets—before
The eyes of the citizens.   I'll follow thee—
Like an avenging spirit I'll follow thee
Even unto death.   Before those whom thou lovest—
Before all Rome I'll taunt thee, villain,—I'll taunt thee,
Dost hear? with *cowardice*—thou *wilt not* fight me?
Thou liest! thou *shalt!*   (*exit.*)

  Cas. Now this indeed is just!
Most righteous, and most just, avenging Heaven!

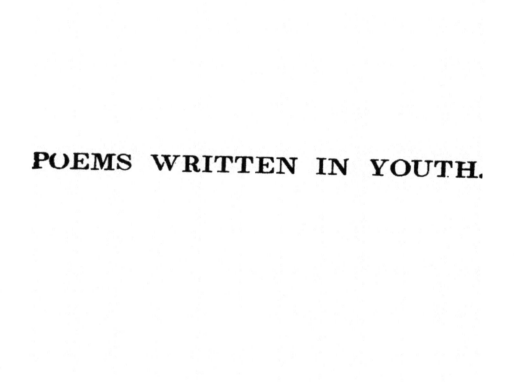

POEMS WRITTEN IN YOUTH.

POEMS WRITTEN IN YOUTH *

SONNET—TO SCIENCE.

Science! true daughter of Old Time thou art!
  Who alterest all things with thy peering eyes.
Why preyest thou thus upon the poet's heart,
  Vulture, whose wings are dull realities?
How should he love thee? or how deem thee wise,
  Who wouldst not leave him in his wandering
To seek for treasure in the jewelled skies,
  Albeit he soared with an undaunted wing?
Hast thou not dragged Diana from her car?
  And driven the Hamadryad from the wood
To seek a shelter in some happier star?
  Hast thou not torn the Naiad from her flood,
The Elfin from the green grass, and from me
The summer dream beneath the tamarind tree?

* Private reasons—some of which have reference to the sin of plagiarism, and others to the date of Tennyson's first poems—have induced me, after some hesitation, to re-publish these, the crude compositions of my earliest boyhood. They are printed *verbatim*—without alteration from the original edition—the date of which is too remote to be judiciously acknowledged.

                                                      E. A. P.

AL AARAAF.*

PART I.

O ! NOTHING earthly save the ray
(Thrown back from flowers) of Beauty's eye,
As in those gardens where the day
Springs from the gems of Circassy—
O ! nothing earthly save the thrill
Of melody in woodland rill—
Or (music of the passion-hearted)
Joy's voice so peacefully departed
That like the murmur in the shell,
Its echo dwelleth and will dwell—
Oh, nothing of the dross of ours—
Yet all the beauty—all the flowers
That list our Love, and deck our bowers—
Adorn yon world afar, afar—
The wandering star.

'Twas a sweet time for Nesace—for there
Her world lay lolling on the golden air,
Near four bright suns—a temporary rest—
An oasis in desert of the blest.

* A star was discovered by Tycho Brahe which appeared suddenly in ʊ
heavens—attained, in a few days, a brilliancy surpassing that of Jupiter—that
as suddenly disappeared, and has never been seen since.

Away—away—'mid seas of rays that roll
Empyrean splendor o'er th' unchained soul—
The soul that scarce (the billows are so dense)
Can struggle to its destin'd eminence—
To distant spheres, from time to time, she rode,
And late to ours, the favour'd one of God—
But, now, the ruler of an anchor'd realm,
She throws aside the sceptre—leaves the helm,
And, amid incense and high spiritual hymns,
Laves in quadruple light her angel limbs.

Now happiest, loveliest in yon lovely Earth,
Whence sprang the " Idea of Beauty" into birth.
(Falling in wreaths thro' many a startled star,
Like woman's hair 'mid pearls, until, afar,
It lit on hills Achaian, and there dwelt)
She look'd into Infinity—and knelt.
Rich clouds, for canopies, about her curled—
Fit emblems of the model of her world—
Seen but in beauty—not impeding sight
Of other beauty glittering thro' the light—
A wreath that twined each starry form around,
And all the opal'd air in color bound.

All hurriedly she knelt upon a bed
Of flowers : of lilies such as rear'd the head
*On the fair Capo Deucato, and sprang
So eagerly around about to hang
Upon the flying footsteps of——deep pride—
†Of her who lov'd a mortal—and so died.
The Sephalica, budding with young bees,
Uprear'd its purple stem around her knees :

* On Santa Maura—olim Deucadia.   † Sappho.

*And gemmy flower, of Trebizond misnam'd—
Inmate of highest stars, where erst it sham'd
All other loveliness : its honied dew
(The fabled nectar that the heathen knew)
Deliriously sweet, was dropp'd from Heaven,
And fell on gardens of the unforgiven
In Trebizond—and on a sunny flower
So like its own above that, to this hour,
It still remaineth, torturing the bee
With madness, and unwonted reverie :
In Heaven, and all its environs, the leaf
And blossom of the fairy plant, in grief
Disconsolate linger—grief that hangs her head,
Repenting follies that full long have fled,
Heaving her white breast to the balmy air,
Like guilty beauty, chasten'd, and more fair :
Nyctanthes too, as sacred as the light
She fears to perfume, perfuming the night :
†And Clytia pondering between many a sun,
While pettish tears adown her petals run :
‡And that aspiring flower that sprang on Earth—
And died, ere scarce exalted into birth,
Bursting its odorous heart in spirit to wing
Its way to Heaven, from garden of a king :

---

* This flower is much noticed by Lewenhoeck and Tournefort. The bee, feeding upon its blossom, becomes intoxicated.

† Clytia—The Chrysanthemum Peruvianum, or, to employ a better-known term, the turnsol—which turns continually towards the sun, covers itself, like Peru, the country from which it comes, with dewy clouds which cool and refresh its flowers during the most violent heat of the day.—*B. de St. Pierre.*

‡ There is cultivated in the king's garden at Paris, a species of serpentine aloes without prickles, whose large and beautiful flower exhales a strong odour of the vanilla, during the time of its expansion, which is very short. It does not blow till towards the month of July—you then perceive it gradually open its petals—expand them—fade and die.—*St. Pierre.*

*And Valisnerian lotus thither flown
From struggling with the waters of the Rhone :
†And thy most lovely purple perfume, Zante !
Isola d'oro !—Fior di Levante !
‡And the Nelumbo bud that floats for ever
With Indian Cupid down the holy river—
Fair flowers, and fairy ! to whose care is given
§To bear the Goddess' song, in odors, up to Heaven :

" Spirit ! that dwellest where,
     In the deep sky,
 The terrible and fair,
     In beauty vie !
 Beyond the line of blue—
     The boundary of the star
 Which turneth at the view
     Of thy barrier and thy bar—
 Of the barrier overgone
     By the comets who were cast
 From their pride, and from their throne
     To be drudges till the last—
 To be carriers of fire
     (The red fire of their heart)
 With speed that may not tire
     And with pain that shall not part—

---

* There is found, in the Rhone, a beautiful lily of the Valisnerian kind. Its stem will stretch to the length of three or four feet—thus preserving its head above water in the swellings of the river.

† The Hyacinth.

‡ It is a fiction of the Indians, that Cupid was first seen floating in one of these down the river Ganges—and that he still loves the cradle of his childhood.

§ And golden vials full of odors which are the prayers of the saints.—Rev St. John.

Who livest—*that* we know—
In Eternity—we feel—
But the shadow of whose brow
What spirit shall reveal ?
Tho' the beings whom thy Nesace,
Thy messenger hath known
Have dream'd for thy Infinity
*A model of their own—
Thy will is done, Oh, God !
The star hath ridden high
Thro' many a tempest, but she rode
Beneath thy burning eye ;
And here, in thought, to thee—
In thought that can alone
Ascend thy empire and so be
A partner of thy throne—

* The Humanitarians held that God was to be understood as having really
a human form.—*Vide Clarke's Sermons*, vol. 1, page 26, fol. edit.

The drift of Milton's argument, leads him to employ language which would
appear, at first sight, to verge upon their doctrine ; but it will be seen immediately, that he guards himself against the charge of having adopted one of
the most ignorant errors of the dark ages of the church.—*Dr. Sumner's Notes
on Milton's Christian Doctrine.*

This opinion, in spite of many testimonies to the contrary, could never have
been very general. Andeus, a Syrian of Mesopotamia, was condemned for
the opinion, as heretical. He lived in the beginning of the fourth century
His disciples were called Anthropmorphites.—*Vide Du Pin.*

Among Milton's minor poems are these lines :—

    Dicite sacrorum præsides nemorum Deæ, &c.
    Quis ille primus cujus ex imagine
    Natura solers finxit humanum genus ?
    Eternus, incorruptus, æquævus polo,
    Unusque et universus exemplar Dei.—And afterwards,
    Non cui profunoum Cœcitas lumen dedit
    Dircæus augur vidit hunc alto sinu, &c.

*"By winged Fantasy,
  My embassy is given,
Till secrecy shall knowledge be
  In the environs of Heaven."

She ceas'd—and buried then her burning cheek
Abash'd, amid the lilies there, to seek
A shelter from the fervour of His eye;
For the stars trembled at the Deity.
She stirr'd not—breath'd not—for a voice was there
How solemnly pervading the calm air!
A sound of silence on the startled ear
Which dreamy poets name "the music of the sphere."
Ours is a world of words: Quiet we call
"Silence"—which is the merest word of all.
All Nature speaks, and ev'n ideal things
Flap shadowy sounds from visionary wings—
But ah! not so when, thus, in realms on high
The eternal voice of God is passing by,
And the red winds are withering in the sky!

   †" What tho' in worlds which sightless cycles run,
Link'd to a little system, and one sun—
Where all my love is folly and the crowd
Still think my terrors but the thunder cloud,
The storm, the earthquake, and the ocean-wrath—
(Ah! will they cross me in my angrier path?)
What tho' in worlds which own a single sun
The sands of Time grow dimmer as they run,

* Seltsamen Tochter Jovis
  Seinem Schosskinde
  Der Phantasie.—*Goethe.*

† Sightless—too small to be seen.—*Legge.*

Yet thine is my resplendency, so given
To bear my secrets thro' the upper Heaven.
Leave tenantless thy crystal home, and fly,
With all thy train, athwart the moony sky—
*Apart—like fire-flies in Sicilian night,
And wing to other worlds another light !
Divulge the secrets of thy embassy
To the proud orbs that twinkle—and so be
To ev'ry heart a barrier and a ban
Lest the stars totter in the guilt of man !"

    Up rose the maiden in the yellow night,
The single-mooned eve !—on Earth we plight
Our faith to one love—and one moon adore—
The birth-place of young Beauty had no more.
As sprang that yellow star from downy hours
Up rose the maiden from her shrine of flowers,
And bent o'er sheeny mountain and dim plain
†Her way—but left not yet her Theræœan reign.

* I have often noticed a peculiar movement of the fire-flies ;—they will col-
lect in a body and fly off, from a common centre, into innumerable radii.

† Theræœa, or Therœa, the island mentioned by Seneca, which, in a moment, arose from the sea to the eyes of astonished mariners.

PART II.

High on a mountain of enamell'd head—
Such as the drowsy shepherd on his bed
Of giant pasturage lying at his ease,
Raising his heavy eyelid, starts and sees
With many a mutter'd "hope to be forgiven"
What time the moon is quadrated in Heaven—
Of rosy head, that towering far away
Into the sunlit ether, caught the ray
Of sunken suns at eve—at noon of night,
While the moon danc'd with the fair stranger light—
Uprear'd upon such height arose a pile
Of gorgeous columns on th' unburthen'd air,
Flashing from Parian marble that twin smile
Far down upon the wave that sparkled there,
And nursled the young mountain in its lair.
*Of molten stars their pavement, such as fall
Thro' the ebon air, besilvering the pall
Of their own dissolution, while they die—
Adorning then the dwellings of the sky.
A dome, by linked light from Heaven let down,
Sat gently on these columns as a crown—
A window of one circular diamond, there,
Look'd out above into the purple air,

* Some star which, from the ruin'd roof
    Of shak'd Olympus, by mischance, did fall.—*Milton.*
    5*

And rays from God shot down that meteor chain
And hallow'd all the beauty twice again,
Save when, between th' Empyrean and that ring,
Some eager spirit flapp'd his dusky wing.
But on the pillars Seraph eyes have seen
The dimness of this world : that greyish green
That Nature loves the best for Beauty's grave
Lurk'd in each cornice, round each architrave—
And every sculptur'd cherub thereabout
That from his marble dwelling peeréd out,
Seem'd earthly in the shadow of his niche—
Achaian statues in a world so rich ?
*Friezes from Tadmor and Persepolis—
From Balbec, and the stilly, clear abyss
†Of beautiful Gomorrah ! O, the wave
Is now upon thee—but too late to save !

Sound loves to revel in a summer night :
Witness the murmur of the grey twilight

---

* Voltaire, in speaking of Persepolis, says, "Je connois bien l'admiration qu'inspirent ces ruines—mais un palais erigé au pied d'une chaine des rochers sterils—peut il être un chef d'œuvre des arts !"

† "Oh ! the wave"—Ula Deguisi is the Turkish appellation ; but, on its own shores, it is called Bahar Loth, or Almotanah. There were undoubtedly more than two cities engulphed in the "dead sea." In the valley of Siddim were five—Adrah, Zeboin, Zoar, Sodom and Gomorrah. Stephen of Byzantium mentions eight, and Strabo thirteen, (engulphed)—but the last is out of all reason.

It is said, [Tacitus, Strabo, Josephus, Daniel of St. Saba, Nau, Maundrell, Troilo, D'Arvieux] that after an excessive drought, the vestiges of columns, walls, &c. are seen above the surface. At any season, such remains may be discovered by looking down into the transparent lake, and at such distances as would argue the existence of many settlements in the space now usurped by the 'Asphaltites.'

*That stole upon the ear, in Eyraco,
Of many a wild star-gazer long ago—
That stealeth ever on the ear of him
Who, musing, gazeth on the distance dim.
And sees the darkness coming as a cloud—
†Is not its form—its voice—most palpable and loud ?

But what is this ?—it cometh—and it brings
A music with it—'tis the rush of wings—
A pause—and then a sweeping, falling strain
And Nesace is in her halls again.
From the wild energy of wanton haste
    Her cheeks were flushing, and her lips apart ;
And zone that clung around her gentle waist
    Had burst beneath the heaving of her heart.
Within the centre of that hall to breathe
She paus'd and panted, Zanthe ! all beneath,
The fairy light that kiss'd her golden hair
And long'd to rest, yet could but sparkle there !

‡ Young flowers were whispering in melody
To happy flowers that night—and tree to tree ;
Fountains were gushing music as they fell
In many a star-lit grove, or moon-lit dell ;
Yet silence came upon material things—
Fair flowers, bright waterfalls and angel wings—
And sound alone that from the spirit sprang
Bore burthen to the charm the maiden sang :

* Eyraco—Chaldea.
  † I have often thought I could distinctly hear the sound of the darkness as it
stole over the horizon.
    ‡ Fairies use flowers for their charactery —*Merry Wives of Windsor.*

" 'Neath blue-bell or streamer—
Or tufted wild spray
That keeps, from the dreamer,
*The moonbeam away—
Bright beings ! that ponder,
With half closing eyes,
On the stars which your wonder
Hath drawn from the skies,
Till they glance thro' the shade, and
Come down to your brow
Like——eyes of the maiden
Who calls on you now—
Arise ! from your dreaming
In violet bowers,
To duty beseeming
These star-litten hours—
And shake from your tresses
Encumber'd with dew
The breath of those kisses
That cumber them too—
(O ! how, without you, Love !
Could angels be blest ?)
Those kisses of true love
That lull'd ye to rest !
Up !—shake from your wing
Each hindering thing :
The dew of the night—
It would weigh down your flight ;
And true love caresses—
O ! leave them apart !

* In Scripture is this passage—" The sun shall not harm thee by day, nor
the moon by night." It is perhaps not generally known that the moon, in
Egypt, has the effect of producing blindness to those who sleep with the face
exposed to its rays, to which circumstance the passage evidently alludes

They are light on the tresses,
But lead on the heart.

Ligeia ! Ligeia !
My beautiful one !
Whose harshest idea
Will to melody run,
O ! is it thy will
On the breezes to toss ?
Or, capriciously still,
*Like the lone Albatross,
Incumbent on night
(As she on the air)
To keep watch with delight
On the harmony there ?

Ligeia ! wherever
Thy image may be,
No magic shall sever
Thy music from thee.
Thou hast bound many eyes
In a dreamy sleep—
But the strains still arise
Which *thy* vigilance keep—
The sound of the rain
Which leaps down to the flower,
And dances again
In the rhythm of the shower—
†The murmur that springs
From the growing of grass

---

* The Albatross is said to sleep on the wing.

† I met with this idea in an old English tale, which I am now unable to obtain and quote from memory :—" The verie essence and, as it were, springe-

Are the music of things—
　　But are modell'd, alas !—
Away, then my dearest,
　　O ! hie thee away
To springs that lie clearest
　　Beneath the moon-ray—
To lone lake that smiles,
　　In its dream of deep rest,
At the many star-isles
　　That enjewel its breast—
Where wild flowers, creeping,
　　Have mingled their shade,
On its margin is sleeping
　　Full many a maid—
Some have left the cool glade, and
　　* Have slept with the bee—
Arouse them my maiden,
　　On moorland and lea—
Go ! breathe on their slumber,
　　All softly in ear,
The musical number
　　They slumber'd to hear—
For what can awaken
　　An angel so soon

heade and origine of all musiche is the verie pleasaunte sounde which the
trees of the forest do make when they growe."
　　* The wild bee will not sleep in the shade if there be moonlight.
　　The rhyme in this verse, as in one about sixty lines before, has an appear-
ance of affectation.　It is, however, imitated from Sir W. Scott, or rather from
Claud Halero—in whose mouth I admired its effect :
　　　　　　　O ! were there an island,
　　　　　　　　Tho' ever so wild
　　　　　　　Where woman might smile, and
　　　　　　　　No man be beguil'd, &c.

Whose sleep hath been taken
　　Beneath the cold moon,
As the spell which no slumbeɪ
　　Of witchery may test,
The rhythmical number
　　Which lull'd him to rest ?"

Spirits in wing, and angels to the view,
A thousand seraphs burst th' Empyrean thro',
Young dreams still hovering on their drowsy flight—
Seraphs in all but " Knowledge," the keen light
That fell, refracted, thro' thy bounds, afar
O Death ! from eye of God upon that star :
Sweet was that error—sweeter still that death—
Sweet was that error—ev'n with *us* the breath
Of Science dims the mirror of our joy—
To them 'twere the Simoom, and would destroy—
For what (to them) availeth it to know
That Truth is Falsehood—or that Bliss is Woe ?
Sweet was their death—with them to die was rife
With the last ecstasy of satiate life—
Beyond that death no immortality—
But sleep that pondereth and is not " to be"—
And there—oh ! may my weary spirit dwell—
*Apart from Heaven's Eternity—and yet how far from Hell !

* With the Arabians there is a medium between Heaven and Hell, where
men suffer no punishment, but yet do not attain that tranquil and even happi-
:ɴess which they suppose to be characteristic of heavenly enjoyment.

　　　　Un no rompido sueno—
　　　　Un dia puro—allegre—libre
　　　　Quiera—
　　　　Libre de amor—de zelo—
　　　　De odio—de esperanza—de rezelo.—*Luis Ponce de Leon.*
Sorrow is not excluded from " Al Aaraaf," but it is that sorrow which the

What guilty spirit, in what shrubbery dim,
Heard not the stirring summons of that hymn ?
But two : they fell : for Heaven no grace imparts
To those who hear not for their beating hearts.
A maiden-angel and her seraph-lover—
O ! where (and ye may seek the wide skies over)
Was Love, the blind, near sober Duty known ?
*Unguided Love hath fallen—'mid "tears of perfect moan "

He was a goodly spirit—he who fell :
A wanderer by moss-y-mantled well—
A gazer on the lights that shine above—
A dreamer in the moonbeam by his love :
What wonder ? for each star is eye-like there,
And looks so sweetly down on Beauty's hair—
And they, and ev'ry mossy spring were holy
To his love-haunted heart and melancholy.
The night had found (to him a night of wo)
Upon a mountain crag, young Angelo—
Beetling it bends athwart the solemn sky,
And scowls on starry worlds that down beneath it lie.
Here sate he with his love—his dark eye bent
With eagle gaze along the firmament :
Now turn'd it upon her—but ever then
It trembled to the orb of EARTH again.

" Ianthe, dearest, see ! how dim that ray !
How lovely 'tis to look so far away !

living love to cherish for the dead, and which, in some minds, resembles the delirium of opium. The passionate excitement of Love and the buoyancy of spirit attendant upon intoxication are its less holy pleasures—the price of which, to those souls who make choice of " Al Aaraaf" as their residence after life, is final death and annihilation.

* There be tears of perfect moan
Wept for thee in Helicon.—*Milton*

She seem'd not thus upon that autumn eve
I left her gorgeous halls—nor mourn'd to leave.
That eve—that eve—I should remember well—
The sun-ray dropp'd, in Lemnos, with a spell
On th' Arabesque carving of a gilded hall
Wherein I sate, and on the draperied wall—
And on my eye-lids—O the heavy light!
How drowsily it weigh'd them into night!
On flowers, before, and mist, and love they ran
With Persian Saadi in his Gulistan:
But O that light!—I slumber'd—Death, the while,
Stole o'er my senses in that lovely isle
So softly that no single silken hair
Awoke that slept—or knew that he was there.

The last spot of Earth's orb I trod upon
*Was a proud temple call'd the Parthenon—
More beauty clung around her column'd wall
†Than ev'n thy glowing bosom beats withal,
And when old Time my wing did disenthral
Thence sprang I—as the eagle from his tower,
And years I left behind me in an hour.
What time upon her airy bounds I hung
One half the garden of her globe was flung
Unrolling as a chart unto my view—
Tenantless cities of the desert too!
Ianthe, beauty crowded on me then,
And half I wish'd to be again of men."

" My Angelo! and why of them to be ?
A brighter dwelling-place is here for thee—

* It was entire in 1687—the most elevated spot in Athens.
† Shadowing more beauty in their airy brows
  Than have the white breasts of the Queen of Love.—Marlowe.

And greener fields than in yon world above,
And woman's loveliness—and passionate love."

" But, list, Ianthe ! when the air so soft
*Fail'd, as my pennon'd spirit leapt aloft,
Perhaps my brain grew dizzy—but the world
I left so late was into chaos hurl'd—
Sprang from her station, on the winds apart,
And roll'd, a flame, the fiery Heaven athwart.
Methought, my sweet one, then I ceased to soar
And fell—not swiftly as I rose before,
But with a downward, tremulous motion thro'
Light, brazen rays, this golden star unto !
Nor long the measure of my falling hours,
For nearest of all stars was thine to ours—
Dread star ! that came, amid a night of mirth,
A red Dædalion on the timid Earth.

" We came—and to thy Earth—but not to us
Be given our lady's bidding to discuss :
We came, my love ; around, above, below,
Gay fire-fly of the night we come and go,
Nor ask a reason save the angel-nod
She grants to us, as granted by her God—
But, Angelo, than thine grey Time unfurl'd
Never his fairy wing o'er fairier world !
Dim was its little disk, and angel eyes
Alone could see the phantom in the skies,
When first Al Aaraaf knew her course to be
Headlong thitherward o'er the starry sea—
But when its glory swell'd upon the sky,
As glowing Beauty's bust beneath man's eye,

* Pennon—for pinion.—*Milton.*

We paus'd before the heritage of men,
And thy star trembled—as doth Beauty then!"

Thus, in discourse, the lovers whiled away
The night that waned and waned and brought no day.
They fell: for Heaven to them no hope imparts
Who hear not for the beating of their hearts.

TO THE RIVER ——.

FAIR river! in thy bright, clear flow
    Of crystal, wandering water,
Thou art an emblem of the glow
        Of beauty—the unhidden heart—
        The playful maziness of art
    In old Alberto's daughter;

But when within thy wave she looks—
    Which glistens then, and trembles—
Why, then, the prettiest of brooks
    Her worshipper resembles;
For in his heart, as in thy stream,
    Her image deeply lies—
His heart which trembles at the beam
    Of her soul-searching eyes.

TAMERLANE.

Kind solace in a dying hour!
   Such, father, is not (now) my theme—
I will not madly deem that power
     Of Earth may shrive me of the sin
     Unearthly pride hath revell'd in—
I have no time to dote or dream:
You call it hope—that fire of fire!
It is but agony of desire:
If I *can* hope—Oh God! I can—
   Its fount is holier—more divine—
I would not call thee fool, old man,
   But such is not a gift of thine.

Know thou the secret of a spirit
   Bow'd from its wild pride into shame.
O yearning heart! I did inherit
   Thy withering portion with the fame,
The searing glory which hath shone
Amid the Jewels of my throne,
Halo of Hell! and with a pain
Not Hell shall make me fear again—
O craving heart, for the lost flowers
And sunshine of my summer hours!
The undying voice of that dead time,
With its interminable chime,

Rings, in the spirit of a spell,
Upon thy emptiness—a knell.

I have not always been as now :
The fever'd diadem on my brow
  I claim'd and won usurpingly——
Hath not the same fierce heirdom given
  Rome to the Cæsar—this to me ?
    The heritage of a kingly mind,
And a proud spirit which hath striven
    Triumphantly with human kind.

On mountain soil I first drew life :
  The mists of the Taglay have shed
  Nightly their dews upon my head,
And, I believe, the winged strife
And tumult of the headlong air
Have nestled in my very hair.

So late from Heaven—that dew—it fell
  ('Mid dreams of an unholy night)
Upon me with the touch of Hell,
  While the red flashing of the light
From clouds that hung, like banners, o'er,
  Appeared to my half-closing eye
  The pageantry of monarchy,
And the deep trumpet-thunder's roar
  Came hurriedly upon me, telling
    Of human battle, where my voice,
  My own voice, silly child !—was swelling
    (O ! how my spirit would rejoice,
And leap within me at the cry)
The battle-cry of Victory !

The rain came down upon my head
  Unshelter'd—and the heavy wind
  Rendered me mad and deaf and blind.
It was but man, I thought, who shed
  Laurels upon me : and the rush—
The torrent of the chilly air
Gurgled within my ear the crush
  Of empires—with the captive's prayer—
The hum of suitors—and the tone
Of flattery 'round a sovereign's throne.

My passions, from that hapless hour,
  Usurp'd a tyranny which men
Have deem'd, since I have reach'd to power,
    My innate nature—be it so :
  But, father, there liv'd one who, then,
Then—in my boyhood—when their fire
    Burn'd with a still intenser glow
(For passion must, with youth, expire)
  E'en *then* who knew this iron heart
  In woman's weakness had a part.

I have no words—alas !—to tell
The loveliness of loving well !
Nor would I now attempt to trace
The more than beauty of a face
Whose lineaments, upon my mind,
Are——shadows on th' unstable wind ·
Thus I remember having dwelt
  Some page of early lore upon,
With loitering eye, till I have felt
The letters—with their meaning—melt
  To fantasies—with none

O, she was worthy of all love !
  Love——as in infancy was mine——
'Twas such as angel minds above
  Might envy ; her young heart the shrine
On which my every hope and thought
  Were incense——then a goodly gift,
    For they were childish and upright——
Pure——as her young example taught :
  Why did I leave it, and, adrift,
    Trust to the fire within, for light ?

We grew in age——and love——together——
  Roaming the forest, and the wild ;
My breast her shield in wintry weather——
  And, when the friendly sunshine smil'd.
And she would mark the opening skies,
I saw no Heaven——but in her eyes.

Young Love's first lesson is——the heart :
  For 'mid that sunshine, and those smiles,
When, from our little cares apart,
  And laughing at her girlish wiles,
I'd throw me on her throbbing breast,
  And pour my spirit out in tears——
There was no need to speak the rest——
  No need to quiet any fears
Of her——who ask'd no reason why,
But turn'd on me her quiet eye !

Yet *more* than worthy of the love
My spirit struggled with, and strove,
When, on the mountain peak, alone,
Ambition lent it a new tone——

I had no being—but in thee :
   The world, and all it did contain
In the earth—the air—the sea—
   Its joy—its little lot of pain
That was new pleasure——the ideal,
   Dim, vanities of dreams by night—
And dimmer nothings which were real—
   (Shadows—and a more shadowy light!)
Parted upon their misty wings,
     And, so, confusedly, became
     Thine image and—a name—a name!
Two separate—yet most intimate things.

I was ambitious—have you known
     The passion, father ?   You have not:
A cottager, I mark'd a throne
Of half the world as all my own,
     And murmur'd at such lowly lot—
But, just like any other dream,
     Upon the vapor of the dew
My own had past, did not the beam
     Of beauty which did while it thro'
The minute—the hour—the day—oppress
My mind with double loveliness.

We walk'd together on the crown
Of a high mountain which look'd down
Afar from its proud natural towers
   Of rock and forest, on the hills—
The dwindled hills! begirt with bowers
   And shouting with a thousand rills.

I spoke to her of power and pride,
   But mystically—in such guise

That she might deem it nought beside
  The moment's converse ; in her eyes
I read, perhaps too carelessly—
  A mingled feeling with my own—
The flush on her bright cheek, to me
  Seem'd to become a queenly throne
Too well that I should let it be
  Light in the wilderness alone.

I wrapp'd myself in grandeur then
  And donn'd a visionary crown——
    Yet it was not that Fantasy
    Had thrown her mantle over me—
But that, among the rabble—men,
    Lion ambition is chain'd down—
And crouches to a keeper's hand—
Not so in deserts where the grand—
The wild—the terrible conspire
With their own breath to fan his fire.

Look 'round thee now on Samarcand !—
  Is she not queen of Earth ? her pride
Above all cities ? in her hand
  Their destinies ? in all beside
Of glory which the world hath known
Stands she not nobly and alone ?
Falling—her veriest stepping-stone
Shall form the pedestal of a throne—
And who her sovereign ? Timour—he
  Whom the astonished people saw
Striding o'er empires haughtily
  A diadem'd outlaw !
    Vol. II.—6.

O, human love ! thou spirit given,
On Earth, of all we hope in Heaven !
Which fall'st into the soul like rain
Upon the Siroc-wither'd plain,
And, failing in thy power to bless,
But leav'st the heart a wilderness !
Idea ! which bindest life around
With music of so strange a sound
And beauty of so wild a birth—
Farewell ! for I have won the Earth.

When Hope, the eagle that tower'd, could see
    No cliff beyond him in the sky,
His pinions were bent droopingly—
    And homeward turn'd his soften'd eye.
'Twas sunset : when the sun will part
There comes a sullenness of heart
To him who still would look upon
The glory of the summer sun.
That soul will hate the ev'ning mist
So often lovely, and will list
To the sound of the coming darkness (known
To those whose spirits harken) as one
Who, in a dream of night, *would* fly
But *cannot* from a danger nigh.

What tho' the moon—the white moon
Shed all the splendor of her noon,
Her smile is chilly—and *her* beam,
In that time of dreariness, will seem
(So like you gather in your breath)
A portrait taken after death.

And boyhood is a summer sun
Whose waning is the dreariest one—
For all we live to know is known
And all we seek to keep hath flown—
Let life, then, as the day-flower, fall
With the noon-day beauty—which is all.

I reach'd my home—my home no more—
  For all had flown who made it so.
I pass'd from out its mossy door,
  And, tho' my tread was soft and low,
A voice came from the threshold stone
Of one whom I had earlier known—
  O, I defy thee, Hell, to show
  On beds of fire that burn below,
  An humbler heart—a deeper wo.

Father, I firmly do believe—
  I *know*—for Death who comes for me
    From regions of the blest afar,
Where there is nothing to deceive,
    Hath left his iron gate ajar,
  And rays of truth you cannot see
  Are flashing thro' Eternity——
I do believe that Eblis hath
A snare in every human path—
Else how, when in the holy grove
I wandered of the idol, Love,
Who daily scents his snowy wings
With incense of burnt offerings
From the most unpolluted things,
Whose pleasant bowers are yet so riven
Above with trellic'd rays from Heaven

No mote may shun—no tiniest fly—
The light'ning of his eagle eye—
How was it that Ambition crept,
    Unseen, amid the revels there,
Till growing bold, he laughed and leapt
    In the tangles of Love's very hair ?

TO ——.

THE bowers whereat, in dreams, I see
    The wantonest singing birds,
Are lips—and all thy melody
    Of lip-begotten words—

Thine eyes, in Heaven of heart enshrined
    Then desolately fall,
O God ! on my funereal mind
    Like starlight on a pall—

Thy heart—*thy* heart !—I wake and sigh
    And sleep to dream till day
Of the truth that gold can never buy—
    Of the baubles that it may.

A DREAM.

In visions of the dark night
  I have dreamed of joy departed—
But a waking dream of life and light
  Hath left me broken-hearted.

Ah! what is not a dream by day
  To him whose eyes are cast
On things around him with a ray
  Turned back upon the past?

That holy dream—that holy dream,
  While all the world were chiding,
Hath cheered me as a lovely beam
  A lonely spirit guiding.

What though that light, thro' storm and night,
  So trembled from afar—
What could there be more purely bright
  In Truth's day-star?

ROMANCE.

Romance, who loves to nod and sing,
With drowsy head and folded wing,
Among the green leaves as they shake
Far down within some shadowy lake,
To me a painted paroquet
Hath been—a most familiar bird—
Taught me my alphabet to say—
To lisp my very earliest word
While in the wild wood I did lie,
A child—with a most knowing eye.

Of late, eternal Condor years
So shake the very Heaven on high
With tumult as they thunder by,
I have no time for idle cares
Through gazing on the unquiet sky.
And when an hour with calmer wings
Its down upon my spirit flings—
That little time with lyre and rhyme
To while away—forbidden things !
My heart would feel to be a crime
Unless it trembled with the strings.

FAIRY-LAND.

Dim vales—and shadowy floods—
And cloudy-looking woods,
Whose forms we can't discover
For the tears that drip all over
Huge moons there wax and wane—
Again—again—again—
Every moment of the night—
Forever changing places—
And they put out the star-light
With the breath from their pale faces.
About twelve by the moon-dial
One more filmy than the rest
(A kind which, upon trial,
They have found to be the best)
Comes down—still down—and down
With its centre on the crown
Of a mountain's eminence,
While its wide circumference
In easy drapery falls
Over hamlets, over halls,
Wherever they may be—
O'er the strange woods—o'er the sea—
Over spirits on the wing—
Over every drowsy thing—
And buries them up quite
In a labyrinth of light—

And then, how deep!—O, deep!
Is the passion of their sleep.
In the morning they arise,
And their moony covering
Is soaring in the skies,
With the tempests as they toss,
Like——almost any thing—
Or a yellow Albatross.
They use that moon no more
For the same end as before—
Videlicet a tent—
Which I think extravagant:
Its atomies, however,
Into a shower dissever,
Of which those butterflies,
Of Earth, who seek the skies,
And so come down again
(Never-contented things!)
Have brought a specimen
Upon their quivering wings.

THE LAKE—TO ———.

In spring of youth it was my lot
To haunt of the wide world a spot
The which I could not love the less—
So lovely was the loneliness
Of a wild lake, with black rock bound,
And the tall pines that towered around.

But when the Night had thrown her pall
Upon that spot, as upon all,
And the mystic wind went by
Murmuring in melody—
Then—ah then I would awake
To the terror of the lone lake.

Yet that terror was not fright,
But a tremulous delight—
A feeling not the jewelled mine
Could teach or bribe me to define—
Nor Love—although the Love were thine.

Death was in that poisonous wave,
And in its gulf a fitting grave
For him who thence could solace bring
To his lone imagining—
Whose solitary soul could make
An Eden of that dim lake.

SONG.

I saw thee on thy bridal day—
    When a burning blush came o'er thee,
Though happiness around thee lay,
    The world all love before thee :

And in thine eye a kindling light
    (Whatever it might be)
Was all on Earth my aching sight
    Of Loveliness could see.

That blush, perhaps, was maiden shame—
    As such it well may pass—
Though its glow heth raised a fiercer flame
    In the breast of him, alas !

Who saw thee on that bridal day,
    When that deep blush *would* come o'er thee,
Though happiness around thee lay,
    The world all love before thee.

TO M. L. S———.

Of all who hail thy presence as the morning—
Of all to whom thine absence is the night—
The blotting utterly from out high heaven
The sacred sun—of all who, weeping, bless thee
Hourly for hope—for life—ah! above all,
For the resurrection of deep-buried faith
In Truth—in Virtue—in Humanity—
Of all who, on Despair's unhallowed bed
Lying down to die, have suddenly arisen
At thy soft-murmured words, " Let there be light !"
At the soft-murmured words that were fulfilled
In the seraphic glancing of thine eyes—
Of all who owe thee most—whose gratitude
Nearest resembles worship—oh, remember
The truest—the most fervently devoted,
And think that these weak lines are written by him—
By him who, as he pens them, thrills to think
His spirit is communing with an angel's.

EUREKA: A PROSE POEM.

EUREKA:

AN ESSAY ON

THE MATERIAL AND SPIRITUAL UNIVERSE.

[To the few who love me and whom I love—to those who feel rather than to those who think—to the dreamers and those who put faith in dreams as in the only realities—I offer this Book of Truths, not in its character of Truth-Teller, but for the Beauty that abounds in its Truth; constituting it true. To these I present the composition as an Art-Product alone:—let us say as a Romance; or, if I be not urging too lofty a claim, as a Poem.

What I here propound is true:—therefore it cannot die:—or if by any means it be now trodden down so that it die, it will "rise again to the Life Everlasting."

Nevertheless it is as a Poem only that I wish this work to be judged after I am dead.]

It is with humility really unassumed—it is with a sentiment even of awe—that I pen the opening sentence of this work: for of all conceivable subjects I approach the reader with the most solemn—the most comprehensive—the most difficult—the most august.

What terms shall I find sufficiently simple in their sublimity—sufficiently sublime in their simplicity—for the mere enunciation of my theme?

I design to speak of the *Physical, Metaphysical and Mathematical—of the Material and Spiritual Universe:—of its Essence, its Origin, its Creation, its Present Condition and its Destiny.* I shall be so rash, moreover, as to challenge the conclusions, and thus, in effect, to question the sagacity, of many of the greatest and most justly reverenced of men.

In the beginning, let me as distinctly as possible announce—not the theorem which I hope to demonstrate—for, whatever the mathematicians may assert, there is, in this world at least, *no such thing* as demonstration—but the ruling idea which, throughout this volume, I shall be continually endeavoring to suggest.

My general proposition, then, is this :—*In the Original Unity of the First Thing lies the Secondary Cause of All Things, with the Germ of their Inevitable Annihilation.*

In illustration of this idea, I propose to take such a survey of the Universe that the mind may be able really to receive and to perceive an individual impression.

He who from the top of Ætna casts his eyes leisurely around, is affected chiefly by the *extent* and *diversity* of the scene. Only by a rapid whirling on his heel could he hope to comprehend the panorama in the sublimity of its *oneness*. But as, on the summit of Ætna, *no* man has thought of whirling on his heel, so no man has ever taken into his brain the full uniqueness of the prospect; and so, again, whatever considerations lie involved in this uniqueness, have as yet no practical existence for mankind.

I do not know a treatise in which a survey of the *Universe*—using the word in its most comprehensive and only legitimate acceptation—is taken at all :—and it may be as well here to mention that by the term "Universe," wherever employed without qualification in this essay, I mean to designate *the utmost conceivable expanse of space, with all things, spiritual and material, that can be imagined to exist within the compass of that expanse.* In speaking of what is *ordinarily* implied by the expression, "Universe," I shall take a phrase of limitation—"the Universe of stars." Why this distinction is considered necessary, will be seen in the sequel.

But even of treatises on the really limited, although always assumed as the *un*limited, Universe of *stars*, I know none in which a survey, even of this limited Universe, is so taken as to warrant deductions from its *individuality*. The nearest approach to such a work is made in the "Cosmos" of Alexander Von Humboldt. He presents the subject, however, *not* in its individuality but in its generality. His theme, in its last result, is the law of *each* portion of the merely physical Universe, as this law is related to the laws of *every other* portion of this merely physical Universe. His design is simply synceretical. In a word, he discusses the universality of material relation, and discloses to the eye of Philosophy whatever inferences have hitherto lain hidden *behind* this universality. But however admirable be the succinctness with which he has treated each particular point of his topic, the mere multiplicity of these points occasions, necessarily, an amount of detail, and thus an involution of idea, which preclude all *individuality* of impression.

It seems to me that, in aiming at this latter effect, and, through it, at the consequences—the conclusions—the suggestions—the speculations—or, if nothing better offer itself, the mere guesses which may result from it—we require something like a mental gyration on the heel. We need so rapid a revolution of all things about the central point of sight that, while the minutiæ vanish altogether, even the more conspicuous objects become blended into one. Among the vanishing minutiæ, in a survey of this kind, would be all exclusively terrestrial matters. The Earth would be considered in its planetary relations alone. A man, in this view, becomes mankind; mankind a member of the cosmical family of Intelligences.

And now, before proceeding to our subject proper, let me beg the reader's attention to an extract or two from a somewhat remarkable letter, which appears to have been found corked in a bottle and floating on the *Mare Tenebrarum*—an ocean well described by the Nubian geographer, Ptolemy Hephestion, but little frequented in modern days unless by the Transcendentalists and some other divers for crotchets. The date of this letter, I confess, surprises me even more particularly than its contents; for it seems to have been written in the year *two* thousand eight hundred and forty-eight. As for the passages I am about to transcribe, they, I fancy, will speak for themselves.

" Do you know, my dear friend," says the writer, addressing, no doubt, a contemporary—" Do you know that it is scarcely more than eight or nine hundred years ago since the metaphysicians first consented to relieve the people of the singular fancy that there exist *but two practicable roads to Truth?* Believe it if you can ! It appears, however, that long, long ago, in the night of Time, there lived a Turkish philosopher called Aries and surnamed Tottle." [Here, possibly, the letter-writer means Aristotle ; the best

names are wretchedly corrupted in two or three thousand years.]
" The fame of this great man depended mainly upon his demonstration that sneezing is a natural provision, by means of which
over-profound thinkers are enabled to expel superfluous ideas
through the nose; but he obtained a scarcely less valuable celeb-
rity as the founder, or at all events as the principal propagator, of
what was termed the *deductive* or *à priori* philosophy. He started
with what he maintained to be axioms, or self-evident truths:—
and the now well-understood fact that *no* truths are *self*-evident,
really does not make in the slightest degree against his speculations :—it was sufficient for his purpose that the truths in question
were evident a all. From axioms he proceeded, logically, to results. His most illustrious disciples were one Tuclid, a geometri-
cian," [meaning Euclid] " and one Kant, a Dutchman, the origi-
nator of that species of Transcendentalism which, with the change
merely of a C for a K, now bears his peculiar name.

" Well, Aries Tottle flourished supreme, until the advent of one
Hog, surnamed ' the Ettrick shepherd,' who preached an entirely
different system, which he called the *à posteriori* or *inductive*.
His plan referred altogether to sensation. He proceeded by observing, analyzing, and classifying facts—*instantiæ Naturæ*, as
they were somewhat affectedly called—and arranging them into
general laws. In a word, while the mode of Aries rested on
noumena, that of Hog depended on *phenomena ;* and so great
was the admiration excited by this latter system that, at its first
introduction, Aries fell into general disrepute. Finally, however,
he recovered ground, and was permitted to divide the empire of
Philosophy with his more modern rival :—the savans contenting
themselves with proscribing all *other* competitors, past, present,
and to come; putting an end to all controversy on the topic by
the promulgation of a Median law, to the effect that the Aristotelian and Baconian roads are, and of right ought to be, the sole
possible avenues to knowledge :—' Baconian,' you must know, my
dear friend," adds the letter-writer at this point, " was an adjective
invented as equivalent to Hog-ian, and at the same time more
dignified and euphonious.

" Now I do assure you most positively"—proceeds the epistle—
" that I represent these matters fairly ; and you can easily under-

stand how restrictions so absurd on their very face must have operated, in those days, to retard the progress of true Science, which makes its most important advances—as all History will show—by seemingly intuitive *leaps*. These ancient ideas confined investigation to crawling; and I need not suggest to you that crawling, among varieties of locomotion, is a very capital thing of its kind:——but because the tortoise is sure of foot, for this reason must we clip the wings of the eagles? For many centuries, so great was the infatuation, about Hog especially, that a virtual stop was put to all thinking, properly so called. No man dared utter a truth for which he felt himself indebted to his soul alone. It mattered not whether the truth was even demonstrably such; for the dogmatizing philosophers of that epoch regarded only *the road* by which it professed to have been attained. The end, with them, was a point of no moment, whatever:—"the means!" they vociferated—"let us look at the means!"—and if, on scrutiny of the means, it was found to come neither under the category Hog, nor under the category Aries (which means ram), why then the savans went no farther, but, calling the thinker a fool and branding him a 'theorist,' would never, thenceforward, have any thing to do either with *him* or with his truths.

"Now, my dear friend," continues the letter-writer, "it cannot be maintained that by the crawling system exclusively adopted, men would arrive at the maximum amount of truth, even in any long series of ages: for the repression of imagination was an evil not to be counterbalanced even by *absolute* certainty in the snail processes. But their certainty was very far from absolute. The error of our progenitors was quite analogous with that of the wiseacre who fancies he must necessarily see an object the more distinctly, the more closely he holds it to his eyes. They blinded themselves, too, with the impalpable, titillating Scotch snuff of *detail*; and thus the boasted facts of the Hog-ites were by no means always facts—a point of little importance but for the assumption that they always *were*. The vital taint, however, in Baconianism—its most lamentable fount of error—lay in its tendency to throw power and consideration into the hands of merely perceptive men—of those inter-Tritonic minnows, the microscopical savans—the diggers and pedlers of minute *facts*, for the most part in physical science—facts, all of which they retailed at the same price upon the highway; their value depending, it was supposed, simply upon the *fact of their fact*, without reference to their applicability or inapplicability in the development of those ultimate and only legitimate facts, called Law.

"Than the persons"—the letter goes on to say—"than the persons thus suddenly elevated by the Hog-ian philosophy into a station for which they were unfitted—thus transferred from the sculleries into the parlors of Science—from its pantries into its pulpits—than these individuals a more intolerant—a more intolerable set of bigots and tyrants never existed on the face of the earth. Their creed, their text, and their sermon were, alike, the one word '*fact*'—but, for the most part, even of this one word, they knew not even the meaning. On those who ventured to *disturb* their facts with the view of putting them in order and to use the disciples of Hog had no mercy whatever. All attempts at generalization were met at once by the words 'theoretical,' 'theory,' 'theorist'—all *thought*, to be brief, was very properly resented as a personal affront to themselves. Cultivating the natural sciences to the exclusion of Metaphysics, the Mathematics, and Logic, many of these Bacon-engendered philosophers—one-idead, one-sided, and lame of a leg—were more wretchedly helpless—more miserably ignorant, in view of all the comprehensible objects of knowledge, than the veriest unlettered hind who proves that he knows something at least, in admitting that he knows absolutely nothing.

"Nor had our forefathers any better right to talk about *certainty*, when pursuing, in blind confidence, the *à priori* path of axioms, or of the Ram. At innumerable points this path was scarcely as straight as a ram's-horn. The simple truth is, that the Aristotelians erected their castles upon a basis far less reliable than air; *for no such things as axioms ever existed or can possibly exist at all.* This they must have been very blind indeed not to see, or at least to suspect; for, even in their own day, many of their long-admitted 'axioms' had been abandoned: '*ex nihilo nihil fit*,' for example, and a 'thing cannot act where it is not,' and 'there cannot be antipodes,' and 'darkness cannot proceed from light.' These and numerous similar propositions formerly accepted, without hesita tion, as axioms, or undeniable truths, were, even at the period of which I speak, seen to be altogether untenable:—how absurd in these people, then, to persist in relying upon a basis, as immutable, whose mutability had become so repeatedly manifest!

"But, even through evidence afforded by themselves against themselves, it is easy to convict these *a priori* reasoners of the grossest unreason—it is easy to show the futility—the impalpability of their axioms in general. I have now lying before me"— it will be observed that we still proceed with the letter—"I have now lying before me a book printed about a thousand years ago. Pundit assures me that it is decidedly the cleverest ancient work on its topic, which is 'Logic.' The author, who was much esteemed in his day, was one Miller, or Mill; and we find it recorded of him, as a point of some importance, that he rode a mill-horse whom he called Jeremy Bentham:—but let us glance at the volume itself.

"Ah! 'Ability or inability to conceive,' says Mr. Mill, very properly, 'is *in no case* to be received as a criterion of axiomatic truth.' Now, that this is a palpable truism, no one in his senses will deny. *Not* to admit the proposition, is to insinuate a charge of variability in Truth itself, whose very title is a synonym of the Steadfast. If ability to conceive be taken as a criterion of Truth, then a truth to *David* Hume would very seldom be a truth to *Joe* ; and ninety-nine hundredths of what is undeniable in Heaven, would be demonstrable falsity upon Earth. The proposition of Mr. Mill, then, is sustained. I will not grant it to be an *axiom* ; and this merely because I am showing that *no* axioms exist ; but, with a distinction which could not have been cavilled at even by Mr. Mill himself, I am ready to grant that, *if* an axiom *there be*, then the proposition of which we speak has the fullest right to be considered an axiom—that no *more* absolute axiom *is*—and, consequently, that any subsequent proposition which shall conflict with this one primarily advanced, must be either a falsity in itself— that is to say, no axiom—or, if admitted axiomatic, must at once neutralize both itself and its predecessor.

"And now, by the logic of their own propounder, let us proceed to test any one of the axioms propounded. Let us give Mr. Mill the fairest of play. We will bring the point to no ordinary issue.

We will select for investigation no common-place axiom—no axiom of what, not the less preposterously because only impliedly, he terms his secondary class—as if a positive truth by definition could be either more or less positively a truth : we will select, I say, no axiom of an unquestionability so questionable as is to be found in Euclid. We will not talk, for example, about such propositions as that two straight lines cannot enclose a space, or that the whole is greater than any one of its parts. We will afford the logician *every* advantage. We will come at once to a proposition which he regards as the acme of the unquestionable—as the quintessence of axiomatic undeniability. Here it is :—'Contradictions cannot *both* be true—that is, cannot coexist in nature.' Here Mr. Mill means, for instance,—and I give the most forcible instance conceivable,—that a tree must be either a tree or *not* a tree—that it cannot be at the same time a tree *and* not a tree : all which is quite reasonable of itself, and will answer remarkably well as an axiom, until we bring it into collation with an axiom insisted upon a few pages before; in other words—words which I have previously employed—until we test it by the logic of its own propounder. 'A tree,' Mr. Mill asserts, 'must be either a tree or *not* a tree.' Very well : and now let me ask him, *why*. To this little query there is but one response—I defy any man living to invent a second. The sole answer is this :—'Because we find it *impossible to conceive* that a tree can be anything else than a tree or not a tree.' This, I repeat, is Mr. Mill's sole answer—he will not *pretend* to suggest another ; and yet, by his own showing, his answer is clearly no answer at all—for has he not already required us to admit, *as an axiom*, that ability or inability to conceive, is *in no case* to be taken as a criterion of axiomatic truth ? Thus all—absolutely *all* his argumentation is at sea without a rudder Let it not be urged that an exception from the general rule is to be made, in cases where the 'impossibility to conceive' is so peculiarly great as when we are called upon to conceive a tree *both* a tree and *not* a tree. Let no attempt, I say, be made at urging this sotticism ; for, in the first place, there are no *degrees* of 'impossibility,' and thus no one impossible conception can be *more* peculiarly impossible than another impossible conception : in the second place, Mr. Mill him-self—no doubt after thorough deliberation—has most distinctly, and most rationally, excluded all opportunity for exception, by the emphasis of his proposition, that, *in no case*, is ability or inability to conceive, to be taken as a criterion of axiomatic truth: in the third place, even were exceptions admissible at all, it remains to be shown how any exception is admissible *here*. That a tree can be both a tree and not a tree, is an idea which the angels, or the devils, *may* entertain, and which no doubt many an earthly Bedlamite, or Transcendentalist, *does*.

"Now I do not quarrel with these ancients," continues the letter-writer, "*so much* on account of the transparent frivolity of their logic—which, to be plain, was baseless, worthless, and fantastic altogether—as on account of their pompous and infatuate proscription of all *other* roads to Truth than the two narrow and crooked paths—the one of creeping and the other of crawling—to which, in their ignorant perversity, they have dared to confine the Soul—the Soul which loves nothing so well as to soar in those regions of illimitable intuition which are utterly incognizant of '*path.*'

"By the by, my dear friend, is it not an evidence of the mental slavery entailed upon those bigoted people by their Hogs and Rams, that in spite of the eternal prating of their savans about *roads* to Truth, none of them fell, even by accident, into what we now so distinctly perceive to be the broadest, the straightest, and most available of all mere roads—the great thoroughfare—the majestic highway of the *Consistent?* Is it not wonderful that they should have failed to deduce from the works of God the vitally momentous consideration that *a perfect consistency can be nothing but an absolute truth!* How plain—how rapid our progress since the late announcement of this proposition! By its means, investigation has been taken out of the hands of the ground-moles, and given as a duty, rather than as a task, to the true—to the *only* true thinkers—to the generally-educated men of ardent imagination. These latter—our Keplers—our Laplaces—'speculate'—'theorize'—these are the terms—can you not fancy the shout of scorn with which they would be received by our progenitors, were it possible for them to be looking over my shoulders as I write? The Keplers, I repeat, speculate—theorize—and their theories are merely corrected—reduced—sifted—cleared, little by little, of their chaff of inconsistency—until at length there stands apparent an unencumbered *Consistency*—a consistency which the most stolid admit—because it *is* a consistency—to be an absolute and unquestionable *Truth*.

" I have often thought, my friend, that it must have puzzled these dogmaticians of a thousand years ago, to determine, even, by which of their two boasted roads it is that the cryptographist attains the solution of the more complicated cyphers—or by which of them Champollion guided mankind to those important and innumerable truths which, for so many centuries, have lain entombed amid the phonetical hieroglyphics of Egypt. In especial, would it not have given these bigots some trouble to determine by which of their two roads was reached the most momentous and sublime of *all* their truths—the truth—the fact of *gravitation ?* Newton deduced it from the laws of Kepler. Kepler admitted that these laws he *guessed*—these laws whose investigation disclosed to the greatest of British astronomers that principle, the basis of all (existing) physical principle, in going behind which we enter at once the nebulous kingdom of Metaphysics. Yes !—these vital laws Kepler *guessed*—that is to say, he *imagined* them. Had he been asked to point out either the *deductive* or *inductive* route by which he attained them, his reply might have been—' I know nothing about *routes*—but I *do* know the machinery of the Universe. Here it is. I grasped it with *my soul*—I reached it through mere dint of *intuition*. Alas, poor ignorant old man ! Could not any metaphysician have told him that what he called ' intuition' was but the conviction resulting from *deductions or inductions of* which the processes were so shadowy as to have escaped his consciousness, eluded his reason, or bidden defiance to his capacity of expression ? How great a pity it is that some ' moral philosopher' had not enlightened him about all this ! How it would have comforted him on his death-bed to know that, instead of having gone intuitively and thus unbecomingly, he had, in fact, proceeded decorously and legitimately—that is to say Hog-ishly, or at least Ram-ishly—into the vast halls where lay gleaming, untended, and hitherto untouched by mortal hand—unseen by mortal eye—the imperishable and priceless secrets of the Universe !

" Yes, Kepler was essentially a *theorist ;* but this title, *now* of so much sanctity, was, in those ancient days, a designation of supreme contempt. It is only *now* that men begin to appreciate that divine old man—to sympathise with the prophetical and poetical rhapsody of his ever memorable words. For *my* part," continues the unknown correspondent, "I glow with a sacred fire when I even think of them, and feel that I shall never grow weary of their repetition :—in concluding this letter, let me have the real pleasure of transcribing them once again :—'*I care not whether my work be read now or by posterity. I can afford to wait a century for readers when God himself has waited six thousand years for an observer. I triumph. I have stolen the golden secret of the Egyptians. I will indulge my sacred fury.*'"

Here end my quotations from this very unaccountable and, perhaps, somewhat impertinent epistle; and perhaps it would be folly to comment, in any respect, upon the chimerical, not to say revolutionary, fancies of the writer—whoever he is—fancies so radically at war with the well-considered and well-settled opinions of this age. Let us proceed, then, to our legitimate thesis, *The Universe.*

This thesis admits a choice between two modes of discussion :—We may *ascend* or *descend.* Beginning at our own point of view, at the Earth on which we stand, we may pass to the other planets of our system, thence to the Sun, thence to our system considered collectively, and thence, through other systems, indefinitely outwards; or, commencing on high at some point as definite as we can make it or conceive it, we may come down to the habitation of Man. Usually, that is to say, in ordinary essays on Astronomy, the first of these two modes is, with certain reservation, adopted: this for the obvious reason that astronomical *facts*, merely, and principles, being the object, that object is best fulfilled in stepping from the known because proximate, gradually onward to the point where all certitude becomes lost in the remote. For my present purpose, however, that of enabling the mind to take in, as if from afar and at one glance, a distant conception of the *individual* Universe—it is clear that a descent to small from great—to the outskirts from the centre (if we could establish a centre)—to the end from the beginning (if we could fancy a beginning) would be the preferable course, but for the difficulty, if not impossibility, of presenting, in this course, to the unastronomical, a picture at all comprehensible in regard to such considerations as are involved in *quantity*—that is to say, in number, magnitude and distance.

Now, distinctness—intelligibility, at all points, is a primary feature in my general design. On important topics it is better to be a good deal prolix than even a very little obscure. But abstruseness is a quality appertaining to no subject *per se*. All are alike, in facility of comprehension, to him who approaches them by properly graduated steps. It is merely because a stepping-stone, here and there, is heedlessly left unsupplied in our road to Differential Calculus, that this latter is not altogether as simple a thing as a sonnet by Mr. Solomon Seesaw.

By way of admitting, then, no *chance* for misapprehension, I think it advisable to proceed as if even the more obvious facts of Astronomy were unknown to the reader. In combining the two modes of discussion to which I have referred, I propose to avail myself of the advantages peculiar to each—and very especially of the *iteration in detail* which will be unavoidable as a consequence of the plan. Commencing with a descent, I shall reserve for the return upwards those indispensable considerations of *quantity* to which allusion has already been made.

Let us begin, then, at once, with that merest of words, " Infinity." This, like " God," " spirit," and some other expressions of which the equivalents exist in all languages, is by no means the expression of an idea, but of an effort at one. It stands for the possible attempt at an impossible conception. Man needed a term by which to point out the *direction* of this effort—the cloud behind which lay, forever invisible, the *object* of this attempt. A word, in fine, was demanded, by means of which one human being might put himself in relation at once with another human being and with a certain *tendency* of the human intellect. Out of this demand arose the word, " Infinity ;" which is thus the representative but of the *thought of a thought*.

As regards *that* infinity now considered— the infinity of space— we often hear it said that " its idea is admitted by the mind—is acquiesced in —is entertained—on account of the greater difficulty which attends the conception of a limit." But this is merely one of those *phrases* by which even profound thinkers, time out of mind, have occasionally taken pleasure in deceiving *themselves*.

The quibble lies concealed in the word "difficulty." "The mind," we are told, "entertains the idea of *limitless*, through the greater *difficulty* which it finds in entertaining that of *limited*, space." Now, were the proposition but fairly *put*, its absurdity would become transparent at once. Clearly, there is no more *difficulty* in the case. The assertion intended, if presented *according* to its intention, and without sophistry, would run thus:—"The mind admits the idea of limitless, through the greater *impossibility* of entertaining that of limited, space."

It must be immediately seen that this is not a question of two statements between whose respective credibilities—or of two arguments between whose respective validities—the *reason* is called upon to decide:—it is a matter of two conceptions, directly conflicting, and each avowedly impossible, one of which the *intellect* is supposed to be capable of entertaining, on account of the greater *impossibility* of entertaining the other. The choice is *not* made between two difficulties; it is merely *fancied* to be made between two impossibilities. Now of the former, there *are* degrees, but of the latter, none:—just as our impertinent letter-writer has already suggested. A task *may* be more or less difficult; but it is either possible or not possible—there are no gradations. It *might* be more *difficult* to overthrow the Andes than an ant-hill; but it *can* be no more *impossible* to annihilate the matter of the one than the matter of the other. A man may jump ten feet with less *difficulty* than he can jump twenty, but the *impossibility* of his leaping to the moon is not a wit less than that of his leaping to the dog-star.

Since all this is undeniable; since the choice of the mind is to be made between *impossibilities* of conception; since one impossibility cannot be greater than another; and since, thus, one cannot be preferred to another: the philosophers who not only maintain, on the grounds mentioned, man's *idea* of infinity but, on account of such suppositions idea, *infinity itself*—are plainly engaged in demonstrating one impossible thing to be possible by showing how it is that some one other thing is impossible too. This, it will be said, is nonsense, and perhaps it is; indeed I think it very capital nonsense, but forego all claim to it as nonsense of mine.

The readiest mode, however, of displaying the fallacy of the philosophical argument on this question, is by simply adverting to a *fact* respecting it which has been hitherto quite overlooked—the fact that the argument alluded to both proves and disproves its own proposition. "The mind is impelled," say the theologians and others, "to admit a *First Cause*, by the superior difficulty it experiences in conceiving cause beyond cause without end." The quibble, as before, lies in the word "difficulty," but *here* what is it employed to sustain? A First Cause. And what is a First Cause? An ultimate termination of causes. And what is an ultimate termination of causes? Finity—the Finite. Thus the one quibble, in two processes, by God knows how many philosophers, is made to support now Finity and now Infinity; could it not be brought to support something besides? As for the quibbles, *they*, at least, are insupportable. But, to dismiss them; what they prove in the one case is the identical nothing which they demonstrate in the other.

Of course, no one will suppose that I here contend for the absolute impossibility of *that* which we attempt to convey in the word "Infinity." My purpose is but to show the folly of endeavoring to prove Infinity itself, or even our conception of it, by any such blundering ratiocination as that which is ordinarily employed.

Nevertheless, as an individual, I may be permitted to say that I *cannot* conceive Infinity, and am convinced that no human being can. A mind not thoroughly self-conscious, not accustomed to the introspective analysis of its own operations, will, it is true, often deceive itself by supposing that it *has* entertained the conception of which we speak. In the effort to entertain it, we proceed step beyond step, we fancy point still beyond point; and so long as we *continue* the effort, it may be said, in fact, that we are *tending* to the formation of the idea designed; while the strength of the impression that we actually form or have formed, is in the ratio of the period during which we keep up the mental endeavor. But it is in the act of discontinuing the endeavor—of fulfilling (as we think) the idea—of putting the finishing stroke (as we suppose) to the conception—that we overthrow at once the whole fabric of our fancy by resting upon some one ultimate, and, therefore, definite point. This fact, however, we fail to perceive, on account of the absolute coincidence, in time, between the settling down upon the

ultimate point and the act of cessation in thinking.   In attempting,
on the other hand, to frame the idea of a *limited* space, we merely
converse the processes which involve the impossibility.

We *believe* in a God.   We may or may not *believe* in finite or in
infinite space; but our belief, in such cases, is more properly designated as *faith*, and is a matter quite distinct from that belief proper—from that *intellectual* belief—which presupposes the mental
conception.

The fact is, that, upon the enunciation of any one of that class
of terms to which "Infinity" belongs—the class representing
thoughts of thought—he who has a right to say that he thinks *at
all*, feels himself called upon, *not* to entertain a conception, but
simply to direct his mental vision toward some given point, in the
intellectual firmament, where lies a nebula never to be resolved.
To solve it, indeed, he makes no effort; for with a rapid instinct
he comprehends, not only the impossibility, but, as regards all
human purposes, the *inessentiality* of its solution.   He perceives
that the Deity has not *designed* it to be solved.   He sees, at once,
that it lies *out* of the brain of man, and even *how*, if not exactly
why, it lies out of it.   There *are* people, I am aware, who, busy-
ing themselves in attempts at the unattainable, acquire very easily,
by dint of the jargon they emit, among those thinkers-that-they-
think with whom darkness and depth are synonymous, a kind of
cuttle-fish reputation for profundity; but the finest quality of
Thought is its self-cognizance; and with some little equivocation,
it may be said that no fog of the mind can well be greater than
that which, extending to the very boundaries of the mental domain, shuts out even these boundaries themselves from comprehension.

It will now be understood that, in using the phrase, "Infinity
of Space," I make no call upon the reader to entertain the impossible conception of an *absolute* infinity.   I refer simply to the
"*utmost conceivable expanse*" of space—a shadowy and fluctuating
domain, now shrinking, now swelling, in accordance with the vacillating energies of the imagination.

Hitherto, the Universe of stars has always been considered as
coincident with the Universe proper, as I have defined it in the
commencement of this Discourse.   It has been always either di-

rectly or indirectly assumed—at least since the dawn of intelligible
Astronomy—that, were it possible for us to attain any given point
in space, we should still find, on all sides of us, an interminable
succession of stars. This was the untenable idea of Pascal when
making perhaps the most successful attempt ever made, at peri-
phrasing the conception for which we struggle in the word
" Universe." " It is a sphere," he says, " of which the centre is
everywhere, the circumference, nowhere." But although this
intended definition is, in fact, *no* definition of the Universe of
stars, we may accept it, with some mental reservation, as a definition (rigorous enough for all practical purposes) of the Universe
proper—that is to say, of the Universe of *space*. This latter,
then, let us regard as " *a sphere of which the centre is everywhere, the circumference nowhere.*" In fact, while we find it impossible to fancy an *end* to space, we have no difficulty in picturing
to ourselves any one of an infinity of *beginnings*.

As our starting point, then, let us adopt the *Godhead*. Of this
Godhead, *in itself*, he alone is not imbecile—he alone is not impious who propounds——nothing. " *Nous ne connaissons rien,*"
says the Baron de Bielfeld—" *Nous ne connaissons rien de la
nature ou de l'essence de Dieu :—pour savior ce qu'il est, il faut
être Dieu même.*"—" We know absolutely *nothing* of the nature
or essence of God :—in order to comprehend what he is, we should
have to be God ourselves."

" *We should have to be God ourselves !*"—With a phrase so
startling as this yet ringing in my ears, I nevertheless venture to
demand if this our present ignorance of the Deity is an ignorance
to which the soul is *everlastingly* condemned.

By *Him*, however—*now*, at least, the Incomprehensible—by
Him—assuming him as *Spirit*—that is to say, as *not Matter*—a
distinction which, for all intelligible purposes, will stand well
instead of a definition—by Him, then, existing as Spirit, let us
content ourselves, to-night, with supposing to have been *created*,
or made out of Nothing, by dint of his Volition—at some point
of Space which we will take as a centre—at some period into
which we do not pretend to inquire, but at all events immensely
remote—by Him, then again, let us suppose to have been created——*what !* This s a vitally momentous epoch in our con-

siderations. *What* is it that we are justified—that alone we are justified in supposing to have been, primarily and solely, *created !*

We have attained a point where only *Intuition* can aid us :— but now let me recur to the idea which I have already suggested as that alone which we can properly entertain of intuition. It is but *the conviction arising from those inductions or deductions of which the processes are so shadowy as to escape our consciousness, elude our reason, or defy our capacity of expression.* With this understanding, I now assert—that an intuition altogether irresistible, although inexpressible, forces me to the conclusion that what God originally created—that that Matter which, by dint of his Volition, he first made from his Spirit, or from Nihility, *could* have been nothing but Matter in its utmost conceivable state of ——what ?—of *Simplicity ?*

This will be found the sole absolute *assumption* of my Discourse. I use the word "assumption" in its ordinary sense ; yet I maintain that even this my primary proposition, is very, very far indeed, from being really a mere assumption. Nothing was ever more certainly—no human conclusion was ever, in fact, more regularly—more rigorously *deduced* :—but, alas ! the processes lie out of the human analysis—at all events are beyond the utterance of the human tongue.

Let us now endeavor to conceive what Matter must be, when, or if, in its absolute extreme of *Simplicity.* Here the Reason flies at once to Imparticularity—to a particle—to *one* particle— a particle of *one* kind—of *one* character—of *one* nature—of *one* size—of one form—a particle, therefore, "*without* form and void" —a particle positively a particle at all points—a particle absolutely unique, individual, undivided, and not indivisible only because He who *created* it, by dint of his Will, can by an infinitely less energetic exercise of the same Will, as a matter of course, divide it.

Oneness, then, is all that I predicate of the originally created Matter ; but I propose to show that this *Oneness is a principle abundantly sufficient to account for the constitution, the existing phænomena and the plainly inevitable annihilation of at least the material Universe.*

The willing into being the primordial particle, has completed the act, or more properly the *conception* of Creation. We now proceed to the ultimate purpose for which we are to suppose the Particle created—that is to say, the ultimate purpose so far as our considerations *yet* enable us to see it—the constitution of the Universe from it, the Particle.

This constitution has been effected by *forcing* the originally and therefore normally *One* into the abnormal condition of *Many*. An action of this character implies rëaction. A diffusion from Unity, under the conditions, involves a tendency to return into Unity—a tendency ineradicable until satisfied. But on these points I will speak more fully hereafter.

The assumption of absolute Unity in the primordial Particle includes that of infinite divisibility. Let us conceive the Particle, then, to be only not totally exhausted by diffusion into Space. From the one Particle, as a centre, let us suppose to be irradiated spherically—in all directions—to immeasurable but still definite distances in the previously vacant space—a certain inexpressibly great yet limited number of unimaginably yet not infinitely minute atoms.

Now, of these atoms, thus diffused, or upon diffusion, what conditions are we permitted—not to assume, but to infer, from consideration as well of their source as of the character of the design apparent in their diffusion? *Unity* being their source, and *difference from Unity* the character of the design manifested in their diffusion, we are warranted in supposing this character to be at least *generally* preserved throughout the design, and to form a portion of the design itself:—that is to say, we shall be warranted in conceiving continual differences at all points from the uniquity and simplicity of the origin. But, for these reasons, shall we be justified in imagining the atoms heterogeneous, dissimilar, unequal, and inequidistant? More explicitly—are we to consider no two atoms as, at their diffusion, of the same nature, or of the same form, or of the same size?—and, after fulfilment of their diffusion into Space, is absolute inequidistance, each from each, to be understood of all of them? In such arrangement, under such conditions, we most easily and immediately comprehend the subsequent most feasible carrying out to completion of any such design as that which I have suggested—the design of variety out of unity—

diversity out of sameness—heterogeneity out of homogeneity—complexity out of simplicity—in a word, the utmost possible multiplicity of *relation* out of the emphatically irrelative *One*. Undoubtedly, therefore, we *should* be warranted in assuming all that has been mentioned, but for the reflection, first, that supererogation is not presumable of any Divine Act : and, secondly, that the object supposed in view, appears as feasible when some of the conditions in question are dispensed with, in the beginning, as when all are understood immediately to exist. I mean to say that some are involved in the rest, or so instantaneous a consequence of them as to make the distinction inappreciable. Difference of *size*, for example, will at once be brought about through the tendency of one atom to a second, in preference to a third, on account of particular inequidistance ; which is to be comprehended as *particular inequidistances between centres of quantity, in neighboring atoms of different form*—a matter not at all interfering with the generally-equable distribution of the atoms. Difference of *kind*, too, is easily conceived to be merely a result of differences in size and form, taken more or less conjointly :—in fact, since the *Unity* of the Particle Proper implies absolute homogeneity, we cannot imagine the atoms, at their diffusion, differing in kind, without imagining, at the same time, a special exercise of the Divine Will, at the emission of each atom, for the purpose of effecting, in each, a change of its essential nature :—so fantastic an idea is the less to be indulged, as the object proposed is seen to be thoroughly attainable without such minute and elaborate interposition. We perceive, therefore, upon the whole, that it would be supererogatory, and consequently unphilosophical, to predicate of the atoms, in view of their purposes, any thing more than *difference of form* at their dispersion, with particular inequidistance after it—all other differences arising at once out of these, in the very first processes of mass-constitution :—We thus establish the Universe on a purely *geometrical* basis. Of course, it is by no means necessary to assume absolute difference, even of form, among *all* the atoms irradiated—any more than absolute particular inequidistance of each from each. We are required to conceive merely that no *neighboring* atoms are of similar form—no atoms which can ever approximate, until their inevitable reünition at the end.

7*

Although the immediate and perpetual *tendency* of the disunited atoms to return into their normal Unity, is implied, as I have said, in their abnormal diffusion. still it is clear that this tendency will be without consequence—a tendency and no more—until the diffusive energy, in ceasing to be exerted, shall leave *it*, the tendency, free to seek its satisfaction. The Divine Act, however, being considered as determinate, and discontinued on fulfilment of the diffusion, we understand, at once, a *rëaction*—in other words, a *satisfiable* tendency of the disunited atoms to return into *One*.

But the diffusive energy being withdrawn, and the rëaction having commenced in furtherance of the ultimate design—*that of the utmost possible Relation*—this design is now in danger of being frustrated, in detail, by reason of that very tendency to return which is to effect its accomplishment in general. *Multiplicity* is the object; but there is nothing to prevent proximate atoms from lapsing *at once*, through the now satisfiable tendency—*before* the fulfilment of any ends proposed in multiplicity—into absolute oneness among themselves :—there is nothing to impede the aggregation of various *unique* masses, at various points of space :—in other words, nothing to interfere with the accumulation of various masses, each absolutely One.

For the effectual and thorough completion of the general design, we thus see the necessity for a repulsion of limited capacity—a separative *something* which, on withdrawal of the diffusive Volition, shall at the same time allow the approach, and forbid the junction, of the atoms ; suffering them infinitely to approximate, while denying them positive contact ; in a word, having the power—*up to a certain epoch*—of preventing their *coalition*, but no ability to interfere with their *coalescence* in any respect *or degree.* The repulsion, already considered as so peculiarly limited in other regards, must be understood, let me repeat, as having power to prevent absolute coalition, *only up to a certain epoch.* Unless we are to conceive that the appetite for Unity among the atoms is doomed to be satisfied *never ;*—unless we are to conceive that what had a beginning is to have no end—a conception which cannot *really* be entertained, however much we may talk or dream of entertaining it—we are forced to conclude that the repulsive influence imagined, will, finally —under pressure of the *Uni-tendency collectively* applied, but never and in no degree *until*, on fulfilment of the Divine purposes, such collective application shall be naturally made—yield to a force which, at that ultimate epoch, shall be the superior force precisely to the extent required, and thus permit the universal subsidence into the inevitable, because original and therefore normal, *One*. The conditions here to be reconciled are difficult indeed :—we cannot even comprehend the possibility of their conciliation ;—nevertheless, the apparent impossibility is brilliantly suggestive.

That the repulsive something actually exists, *we see*. Man neither employs, nor knows, a force sufficient to bring two atoms into contact. This is but the well-established proposition of the impenetrability of matter. All Experiment proves—all Philosophy admits it. The *design* of the repulsion—the necessity for its existence—I have endeavored to show ; but from all attempt at investigating its nature have religiously abstained ; this on account of an intuitive conviction that the principle at issue is strictly spiritual—lies in a recess impervious to our present understanding—lies involved in a consideration of what now—in our human state—is *not* to be considered—in a consideration of *Spirit in itself*. I feel, in a word, that here the God has interposed, and here only, because here and here only the knot demanded the interposition of the God.

In fact, while the tendency of the diffused atoms to return into Unity, will be recognised, at once, as the principle of the Newtonian Gravity, what I have spoken of as a repulsive influence prescribing limits to the (immediate) satisfaction of the tendency, will be understood as *that* which we have been in the practice of designating now as heat, now as magnetism, now as *electricity ;* displaying our ignorance of its awful character in the vacillation of the phraseology with which we endeavor to circumscribe it.

Calling it, merely for the moment, electricity, we know that all experimental analysis of electricity has given, as an ultimate result, the principle, or seeming principle, *heterogeneity*. *Only* where things differ, is electricity apparent ; and it is presumable that they *never* differ where it is not developed at least, if not apparent. Now, this result is in the fullest keeping with that which I have reached unempirically. The design of the repulsive influence I have maintained to be that of preventing immediate Unity among the diffused atoms; and these atoms are represented as different each from each. *Difference* is their character—their essentiality—just as *no-difference* was the essentiality of their course. When we say, then, that an attempt to bring any two of these atoms together would induce an effort, on the part of the repulsive influence, to prevent the contact, we may as well use the strictly convertible sentence that an attempt to bring together any two differences will result in a development of electricity. All existing bodies, of course, are composed of these atoms in proximate contact, and are therefore to be considered as mere assemblages of more or fewer differences; and the resistance made by the repulsive spirit, on bringing together any two such assemblages, would be in the ratio of the two sums of the differences in each :—an expression which, when reduced, is equivalent to this :—*The amount of electricity developed on the approximation of two bodies, is proportional to the difference between the respective sums of the atoms of which the bodies are composed.* That *no* two bodies are absolutely alike, is a simple corollary from all that has been here said. Electricity, therefore, existing always, is *developed* whenever *any* bodies, but *manifested* only when bodies of appreciable difference, are brought into approximation.

To electricity—so, for the present, continuing to call it—we *may* not be wrong in referring the various physical appearances of light, heat and magnetism; but far less shall we be liable to err in attributing to this strictly spiritual principle the more important phænomena of vitality, consciousness and *Thought.* On this topic, however, I need pause *here* merely to suggest that these phænomena, whether observed generally or in detail, seem to proceed *at least in the ratio of the heterogeneous.*

Discarding now the two equivocal terms, "gravitation" and "electricity," let us adopt the more definite expressions, "*attraction*" and "*repulsion.*" The former is the body; the latter the soul: the one is the material; the other the spiritual, principle of the Universe. *No other principles exist.* All phænomena are referable to one, or to the other, or to both combined. So rigorously is this the case—so thoroughly demonstrable is it that attraction and repulsion are the *sole* properties through which we perceive the Universe—in other words, by which Matter is manifested to Mind—that, for all merely argumentative purposes, we are fully justified in assuming that matter *exists* only as attraction and repulsion—that attraction and repulsion *are* matter :—there being no conceivable case in which we may not employ the term " matter" and the terms " attraction" and " repulsion," taken together, as equivalent, and therefore convertible, expressions in Logic.

I said, just now, that what I have described as the tendency of the diffused atoms to return into their original unity, would be understood as the principle of the Newtonian law of gravity; and, in fact, there can be but little difficulty in such an understanding, if we look at the Newtonian gravity in a merely general view, as a force impelling matter to seek matter; that is to say, when we pay no attention to the known *modus operandi* of the Newtonian force. The general coincidence satisfies us; but, upon looking closely, we see, in detail, much that appears *incoincident*, and much in regard to which no coincidence, at least, is established. For example : the Newtonian gravity, when we think of it in certain moods, does *not* seem to be a tendency to *oneness* at all, but rather a tendency of all bodies in all directions—a phrase apparently expressive of a tendency to diffusion. Here, then, is an *incoincidence*. Again; when we reflect on the mathematical *law* governing the Newtonian tendency, we see clearly that no coincidence has been made good, in respect of the *modus operandi*, at least, between gravitation as known to exist and that seemingly simple and direct tendency which I have assumed.

In fact, I have attained a point at which it will be advisable to strengthen my position by reversing my processes. So far, we have gone on *à priori*, from an abstract consideration of *Simplicity*, as that quality most likely to have characterized the original action of God. Let us now see whether the established facts of the Newtonian Gravitation may not afford us, *à posteriori*, some legitimate inductions.

What does the Newtonian law declare? That all bodies attract each other with forces proportional to the squares of their distances. Purposely, I have given, in the first place, the vulgar version of the law; and I confess that in this, as in most other vulgar ver sions of great truths, we find little of a suggestive character. Let us now adopt a more philosophical phraseology :—*Every atom, of every body, attracts every other atom, both of its own and of every other body, with a force which varies inversely as the squares of the distances between the attracting and attracted atom.* Here, indeed, a flood of suggestion bursts upon the mind.

But let us see distinctly what it was that Newton *proved*—according to the grossly irrational definitions of *proof* prescribed by the metaphysical schools. He was forced to content himself with showing how thoroughly the motions of an imaginary Universe, composed of attracting and attracted atoms obedient to the law he announced, coincide with those of the actually existing Universe so far as it comes under our observation. This was the amount of his *demonstration*—that is to say, this was the amount of it, according to the conventional cant of the " philosophies." His successes added proof multiplied by proof—such proof as a sound intellect admits—but the *demonstration* of the law itself, persist the metaphysicians, had not been strengthened in any degree. " *Ocular, physical* proof," however, of attraction, here upon Earth, in accordance with the Newtonian theory, was, at length, much to the satisfaction of some intellectual grovellers, afforded. This proof arose collaterally and incidentally (as nearly all important truths have arisen) out of an attempt to ascertain the mean density of the Earth. In the famous Maskelyne, Cavendish and Bailly experiments for this purpose, the attraction of the mass of a mountain was seen, felt, measured, and found to be mathematically consistent with the immortal theory of the British astronomer.

But in spite of this confirmation of that which needed none—in spite of the so-called corroboration of the " theory" by the so-called " ocular and physical proof"—in spite of the *character* of this corroboration—the ideas which even really philosophical men cannot help imbibing of gravity—and, especially, the ideas of it which ordinary men get and contentedly maintain, are *seen* to have been derived, for the most part, from a consideration of the principle as they find it developed—*merely in the planet upon which they stand.*

Now, to what does so partial a consideration tend—to what species of error does it give rise? On the Earth we *see* and *feel* only that gravity impels all bodies towards the *centre* of the Earth. No man in the common walks of life could be *made* to see or feel anything else—could be made to perceive that anything, anywhere, has a perpetual, gravitating tendency in any *other* direction than to the centre of the Earth; yet (with an exception hereafter to be specified) it is a fact that every earthly thing (not to speak now of every heavenly thing) has a tendency not *only* to the Earth's centre but in every conceivable direction besides.

Now, although the philosophic cannot be said to *err with* the vulgar in this matter, they nevertheless permit themselves to be influenced, without knowing it, by the *sentiment* of the vulgar idea. "Although the Pagan fables are not believed," says Bryant, in his very erudite "Mythology," "yet we forget ourselves continually and make inferences from them as from existing realities." I mean to assert that the merely *sensitive perception* of gravity as we experience it on Earth, beguiles mankind into the fancy of *concentralization* or *especiality* respecting it—has been continually biasing towards this fancy even the mightiest intellects—perpetually, although imperceptibly, leading them away from the real characteristics of the principle; thus preventing them, up to this date, from ever getting a glimpse of that vital truth which lies in a diametrically opposite direction—behind the principle's *essential* characteristics—those, *not* of concentralization or especiality—but of *universality* and *diffusion*. This "vital truth" is *Unity* as the *source* of the phænomenon.

Let me now repeat the definition of gravity:—*Every atom, of every body, attracts every other atom, both of its own and of every other body*, with a force which varies inversely as the squares of the distances of the attracting and attracted atom.

Here let the reader pause with me, for a moment, in contemplation of the miraculous—of the ineffable—of the altogether unimaginable complexity of relation involved in the fact that *each atom attracts every other atom*—involved merely in this fact of the attraction, without reference to the law or mode in which the attraction is manifested—involved *merely* in the fact that each atom attracts every other atom *at all*, in a wilderness of atoms so numerous that those which go to the composition of a cannon-ball exceed, probably, in mere point of number, all the stars which go to the constitution of the Universe.

Had we discovered, simply, that each atom tended to some one favorite point—to some especially attractive atom—we should still have fallen upon a discovery which, in itself, would have sufficed to overwhelm the mind:—but what is it that we are actually called upon to comprehend? That each atom attracts —sympathizes with the most delicate movements of every other atom, and with each and with all at the same time, and forever, and according to a determinate law of which the complexity, even considered by itself solely, is utterly beyond the grasp of the imagination of man. If I propose to ascertain the influence of one mote in a sunbeam upon its neighboring mote, I cannot accomplish my purpose without first counting and weighing all the atoms in the Universe, and defining the precise positions of all at one particular moment. If I venture to displace, by even the billionth part of an inch, the microscopical speck of dust which lies now upon the point of my finger, what is the character of that act upon which I have adventured? I have done a deed which shakes the Moon in her path, which causes the Sun to be no longer the sun, and which alters forever the destiny of the multitudinous myriads of stars that roll and glow in the majestic presence of their Creator.

These ideas—conceptions such as *these*—unthoughtlike thoughts —soul-reveries rather than conclusions or even considerations of the intellect:—ideas, I repeat, such as these, are such as we can alone hope profitably to entertain in any effort at grasping the great principle, *Attraction.*

But now, *with* such ideas—with such a *vision* of the marvellous complexity of Attraction fairly in his mind—let any person competent of thought on such topics as these, set himself to the task of imagining a *principle* for the phænomena observed—a condition from which they sprang.

Does not so evident a brotherhood among the atoms point to a common parentage? Does not a sympathy so omniprevalent, so ineradicable, and so thoroughly irrespective, suggest a common paternity as its source? Does not one extreme impel the reason to the other? Does not the infinitude of division refer to the utterness of individuality? Does not the entireness of the complex hint at the perfection of the simple? It is *not* that the atoms, as we see them, are divided or that they are complex in their relations—but that they are inconceivably divided and un-utterably complex: it is the extremeness of the conditions to which I now allude, rather than to the conditions themselves. In a word, is it not because the atoms were, at some remote epoch of time, even *more than together*—is it not because originally, and therefore normally, they were *One*—that now, in all circumstances—at all points—in all directions—by all modes of approach—in all relations and through all conditions— they struggle *back* to this absolutely, this irrelatively, this unconditionally *one?*

Some person may here demand:—" Why—since it is to the *One* that the atoms struggle back—do we not find and define Attraction ' a merely general tendency to a centre?'—why, in especial, do not *your* atoms—the atoms which you describe as having been irradiated from a centre—proceed at once, rectilinearly back to the central point of their origin?"

I reply that *they do :* as will be distinctly shown ; but that the cause of their so doing is quite irrespective of the centre *as such.* They all tend rectilinearly towards a centre, because of the sphericity with which they have been irradiated into space. Each atom, forming one of a generally uniform globe of atoms, finds more atoms in the direction of the centre, of course, than in any other, and in that direction, therefore, is impelled—but is *not* thus impelled because the centre is *the point of its origin.* It is not to any *point* that the atoms are allied. It is not any *locality*, either in the concrete or in the abstract, to which I suppose them bound. Nothing like *location* was conceived as their origin. Their source lies in the principle, *Unity.* *This* is their lost parent. *This* they seek always—immediately—in all directions—wherever it is even partially to be found : thus appeasing, in some measure, the inera lizable tendency, while on the way to its absolute satisfaction in the end. It follows from all this, that any principle which shall be adequate to account for the *law*, or *modus operandi*, of the attractive force in general, will account for this law in particular :—that is to say, any principle which will show why the atoms should tend to their *general centre of irradiation* with forces inversely proportional to the squares of the distances will be admitted as satisfactorily accounting, at the same time, for the tendency according to the same law, of these atoms each to each ;—*for the* tendency to the centre *is* merely the tendency each to each, and not any tendency to a centre as such.—Thus it will be seen, also, that the establishment of my propositions would involve no *necessity* of modification in the terms of the Newtonian definition of Gravity, which declares that each atom attracts each other atom and so forth, and declares this merely ; but (always under the supposition that what I propose be, in the end, admitted) it seems clear that some error might occasionally be avoided, in the future processes of Science, were a more ample phraseology adopted :— for instance :—" Each atom tends to every other atom, &c., with a force &c. : *the general result being a tendency of all, with a similar force, to a general centre.*"

The reversal of our processes has thus brought us to an identical result ; but while in the one process *intuition* was the starting point, in the other it was the goal. In commencing the former journey I could only say that, with an irresistible intuition, I *felt* Simplicity to have been made the characteristic of the original action of God :—in ending the letter I can only declare that with an irresistible intuition, I perceive Unity to have been the source of the observed phænomena of the Newtonian gravitation. Thus, according to the schools, I *prove* nothing. So be it :—I design but to suggest—and to *convince* through the suggestion. I am proudly aware that there exist many of the most profound and cautiously discriminative human intellects which cannot *help* being abundantly content with my—suggestions. To these intellects— as to my own—there is no mathematical demonstration which *could* bring the least additional *true proof* of the great *Truth* which I have advanced—*the truth of Original Unity as the source —as the principle of the Universal Phænomena.* For my part I am not sure that I speak and see—I am not so sure that my heart beats and that my soul lives :—of the rising of to-morrow's sun— a probability that as yet lies in the Future—I do not pretend to be one thousandth part as sure—as I am of the irretrievably by-gone *Fact* that All Things and All Thoughts of Things, with all their ineffable Multiplicity of Relation, sprang at once into being from the primordial and irrelative *One*.

Referring to the Newtonian Gravity, Dr. Nichol, the eloquent author of " The Architecture of the Heavens," says :—" In truth we have no reason to suppose this great Law, as now revealed, to be the ultimate or simplest, and therefore the universal and all-comprehensive, form of a great Ordinance. The mode in which its intensity diminishes with the element of distance, has not the aspect of an ultimate *principle ;* which always assumes the simplicity and self-evidence of those axioms which constitute the basis of Geometry."

Now, it is quite true that " ultimate principles," in the common understanding of the words, always assume the simplicity of geometrical axioms—(as for " self-evidence," there is no such thing)—but these principles are clearly *not* " ultimate ;" in other terms, what we are in the habit of calling principles are no principles, properly speaking—since there can be but one *principle*, the Volition of God. We have no right to assume, then, from what we observe in rules that we choose foolishly to name " principles," anything at all in respect to the characteristics of a principle proper. The " ultimate principles" of which Dr. Nichol speaks as having geometrical simplicity, may and do have this geometrical turn, as being part and parcel of a vast geometrical system, and thus a system of simplicity itself—in which, nevertheless, the *truly* ultimate principle is, *as we know*, the consummation of the complex—that is to say, of the unintelligible—for is it not the Spiritual Capacity of God ?

I quoted Dr. Nichol's remark, however, not so much to question its philosophy, as by way of calling attention to the fact that while all men have admitted *some* principle as existing behind the law of Gravity, no attempt has been yet made to point out what this principle in particular *is* :—if we except, perhaps, occasional fantas : efforts at referring it to Magnetism, or Mesmerism, or Swedenborgianism, or Trancendentalism, or some other equally delicious *ism* of the same species, and invariably patronized by one and the same species of people. The great mind of Newton, while boldly grasping the Law itself, shrank from the principle of the Law. The more fluent and comprehensive at least, if not the more patient and profound, sagacity of Laplace, had not the courage to attack it. But hesitation on the part of these two astronomers it is, perhaps, not so very difficult to understand. They, as well as all the first class of mathematicians, were mathematicians *solely :*—their intellect at least had a firmly-pronounced mathematico-physical tone. What lay not distinctly within the domain of Physics, or of Mathematics, seemed to them either Non-Entity or Shadow. Nevertheless, we may well wonder that Leibnitz, who was a marked exception to the general rule in these respects, and whose mental temperament was a singular admixture of the mathematical with the physico-metaphysical, did not at once investigate and establish the point at issue. Either Newton or Laplace, seeking a principle and discovering none *physical*, would have rested contentedly in the conclusion that there was absolutely none ; but it is almost impossible to fancy, of Liebnitz, that, having exhausted in his search the physical dominions, he would not have stepped at once, boldly and hopefully, amid his old familiar haunts in the kingdom of Metaphysics. Here, indeed, it is clear that he *must* have adventured in search of the treasure :—that he did not find it after all, was, perhaps, because his fairy guide, Imagination, was not sufficiently well-grown, or well-educated, to direct him aright.

I observed, just now, that, in fact, there had been certain vague attempts at referring Gravity to some very uncertain *isms*. These attempts, however, although considered bold, and justly so considered, looked no farther than to the generality—the merest generality—of the Newtonian Law. Its *modus operandi* has never, to my knowledge, been approached in the way of an effort at explanation. It is therefore, with no unwarranted fear of being taken for a madman at the outset, and before I can bring my propositions fairly to the eye of those who alone are competent to decide upon them, that I here declare the *modus operandi* of the Law of Gravity to be an exceedingly simple and perfectly explicable thing—that is to say, when we make our advances towards it in just gradations and in the true direction—when we regard it from the proper point of view.

Whether we reach the idea of absolute *Unity* as the source of

All Things, from a consideration of Simplicity as the most probable characteristic of the original action of God;—whether we arrive at it from an inspection of the universality of relation in the gravitating phaenomena;—or whether we attain it as a result of the mutual corroboration afforded by both processes;—still, the idea itself, if entertained at all, is entertained in inseparable connection with another idea—that of the condition of the Universe of stars as we *now* perceive it—that is to say, a condition of immeasurable *diffusion* through space. Now a connection between these two ideas—unity and diffusion—cannot be established unless through the entertainment of a third idea—that of *irradiation*. Absolute Unity being taken as a centre, then the existing Universe of stars is the result of *irradiation* from that centre.

Now, the laws of irradiation are *known*. They are part and parcel of the *sphere*. They belong to the class of *indisputable geometrical properties*. We say of them, "they are true—they are evident." To demand *why* they are true, would be to demand why the axioms are true upon which their demonstration is based. *Nothing* is demonstrable, strictly speaking; but *if* anything *be*, then the properties—the laws in question are demonstrated.

But these laws—what do they declare? Irradiation—how—by what steps does it proceed outwardly from a centre?

From a *luminous* centre, *Light* issues by irradiation; and the quantities of light received upon any given plane, supposed to be shifting its position so as to be now nearer the centre and now farther from it, will be diminished in the same proportion as the squares of the distances of the plane from the luminous body, are increased; and will be increased in the same proportion as these squares are diminished.

The expression of the law may be thus generalized:—the number of light-particles (or, if the phrase be preferred, the number of light-impressions) received upon the shifting plane, will be *inversely* proportional with the squares of the distances of the plane. Generalizing yet again, we may say that the diffusion—the scattering—the irradiation, in a word—is *directly* proportional with the squares of the distances.

For example: at the distance B, from the luminous centre A, a certain number of particles are so diffused as to occupy the sur

face B. Then at double the distance—that is to say, at C—they
will be so much farther diffused as to occupy four such surfaces :

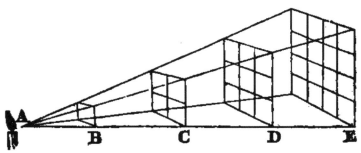

—at treble the distance, or at D, they will be so much farther
separated as to occupy nine such surfaces ;—while, at quadruple
the distance, or at E, they will have become so scattered as to
spread themselves over sixteen such surfaces—and so on forever.

In saying, generally, that the irradiation proceeds in direct proportion with the squares of the distances, we use the term irradiation to express *the degree of the diffusion* as we proceed outwardly from the centre.   Conversing the idea, and employing
the word "concentralization," to express *the degree of the drawing
together* as we come back toward the centre from an outward position, we may say that concentralization proceeds *inversely* as the
squares of the distances.   In other words, we have reached the
conclusion that, on the hypothesis that matter was originally irradiated from a centre, and is now returning to it, the concentralization, in the return, proceeds *exactly as we know the force of gravitation to proceed.*

Now here, if we could be permitted to assume that concentralization exactly represented the *force of the tendency to the centre*—
that the one was exactly proportional to the other, and that the
two proceeded together—we should have shown all that is required.
The sole difficulty existing, then, is to establish a direct proportion
between "concentralization" and the *force* of concentralization ;
and this is done, of course, if we establish such proportion between
"irradiation" and the *force* of irradiation.

A very slight inspection of the Heavens assures us that the stars
have a certain general uniformity, equability, or equidistance, of
distribution through that region of space in which, collectively

and in a roughly globular form, they are situated:—this species of very general, rather than absolute, equability, being in full keeping with my deduction of inequidistance, within certain limits among the originally diffused atoms, as a corollary from the evident design of infinite complexity of relation out of irrelation. I started, it will be remembered, with the idea of a generally uniform but particularly *ununiform* distribution of the atoms;—an idea, I repeat, which an inspection of the stars, as they exist, confirms.

But even in the merely general equability of distribution, as regards the atoms, there appears a difficulty which, no doubt, has already suggested itself to those among my readers who have borne in mind that I suppose this equability of distribution *effected* through *irradiation from a centre*. The very first glance at the idea, irradiation, forces us to the entertainment of the hitherto unseparated and seemingly inseparable idea of agglomeration about a centre, with dispersion as we recede from it—the idea, in a word, of *inequability* of distribution in respect to the matter irradiated.

Now, I have elsewhere * observed, that it is by just such difficulties as the one now in question—such roughnesses—such peculiarities—such protuberances above the plane of the ordinary—that Reason feels her way, if at all, in her search for the True. By the difficulty—the "peculiarity"—now presented, I leap at once to *the* secret—a secret which I might never have attained *but* for the peculiarity and the inference which, *in its mere character of peculiarity*, it affords me.

The process of thought, at this point, may be thus roughly sketched:—I say to myself—"Unity, as I have explained it, is a truth—I feel it. Diffusion is a truth—I see it. Irradiation, by which alone these two truths are reconciled, is a consequent truth—I perceive it. *Equability* of diffusion, first deduced *à priori* and then corroborated by the inspection of phenomena, is also a truth—I fully admit it. So far all is clear around me:—there are no clouds behind which the *secret*—the great secret of the gravitating *modus operandi*—can possibly lie hidden;—but this secret lies *hereabouts*, most assuredly; and *were* there but a cloud in view

* "*Murders in the Rue Morgue*"—p. 109

I should be driven to suspicion of that cloud." And now, just as I say this, there actually comes a cloud into view. This cloud is the seeming impossibility of reconciling my truth, *irradiation*, with my truth, *equability of diffusion*. I say now :—" Behind this *seeming* impossibility is to be found what I desire." I do not say " *real* impossibility ;" for invincible faith in my truths assures me that it is a mere difficulty after all ; but I go on to say, with unflinching confidence, that, *when* this *difficulty* shall be solved, we shall find, *wrapped up in the process of solution*, the key to the secret at which we aim. Moreover—I *feel* that we shall discover *but one* possible solution of the difficulty ; this for the reason that, were there two, one would be supererogatory—would be fruitless— would be empty—would contain no key—since no duplicate key can be needed to any secret of Nature.

And now, let us see :—Our usual notions of irradiation—in fact, *all* our distinct notions of it—are caught merely from the process as we see it exemplified in *Light*. Here there is a *continuous* outpouring of *ray-streams*, and *with a force which we have at least no right to suppose varies at all*. Now, in any such irradiation *as this*—continuous and of unvarying force—the regions nearer the centre must *inevitably* be always more crowded with the irradiated matter than the regions more remote. But I have assumed *no* such irradiation *as this*. I assumed no *continuous* irradiation ; and for the simple reason that such an assumption would have involved, first, the necessity of entertaining a conception which I have shown no man *can* entertain, and which (as I will more fully explain hereafter) all observation of the firmament refutes—the conception of the absolute infinity of the Universe of stars—and would have involved, secondly, the impossibility of understanding a reäction—that is, gravitation—as existing now—since, while an act is continued, no reäction, of course, can take place. My assumption, then, or rather my inevitable deduction from just premises,—was that of a *determinate* irradiation—one finally discontinued.

Let me now describe the sole possible mode in which it is conceivable that matter could have been diffused through space so as to fulfil the conditions at once of irradiation and of generally equable distribution.

For convenience of illustration, let us imagine, in the first place, a hollow sphere of glass, or of anything else, occupying the space throughout which the universal matter is to be thus equally diffused, by means of irradiation, from the absolute, irrelative, unconditional particle, placed in the centre of the sphere.

Now, a certain exertion of the diffusive power (presumed to be the Divine Volition)—in other words, a certain *force*—whose measure is the quantity of matter—that is to say, the number of atoms—emitted; emits, by irradiation, this certain number of atoms; forcing them in all directions outwardly from the centre—their proximity to each other diminishing as they proceed—until, finally, they are distributed, loosely, over the interior surface of the sphere.

When these atoms have attained this position, or while proceeding to attain it, a second and inferior exercise of the same force—or a second and inferior force of the same character—emits, in the same manner—that is to say, by irradiation as before—a second stratum of atoms which proceeds to deposit itself upon the first; the number of atoms, in this case as in the former, being of course the measure of the force which emitted them ; in other words, the force being precisely adapted to the purpose it effects—the force, and the number of atoms sent out by the force, being *directly proportional.*

When this second stratum has reached its destined position—or while approaching it—a third still inferior exertion of the force, or a third inferior force of a similar character—the number of atoms emitted being in *all* cases the measure of the force—proceeds to deposit a third stratum upon the second :—and so on, until these concentric strata, growing gradually less and less, come down at length to the central point; and the diffusive matter, simultaneously with the diffusive force, is exhausted.

We have now the sphere filled, through means of irradiation, with atoms equably diffused. The two necessary conditions—those of irradiation and of equable diffusion—are satisfied ; and by the *sole* process in which the possibility of their simultaneous satisfaction is conceivable. For this reason, I confidently expect to find, lurking in the present condition of the atoms as distributed throughout the sphere, the secret of which I am in search—the all-important principle of the *modus operandi* of the Newt *n*ian law. Let us examine, then, the actual condition of the atoms.

They lie in a series of concentric strata. They are equably diffused throughout the sphere. They have been irradiated into these states.

The atoms being *equably* distributed, the greater the superficial extent of any of *these* concentric strata, or spheres, the more atoms will lie upon it. In other words, the number of atoms lying upon the surface of any one of the concentric spheres, is directly proportional with the extent of that surface.

But, in any series of concentric spheres, the surfaces are directly proportional with the squares of the distances from the centre.*

Therefore the number of atoms in any stratum is directly proportional with the square of that stratum's distance from the centre.

But the number of atoms in any stratum is the measure of the force which emitted that stratum—that is to say, is *directly proportional* with the force.

Therefore the force which irradiated any stratum is directly proportional with the square of that stratum's distance from the centre :—or, generally,

The force of the irradiation has been directly proportional with the squares of the distances.

Now, Reaction, as far as we know any thing of it, is Action conversed. The *general* principle of Gravity being, in the first place, understood as the reaction of an act—as the expression of a desire on the part of Matter, while existing in a state of diffusion, to return into the Unity whence it was diffused ; and, in the second place, the mind being called upon to determine the *character* of the desire—the manner in which it would, naturally, be manifested ; in other words, being called upon to conceive a probable law, or *modus operandi*, for the return ; could not well help arriving at the conclusion that this law of return would be precisely the converse of the law of departure. That such would be the case, any one, at least, would be abundantly justified in taking for granted, until such time as some person should suggest some-

---

* Succinctly—The surfaces of spheres are as the squares of their radii.

thing like a plausible reason why it should *not* be the case—until such period as a law of return shall be imagined which the intellect can consider as preferable.

Matter, then, irradiated into space with a force varying as the squares of the distances, might *à priori*, be supposed to return towards its centre of irradiation with a force varying *inversely* as the squares of the distances: and I have already shown* that any principle which will explain why the atoms should tend, according to any law, to the general centre, must be admitted as satisfactorily explaining, at the same time, why, according to the same law, they should tend each to each. For, in fact, the tendency to the general centre is not to a centre as such, but because of its being a point in tending towards which each atom tends most directly to its real and essential centre, *Unity*—the absolute and final Union of all.

The consideration here involved presents to my own mind no embarrassment whatever—but this fact does not blind me to the possibility of its being obscure to those who may have been less in the habit of dealing with abstractions :—and, upon the whole, **it may be as well to look at the matter from one or two other points of view.**

The absolute, irrelative particle primarily created by the Volition of God, must have been in a condition of positive *normality*, or rightfulness—for wrongfulness implies *relation*. Right is positive ; wrong is negative—is merely the negation of right ; as cold is the negation of heat—darkness of light. That a thing may be wrong, it is necessary that there be some other thing in *relation* to which it *is* wrong—some condition which it fails to satisfy ; some law which it violates ; some being whom it aggrieves. If there be no such being, law, or condition, in respect to which the thing is wrong—and, still more especially, if no beings, laws, or conditions exist at all—then the thing can*not* be wrong, and consequently must be *right*. Any deviation from normality involves a tendency to return to it. A difference from the normal—from the right— from the just—can be understood as effected only by the overcoming a difficulty ; and if the force which overcomes the diffi-

* Page 143

culty be not infinitely continued, the ineradicable tendency to
return will at length be permitted to act for its own satisfaction.
Upon withdrawal of the force, the tendency acts. This is the
principle of reäction as the inevitable consequence of finite
action. Employing a phraseology of which the seeming affectation will be pardoned for its expressiveness, we may say that
Reäction is the return from the condition of *as it is and ought
not to be* into the condition of *as it was, originally, and therefore
ought to be:*—and let me add here that the *absolute* force of
Reäction would no doubt be always found in direct proportion
with the reality—the truth—the absoluteness—of the *originality*
—if ever it were possible to measure this latter:—and, conse·
quently, the greatest of all conceivable reäctions must be that
produced by the tendency which we now discuss—the tendency to
return into the *absolutely original*—into the *supremely* primitive.
Gravity, then, *must be the strongest of forces*—an idea reached
à priori and abundantly confirmed by induction. What use I
make of the idea, will be seen in the sequel.

The atoms, now, having been diffused from their normal condition of Unity, seek to return to——what? Not to any particular
point, certainly; for it is clear that if, upon the diffusion, the whole
Universe of matter had been projected, collectively, to a distance
from the point of irradiation, the atomic tendency to the general
centre of the sphere would not have been disturbed in the least:—
the atoms would not have sought the point *in absolute space* from
which they were originally impelled. It is merely the *condition*,
and not the point or locality at which this condition took its rise,
that these atoms seek to re-establish;—it is merely *that condition
which is their normality*, that they desire. "But they seek a
centre," it will be said, "and a centre is a point." True; but
they seek this point not in its character of point—(for, were the
whole sphere moved from its position, they would seek, equally,
the centre; and the centre *then* would be a *new* point)—but because it so happens, on account of the form in which they collectively exist—(that of the sphere)—that only *through* the point
in question—the sphere's centre—they can attain their true object,
Unity. In the direction of the centre each atom perceives more
atoms than in any other direction. Each atom is impelled towards

the centre because along the straight line joining it and the centre and passing on to the circumference beyond, there lie a greater number of atoms than along any other straight line—a greater number of objects that seek it, the individual atom—a greater number of tendencies to Unity—a greater number of satisfactions for its own tendency to Unity—in a word, because in the direction of the centre lies the utmost possibility of satisfaction, generally, for its own individua¹ appetite. To be brief, the *condition*, Unity, is all that is really sought; and if the atoms *seem* to seek the centre of the sphere, it is only impliedly, through implication—because such centre happens to imply, to include, or to involve, the only essential centre, Unity. But *on account of* this implication or involution, there is no possibility of practically separating the tendency to Unity in the abstract, from the tendency to the concrete centre. Thus the tendency of the atoms to the general centre *is*, to all practical intents and for all logical purposes, the tendency each to each; and the tendency each to each *is* the tendency to the centre; and the one tendency may be assumed *as the other*; whatever will apply to the one must be thoroughly applicable to the other; and, in conclusion, whatever principle will satisfactorily explain the one, cannot be questioned as an explanation of the other.

In looking carefully around me for a rational objection to what I have advanced, I am able to discover *nothing ;*—but of that class of objections usually urged by the doubters for Doubt's sake, I very readily perceive *three ;* and proceed to dispose of them in order.

It may be said, first : " That the proof that the force of irradiation (in the case described) is directly proportional to the squares of the distances, depends upon an unwarranted assumption—that of the number of atoms in each stratum being the measure of the force with which they are emitted."

I reply, not only that I am warranted in such assumption, but that I should be utterly *unwarranted* in any other. What I assume is, simply, that an effect is the measure of its cause—that every exercise of the Divine Will will be proportional to that which demands the exertion—that the means of Omnipotence, or of Omniscience, will be exactly adapted to its purposes. Neither can a deficiency nor an excess of cause bring to pass any effect. Had the force which irradiated any stratum to its position, been either more or less than was needed for the purpose—that is to say, not *directly proportional* to the purpose—then to its position that stratum could not have been irradiated. Had the force which, with a view to general equability of distribution, emitted the proper number of atoms for each stratum, been not *directly proportional* to the number, then the number would *not* have been the number demanded for the equable distribution.

The second supposable objection is somewhat better entitled to an answer.

It is an admitted principle in Dynamics that every body, on receiving an impulse, or disposition to move, will move onward in a straight line, in the direction imparted by the impelling force, until deflected, or stopped, by some other force. How then, it may be asked, is my first or external stratum of atoms to be understood as discontinuing their movement at the circumference of the imaginary glass sphere, when no second force, of more than an imaginary character, appears, to account for the discontinuance?

I reply that the objection, in this case, actually does arise out of "an unwarranted assumption"—on the part of the objector—the assumption of a principle, in Dynamics, at an epoch when *no* "principles," in *anything*, exist:—I use the word "principle," of course, in the objector's understanding of the word.

"In the beginning" we can admit—indeed we can comprehend —but one *First Cause*—the truly ultimate *Principle*—the Volition of God. The primary *act*—that of Irradiation from Unity— must have been independent of all that which the world now calls "principle"—because all that we so designate is but a consequence of the reaction of that primary act:—I say "*primary*" act; for the creation of the absolute material particle is more properly to be regarded as a *conception* than as an "*act*" in the ordinary meaning of the term. Thus, we must regard the primary act as an act for the establishment of what we now call "principles." But this primary act itself is to be considered as *continuous Volition*. The Thought of God is to be understood as originating the

Diffusion—as proceeding with it—as regulating it—and, finally, as being withdrawn from it upon its completion. *Then* commences Reaction, and through Reaction, "Principle," as we employ the word. It will be advisable, however, to limit the application of this word to the two *immediate* results of the discontinuance of the Divine Volition—that is, to the two agents, *Attraction* and *Repulsion*. Every other Natural agent depends, either more or less immediately, upon these two, and therefore would be more conveniently designated as *sub*-principle.

It may be objected, thirdly, that, in general, the peculiar mode of distribution which I have suggested for the atoms, is "an hypothesis and nothing more."

Now, I am aware that the word hypothesis is a ponderous sledge-hammer, grasped immediately, if not lifted, by all very diminutive thinkers, upon the first appearance of any proposition wearing, in any particular, the garb of *a theory*. But "hypothesis" cannot be wielded *here* to any good purpose, even by those who succeed in lifting it—little men or great.

I maintain, first, that *only* in the mode described is it conceivable that Matter could have been diffused so as to fulfil at once the conditions of irradiation and of generally equable distribution. I maintain, secondly, that these conditions themselves have been imposed upon me, as necessities, in a train of ratiocination *as rigorously logical as that which establishes any demonstration in Euclid ;* and I maintain, thirdly, that even if the charge of "hypothesis" were as fully sustained as it is, in fact, unsustained and untenable, still the validity and indisputability of my result would not, even in the slightest particular, be disturbed.

To explain :—The Newtonian Gravity—a law of Nature—a law whose existence as such no one out of Bedlam questions—a law whose admission as such enables us to account for nine-tenths of the Universal phænomena—a law which, merely because it does so enable us to account for these phænomena, we are perfectly willing, without reference to any other considerations, to admit, and cannot help admitting, as a law—a law, nevertheless, of which neither the principle nor the *modus operandi* of the principle, has ever yet been traced by the human analysis—a law, in short, which, neither in its detail nor in its generality, has been found susceptible of explanation *at all*—is at length seen to be at every point thoroughly explicable, provided we only yield our assent to ——what ? To an hypothesis ! Why *if* an hypothesis—if the merest hypothesis—if an hypothesis for whose assumption—as in the case of that *pure* hypothesis the Newtonian law itself—no shadow of *à priori* reason could be assigned—if an hypothesis, even so absolute as all this implies, would enable us to perceive a principle for the Newtonian law—would enable us to understand as satisfied, conditions so miraculously—so ineffably complex and seemingly irreconcileable as those involved in the relations of which Gravity tells us,—what rational being *could* so expose his fatuity as to call 'even this absolute hypothesis an hypothesis any longer—unless, indeed, he were to persist in so calling it, with the understanding that he did so, simply for the sake of consistency *in words ?*

But what is the true state of our present case ? What is *the fact ?* Not only that is *not* an hypothesis which we are required *to adopt*, in order to admit the principle at issue explained, but that it *is* a logical conclusion which we are requested *not* to adopt if we can avoid it—which we are simply invited to *deny if we can :* —a conclusion of so accurate a logicality that to dispute it would be the effort—to doubt its validity, beyond our power :—a conclusion from which we see no mode of escape, turn as we will ; a result which confronts us either at the end of an *in*ductive journey from the phænomena of the very Law discussed, or at the close of a *de*ductive career from the most rigorously simple of all conceivable assumptions—*the assumption, in a word, of Simplicity itself.*

And if here, for the mere sake of cavilling, it be urged, that although my starting-point is, as I assert, the assumption of absolute Simplicity, yet Simplicity, considered merely in itself, is no axiom ; and that only deductions from axioms are indisputable— it is thus that I reply :—

Every other science than Logic is the science of certain concrete relations. Arithmetic, for example, is the science of the relations of number—Geometry, of the relations of form—Mathematics in general, of the relations of quantity in general—of whatever can be increased or diminished. Logic, however, is the science of

Relation in the abstract—of absolute Relation—of Relation considered solely in itself. An axiom in any particular science other than Logic is, thus, merely a proposition announcing certain concrete relations which seem to be too obvious for dispute—as when we say, for instance, that the whole is greater than its part;—and, thus again, the principle of the *Logical* axiom—in other words, of an axiom in the abstract—is, simply, *obviousness of relation*. Now, it is clear, not only that what is obvious to one mind may not be obvious to another, but that what is obvious to one mind at one epoch, may be anything but obvious, at another epoch, to the same mind. It is clear, moreover, that what, to-day, is obvious even to the majority of mankind, or to the majority of the best intellects of mankind, may to-morrow be, to either majority, more or less obvious, or in no respect obvious at all. It is seen, then, that the *axiomatic principle* itself is susceptible of variation, and of course that axioms are susceptible of similar change. Being mutable, the "truths" which grow out of them are necessarily mutable too; or, in other words, are never to be positively depended upon as truths at all—since Truth and Immutability are one.

It will now be readily understood that no axiomatic idea—no **idea founded in the fluctuating principle, obviousness of relation— can possibly be so secure—so reliable a basis for any structure erected by the Reason, as** *that* **idea—(whatever it is, wherever we can find it, or** *if* **it be practicable to find it anywhere)—which is** *ir***relative altogether—which not only presents to the understanding** *no obviousness* **of relation, either greater or less, to be considered, but subjects the intellect, not in the slightest degree, to the necessity of even looking at** *any relation at all.* **If such an idea be not what we too heedlessly term "an axiom," it is at least preferable, as a Logical basis, to any axiom ever propounded, or to all imaginable axioms combined:—and such, precisely, is the idea with which my deductive process, so thoroughly corroborated by induction, commences.** My *particle proper* **is but** *absolute Irrelation.* **To sum up what has been advanced:—As a starting point I have taken it for granted, simply, that the Beginning had nothing behind it or before it—that it was a Beginning in fact— that it was a beginning and nothing different from a beginning—**
8*

In short, that this Beginning was—*that which it was.* If this be a "mere assumption" then a "mere assumptioh" let it be.

To conclude this branch of the subject:—I am fully warranted in announcing that *the Law which we have been in the habit of calling Gravity exists on account of Matter's having been irradiated, at its origin, atomically, into a limited* sphere of Space, from one, individual, unconditional, irrelative, and absolute Particle Proper, by the sole process in which it was possible to satisfy, at the same time, the two conditions, irradiation, and generally-equable distribution throughout the sphere—that is to say, by a force varying in direct proportion with the squares of the distances between the irradiated atoms, respectively, and the Particular centre of Irradiation.*

I have already given my reasons for presuming Matter to have been diffused by a determinate rather than by a continuous or infinitely continued force. Supposing a continuous force, we should be unable, in the first place, to comprehend a rëaction at all; and we should be required, in the second place, to entertain the impossible conception of an infinite extension of Matter. Not to dwell upon the impossibility of the conception, the infinite extension of Matter is an idea which, if not positively disproved, is at least not in any respect warranted by telescopic observation of the stars—a point to be explained more fully hereafter; and this empirical reason for believing in the original finity of Matter is unempirically confirmed. For example:—Admitting, for the moment, the possibility of understanding Space *filled* with the irradiated atoms—that is to say, admitting, as well as we can, for argument's sake, that the succession of the irradiated atoms had absolutely *no end*—then it is abundantly clear that, even when the Volition of God had been withdrawn from them, and thus the tendency to return into Unity permitted (abstractly) to be satisfied, this permission would have been nugatory and invalid—practically valueless and of no effect whatever. No Rëaction could have taken place; no movement toward Unity could have been made; no Law of Gravity could have obtained.

---

* "Limited sphere"—A sphere is *necessarily* limited. I prefer tautology to a chance of misconception.

To explain :—Grant the *abstract* tendency of any one atom to any one other as the inevitable result of diffusion from the normal Unity :—or, what is the same thing, admit any given atom as *proposing* to move in any given direction —it is clear that, since there is an *infinity* of atoms on all sides of the atom proposing to move, it never can actually move toward the satisfaction of its tendency in the direction given, on account of a precisely equal and counter-balancing tendency in the direction diametrically opposite. In other words, exactly as many tendencies to Unity are behind the hesitating atom as before it ; for it is a mere sotticism to say that one infinite line is longer or shorter than another infinite line, or that one infinite number is greater or less than another number that is infinite. Thus the atom in question must remain stationary forever. Under the impossible circumstances which we have been merely endeavoring to conceive for argument's sake, there could have been no aggregation of Matter—no stars—no worlds—nothing but a perpetually atomic and inconsequential Universe. In fact, view it as we will, the whole idea of unlimited Matter is not only untenable, but impossible and preposterous.

With the understanding of a *sphere* of atoms, however, we perceive, at once, a *satisfiable* tendency to union. The general result of the tendency each to each, being a tendency of all to the centre, the *general* process of condensation, or approximation, commences immediately, by a common and simultaneous movement, on withdrawal of the Divine Volition ; the *individual* approximations, or coalescences—*not* coalitions—of atom with atom, being subject to almost infinite variations of time, degree, and condition, on account of the excessive multiplicity of relation, arising from the differences of form assumed as characterizing the atoms at the moment of their quitting the Particle Proper ; as well as from the subsequent particular inequidistance, each from each.

What I wish to impress upon the reader is the certainty of there arising, at once, (on withdrawal of the diffusive force, or Divine Volition,) out of the condition of the atoms as described, at innumerable points throughout the Universal sphere, innumerable agglomerations, characterized by innumerable specific differences of form, size, essential nature, and distance each from each. The development of Repulsion (Electricity) must have commenced, of course, with the very earliest particular efforts at Unity, and must have proceeded constantly in the ratio of Coalescence—that is to say, *in that of Condensation*, or, again, of Heterogeneity.

Thus the two Principles Proper, *Attraction* and *Repulsion*— the Material and the Spiritual—accompany each other, in the strictest fellowship, forever. Thus *The Body and The Soul walk hand in hand.*

If now, in fancy, we select *any one* of the agglomerations considered as in their primary stages throughout the Universal sphere, and suppose this incipient agglomeration to be taking place at that point where the centre of our Sun exists—or rather where it *did* exist originally; for the Sun is perpetually shifting his position—we shall find ourselves met, and borne onward for a time at least, by the most magnificent of theories—by the Nebular Cosmogony of Laplace :—although " Cosmogony" is far too comprehensive a term for what he really discusses—which is the constitution of our solar system alone—of one among the myriad of similar systems which make up the Universe Proper—that Universal sphere—that all-inclusive and absolute *Kosmos* which forms the subject of my present Discourse.

Confining himself to an *obviously limited* region—that of our solar system with its comparatively immediate vicinity—and *merely* assuming—that is to say, assuming without any basis whatever, either deductive or inductive—*much* of what I have been just endeavoring to place upon a more stable basis than assumption ; assuming, for example, matter as diffused (without pretending to account for the diffusion) throughout, and somewhat beyond, the space occupied by our system—diffused in a state of heterogeneous nebulosity and obedient to that omniprevalent law of Gravity at whose principle he ventured to make no guess ; assuming all this (which is quite true, although he had no logical right to its assumption) Laplace has shown, dynamically and mathematically, that the results in such case necessarily ensuing, are those and those alone which we find manifested in the actually existing condition of the system itself.

To explain :—Let us conceive *that* particular agglomeration of which we have just spoken—the one at the point designated by our Sun's centre—to have so far proceeded that a vast quantity of nebulous matter has here assumed a roughly globular form; its centre being, of course, coincident with what is now, or rather was originally, the centre of our Sun; and its periphery extending out beyond the orbit of Neptune, the most remote of our planets:—in other words, let us suppose the diameter of this rough sphere to be some 6000 millions of miles. For ages, this mass of matter has been undergoing condensation, until at length it has become reduced into the bulk we imagine; having proceeded gradually, of course, from its atomic and imperceptible state, into what we understand of visible, palpable, or otherwise appreciable nebulosity.

Now, the condition of this mass implies a rotation about an imaginary axis—a rotation which, commencing with the absolute incipiency of the aggregation, has been ever since acquiring velocity. The very first two atoms which met, approaching each other from points not diametrically opposite, would, in rushing partially past each other, form a nucleus for the rotary movement described. How this would increase in velocity, is readily seen. The two atoms are joined by others:—an aggregation is formed. The mass continues to rotate while condensing. But any atom at the circumference has, of course, a more rapid motion than one nearer the centre. The outer atom, however, with its superior velocity, approaches the centre; carrying this superior velocity with it as it goes. Thus every atom, proceeding inwardly, and finally attaching itself to the condensed centre, adds something to the original velocity of that centre—that is to say, increases the rotary movement of the mass.

Let us now suppose this mass so far condensed that it occupies *precisely* the space circumscribed by the orbit of Neptune, and that the velocity with which the surface of the mass moves, in the general rotation, is precisely that velocity with which Neptune now revolves about the Sun. At this epoch, then, we are to understand that the constantly increasing centrifugal force, having gotten the better of the non-increasing centripetal, loosened and separated the exterior and least condensed stratum, or a few of the exterior and least condensed strata, at the equator of the sphere, where the tangential velocity predominated; so that these strata formed about the main body an independent ring encircling the equatorial regions :—just as the exterior portion thrown off by excessive velocity of rotation, from a grindstone, would form a ring about the grindstone, but for the solidity of the superficial material : were this caoutchouc, or anything similar in consistency precisely the phænomenon I describe would be presented.

The ring thus whirled from the nebulous mass, *revolved*, of course, *as* a separate ring, with just that velocity with which, while the surface of the mass, it *rotated*. In the meantime, condensation still proceeding, the interval between the discharged ring and the main body continued to increase, until the former was left at a vast distance from the latter.

Now, admitting the ring to have possessed, by some seemingly accidental arrangement of its heterogeneous materials, a constitution nearly uniform, then this ring, *as* such, would never have ceased revolving about its primary ; but, as might have been anticipated, there appears to have been enough irregularity in the disposition of the materials, to make them cluster about centres of superior solidity ; and thus the annular form was destroyed.* No doubt, the band was soon broken up into several portions, and one of these portions, predominating in mass, absorbed the others into itself; the whole settling, spherically, into a planet. That this latter, *as* a planet, continued the revolutionary movement which characterized it while a ring, is sufficiently clear ; and that it took upon itself, also, an additional movement in its new condition of sphere, is readily explained. The ring being understood as yet unbroken, we see that its exterior, while the whole revolves about the parent body, moves more rapidly than its interior. When the rupture occurred, then, some portion in each fragment must have been moving with greater velocity than the others. The superior movement prevailing, must have whirled each fragment round—that is to say, have caused it to rotate ; and the di-

* Laplace assumed his nebulosity heterogeneous, merely that he might be thus enabled to account for the breaking up of the rings ; for had the nebulosity been homogeneous, they would not have broken. I reach the same result—heterogeneity of the secondary masses immediately resulting from the atoms—purely from an *à priori* consideration of their general design— Relation.

rection of the rotation must, of course, have been the direction of the revolution whence it arose. *All* the fragments having become subject to the rotation described, must, in coalescing, have imparted it to the one planet constituted by their coalescence.—This planet was Neptune. Its material continuing to undergo condensation, and the centrifugal force generated in its rotation, getting, at length, the better of the centripetal, as before in the case of the parent orb, a ring was whirled also from the equatorial surface of this planet: this ring, having been uniform in its constitution, was broken up, and its several fragments, being absorbed by the most massive, were collectively spherified into a moon. Subsequently, the operation was repeated, and a second moon was the result. We thus account for the planet Neptune, with the two satellites which accompany him.

In throwing off a ring from its equator, the Sun re-established that equilibrium between its centripetal and centrifugal forces which had been disturbed in the process of condensation; but, as this condensation still proceeded, the equilibrium was again immediately disturbed, through the increase of rotation. By the time the mass had so far shrunk that it occupied a spherical space just that circumscribed by the orbit of Uranus, we are to understand that the centrifugal force had so far obtained the ascendency that new relief was needed: a second equatorial band was, consequently, thrown off, which, proving ununiform, was broken up, as before in the case of Neptune; the fragments settling into the planet Uranus; the velocity of whose actual revolution about the Sun indicates, of course, the rotary speed of that Sun's equatorial surface at the moment of the separation. Uranus, adopting a rotation from the collective rotations of the fragments composing it, as previously explained, now threw off ring after ring; each of which, becoming broken up, settled into a moon:—three moons, at different epochs, having been formed, in this manner, by the rupture and general spherification of as many distinct ununiform rings.

By the time the Sun had shrunk until it occupied a space just that circumscribed by the orbit of Saturn, the balance, we are to suppose, between its centripetal and centrifugal forces had again become so far disturbed, through increase of rotary velocity, the result of condensation, that a third effort at equilibrium became necessary; and an annular band was therefore whirled off, as twice before; which, on rupture through ununiformity, became consolidated into the planet Saturn. This latter threw off, in the first place, seven uniform bands, which, on rupture, were spherified respectively into as many moons; but, subsequently, it appears to have discharged, at three distinct but not very distant epochs, three rings whose equability of constitution was, by apparent accident, so considerable as to present no occasion for their rupture; thus they continue to revolve as rings. I use the phrase "*apparent* accident;" for of accident in the ordinary sense there was, of course, nothing:—the term is properly applied only to the result of indistinguishable or not immediate traceable *law*.

Shrinking still farther, until it occupied just the space circumscribed by the orbit of Jupiter, the Sun now found need of farther effort to restore the counterbalance of its two forces, continually disarranged in the still continued increase of rotation. Jupiter, accordingly, was now thrown off; passing from the annular to the planetary condition; and, on attaining this latter, threw off in its turn, at four different epochs, four rings, which finally resolved themselves into so many moons.

Still shrinking, until its sphere occupied just the space defined by the orbit of the Asteroids, the Sun now discarded a ring which appears to have had *eight* centres of superior solidity, and, on breaking up, to have separated into eight fragments, no one of which so far predominated in mass as to absorb the others. All therefore, as distinct although comparatively small planets, proceeded to revolve in orbits whose distances, each from each, may be considered as in some degree the measure of the force which drove them asunder:—all the orbits, nevertheless, being so closely coincident as to admit of our calling them *one*, in view of the other planetary orbits.

Continuing to shrink, the Sun, on becoming so small as just to fill the orbit of Mars, now discharged this planet—of course by the process repeatedly described. Having no moon, however, Mars could have thrown off no ring. In fact, an epoch had now arrived in the career of the parent body, the centre of the system. The *decrease* of its nebulosity, which is the *increase* of its density, and which aga'n is the *decrease* of its condensation, out of which latter arose the constant disturbance of equilibrium—must, by this period, have attained a point at which the efforts for restoration would have been more and more ineffectual just in proportion as they were less frequently needed. Thus the processes of which we have been speaking would everywhere show signs of exhaustion—in the planets, first, and secondly, in the original mass. We must not fall into the error of supposing the decrease of interval observed among the planets as we approach the Sun, to be in any respect indicative of an increase of frequency in the periods at which they were discarded. Exactly the converse is to be understood. The longest interval of time must have occurred between the discharges of the two interior; the shortest, between those of the two exterior, planets. The decrease of the interval of space is, nevertheless, the measure of the density, and thus inversely of the condensation, of the Sun, throughout the processes detailed.

Having shrunk, however, so far as to fill only the orbit of our Earth, the parent sphere whirled from itself still one other body —the Earth—in a condition so nebulous as to admit of this body's discarding, in its turn, yet another, which is our Moon;— but here terminated the lunar formations.

Finally, subsiding to the orbits first of Venus and then of Mercury, the Sun discarded these two interior planets; neither of which has given birth to any moon.

Thus from his original bulk—or, to speak more accurately, from the condition in which we first considered him—from a partially spherified nebular mass, *certainly* much more than 5,600 millions of miles in diameter—the great central orb and origin of our solar-planetary-lunar system, has gradually descended, by condensation, in obedience to the law of Gravity, to a globe only 882,000 miles in diameter; but it by no means follows, either that its condensation is yet complete, or that it may not still possess the capacity of whirling from itself another planet.

I have here given—in outline of course, but still with all the detail necessary for distinctness—a view of the Nebular Theory as its author himself conceived it. From whatever point we regard it, we shall find it *beautifully true*. It is by far too beautiful, indeed, *not to possess* Truth as its essentiality—and here I am

very profoundly serious in what I say. In the revolution of the
satellites of Uranus, there does appear something seemingly inconsistent with the assumptions of Laplace ; but that *one* inconsistency
can invalidate a theory constructed from a million of intricate
consistencies, is a fancy fit only for the fantastic. In prophecying,
confidently, that the apparent anomaly to which I refer, will, sooner
or later, be found one of the strongest possible corroborations of
the general hypothesis, I pretend to no especial spirit of divina-
tion. It is a matter which the only difficulty seems *not* to
foresee.*

The bodies whirled off in the processes described, would exchange, it has been seen, the superficial *rotation* of the orbs whence
they originated, for a *revolution* of equal velocity about these
orbs as distant centres ; and the revolution thus engendered must
proceed, so long as the centripetal force, or that with which the
discarded body gravitates toward its parent, is neither greater nor
less than that by which it was discarded ; that is, than the centrifugal, or, far more properly, than the tangential, velocity. From
the unity, however, of the origin of these two forces, we might
have expected to find them as they are found—the one accurately
counterbalancing the other. It has been shown, indeed, that the
act of whirling-off is, in every case, merely an act for the preservation of the counterbalance.

After referring, however, the centripetal force to the omniprevalent law of Gravity, it has been the fashion with astronomical
treatises, to seek beyond the limits of mere Nature—that is to say,
of *Secondary* Cause—a solution of the phænomenon of tangential velocity. This latter they attribute directly to a *First* Cause
—to God. The force which carries a steller body around its primary they assert to have originated in an impulse given immediately by the finger—this is the childish phraseology employed—
by the finger of Deity itself. In this view, the planets, fully
formed, are conceived to have been hurled from the Divine hand,
to a position in the vicinity of the suns, with an impetus mathe-

---

* I am prepared to show that the anomalous revolution of the satellites
of Uranus is a simply perspective anomaly arising from the inclination of
the axis of the planet.

matically adapted to the masses, or attractive capacities, of the suns themselves. An idea so grossly unphilosophical, although so supinely adopted, could have arisen only from the difficulty of otherwise accounting for the absolutely accurate adaptation, each to each, of two forces so seemingly independent, one of the other, as are the gravitating and tangential. But it should be remembered that, for a long time, the coincidence between the moon's rotation and her sidereal revolution—two matters seemingly far more independent than those now considered—was looked upon as positively miraculous; and there was a strong disposition, even among astronomers, to attribute the marvel to the direct and continual agency of God—who, in this case, it was said, had found it necessary to interpose, specially, among his general laws, a set of subsidiary regulations, for the purpose of forever concealing from mortal eyes the glories, or perhaps the horrors, of the other side of the Moon—of that mysterious hemisphere which has always avoided, and must perpetually avoid, the telescopic scrutiny of mankind. The advance of Science, however, soon demonstrated —what to the philosophical instinct needed *no* demonstration— that the one movement is but a portion—something more, even, than a consequence—of the other.

For my part, I have no patience with fantasies at once so timorous, so idle, and so awkward. They belong to the veriest *cowardice* of thought. That Nature and the God of Nature are distinct, no thinking being can long doubt. By the former we imply merely the laws of the latter. But with the very idea of God, omnipotent, omniscient, we entertain, also, the idea of *the infallibility* of his laws. With Him there being neither Past nor Future—with Him all being *Now*—do we not insult him in supposing his laws so contrived as not to provide for every possible contingency?—or, rather, what idea *can* we have of *any* possible contingency, except that it is at once a result and a manifestation of his laws? He who, divesting himself of prejudice, shall have the rare courage to think absolutely for himself, cannot fail to arrive, in the end, at the condensation of *laws* into *Law*—cannot fail of reaching the conclusion that *each law of Nature is dependent at all points upon all other laws*, and that all are but consequences of one primary exercise of the Divine Volition. Such is the principle of the Cosmogony which, with all necessary deference, I here venture to suggest and to maintain.

In this view, it will be seen that, dismissing as frivolous, and even impious, the fancy of the tangential force having been imparted to the planets immediately by "the finger of God," I consider this force as originating in the rotation of the stars :—this rotation as brought about by the in-rushing of the primary atoms, towards their respective centres of aggregation :—this in-rushing as the consequence of the law of Gravity :—this law as but the mode in which is necessarily manifested the tendency of the atoms to return into imparticularity :—this tendency to return as but the inevitable reaction of the first and most sublime of Acts—that act by which a God, self-existing and alone existing, became all things at once, through dint of his volition, while all things were thus constituted a portion of God.

The radical assumptions of this Discourse suggest to me, and in fact imply, certain important *modifications* of the Nebular Theory as given by Laplace. The efforts of the repulsive power I have considered as made for the purpose of preventing contact among the atoms, and thus as made in the ratio of the approach to contact—that is to say, in the ratio of condensation.* In other words, *Electricity*, with its involute phænomena, heat, light and magnetism, is to be understood as proceeding as condensation proceeds, and, of course, inversely, as destiny proceeds, or the *cessation to condense.* Thus the Sun, in the process of its aggregation, must soon, in developing repulsion, have become excessively heated—perhaps incandescent: and we can perceive how the operation of discarding its rings must have been materially assisted by the slight incrustation of its surface consequent on cooling. Any common experiment shows us how readily a crust of the character suggested, is separated, through heterogeneity, from the interior mass. But, on every successive rejection of the crust, the new surface would appear incandescent as before; and the period at which it would again become so far incrusted as to be readily loosened and discharged, may well be imagined as exactly coincident with that as which a new effort would be

* See page 162.

needed, by the whole mass, to restore the equilibrium of its two forces, disarranged through condensation. In other words:—by the time the electric influence (Repulsion) has prepared the surface for rejection, we are to understand that the gravitating influence (Attraction) is precisely ready to reject it. Here, then, as everywhere, *the Body and the Soul walk hand in hand.*

These ideas are empirically confirmed at all points. Since condensation can never, in any body, be considered as absolutely at an end, we are warranted in anticipating that, whenever we have an opportunity of testing the matter, we shall find indications of resident luminosity in *all* the stellar bodies—moons and planets as well as suns. That our Moon is strongly self-luminous, we see at every total eclipse, when, if not so, she would disappear. On the dark part of the satellite, too, during her phases, we often observe flashes like our own Auroras; and that these latter, with our various other so-called electrical phænomena, without reference to any more steady radiance, must give our Earth a certain appearance of luminosity to an inhabitant of the Moon, is quite evident. In fact, we should regard all the phænomena referred to, as mere manifestations, in different moods and degrees, of the Earth's feebly-continued condensation.

If my views are tenable, we should be prepared to find the newer planets—that is to say, those nearer the Sun—more luminous than those older and more remote:—and the extreme brilliancy of Venus (on whose dark portions, during her phases, the Auroras are frequently visible) does not seem to be altogether accounted for by her mere proximity to the central orb. She is no doubt vividly self-luminous, although less so than Mercury: while the luminosity of Neptune may be comparatively nothing.

Admitting what I have urged, it is clear that, from the moment of the Sun's discarding a ring, there must be a continuous diminution both of his heat and light, on account of the continuous incrustation of his surface; and that a period would arrive—the period immediately previous to a new discharge—when a *very material* decrease of both light and heat, must become apparent. Now, we know that tokens of such changes are distinctly recognisable. On the Melville islands—to adduce merely one out of a hundred examples—we find traces of *ultra-tropical* vegetation—of plants that never could have flourished without immensely more light and heat than are at present afforded by our Sun to any portion of the surface of the Earth. Is such vegetation referable to an epoch immediately subsequent to the whirling-off of Venus? At this epoch must have occurred to us our greatest access of solar influence; and, in fact, this influence must then have attained its maximum:—leaving out of view, of course, the period when the Earth itself was discarded—the period of its mere organization.

Again:—we know that there exist *non-luminous suns*—that is to say, suns whose existence we determine through the movements of others, but whose luminosity is not sufficient to impress us. Are these suns invisible merely on account of the length of time elapsed since their discharge of a planet? And yet again:—may we not—at least in certain cases—account for the sudden appearances of suns where none had been previously suspected, by the hypothesis that, having rolled with incrusted surfaces throughout the few thousand years of our astronomical history, each of these suns, in whirling off a new secondary, has at length been enabled to display the glories of its still incandescent interior?—To the well-ascertained fact of the proportional increase of heat as we descend into the Earth, I need of course, do nothing more than refer:—it comes in the strongest possible corroboration of all that I have said on the topic now at issue.

In speaking, not long ago, of the repulsive or electrical influence, I remarked that "the important phænomena of vitality, consciousness, and thought, whether we observe them generally or in detail, seem to proceed *at least in the ratio of the heterogeneous*."* I mentioned, too, that I would recur to the suggestion:— and this is the proper point at which to do so. Looking at the matter, first, in detail, we perceive that not merely the *manifestation* of vitality, but its importance, consequences, and elevation of character, keep pace, very closely, with the heterogeneity, or complexity, of the animal structure. Looking at the question, now, in its generality, and referring to the first movements of the atoms towards mass-constitution, we find that heterogeneousness,

* Page 138.

brought about directly through condensation, is proportional with it forever. We thus reach the proposition that *the importance of the development of the terrestrial vitality proceeds equably with the terrestrial condensation.*

Now this is in precise accordance with what we know of the succession of animals on the Earth. As it has proceeded in its condensation, superior and still superior races have appeared. Is t impossible that the successive geological revolutions which have attended, at least, if not immediately caused, these successive elevations of vitalic character—is it improbable that these revolutions have themselves been produced by the successive planetary discharges from the Sun—in other words, by the successive variations in the solar influence on the Earth ? Were this idea tenable, we should not be unwarranted in the fancy that the discharge of yet a new planet, interior to Mercury, may give rise to yet a new modification of the terrestrial surface—a modification from which may spring a race both materially and spiritually superior to Man. These thoughts impress me with all the force of truth—but I throw them out, of course, merely in their obvious character of suggestion.

The Nebular Theory of Laplace has lately received far more confirmation than it needed, at the hands of the philosopher, Compte. These two have thus together shown—*not*, to be sure, that Matter at any period actually existed as described, in a state of nebular diffusion, but that, admitting it so to have existed throughout the space and much beyond the space now occupied by our solar system, *and to have commenced a movement towards a centre*—it must gradually have assumed the various forms and motions which are now seen, in that system, to obtain. A demonstration such as this—a dynamical and mathematical demonstration, as far as demonstration can be—unquestionable and unquestioned—unless, indeed, by that unprofitable and disreputable tribe, the professional questioners—the mere madmen who deny the Newtonian law of Gravity on which the results of the French mathematicians are based—a demonstration, I say, such as this, would to most intellects be conclusive—and I confess that it is so to mine—of the validity of the nebular hypothesis upon which the demonstration depends.

That the demonstration does not *prove* the hypothesis, according to the common understanding of the word "proof," I admit, of course. To show that certain existing results—that certain established facts —may be, even mathematically, accounted for by the assumption of a certain hypothesis, is by no means to establish the hypothesis itself. In other words :—to show that, certain data being given, a certain existing result might, or even *must*, have ensued, will fail to prove that this result *did* ensue, *from the data*, until such time as it shall be also shown that there are, *and can be*, no other data from which the result in question might *equally* have ensued. But, in the case now discussed, although all must admit the deficiency of what we are in the habit of terming "proof," still there are many intellects, and those of the loftiest order, to which *no* proof could bring one iota of additional *conviction*. Without going into details which might impinge upon the Cloud-Land of Metaphysics, I may as well here observe, that the force of conviction, in cases such as this, will always, with the right-thinking, be proportional to the amount of *complexity* intervening between the hypothesis and the result. To be less abstract :— The greatness of the complexity found existing among cosmical conditions, by rendering great in the same proportion the difficulty of accounting for all these conditions, *at once*, strengthens, also in the same proportion, our faith in that hypothesis which does, in such manner, satisfactorily account for them :—and as *no* complexity can well be conceived greater than that of the astronomical conditions, so no conviction can be stronger—to *my* mind at least —than that with which I am impressed by an hypothesis that not only reconciles these conditions, with mathematical accuracy, and reduces them into a consistent and intelligible whole, but is, at the same time, the *sole* hypothesis by means of which the human intellect has been ever enabled to account for them *at all*.

A most unfounded opinion has been latterly current in gossiping and even in scientific circles—the opinion that the so-called Nebular Cosmogony has been overthrown. This fancy has arisen from the report of late observations made, among what hitherto have been termed the "nebulæ," through the large telescope of Cincinnati, and the world-renowned instrument of Lord Rosse. Certain spots in the firmament which presented, even to the most powerful of the old telescopes, the appearance of nebulosity, or haze, had been regarded for a long time as confirming the theory of Laplace. They were looked upon as stars in that very process of condensation which I have been attempting to describe. Thus it was supposed that we "had ocular evidence"—an evidence, by the way, which has always been found very questionable—of the truth of the hypothesis; and, although certain telescopic improvements, every now and then, enabled us to perceive that a spot, here and there, which we had been classing among the nebulæ, was, in fact, but a cluster of stars deriving its nebular character only from its immensity of distance—still it was thought that no doubt could exist as to the actual nebulosity of numerous other masses, the strong-holds of the nebulists, bidding defiance to every effort at segregation. Of these latter the most interesting was the great "nebula" in the constellation Orion :—but this, with innumerable other miscalled "nebulæ," when viewed through the magnificent modern telescopes, has become resolved into a simple collection of stars. Now this fact has been very generally understood as conclusive against the Nebular Hypothesis of Laplace ; and, on announcement of the discoveries in question, the most enthusiastic defender and most eloquent popularizer of the theory, Dr. Nichol, went so far as to "admit the necessity of abandoning" an idea which had formed the material of his most praiseworthy book.*

Many of my readers will no doubt be inclined to say that the result of these new investigations *has* at least a strong *tendency* to overthrow the hypothesis ; while some of them, more thoughtful, will suggest that, although the theory is by no means disproved through the segregation of the particular "nebulæ" alluded to, still a *failure* to segregate them, with such telescopes, might well

---

* *"Views of the Architecture of the Heavens."* A letter, purporting to be from Dr. Nichol to a friend in America, went the rounds of our newspapers, about two years ago, I think, admitting "the necessity" to which I refer. In a subsequent Lecture, however, Dr. N. appears in some manner to have gotten the better of the necessity, and does not quite *renounce* the theory, although he seems to wish that he could sneer at it as "a purely hypothetical one." What else was the Law of Gravity before the Maskelyne experiments ? and who questioned the Law of Gravity, even then !

have been understood as a triumphant *corroboration* of the theory: and this latter class will be surprised, perhaps, to hear me say that even with *them* I disagree. If the propositions of this Discourse have been comprehended, it will be seen that, in my view, a failure to segregate the "nebulæ" would have tended to the refutation, rather than to the confirmation, of the Nebular Hypothesis.

Let me explain:—The Newtonian Law of Gravity we may, of course, assume as demonstrated. This law, it will be remembered, I have referred to the reäction of the first Divine Act—to the reäction of an exercise of the Divine Volition temporarily overcoming a difficulty. This difficulty is that of forcing the normal into the abnormal—of impelling that whose originality, and therefore whose rightful condition, was *One*, to take upon itself the wrongful condition of *Many*. It is only by conceiving this difficulty as *temporarily* overcome, that we can comprehend a reäction. There could have been no reäction had the act been infinitely continued. So long as the act *lasted*, no reäction, of course, could commence; in other words, no *gravitation* could take place—for we have considered the one as but the manifestation of the other. But gravitation *has* taken place; therefore the act of Creation has ceased: and gravitation has long ago taken place; therefore the act of Creation has long ago ceased. We can no more expect, then, to observe *the primary processes* of Creation; and to these primary processes the condition of nebulosity has already been explained to belong.

Through what we know of the propagation of light, we have direct proof that the more remote of the stars have existed, under the forms in which we now see them, for an inconceivable number of years. So far back *at least*, then, as the period when these stars underwent condensation, must have been the epoch at which the mass-constitutive processes began. That we may conceive these processes, then, as still going on in the case of certain "nebulæ," while in all other cases we find them thoroughly at an end, we are forced into assumptions for which we have really *no* basis whatever—we have to thrust in, again, upon the revolting Reason, the blasphemous idea, of special interposition—we have to suppose that, in the particular instances of these "nebulæ," an un

erring God found it necessary to introduce certain supplementary regulations—certain improvements of the general law—certain re-touchings and emendations, in a word, which had the effect of deferring the completion of these individual stars for centuries of centuries beyond the æra during which all the other stellar bodies had time, not only to be fully constituted, but to grow hoary with an unspeakable old age.

Of course, it will be immediately objected that since the light by which we recognise the nebulæ now, must be merely that which left their surfaces a vast number of years ago, the processes at present observed, or supposed to be observed, are, in fact, *not* processes now actually going on, but the phantoms of processes completed long in the Past—just as I maintain all these mass-constitutive processes *must* have been.

To this I reply that neither is the now-observed condition of the condensed stars their actual condition, but a condition completed long in the Past; so that my argument drawn from the *relative* condition of the stars and the "nebulæ," is in no manner disturbed. Moreover, those who maintain the existence of nebulæ, do *not* refer the nebulosity to extreme distance; they declare it a real and not merely a perspective nebulosity. That we may conceive, indeed, a nebular mass as visible at all, we must conceive it as *very near us* in comparison with the condensed stars brought into view by the modern telescopes. In maintaining the appearances in question, then, to be really nebulous, we maintain their comparative vicinity to our point of view. Thus, their condition, as we see them now, must be referred to an epoch *far less remote* than that to which we may refer the now-observed condition of at least the majority of the stars.—In a word, should Astronomy ever demonstrate a "nebula," in the sense at present intended, I should consider the Nebular Cosmogony—*not*, indeed, as corroborated by the demonstration—but as thereby irretrievably overthrown.

By way, however, of rendering unto Cæsar *no more* than the things that are Cæsar's, let me here remark that the assumption of the hypothesis which led him to so glorious a result, seems to have been suggested to Laplace in great measure by a misconception—by the very misconception of which we have just been speaking—by the generally prevalent misunderstanding of the character of the nebulæ, so mis-named. These he supposed to be, in reality, what their designation implies. The fact is, this great man had, very properly, an inferior faith in his own merely *perceptive* powers. In respect, therefore, to the actual existence of nebulæ—an existence so confidently maintained by his telescopic contemporaries—he depended less upon what he saw than upon what he heard.

It will be seen that the only valid objections to his theory, are those made to its hypothesis *as* such—to what suggested it—not to what it suggests; to its propositions rather than to its results. His most unwarranted assumption was that of giving the atoms a movement towards a centre, in the very face of his evident understanding that these atoms, in unlimited succession, extended throughout the Universal space. I have already shown that, under such circumstances, there could have occurred no movement at all; and Laplace, consequently, assumed one on no more philosophical ground than that something of the kind was necessary for the establishment of what he intended to establish.

His original idea seems to have been a compound of the true Epicurean atoms with the false nebulæ of his contemporaries; and thus his theory presents us with the singular anomaly of absolute truth deduced, as a mathematical result, from a hybrid datum of ancient imagination intertangled with modern inacumen. Laplace's real strength lay, in fact, in an almost miraculous mathematical instinct:—on this he relied; and in no instance did it fail or deceive him:—in the case of the Nebular Cosmogony, it led him, blindfolded, through a labyrinth of Error, into one of the most luminous and stupendous temples of Truth.

Let us now fancy, for the moment, that the ring first thrown off by the Sun—that is to say, the ring whose breaking-up constituted Neptune—did not, in fact, break up until the throwing-off of the ring out of which Uranus arose; that this latter ring, again, remained perfect until the discharge of that out of which sprang Saturn; that this latter, again, remained entire until the discharge of that from which originated Jupiter—and so on. Let us imagine, in a word, that no dissolution occurred among the rings until the final rejection of that which gave birth to Mercury.

We thus paint to the eye of the mind a series of coexistent concentric circles; and looking as well at *them* as at the processes by which, according to Laplace's hypothesis, they were constructed, we perceive at once a very singular analogy with the atomic strata and the process of the original irradiation as I have described it. Is it impossible that, on measuring the *forces*, respectively, by which each successive planetary circle was thrown off—that is to say, on measuring the successive excesses of rotation over gravitation which occasioned the successive discharges—we should find the analogy in question more decidedly confirmed? *Is it improbable that we should discover these forces to have varied—as in the original radiation—proportionally to the squares of the distances?*

Our solar system, consisting, in chief, of one sun, with sixteen planets certainly, and possibly a few more, revolving about it at various distances, and attended by seventeen moons assuredly, but *very* probably by several others—is now to be considered as *an example* of the innumerable agglomerations which proceeded to take place throughout the Universal Sphere of atoms on withdrawal of the Divine Volition. I mean to say that our solar system is to be understood as affording a *generic instance* of these agglomerations, or, more correctly, of the ulterior conditions at which they arrived. If we keep our attention fixed on the idea of *the utmost possible Relation* as the Omnipotent design, and on the precautions taken to accomplish it through difference of form, among the original atoms, and particular inequidistance, we shall find it impossible to suppose for a moment that even any two of the incipient agglomerations reached precisely the same result in the end. We shall rather be inclined to think that *no two* stellar bodies in the Universe—whether suns, planets or moons—are particularly, while *all* are generally, similar. Still less, then, can we imagine any two *assemblages* of such bodies—any two "systems"—as having more than a general resemblance.* Our teles-

---

* It is not *impossible* that some unlooked-for optical improvement may disclose to us, among innumerable varieties of systems, a luminous sun, encircled by luminous and non-luminous rings, within and without and between which, revolve luminous and non-luminous planets, attended by moons having moons—and even these latter again having moons.

copes, at this point, thoroughly confirm our deductions. Taking our own solar system, then, as merely a loose or general type of all, we have so far proceeded in our subject as to survey the Universe under the aspect of a spherical space, throughout which, dispersed with merely general equability, exist a number of but generally similar *systems*.

Let us now, expanding our conceptions, look upon each of these systems as in itself an atom; which in fact it is, when we consider it as but one of the countless myriads of systems which constitute the Universe. Regarding all, then, as but colossal atoms, each with the same ineradicable tendency to Unity which characterizes the actual atoms of which it consists—we enter at once upon a new order of aggregations. The smaller systems, in the vicinity of a larger one, would, inevitably, be drawn into still closer vicinity. A thousand would assemble here; a million there—perhaps here, again, even a billion—leaving, thus, immeasurable vacancies in space. And if, now, it be demanded why, in the case of these systems—of these merely Titanic atoms—I speak, simply, of an "assemblage," and not, as in the case of the actual atoms, of a more or less consolidated agglomeration:—if it be asked, for instance, why I do not carry what I suggest to its legitimate conclusion, and describe, at once, these assemblages of system-atoms as rushing to consolidation in spheres—as each becoming condensed into one magnificent sun—my reply is that μελλοντα ταυτα—I am but pausing, for a moment, on the awful threshold of *the Future*. For the present, calling these assemblages "clusters," we see them in the incipient stages of their consolidation. Their *absolute* consolidation is *to come.*

We have now reached a point from which we behold the Universe as a spherical space, interspersed, *unequably*, with *clusters.* It will be noticed that I here prefer the adverb "unequably" to the phrase "with a merely general equability," employed before. It is evident, in fact, that the equability of distribution will diminish in the ratio of the agglomerative processes—that is to say, as the things distributed diminish in number. Thus the increase of *inequability*—an increase which must continue until, sooner or later, an epoch will arrive at which the largest agglomeatron will absorb all the others—should be viewed as, simply, a corroborative indication of the *tendency to One*.

And here, at length, it seems proper to inquire whether the ascertained *facts* of Astronomy confirm the general arrangement which I have thus, deductively, assigned to the Heavens. Thoroughly, they *do*. Telescopic observation, guided by the laws of perspective, enables us to understand that the perceptible Universe exists as *a cluster of clusters, irregularly disposed.*

The "clusters" of which this Universal "*cluster of clusters*" consists, are merely what we have been in the practice of designating "nebulæ"—and, of these "nebulæ," *one* is of paramount interest to mankind. I allude to the Galaxy, or Milky Way. This interests us, first and most obviously, on account of its great superiority in apparent size, not only to any one other cluster in the firmament, but to all the other clusters taken together. The largest of these latter occupies a mere point, comparatively, and is distinctly seen only with the aid of a telescope. The Galaxy sweeps throughout the Heaven and is brilliantly visible to the naked eye. But it interests man chiefly, although less immediately, on account of its being his home: the home of the Earth on which he exists; the home of the Sun about which this Earth revolves; the home of that "system" of orbs of which the Sun is the centre and primary—the Earth one of sixteen secondaries, or planets—the Moon one of seventeen tertiaries, or satellites. The Galaxy, let me repeat, is but one of the *clusters* which I have been describing—but one of the mis-called "nebulæ" revealed to us—by the telescope alone, sometimes—as faint hazy spots in various quarters of the sky. We have no reason to suppose the Milky Way *really* more extensive than the least of these "nebulæ." Its vast superiority in size is but an apparent superiority arising from our position in regard to it—that is to say, from our position in its midst. However strange the assertion may at first appear to those unversed in Astronomy, still the astronomer himself has no hesitation in asserting that we are *in the midst* of that inconceivable host of stars—of suns—of systems—which constitute the Galaxy. Moreover, not only have *we*—not only has *our* Sun a right to claim the Galaxy as its own especial cluster, but, with slight reservation, it may be said that all the distinctly visible stars of the firmament,

—all the stars visible to the naked eye—have equally a right to claim it as *their* own.

There has been a great deal of misconception in respect to the *shape* of the Galaxy; which, in nearly all our astronomical treatises, is said to resemble that of a capital Y. The cluster in question has, in reality, a certain general—*very* general resemblance to the planet Saturn, with its encompassing triple ring. Instead of the solid orb of that planet, however, we must picture to ourselves a lenticular star-island, or collection of stars; our Sun lying excentrically—near the shore of the island—on that side of it which is nearest the constellation of the Cross and farthest from that of Cassiopeia. The surrounding ring, where it approaches our position, has in it a longitudinal *gash*, which does, in fact, cause *the ring, in our vicinity*, to assume, loosely, the appearance of a capital Y.

We must not fall into the error, however, of conceiving the somewhat indefinite girdle as at all *remote*, comparatively speaking, from the also indefinite lenticular cluster which it surrounds; and thus, for mere purpose of explanation, we may speak of our Sun as actually situated at that point of the Y where its three component lines unite; and, conceiving this letter to be of a certain solidity—of a certain thickness, very trivial in comparison with its length—we may even speak of our position as *in the middle* of this thickness. Fancying ourselves thus placed, we shall no longer find difficulty in accounting for the phænomena presented—which are perspective altogether. When we look upward or downward—that is to say, when we cast our eyes in the direction of the letter's *thickness*—we look through fewer stars than when we cast them in the direction of its *length*, or *along* either of the three component lines. Of course, in the former case, the stars appear scattered—in the latter, crowded.—To reverse this explanation:—An inhabitant of the Earth, when looking, as we commonly express ourselves, *at* the Galaxy, is then beholding it in some of the directions of its length—is looking *along* the lines of the Y—but when, looking out into the general Heaven, he turns his eyes *from* the Galaxy, he is then surveying it in the direction of the letter's thickness; and on this account the stars seem to him scattered · while, in fact, they are as close together, on an average, as in the mass of the cluster. *No consideration could be better adapted to convey an idea of this cluster's stupendous extent.*

If, with a telescope of high space-penetrating power, we carefully inspect the firmament, we shall become aware of *a belt of clusters*—of what we have hitherto called "nebulæ"—a *band*, of varying breadth, stretching from horizon to horizon, at right angles to the general course of the Milky Way. This band is the ultimate *cluster of clusters*. This belt is *The Universe.* Our Galaxy is but one, and perhaps one of the most inconsiderable, of the clusters which go to the constitution of this ultimate, Universal *belt* or *band*. The appearance of this cluster of clusters, to our eyes, *as* a belt or band, is altogether a perspective phænomenon of the same character as that which causes us to behold our own individual and roughly-spherical cluster, the Galaxy, under guise also of a belt, traversing the Heavens at right angles to the Universal one. The shape of the all-inclusive cluster is, of course *generally*, that of each individual cluster which it includes. Just as the scattered stars which, on looking *from* the Galaxy, we see in the general sky, are, in fact, but a portion of that Galaxy itself, and as closely intermingled with it as any of the telescopic points in what seems the densest portion of its mass—so are the scattered "nebulæ" which, on casting our eyes *from* the Universal *belt*, we perceive at all points of the firmament—so, I say, are these scattered "nebulæ" to be understood as only perspectively scattered, and as part and parcel of the one supreme and Universal *sphere.*

No astronomical fallacy is more untenable, and none has been more pertinaciously adhered to, than that of the absolute *illimitation* of the Universe of Stars. The reasons for limitation, as I have already assigned them, *à priori*, seem to me unanswerable; but, not to speak of these, *observation* assures us that there is, in numerous directions around us, certainly, if not in all, a positive limit—or, at the very least, affords us no basis whatever for thinking otherwise. Were the succession of stars endless, then the background of the sky would present us an uniform luminosity, like that displayed by the Galaxy—*since there could be absolutely no point, in all that background, at which would not exist a star.* The only mode, therefore, in which, under such

state of affairs, we could comprehend the *voids* which our tele
scopes find in innumerable directions, would be by supposing the
distance of the invisible background so immense that no ray from
it has yet been able to reach us at all.   That this *may* be so, who
shall venture to deny ?   I maintain, simply, that we have not even
the shadow of a reason for believing that it *is* so.

When speaking of the vulgar propensity to regard all bodies
on the Earth as tending merely to the Earth's centre, I observed
that, " with certain exceptions to be specified hereafter, every body
on the Earth tended not only to the Earth's centre, but in every
conceivable direction besides."*   The " exceptions " refer to those
frequent gaps in the Heavens, where our utmost scrutiny can detect not only no stellar bodies, but no indications of their existence :—where yawning chasms, blacker than Erebus, seem to
afford us glimpses, through the boundary walls of the Universe
of Stars, into the illimitable Universe of Vacancy, beyond.   Now
as any body, existing on the Earth, chances to pass, either through
its own movement or the Earth's, into a line with any one of these
voids, or cosmical abysses, it clearly is no longer attracted *in the
direction of that void*, and for the moment, consequently, is " heavier" than at any period, either after or before.   Independently
of the consideration of these voids, however, and looking only at
the generally unequable distribution of the stars, we see that the
absolute tendency of bodies on the Earth to the Earth's centre, is
in a state of perpetual variation.

We comprehend, then, the insulation of our Universe.   We perceive the isolation of *that*—of *all* that which we grasp with the
senses.   We know that there exists one *cluster of clusters*—a collection around which, on all sides, extend the immeasureable wildernesses
of a Space *to all human perception* untenanted.   But *because*
upon the confines of this Universe of Stars we are compelled to
pause, through want of farther evidence from the senses, is it right
to conclude that, in fact, there *is* no material point beyond that
which we have thus been permitted to attain ?   Have we, or have
we not, an analogical right to the inference that this perceptible
Universe—that this cluster of clusters—is but one of *a series of*

---

* Page 156.

clusters of clusters, the rest of which are invisible through dis-
tance—through the diffusion of their light being so excessive, ere
it reaches us, as not to produce upon our retinas a light-impression
—or from there being no such emanation as light at all, in those
unspeakably distant worlds—or, lastly, from the mere interval
being so vast, that the electric tidings of their presence in
Space, have not yet—through the lapsing myriads of years—been
enabled to traverse that interval ?

Have we any right to inferences—have we any ground whatever for visions such as these ? If we have a right to them in
any degree, we have a right to their infinite extension.

The human brain has obviously a leaning to the "*Infinite*," and
fondles the phantom of the idea. It seems to long with a passionate fervor for this impossible conception, with the hope of
intellectually believing it when conceived. What is general among
the whole race of Man, of course no individual of that race can be
warranted in considering abnormal : nevertheless, there *may* be a
class of superior intelligences, to whom the human bias alluded to
may wear all the character of monomania.

My question, however, remains unanswered :—Have we any
right to infer—let us say, rather, to imagine—an interminable
succession of the "clusters of clusters," or of "Universes" more
or less similar ?

I reply that the "right," in a case such as this, depends absolutely upon the hardihood of that imagination which ventures to
claim the right. Let me declare, only, that, as an individual, I
myself feel impelled to *fancy*—without daring to call it more—
that there *does* exist a *limitless* succession of Universes, more or
less similar to that of which we have cognizance—to that of which
alone we shall ever have cognizance—at the very least until the
return of our own particular Universe into Unity. *If* such clusters of clusters exist, however—*and they do*—it is abundantly
clear that, having had no part in our origin, they have no portion in our laws. They neither attract us, nor we them. Their
material—their spirit is not ours—is not that which obtains
in any part of our Universe. They could not impress our senses
or our souls. Among them and us—considering all, for the
moment, collectively—there are no influences in common. Each

exists, apart and independently, *in the bosóm of its proper and particular God.*

In the conduct of this Discourse, I am aiming less at physical than at metaphysical order. The clearness with which even material phænomena are presented to the understanding, depends very little, I have long since learned to perceive, upon a merely natural, and almost altogether upon a moral, arrangement. If then I seem to step somewhat too discursively from point to point of my topic, let me suggest that I do so in the hope of thus the better keeping unbroken that chain of *graduated impression* by which alone the intellect of Man can expect to encompass the grandeurs of which I speak, and, in their majestic totality, to comprehend them.

So far, our attention has been directed, almost exclusively, to a general and relative grouping of the stellar bodies in space. Of specification there has been little; and whatever ideas of *quantity* have been conveyed—that is to say, of number, magnitude, and distance—have been conveyed incidentally and by way of preparation for more definitive conceptions. These latter let us now attempt to entertain.

Our solar system, as has been already mentioned, consists, in chief, of one sun and sixteen planets certainly, but in all probability a few others, revolving around it as a centre, and attended by seventeen moons of which we know, with possibly several more of which as yet we know nothing. These various bodies are not true spheres, but oblate spheroids—spheres flattened at the poles of the imaginary axes about which they rotate:—the flattening being a consequence of the rotation. Neither is the Sun absolutely the centre of the system; for this Sun itself, with all the planets, revolves about a perpetually shifting point of space, which is the system's general centre of gravity. Neither are we to consider the paths through which these different spheroids move—the moons about the planets, the planets about the Sun, or the Sun about the common centre—as circles in an accurate sense. They are, in fact, *ellipses—one of the foci being the point about which the revolution is made.* An ellipse is a curve, returning into itself, one of whose diameters is longer than the other. In the longer diameter are two points, equidistant from the middle of the line, and

so situated otherwise that if, from each of them a straight line be
drawn to any one point of the curve, the two lines, taken together,
will be equal to the long diameter itself. Now let us conceive
such an ellipse. At one of the points mentioned, which are the
foci, let us fasten an orange. By an elastic thread let us connect
this orange with a pea; and let us place this latter on the circumference of the ellipse. Let us now move the pea continuously
around the orange—keeping always on the circumference of the
ellipse. The elastic thread, which, of course, varies in length as we
move the pea, will form what in geometry is called a *radius vector*.
Now, if the orange be understood as the Sun, and the pea as a
planet revolving about it, then the revolution should be made at
such a rate—with a velocity so varying—that the *radius vector*
may pass over *equal areas of space in equal times*. The progress
of the pea *should be*—in other words, the progress of the planet
is, of course,—slow in proportion to its distance from the Sun—
swift in proportion to its proximity. Those planets, moreover,
move the more slowly which are the farther from the Sun; *the
squares of their periods of revolution having the same proportion
to each other, as have to each other the cubes of their mean distances
from the Sun.*

The wonderfully complex laws of revolution here described,
however, are not to be understood as obtaining in our system
alone. They *everywhere* prevail where Attraction prevails. They
control *the Universe*. Every shining speck in the firmament is,
no doubt, a luminous Sun, resembling our own, at least in its
general features, and having in attendance upon it a greater or less
number of planets, greater or less, whose still lingering luminosity
is not sufficient to render them visible to us at so vast a distance,
but which, nevertheless, revolve, moon-attended, about their starry
centres, in obedience to the principles just detailed—in obedience
to the three omniprevalent laws of revolution—the three immortal
laws *guessed* by the imaginative Kepler, and but subsequently
demonstrated and accounted for by the patient and mathematical
Newton. Among a tribe of philosophers who pride themselves
excessively upon matter-of-fact, it is far too fashionable to sneer at
all speculation under the comprehensive *sobriquet*, "guess-work."
The point to be considered is, *who* guesses. In guessing with Plato,

we spend our time to better purpose, now and then, than in hark-
ening to a demonstration by Alcmæon.

In many works on Astronomy I find it distinctly stated that the
laws of Kepler are *the basis* of the great principle, Gravitation.
This idea must have arisen from the fact that the suggestion of
these laws by Kepler, and his proving them *à posteriori* to have
an actual existence, led Newton to account for them by the
hypothesis of Gravitation, and, finally, to demonstrate them *à
priori*, as necessary consequences of the hypothetical principle.
Thus so far from the laws of Kepler being the basis of Gravity,
Gravity is the basis of these laws—as it is, indeed, of all the laws,
of the material Universe which are not referable to Repulsion
alone.

The mean distance of the Earth from the Moon—that is to say,
from the heavenly body in our closest vicinity—is 237,000 miles.
Mercury, the planet nearest the Sun, is distant from him 37
millions of miles. Venus, the next, revolves at a distance of 68
millions:—the Earth, which comes next, at a distance of 95
millions:—Mars, then, at a distance of 144 millions. Now come
the eight Asteroids (Ceres, Juno, Vesta, Pallas, Astraea, Flora, Iris,
and Hebe) at an average distance of about 250 millions. Then
we have Jupiter, distant 490 millions; then Saturn, 900 millions;
then Uranus, 19 hundred millions; finally Neptune, lately discovered, and revolving at a distance, say of 28 hundred millions.
Leaving Neptune out of the account—of which as yet we know
little accurately and which is, possibly, one of a system of Asteroids—it will be seen that, within certain limits, there exists an
order of interval among the planets. Speaking loosely, we may
say that each outer planet is twice as far from the Sun as is the
next inner one. May not the *order* here mentioned—*may not the
law of Bode*—*be deduced from consideration of the analogy suggested by me as having place between the solar discharge of rings and
the mode of the atomic irradiation?*

The numbers hurriedly mentioned in this summary of distances,
it is folly to attempt comprehending, unless in the light of abstract
arithmetical facts. They are not practically tangible ones. They
convey no precise ideas. I have stated that Neptune, the planet
farthest from the Sun, revolves about him at a distance of 28

hundred millions of miles. So far good :—I have stated a mathematical fact ; and, without comprehending it in the least, we may put it to use—mathematically. But in mentioning, even, that the Moon revolves about the Earth at the comparatively trifling distance of 237,000 miles, I entertained no expectation of giving any one to understand—to know—to feel—how far from the Earth the Moon actually *is*. 237,000 *miles !* There are, perhaps, few of my readers who have not crossed the Atlantic ocean ; yet how many of them have a distinct idea of even the 3,000 miles intervening between shore and shore ? I doubt, indeed, whether the man lives who can force into his brain the most remote conception of the interval between one milestone and its next neighbor upon the turnpike. We are in some measure aided, however, in our consideration of distance, by combining this consideration with the kindred one of velocity. Sound passes through 1100 feet of space in a second of time. Now were it possible for an inhabitant of the Earth to see the flash of a cannon discharged in the Moon, and to hear the report, he would have to wait, after perceiving the former, more than 13 entire days and nights before getting any intimation of the latter.

However feeble be the impression, even thus conveyed, of the Moon's real distance from the Earth, it will, nevertheless, effect a good object in enabling us more clearly to see the futility of attempting to grasp such intervals as that of the 28 hundred millions of miles between our Sun and Neptune ; or even that of the 95 millions between the Sun and the Earth we inhabit. A cannon-ball, flying at the greatest velocity with which such a ball has ever been known to fly, could not traverse the latter interval in less than 20 years ; while for the former it would require 590.

Our Moon's real diameter is 2160 miles ; yet she is comparatively so trifling an object that it would take nearly 50 such orbs to compose one as great as the Earth.

The diameter of our own globe is 7912 miles—but from the enunciation of these numbers what positive idea do we derive ?

If we ascend an ordinary mountain and look around us from its summit, we behold a landscape stretching, say 40 miles, in every direction ; forming a circle 250 miles in circumference ; and including an area of 5000 square miles. The extent of such a prospect, on account of the *successiveness* with which its portions necessarily present themselves to view, can be only very feebly and very partially appreciated:—yet the entire panorama would comprehend no more than one 40,000th part of the mere *surface* of our globe. Were this panorama, then, to be succeeded, after the lapse of an hour, by another of equal extent; this again by a third, after the lapse of an hour; this again by a fourth after lapse of another hour—and so on, until the scenery of the whole Earth were exhausted; and were we to be engaged in examining these various panoramas for twelve hours of every day; we should nevertheless, be 9 years and 48 days in completing the general survey.

But if the mere surface of the Earth eludes the grasp of the imagination, what are we to think of its cubical contents? It embraces a mass of matter equal in weight to at least two sextillions, two hundred quintillions of tons. Let us suppose it in a state of quiescence; and now let us endeavor to conceive a mechanical force sufficient to set it in motion! Not the strength of all the myriads of beings whom we may conclude to inhabit the planetary worlds of our system—not the combined physical strength of *all* these beings—even admitting all to be more pow erful than man—would avail to stir the ponderous mass *a single inch* from its position.

What are we to understand, then, of the force, which under similar circumstances, would be required to move the *largest* of our planets, Jupiter? This is 86,000 miles in diameter, and would include within its periphery more than a thousand orbs of the magnitude of our own. Yet this stupendous body is actually flying around the sun at the rate of 29,000 miles an hour—that is to say, with a velocity forty times greater than that of a cannon-ball! The thought of such a phænomenon cannot well be said to *startle* the mind:—it palsies and appals it. Not unfrequently we task our imagination in picturing the capacities of an angel. Let us fancy such a being at a distance of some hundred miles from Jupiter—a close eye-witness of this planet as it speeds on its annual revolution. Now *can* we, I demand, fashion for ourselves any conception so distinct of this ideal being's spiritual exaltation as *that* involved in the supposition that, even by this immeasurable mass of matter, whirled immediately before his eyes, with a velocity so unutterable, he—an angel—angelic though he be—is not at once struck in a nothingness and overwhelmed!

At this point, however, it seems proper to suggest that, in fact, we have been speaking of comparative trifles. Our Sun—the central and controlling orb of the system to which Jupiter belongs—is not only greater than Jupiter, but greater by far than all the planets of the system taken together. This fact is an essential condition, indeed, of the stability of the system itself. The diameter of Jupiter has been mentioned: it is 86,000 miles:—that of the Sun is 882,000 miles. An inhabitant of the latter, travelling ninety miles a day, would be more than eighty years in going round a great circle of its circumference. It occupies a cubical space of 681 quadrillions, 472 trillions of miles. The Moon, as has been stated, revolves about the Earth at a distance of 237,000 miles—in an orbit, consequently, of nearly a million and a half. Now, were the Sun placed upon the Earth, centre over centre, the body of the former would extend, in every direction, not only to the line of the Moon's orbit, but beyond it, a distance of 200,000 miles.

And here, once again, let me suggest that, in fact, we have *still* been speaking of comparative trifles. The distance of the planet Neptune from the Sun has been stated: it is 28 hundred millions of miles: the circumference of its orbit, therefore, is about 17 billions. Let this be borne in mind while we glance at some one of the brightest stars. Between this and the star of *our* system, (the Sun,) there is a gulf of space, to convey any idea of which, we should need the tongue of an archangel. From *our* system, then, and from *our* Sun, or star, the star at which we suppose ourselves glancing is a thing altogether apart:—still, for the moment, let us imagine it placed upon our Sun, centre over centre, as we just now imagined this Sun itself placed upon the Earth. Let us now conceive the particular star we have in mind, extending, in every direction, beyond the orbit of Mercury—of Venus—of the Earth:—still *on*, beyond the orbit of Mars—of Jupiter—of Uranus—until, finally, we fancy it filling the circle—*seventeen billions of miles in circumference*—which is described by the revolution of Leverrier's planet. When we have conceived all this, we shall have entertained no extravagant conception. There is the very best reason for believing that many of the stars are even far larger than the one we have imagined. I mean to say, that we have the very best *empirical* basis for such belief:—and, in looking back at the original, atomic arrangements for *diversity*, which have been assumed as a part of the Divine plan in the constitution of the Universe, we shall be enabled easily to understand, and to credit, the existence of even far vaster disproportions in stellar size than any to which I have hitherto alluded. The largest orbs, of course, we must expect to find rolling through the widest vacancies of Space.

I remarked, just now, that to convey an idea of the interval between our Sun and any one of the other stars, we should require the eloquence of an archangel. In so saying, I should not be accused of exaggeration; for, in simple truth, these are topics on which it is scarcely possible to exaggerate. But let us bring the matter more distinctly before the eye of the mind.

In the first place, we may get a general, *relative* conception of the interval referred to, by comparing it with the inter-planetary spaces. If, for example, we suppose the Earth, which is, in reality, 95 millions of miles from the Sun, to be only *one foot* from that luminary; then Neptune would be forty feet distant; *and the star Alpha Lyræ, at the very least, one hundred and fifty-nine.*

Now I presume that, in the termination of my last sentence, few of my readers have noticed anything especially objectionable—particularly wrong. I said that the distance of the Earth from the Sun being taken at *one foot*, the distance of Neptune would be forty feet, and that of Alpha Lyræ, one hundred and fifty-nine. The proportion between one foot and one hundred and fifty nine, has appeared, perhaps, to convey a sufficiently definite impression of the proportion between the two intervals—that of the Earth from the Sun, and that of Alpha Lyræ from the same luminary. But my account of the matter should, in reality, have run thus :— The distance of the Earth from the Sun being taken at one foot, the distance of Neptune would be forty feet, and that of Alpha Lyræ, one hundred and fifty-nine——*miles :*—that is to say, I had assigned to Alpha Lyræ, in my first statement of the case, only the 5280*th part* of that distance which is the *least distance possible* at which it can actually lie.

To proceed:—However distant a mere *planet* is, yet when we look at it through a telescope, we see it under a certain form—of a certain appreciable size. Now I have already hinted at the probable bulk of many of the stars; nevertheless, when we view any one of them, even through the most powerful telescope, it is found to present us with *no form*, and consequently with *no magnitude* whatever. We see it as a point, and nothing more.

Again:—Let us suppose ourselves walking, at night, on a highway. In a field on one side of the road, is a line of tall objects, say trees, the figures of which are distinctly defined against the background of the sky. This line of objects extends at right angles to the road, and from the road to the horizon. Now, as we proceed along the road, we see these objects changing their positions, respectively, in relation to a certain fixed point in that portion of the firmament which forms the background of the view. Let us suppose this fixed point—sufficiently fixed for our purpose—to be the rising moon. We become aware, at once, that while the tree nearest us so far alters its position in respect to the moon, as to seem flying behind us, the tree in the extreme distance has scarcely changed at all its relative position with the satellite. We then go on to perceive that the farther the objects are from us, the less they alter their positions; and the converse. Then we begin, unwittingly, to estimate the distances of individual trees by the degrees in which they evince the relative alteration. Finally, we come to understand how it might be possible to ascertain the actual distance of any given tree in the line, by using the amount of relative alteration as a basis in a simple geometrical problem. Now, this relative alteration is what we call "parallax;" and by parallax we calculate the distances of the heavenly bodies. Applying the principle to the trees in question, we should, of course, be very much at a loss to comprehend the distance of *that* tree, which, however far we proceeded along the road, should evince *no* parallax at all. This, in the case described, is a thing impossible; but impossible only because all distances on our Earth are trivial indeed:—in comparison with the vast cosmical quantities, we may speak of them as absolutely nothing.

Now, let us suppose the star Alpha Lyræ directly overhead; and let us imagine that, instead of standing on the Earth, we stand at one end of a straight road stretching through Space to a distance equalling the diameter of the Earth's orbit—that is to say, to a distance of *one hundred and ninety millions of miles.* Having observed, by means of the most delicate micrometrical instruments, the exact position of the star, let us now pass along this inconceivable road, until we reach the other extremity. Now, once again, let us look at the star. It is *precisely* where we left it. Our instruments, however delicate, assure us that its relative position is absolutely—is identically the same, as at the commencement of our unutterable journey. *No* parallax—none whatever—has been found.

The fact is, that, in regard to the distance of the fixed stars—of any one of the myriads of suns glistening on the farther side of that awful chasm which separates our system from its brothers in the cluster to which it belongs—astronomical science, until very lately, could speak only with a negative certainty. Assuming the brightest as the nearest, we could say, even of *them,* only that there is a certain incomprehensible distance on the *hither* side of which they cannot be:—how far they are beyond it we had in no case been able to ascertain. We perceived, for example, that Alpha Lyræ cannot be nearer to us than 19 trillions, 200 billions of miles; but, for all we knew, and indeed for all we now know, it may be distant from us the square, or the cube, or any other power of the number mentioned. By dint, however, of wonderfully minute and cautious observations, continued, with novel instruments, for many laborious years, *Bessel,* not long ago deceased, has lately succeeded in determining the distance of six or seven stars; among others, that of the star numbered 61 in the constellation of the Swan. The distance in this latter instance ascertained, is 670,000 times that of the Sun; which last it will be remembered, is 95 millions of miles. The star 61 Cygni, then, is nearly 64 trillions of miles from us—or more than three times the distance assigned, *as the least possible,* for Alpha Lyræ.

In attempting to appreciate this interval by the aid of any considerations of *velocity,* as we did in endeavoring to estimate the distance of the moon, we must leave out of sight, altogether, such nothings as the speed of a cannon ball, or of sound. Light, however, according to the latest calculations of Struve, proceeds at the rate of 167,000 miles in a second. Thought itself cannot pass through this interval more speedily—if, indeed, thought can traverse it at all. Yet, in coming from 61 Cygni to us, even at this inconceivable rate, light occupies more than *ten years;* and, consequently, were the star this moment blotted out from the Universe, still, *for ten years,* would it continue to sparkle on, undimmed in its paradoxical glory.

Keeping now in mind whatever feeble conception we may have attained of the interval between our Sun and 61 Cygni, let us remember that this interval, however unutterably vast, we are permitted to consider as but the *average* interval among the countless host of stars composing that cluster, or "nebula," to which our system, as well as that of 61 Cygni, belongs. I have, in fact, stated the case with great moderation:—we have excellent reason for believing 61 Cygni to be one of the *nearest* stars, and thus for concluding, at least for the present, that its distance from us is *less* than the average distance between star and star in the magnificent cluster of the Milky Way.

And here, once again and finally, it seems proper to suggest that even as yet we have been speaking of trifles. Ceasing to wonder at the space between star and star in our own or in any particular cluster, let us rather turn our thoughts to the intervals between cluster and cluster, in the all-comprehensive cluster of the Universe.

. I have already said that light proceeds at the rate of 167,000 miles in a second—that is, about 10 millions of miles in a minute, or about 600 millions of miles in an hour:—yet so far removed from us are some of the "nebulæ" that even light, speeding with this velocity, could not and does nor reach us, from those mysterious regions, in less than 3 *millions of years.* This calculation, moreover, is made by the elder Herschel, and in reference merely to those comparatively proximate clusters within the scope of his own telescope. There *are* "nebulæ," however, which, through the magical tube of Lord Rosse, are this instant whispering in our ears the secrets of *a million of ages* by-gone. In a word, the events which we behold now—at this moment—in those worlds— are the identical events which interested their inhabitants *ten hundred thousand centuries* ago. In intervals—in distances such as this suggestion forces upon the *soul*—rather than upon the mind—we find, at length, a fitting climax to all hitherto frivolous considerations of *quantity.*

Our fancies thus occupied with the cosmical distances, let us take the opportunity of referring to the difficulty which we have so often experienced, while pursuing *the beaten path* of astronomical reflection, *in accounting* for the immeasurable voids alluded to—in comprehending why chasms so totally unoccupied and therefore apparently so needless, have been made to intervene between star and star—between cluster and cluster—in understanding, to be brief, a sufficient reason for the Titanic scale, in respect of mere *Space,* on which the Universe is seen to be constructed. A rational cause for the phænomenon, I maintain that Astronomy has palpably failed to assign:—but the considerations through which, in this Essay, we have proceeded step by step, enable us clearly and immediately to perceive that *Space and Duration are one.* That the Universe might *endure* throughout an æra at all commensurate with the grandeur of its component material portions and with the high majesty of its spiritual purposes, it was necessary that the original atomic diffusion be made to so inconceivable an extent as to be only not infinite. It was required, in a word, that the stars should be gathered into visibility from invisible nebulosity—proceed from nebulosity to consolidation—and so grow grey in giving birth and death to unspeakably numerous and complex variations of vitalic development:—it was required that the stars should do all this—should have time thoroughly to accomplish all these Divine purposes—*during the period* in which all things were effecting their return into Unity with a velocity accumulating in the inverse proportion of the squares of the distances at which lay the inevitable End.

Throughout all this we have no difficulty in understanding the absolute accuracy of the Divine *adaptation.* The density of the stars, respectively, proceeds, of course, as their condensation diminishes; condensation and heterogeneity keep pace with each other, through the latter, which is the index of the former, we estimate the vitalic and spiritual development. Thus, in the density of the globes, we have the measure in which their purposes are fulfilled. *As* density proceeds—*as* the divine intentions *are* accomplished—

as less and still less remains *to be* accomplished—so—in the same ratio—should we expect to find an acceleration of *the End*:—and thus the philosophical mind will easily comprehend that the Divine designs in constituting the stars, advance *mathematically* to their fulfilment:—and more; it will readily give the advance a mathematical expression; it will decide that this advance is inversely proportional with the squares of the distances of all created things from the starting-point and goal of their creation.

Not only is this Divine adaptation, however, mathematically accurate, but there is that about it which stamps it *as divine*, in distinction from that which is merely the work of human constructiveness. I allude to the complete *mutuality* of adaptation. For example: in human constructions a particular cause has a particular effect; a particular intention brings to pass a particular object; but this is all; we see no reciprocity. The effect does not re-act upon the cause; the intention does not change relations with the object. In Divine constructions the object is either design or object as we choose to regard it—and we may take at any time a cause for an effect, or the converse—so that we can never absolutely decide which is which.

To give an instance:—In polar climates the human frame, to maintain its animal heat, requires, for combustion in the capillary system, an abundant supply of highly azotized food, such as train-oil. But again:—in polar climates nearly the sole food afforded man is the oil of abundant seals and whales. Now, whether is oil at hand because imperatively demanded, or the only thing demanded because the only thing to be obtained? It is impossible to decide. There is an absolute *reciprocity of adaptation*.

The pleasure which we derive from any display of human ingenuity is in the ratio of *the approach* to this species of reciprocity. In the construction of *plot*, for example, in fictitious literature, we should aim at so arranging the incidents that we shall not be able to determine, of any one of them, whether it depends from any one other or upholds it. In this sense, of course, *perfection of plot* is really, or practically, unattainable—but only because it is a finite intelligence that constructs. The plots of God are perfect. The Universe is a plot of God.

And now we have reached a point at which the intellect is forced, again, to struggle against its propensity for analogical inference—against its monomaniac grasping at the infinite. Means have been seen *revolving* about planets; planets about stars; and the poetical instinct of humanity—its instinct of the symmetrical, if the symmetry be but a symmetry of surface:—this *instinct*, which the Soul, not only of Man but of all created beings, took up, in the beginning, from the *geometrical* basis of the Universal irradiation—impels us to the fancy of an endless extension of this system of *cycles*. Closing our eyes equally to *deduction* and *induction*, we insist upon imagining a *revolution* of all the orbs of the Galaxy about some gigantic globe which we take to be the central pivot of the whole. Each cluster in the great cluster of clusters is imagined, of course, to be similarly supplied and constructed; while, that the "analogy" may be wanting at no point, we go on to conceive these clusters themselves, again, as *revolving* about some still more august sphere;— this latter, still again, *with* its encircling clusters, as but one of a yet more magnificent series of agglomerations, *gyrating* about yet another orb central *to them* —some orb still more unspeakably sublime—some orb, let us rather say, of infinite sublimity endlessly multiplied by the infinitely sublime. Such are the conditions, continued in perpetuity, which the voice of what some people term "analogy" calls upon the Fancy to depict and the Reason to contemplate, if possible, without becoming dissatisfied with the picture. Such, *in general*, are the interminable gyrations beyond gyration which we have been instructed by Philosophy to comprehend and to account for, at least in the best manner we can. Now and then, however, a philosopher proper—one whose frenzy takes a very determinate turn—whose genius, to speak more reverentially, has a strongly-pronounced washer-womanish bias, doing every thing up by the dozen—enables us to see *precisely* that point out of sight, at which the revolutionary processes in question do, and of right ought to, come to an end.

It is hardly worth while, perhaps, even to sneer at the reveries of Fourrier:—but much has been said, latterly, of the hypothesis of Mädler—that there exists, in the centre of the Galaxy, a stupendous globe about which all the systems of the cluster revolve

The *period* of our own, indeed, has been stated—117 millions of years.

That our Sun has a motion in space, independently of its rotation, and revolution about the system's centre of gravity, has long been suspected. This motion, granting it to exist, would be manifested perspectively. The stars in that firmamental region which we were leaving behind us, would, in a very long series of years, become crowded; those in the opposite quarter, scattered. Now, by means of astronomical History, we ascertain, cloudily, that some such phænomena have occurred. On this ground it has been declared that our system is moving to a point in the heavens diametrically opposite the star Zeta Herculis:—but this inference is, perhaps, the maximum to which we have any logical right. Mädler, however, has gone so far as to designate a particular star, Alcyone in the Pleiades, as being at or about the very spot around which a general *revolution* is performed.

Now, since by "analogy" we are led, in the first instance, to these dreams, it is no more than proper that we should abide by analogy, at least in some measure, during their development; and that analogy which suggests the revolution, suggests at the same time a central orb about which it should be performed:—so far the astronomer was consistent. This central orb, however, should, dynamically, be greater than all the orbs, taken together, which surround it. Of these there are about 100 millions. "Why, then," it was of course demanded, "do we not *see* this vast central sun—*at least equal* in mass to 100 millions of such suns as ours—why do we not *see* it—*we*, especially, who occupy the mid region of the cluster—the very locality *near* which, at all events, must be situated this incomparable star?" The reply was ready—"It must be non-luminous, as are our planets." Here, then, to suit a purpose, analogy is suddenly let fall. "Not so," it may be said—"we know that non-luminous suns actually exist." It is true that we have reason at least for supposing so; but we have certainly no reason whatever for supposing that the non-luminous suns in question are encircled by *luminous* suns, while these again are surrounded by non-luminous planets:—and it is precisely all this with which Mädler is called upon to find any thing analogous in the heavens—for it is precisely all this which he imagines in the case of the Galaxy.

Admitting the thing to be so, we cannot help here picturing to ourselves how sad a puzzle the *why is it so* must prove to all *à priori* philosophers.

But granting, in the very teeth of analogy and of every thing else, the non-luminosity of the vast central orb, we may still inquire how this orb, so enormous, could fail of being rendered visible by the flood of light thrown upon it from the 100 millions of glorious suns glaring in all directions about it. Upon the urging' of this question, the idea of an actually solid central sun appears, in some measure, to have been abandoned; and speculation proceeded to assert that the systems of the cluster perform their revolutions merely about an immaterial centre of gravity common to all. Here again then, to suit a purpose, analogy is let fall. The planets of our system revolve, it is true, about a common centre of gravity; but they do this in connexion with, and in consequence of, a material sun whose mass more than counterbalances the rest of the system.

The mathematical circle is a curve composed of an infinity of straight lines. But this idea of the circle—an idea which, in view of all ordinary geometry, is merely the mathematical, as contradistinguished from the practical, idea—is, in sober fact, the *practical* conception which alone we have any right to entertain in regard to the majestic circle with which we have to deal, at least in fancy, when we suppose our system revolving about a point in the centre of the Galaxy. Let the most vigorous of human imaginations attempt but to take a single step towards the comprehension of a sweep so ineffable! It would scarcely be paradoxical to say that a flash of lightning itself, travelling *forever* upon the circumference of this unutterable circle, would still, *forever*, be travelling in a straight line. That the path of our Sun in such an orbit would, to any human perception, deviate in the slightest degree from a straight line, even in a million of years, is a proposition not to be entertained :—yet we are required to believe that a curvature has become apparent during the brief period of our astronomical history—during a mere point—during the utter nothingness of two or three thousand years.

It may be said that Mädler *has* really ascertained a curvature in the direction of our system's now well-established progress through Space. Admitting, if necessary, this fact to be in reality such, I maintain that nothing is thereby shown except the reality of this fact—the fact of a curvature. For its *thorough* determination, ages will be required; and, when determined, it will be found indicative of some binary or other multiple relation between our Sun and some one or more of the proximate stars. I hazard nothing however, in predicting, that, after the lapse of many centuries, all efforts at determining the path of our Sun through Space, will be abandoned as fruitless. This is easily conceivable when we look at the infinity of perturbation it must experience, from its perpetually-shifting relations with other orbs, in the common approach of all to the nucleus of the Galaxy.

But in examining other "nebulæ" than that of the Milky Way —in surveying, generally, the clusters which overspread the heavens—do we or do we not find confirmation of Mädler's hypothesis? We do *not*. The forms of the clusters are exceedingly diverse when casually viewed; but on close inspection, through powerful telescopes, we recognise the sphere, very distinctly, as at least the proximate form of all:—their constitution, in general, being at variance with the idea of revolution about a common centre.

"It is difficult," says Sir John Herschel, "to form any conception of the dynamical state of such systems. On one hand, without a rotary motion and a centrifugal force, it is hardly possible not to regard them as in a state of *progressive collapse*. On the other, granting such a motion and such a force, we find it no less difficult to reconcile their forms with the rotation of the whole system [meaning cluster] around any single axis, without which internal collision would appear to be inevitable."

Some remarks lately made about the "nebulæ" by Dr. Nichol, in taking quite a different view of the cosmical conditions from any taken in this Discourse have a very peculiar applicability to the point now at issue. He says :

"When our greatest telescopes are brought to bear upon them, we find that those which were thought to be irregular, are not so; they approach nearer to a globe. Here is one that looked oval : but Lord Rosse's telescope brought it into a circle . . . . Now there occurs a very remarkable circumstance in reference to these comparatively sweeping circular masses of nebulæ. We find they are not entirely circular, but the reverse; and that all around them, on every side, there are volumes of stars, *stretching out apparently as if they were rushing towards a great central mass in consequence of the action of some great power.*" [*]

Were I to describe, in my own words, what must necessarily be the existing condition of each nebula on the hypothesis that all matter is, as I suggest, now returning to its original Unity, I should simply be going over, nearly verbatim, the language here employed by Dr. Nichol, without the faintest suspicion of that stupendous truth which is the key to these nebular phænomena.

And here let me fortify my position still farther, by the voice of a greater than Mädler—of one, moreover, to whom all the data of Mädler have long been familiar things, carefully and thoroughly considered. Referring to the elaborate calculations of Argelander—the very researches which form Mädler's basis—*Humboldt*, whose generalizing powers have never, perhaps, been equalled, has the following observation:

"When we regard the real, proper, or non-perspective motions of the stars, we find *many groups of them moving in opposite directions;* and the data as yet in hand render it not necessary, at least, to conceive that the systems composing the Milky Way, or the clusters, generally, composing the Universe, are revolving about any particular centre unknown, whether luminous or non-luminous. It is but Man's longing for a fundamental First Cause, that impels both his intellect and fancy to the adoption of such an hypothesis." [†]

---

[*] I must be understood as denying, *especially*, only the *revolutionary* portion of Mädler's hypothesis. Of course, if no great central orb exists *now* in our cluster, such will exist hereafter. Whenever existing, it will be merely the *nucleus* of the consolidation.

[†] Betrachtet man die nicht perspectivischen eigenen Bewegungen der Sterne, so scheinen viele gruppenweise in ihrer Richtung entgegengesetzt; und die bisher gesammelten Thatsachen machen es auf's wenigste nicht nothwendig, anzunehmen, dass alle Theile unserer Sternenschicht oder gar der gesammten Sterneninseln, welche den Weltraum füllen, sich um einen grossen, unbekannten, leuchtenden oder, dunkeln Centralkörper bewegen. Das Streben nach den letzten und höchsten Grundursachen macht freilich die reflectirende Thätigkeit des Menschen, wie seine Phantasie, zu einer solchen Annahme geneigt.

The phænomenon here alluded to—that of "many groups moving in opposite directions"—is quite inexplicable by Mädler's idea; but arises, as a necessary consequence, from that which forms the basis of this Discourse. While the *merely general direction* of each atom—of each moon, planet, star, or cluster—would, on my hypothesis, be, of course, absolutely rectilinear, while the *general* path of all bodies would be a right line leading to the centre of all; it is clear, nevertheless, that this general rectilinearity would be compounded of what, with scarcely any exaggeration, we may term an infinity of particular curves—an infinity of local deviations from rectilinearity—the result of continuous differences of relative position among the multitudinous masses, as each proceeded on its own proper journey to the End.

I quoted, just now, from Sir John Herschel, the following words, used in reference to the clusters :—" On one hand, without a rotary motion and a centrifugal force, it is hardly possible not to regard them as in a state of *progressive collapse.*" The fact is, that, in surveying the " nebulæ" with a telescope of high power, we shall find it quite impossible, having once conceived this idea of "collapse," not to gather, at all points, corroboration of the idea. A nucleus is always apparent, in the direction of which the stars seem to be precipitating themselves; nor can these nuclei be mistaken for merely perspective phænomena :—the clusters are *really* denser near the centre—sparser in the regions more remote from it. In a word, we see every thing as we *should* see it were a collapse taking place; but, in general, it may be said of these clusters, that we can fairly entertain, while looking at them, the idea of *orbitual movement about a centre*, only by admitting the *possible* existence, in the distant domains of space, of dynamical laws with which *we* are unacquainted.

On the part of Herschel, however, there is evidently *a reluctance* to regard the nebulæ as in " a state of progressive collapse." But if facts—if even appearances justify the supposition of their being in this state, *why*, it may well be demanded, is he disinclined to admit it ? Simply on account of a prejudice ;—merely because the supposition is at war with a pre-conceived and utterly baseless notion—that of the endlessness—that of the eternal stability of the Universe.

If the propositions of this Discourse are tenable, the "state of progressive collapse" is *precisely* that state in which alone we are warranted in considering All Things; and, with due humility, let me here confess that, for my part, I am at a loss to conceive how any *other* understanding of the existing condition of affairs, could ever have made its way into the human brain. "The tendency to collapse" and "the attraction of gravitation" are convertible phrases. In using either, we speak of the reaction of the First Act. Never was necessity less obvious than that of supposing Matter imbued with an ineradicable *quality* forming part of its material nature—a quality, or instinct, *forever* inseparable from it, and by dint of which inalienable principle every atom is *perpetually* impelled to seek its fellow-atom. Never was necessity less obvious than that of entertaining this unphilosophical idea. Going boldly behind the vulgar thought, we have to conceive, metaphysically, that the gravitating principle appertains to Matter *temporarily*—only while diffused—only while existing as Many instead of as One—appertains to it by virtue of its state of irradiation alone—appertains, in a word, altogether to its *condition*, and not in the slightest degree to *itself*. In this view, when the irradiation shall have returned into its source—when the reaction shall be completed—the gravitating principle will no longer exist. And, in fact, astronomers, without at any time reaching the idea here suggested, seem to have been approximating it, in the assertion that "if there were but one body in the universe, it would be impossible to understand how the principle, Gravity, could obtain:" that is to say, from a consideration of Matter as they find it, they reach a conclusion at which I deductively arrive. That so pregnant a suggestion as the one quoted should have been permitted to remain so long unfruitful, is, nevertheless, a mystery which I find it difficult to fathom.

It is, perhaps, in no little degree, however, our propensity for the continuous—for the analogical—in the present case more particularly for the symmetrical—which has been leading us astray. And, in fact, the sense of the symmetrical is an instinct which may be depended upon with an almost blindfold reliance. It is the poetical essence of the Universe—*of the Universe* which, in the supremeness of its symmetry, is but the most sublime of poems. Now symmetry and consistency are convertible terms:—thus Poetry and Truth are one. A thing is consistent in the ratio of its truth—true in the ratio of its consistency. *A perfect consistency, I repeat, can be nothing but an absolute truth.* We may take it for granted, then, that Man cannot long or widely err, if he suffer himself to be guided by his poetical, which I have maintained to be his truthful, in being his symmetrical, instinct. He must have a care, however, lest, in pursuing too heedlessly the superficial symmetry of forms and motions, he leave out of sight the really essential symmetry of the principles which determine and control them.

That the stellar bodies would finally be merged in one—that, at last, all would be drawn into the substance of *one stupendous central orb already existing*—is an idea which, for some time past, seems, vaguely and indeterminately, to have held possession of the fancy of mankind. It is an idea, in fact, which belongs to the class of the *excessively obvious.* It springs, instantly, from a superficial observation of the cyclic and seemingly *gyrating* or *vortical* movements of those individual portions of the Universe which come most immediately and most closely under our observation. There is not, perhaps, a human being, of ordinary education and of average reflective capacity, to whom, at some period, the fancy in question has not occurred, as if spontaneously, or intuitively, and wearing all the character of a very profound and very original conception. This conception, however, so commonly entertained, has never, within my knowledge, arisen out of any abstract considerations. Being, on the contrary, always suggested, as I say, by the vortical movements about centres, a reason for it, also,—a *cause* for the ingathering of all the orbs into one, *imagined to be already existing*, was naturally sought in the same direction—among these cyclic movements themselves.

Thus it happened that, on announcement of the gradual and perfectly regular decrease observed in the orbit of Encke's comet, at every successive revolution about our Sun, astronomers were nearly unanimous in the opinion that the cause in question was found—that a principle was discovered sufficient to account, physically, for that final, universal agglomeration which, I repeat, the analogical, symmetrical, or poetical instinct of man had predetermined to understand as something more than a simple hypothesis.

This cause—this sufficient reason for the final ingathering—was declared to exist in an exceedingly rare but still material medium pervading space; which medium, by retarding, in some degree, the progress of the comet, perpetually weakened its tangential force; thus giving a predominance to the centripetal; which, of course, drew the comet nearer and nearer at each revolution, and would eventually precipitate it upon the Sun.

All this was strictly logical—admitting the medium or ether; but this ether was assumed, most illogically, on the ground that no *other* mode than the one spoken of could be discovered, of accounting for the observed decrease in the orbit of the comet :—as if from the fact that we could *discover* no other mode of accounting for it, it followed, in any respect, that no other mode of accounting for it existed. It is clear that innumerable causes might operate, in combination, to diminish the orbit, without even a possibility of our ever becoming acquainted with one of them. In the meantime, it has never been fairly shown, perhaps, why the retardation occasioned by the skirts of the Sun's atmosphere, through which the comet passes at perihelion, is not enough to account for the phænomenon. That Encke's comet will be absorbed into the Sun, is probable; that all the comets of the system will be absorbed, is more than merely possible; but, in such case, the principle of absorption must be referred to eccentricity of orbit—to the close approximation to the Sun, of the comets at their perihelia; and is a principle not affecting, in any degree, the ponderous *spheres*, which are to be regarded as the true material constituents of the Universe. Touching comets in general, let me here suggest, in passing, that we cannot be far wrong in looking upon them as the *lightning-flashes of the cosmical Heaven.*

The idea of a retarding ether, and, through it, of a final agglomeration of all things, seemed at one time, however, to be confirmed by the observation of a positive decrease in the orbit of the solid moon. By reference to eclipses recorded 2500 years ago, it was found that the velocity of the satellite's revolution *then* was considerably less than it is *now;* that on the hypothesis that its motions in its orbit is uniformly in accordance with Kepler's law, and was accurately determined *then*—2500 years ago—it is now in advance of the position it *should* occupy, by nearly 9000 miles. The increase of velocity proved, of course, a diminution of orbit; and astronomers were fast yielding to a belief in an ether, as the sole mode of accounting for the phænomenon, when Lagrange came to the rescue. He showed that, owing to the configurations of the spheroids, the shorter axes of their ellipses are subject to variation in length; the longer axes being permanent; and that this variation is continuous and vibratory—so that every orbit is in a state of transition, either from circle to ellipse, or from ellipse to circle. In the case of the moon, where the shorter axis is *decreasing*, the orbit is passing from circle to ellipse, and, consequently, is *decreasing* too; but, after a long series of ages, the ultimate eccentricity will be attained; then the shorter axis will proceed to *increase*, until the orbit becomes a circle; when the process of shortening will again take place:—and so on forever. In the case of the Earth, the orbit is passing from ellipse to circle. The facts thus demonstrated do away, of course, with all necessity for supposing an ether, and with all apprehension of the system's instability—on the ether's account.

It will be remembered that I have myself assumed what we may term *an ether*. I have spoken of a subtle *influence* which we know to be ever in attendance upon matter, although becoming manifest only through matter's heterogeneity. To this *influence* —without daring to touch it at all in any effort at explaining its awful *nature*—I have referred the various phænomena of electricity, heat, light, magnetism; and more—of vitality, consciousness, and thought—in a word, of spirituality. It will be seen, at once, then, that the ether thus conceived is radically distinct from the ether of the astronomers; inasmuch as theirs is *matter* and mine *not.*

With the idea of material ether, seems, thus, to have departed altogether the thought of that universal agglomeration so long predetermined by the poetical fancy of mankind:—an agglomeration in which a sound Philosophy might have been warranted in putting faith, at least to a certain extent, if for no other reason than that by this poetical fancy it *had* been so predetermined. But so far as Astronomy—so far as mere Physics have yet spoken,

10*

the cycles of the Universe has no conceivable end. Had an end
been demonstrated, however, from so purely collateral a cause as
an ether, Man's instinct of the Divine *capacity to adapt*, would
have rebelled against the demonstration. We should have been
forced to regard the Universe with some such sense of dissatisfaction as we experience in contemplating an unnecessarily complex
work of human art. Creation would have affected us as an imperfect *plot* in a romance, where the *dénoûment* is awkwardly brought
about by interposed incidents external and foreign to the main
subject; instead of springing out of the bosom of the thesis—
out of the heart of the ruling idea—instead of arising as a result
of the primary proposition—as inseparable and inevitable part
and parcel of the fundamental conception of the book.

What I mean by the symmetry of mere surface will now be
more clearly understood. It is simply by the blandishment of
this symmetery that we have been beguiled into the general idea
of which Mädler's hypothesis is but a part—the idea of the vor-
ticial indrawing of the orbs. Dismissing this nakedly physical
conception, the symmetry of principle sees the end of all things
metaphysically involved in the thought of a beginning; seeks and
finds in this origin of all things the *rudiment* of this end; and
perceives the impiety of supposing this end likely to be brought
about less simply—less directly—less obviously—less artistically
—than through *the reaction of the originating Act.*

Recurring, then, to a previous suggestion, let us understand the
systems—let us understand each star, with its attendant planets—
as but a Titanic atom existing in space with precisely the same inclination for Unity which characterized, in the beginning, the actual
atoms after their irradiation throughout the Universal sphere. As
these original atoms rushed towards each other in generally straight
lines, so let us conceive as at least generally rectilinear, the paths
of the system-atoms towards their respective centres of aggregation:—and in this direct drawing together of the systems into
clusters, with a similar and simultaneous drawing together of the
clusters themselves while undergoing consolidation, we have at
length attained the great *Now*—the awful Present—the Existing
Condition of the Universe.

Of the still more awful Future a not irrational analogy may

guide us in framing an hypothesis. The equilibrium between the centripetal and centrifugal forces of each system, being necessarily destroyed upon attainment of a certain proximity to the nucleus of the cluster to which it belongs, there must occur, at once, a chaotic or seemingly chaotic precipitation, of the moons upon the planets, of the planets upon the suns, and of the suns upon the nuclei; and the general result of this precipitation must be the gathering of the myriad now-existing stars of the firmament into an almost infinitely less number of almost infinitely superior spheres. In being immeasurably fewer, the worlds of that day will be immeasurably greater than our own. Then, indeed, amid unfathomable abysses, will be glaring unimaginable suns. But all this will be merely a climacic magnificence foreboding the great End. Of this End the new genesis described, can be but a very partial postponement. While undergoing consolidation, the clusters themselves, with a speed prodigiously accumulative, have been rushing towards their own general centre— and now, with a thousand-fold electric velocity, commensurate only with their material grandeur and with the spiritual passion of their appetite for oneness, the majestic remnants of the tribe of Stars flash, at length, into a common embrace. The inevitable catastrophe is at hand.

But this catastrophe—what is it? We have seen accomplished the ingathering of the orbs. Henceforward, are we not to understand *one material globe of globes* as constituting and comprehending the Universe? Such a fancy would be altogether at war with every assumption and consideration of this Discourse.

I have already alluded to that absolute *reciprocity of adaptation* which is the idiosyncrasy of the divine Art—stamping it divine. Up to this point of our reflections, we have been regarding the electrical influence as a something by dint of whose repulsion alone Matter is enabled to exist in that state of diffusion demanded for the fulfilment of its purposes:—so far, in a word, we have been considering the influence in question as ordained for Matter's sake to subserve the objects of matter. With a perfectly legitimate reciprocity, we are now permitted to look at Matter, as created *solely for the sake of this influence*—solely to serve the objects of this spiritual Ether. Through the aid - by the means - through the agency of Matter, and by dint of its heterogeneity—is this Ether manifested—is *Spirit individualized*. It is merely in the development of this Ether, through heterogeneity, that particular masses of Matter become animate—sensitive—and in the ratio of their heterogeneity;—some reaching a degree of sensitiveness involving what we call *Thought*, and thus attaining Conscious Intelligence.

In this view, we are enabled to perceive Matter as a Means— not as an End. Its purposes are thus seen to have been comprehended in its diffusion; and with the return into Unity these purposes cease. The absolutely consolidated globe of globes would be *objectless :*—therefore not for a moment could it continue to exist. Matter, created for an end, would unquestionably, on fulfilment of that end, be Matter no longer. Let us endeavor to understand that it would disappear, and that God would remain all in all.

That every work of Divine conception must cöexist and cöexpire with its particular design, seems to me especially obvious; and I make no doubt that, on perceiving the final globe of globes to be *objectless*, the majority of my readers will be satisfied with my " *therefore* it cannot continue to exist." Nevertheless, as the startling thought of its instantaneous disappearance is one which the most powerful intellect cannot be expected readily to entertain on grounds so decidedly abstract, let us endeavor to look at the idea from some other and more ordinary point of view:—let us see how thoroughly and beautifully it is corroborated in an *à posteriori* consideration of Matter as we actually find it.

I have before said that " Attraction and Repulsion being undeniably the sole properties by which Matter is manifested to Mind, we are justified in assuming that Matter *exists* only as Attraction and Repulsion—in other words that Attraction and Repulsion *are* Matter; there being no conceivable case in which we may not employ the term Matter and the terms ' Attraction' and ' Repulsion' taken together, as equivalent, and therefore convertible, expressions of Logic."*

Now the very definition of Attraction implies particularity—

* Page 188.

the existence of parts, particles, or atoms; for we define it as the tendency of "each atom &c. to every other atom," &c. according to a certain law. Of course where there are *no* parts—where there is absolute Unity—where the tendency to oneness is satisfied—there can be no Attraction:—this has been fully shown, and all Philosophy admits it. When, on fulfilment of its purposes, then, Matter shall have returned into its original condition of *One* —a condition which presupposes the expulsion of the separative ether, whose province and whose capacity are limited to keeping the atoms apart until that great day when, this ether being no longer needed, the overwhelming pressure of the finally collective Attraction shall at length just sufficiently predominate* and expel it:—when, I say, Matter, finally, expelling the Ether, shall have returned into absolute Unity,—it will then (to speak paradoxically for the moment) be Matter without Attraction and without Repulsion—in other words, Matter without Matter—in other words, again, *Matter no more.* In sinking into Unity, it will sink at once into that Nothingness which, to all Finite Perception, Unity must be—into that Material Nihility from which alone we can conceive it to have been evoked—to have been *created* by the Volition of God.

I repeat, then—Let us endeavor to comprehend that the final globe of globes will instantaneously disappear, and that God will remain all in all.

But are we here to pause? Not so. On the Universal agglomeration and dissolution, we can readily conceive that a new and perhaps totally different series of conditions may ensue—another creation and irradiation, returning into itself—another action and reaction of the Divine Will. Guiding our imaginations by that omniprevalent law of laws, the law of periodicity, are we not, indeed, more than justified in entertaining a belief—let us say, rather, in indulging a hope—that the processes we have here ventured to contemplate will be renewed forever, and forever, and forever; a novel Universe swelling into existence, and then subsiding into nothingness, at every throb of the Heart Divine?

And now—this Heart Divine—what is it? *It is our own.*

---

* "**Gravity, therefore, must be the strongest of forces.**"—See page 140.

Let not the merely seeming irreverence of this idea frighten our souls from that cool exercise of consciousness—from that deep tranquillity of self-inspection—through which alone we can hope to attain the presence of this, the most sublime of truths, and look it leisurely in the face.

The *phænomena* on which our conclusions must at this point depend, are merely spiritual shadows, but not the less thoroughly substantial.

We walk about, amid the destinies of our world-existence, encompassed by dim but ever present *Memories* of a Destiny more vast—very distant in the by-gone time, and infinitely awful.

We live out a Youth peculiarly haunted by such dreams; yet never mistaking them for dreams. As Memories we *know* them. *During our Youth* the distinction is too clear to deceive us even for a moment.

So long as this Youth endures, the feeling *that we exist,* is the most natural of all feelings. We understand it *thoroughly.* That there was a period at which we did *not* exist—or, that it might so have happened that we never had existed at all—are the considerations, indeed, which *during this youth,* we find difficulty in understanding. Why we should *not* exist, is, *up to the epoch of our Manhood,* of all queries the most unanswerable. Existence—self-existence—existence from all Time and to all Eternity—seems, up to the epoch of Manhood, a normal and unquestionable condition: —*seems, because it is.*

But now comes the period at which a conventional World-Reason awakens us from the truth of our dream. Doubt, Surprise and Incomprehensibility arrive at the same moment. They say:—" You live, and the time was when you lived not. You have been created. An Intelligence exists greater than your own; and it is only through this Intelligence you live at all." These things we struggle to comprehend and cannot:—*cannot,* because these things, being untrue, are thus, of necessity, incomprehensible.

No thinking being lives who, at some luminous point of his life of thought, has not felt himself lost amid the surges of futile efforts at understanding or believing, that anything exists *greater than his own soul.* The utter impossibility of any one's soul feeling itself inferior to another; the intense, overwhelming dissatisfaction and rebellion at the thought;—these, with the omniprevalent aspirations at perfection, are but the spiritual, coincident with the material, struggles towards the original Unity—are, to my mind at least, a species of proof far surpassing what Man terms demonstration, that no one soul *is* inferior to another—that nothing is, or can be, superior to any one soul—that each soul is, in part, its own God—its own Creator:—in a word, that God—the material *and* spiritual God—*now* exists solely in the diffused Matter and Spirit of the Universe; and that the regathering of this diffused Matter and Spirit will be but the re-constitution of the *purely* Spiritual and Individual God.

In this view, and in this view alone, we comprehend the riddles of Divine Injustice—of Inexorable Fate. In this view alone the existence of Evil becomes intelligible; but in this view it becomes more—it becomes endurable. Our souls no longer rebel at a *Sorrow* which we ourselves have imposed upon ourselves, in furtherance of our own purposes—with a view—if even with a futile view—to the extension of our own *Joy*.

I have spoken of *Memories* that haunt us during our youth. They sometimes pursue us even in our Manhood:—assume gradually less and less indefinite shapes:—now and then speak to us with low voices, saying:

"There was an epoch in the Night of Time, when a still-existent Being existed—one of an absolutely infinite number of similar Beings that people the absolutely infinite domains of the absolutely infinite space.* It was not and is not in the power of this Being—any more than it is in your own—to extend, by actual increase, the joy of his Existence; but just as it *is* in your power to expand or to concentrate your pleasures (the absolute amount of happiness remaining always the same) so did and does a similar capability appertain to this Divine Being, who thus passes his Eternity in perpetual variation of Concentrated Self and almost Infinite Self-Diffusion. What you call The Universe is but his present expansive existence. He now feels his life through an in-

* See pages 185–186—Paragraph commencing "I reply that the right," and ending "proper and particular God."

finity of imperfect pleasures—the partial and pain-intertangled pleasures of those inconceivably numerous things which you designate as his creatures, but which are really but infinite individualizations of Himself. All these creatures—*all*—those which you term animate, as well as those to whom you deny life for no better reason than that you do not behold it in operation—*all* these creatures have, in a greater or less degree, a capacity for pleasure and for pain:—*but the general sum of their sensations is precisely that amount of Happiness which appertains by right to the Divine Being when concentrated within Himself.* These creatures are all too, more or less conscious Intelligences; conscious, first, of a proper identity; conscious, secondly, and by faint indeterminate glimpses, of an identity with the Divine Being of whom we speak —of an identity with God. Of the two classes of consciousness, fancy that the former will grow weaker, the latter stronger, during the long succession of ages which must elapse before these myriads of individual Intelligences become blended—when the bright stars become blended—into One. Think that the sense of individual identity will be gradually merged in the general consciousness— that Man, for example, ceasing imperceptibly to feel himself Man, will at length attain that awfully triumphant epoch when he shall recognise his existence as that of Jehovah. In the meantime bear in mind that all is Life—Life—Life within Life—the less **within** the greater, and all within the *Spirit Divine.*

THE RATIONALE OF VERSE.

THE word "Verse" is here used not in its strict or primitive sense, but as the term most convenient for expressing generally and without pedantry all that is involved in the consideration of rhythm, rhyme, metre, and versification.

There is, perhaps, no topic in polite literature which has been more pertinaciously discussed, and there is certainly not one about which so much inaccuracy, confusion, misconception, misrepresentation, mystification, and downright ignorance on all sides, can be fairly said to exist. Were the topic really difficult, or did it lie, even, in the cloud-land of metaphysics, where the doubt-vapors may be made to assume any and every shape at the will or at the fancy of the gazer, we should have less reason to wonder at all this contradiction and perplexity; but in fact the subject is exceedingly simple; one tenth of it, possibly, may be called ethical; nine tenths, however, appertain to the mathematics; and the whole is included within the limits of the commonest common sense.

"But, if this is the case, how," it will be asked, "can so much misunderstanding have arisen? Is it conceivable that a thousand profound scholars, investigating so very simple a matter for centuries, have not been able to place it in the fullest light, at least, of which it is susceptible?" These queries, I confess, are not easily answered:—at all events, a satisfactory reply to them might cost more trouble than would, if properly considered, the whole *vexata quæstio* to which they have reference. Nevertheless, there is little difficulty or danger in suggesting that the "thousand profound scholars" *may* have failed, first, because they were scholars, secondly, because they were profound, and thirdly, because they were a thousand—the impotency of the scholarship and profundity having been thus multiplied a thousand fold. I am serious in these suggestions; for, first again, there is something in "scholarship" which seduces us into blind worship of Bacon's Idol of the Theatre—into irrational deference to antiquity; secondly, the proper "profundity" is rarely profound—it is the nature of Truth in general, as of some ores in particular, to be richest when most superficial; thirdly, the clearest subject may be overclouded by mere superabundance of talk. In chemistry, the best way of separating two bodies is to add a third; in speculation, fact often agrees with fact and argument with argument, until an additional well-meaning fact or argument sets every thing by the ears. In one case out of a hundred a point is excessively discussed because it is obscure; in the ninety-nine remaining it is obscure because excessively discussed. When a topic is thus circumstanced, the readiest mode of investigating it is to forget that any previous investigation has been attempted.

But, in fact, while much has been written on the Greek and Latin rhythms, and even on the Hebrew, little effort has been made at examining that of any of the modern tongues. As regards the English, comparatively nothing has been done. It may be said, indeed, that we are without a treatise on our own verse. In our ordinary grammars and in our works on rhetoric or prosody in general, may be found occasional chapters, it is true, which have the heading, "Versification," but these are, in all instances, exceedingly meagre. They pretend to no analysis; they propose nothing like system; they make no attempt at even rule; every thing depends upon "authority." They are confined, in fact, to mere exemplification of the supposed varieties of English feet and English lines;—although in no work with which I am acquainted are these feet correctly given or these lines detailed in anything like their full extent. Yet what has been mentioned is all—if we except the occasional introduction of some pedagogue-ism, such as this, borrowed from the Greek Prosodies: "When a syllable is wanting, the verse is said to be catalectic; when the measure is exact, the line is acatalectic; when there is a redundant syllable it forms hypermeter." **Now whether a line be termed catalectic or acatalectic is, perhaps, a point of no vital** importance:—it is even possible that the student may be able to decide, promptly, when the *a* should be employed and when omitted, yet be incognizant, at the same time, of *all* that is worth knowing in regard to the structure of verse.

A leading defect in each of our treatises, (if treatises they can be called,) is the confining the subject to mere *Versification*, while *Verse* in general, with the understanding given to the term in the heading of this paper, is the real question at issue. Nor am I aware of even one of our Grammars which so much as properly defines the word versification itself. " Versification," says a work now before me, of which the accuracy is far more than usual—the "English Grammar" of Goold Brown—" Versification is the art of arranging words into lines of correspondent length, so as to produce harmony by the regular alternation of syllables differing in quantity." The commencement of this definition might apply, indeed, to the *art* of versification, but not versification itself. Versification is not the art of arranging, &c., but the actual arranging —a distinction too obvious to need comment. The error here is identical with one which has been too long permitted to disgrace the initial page of every one of our school grammars. I allude to the definitions of English Grammar itself. " English Grammar," it is said, " is the art of speaking and writing the English language correctly." This phraseology, or something essentially similar, is employed, I believe, by Bacon, Miller, Fisk, Greenleaf, Ingersoll, Kirkland, Cooper, Flint, Pue, Comly and many others. These gentlemen, it is presumed, adopted it without examination from Murray, who derived it from Lily, (whose work was " *quam solam Regia Majestas in omnibus scholis docendam præcipit*,") and who appropriated it without acknowledgment, but with some unimportant modification, from the Latin Grammar of Leoniceno. It may be shown, however, that this definition, so complacently received, is not, and cannot be, a proper definition of English Grammar. A definition is that which so describes its object as to distinguish it from all others:—it is no definition of any one thing if its terms are applicable to any one other. But if it be asked—" What is the design—the end—the aim of English

Grammar?" our obvious answer is, "The art of speaking and
writing the English language correctly:"—that is to say, we must
use the precise words employed as the definition of English Grammar itself. But the object to be obtained by any means is, assuredly, not the means. English Grammar and the end contemplated
by English Grammar, are two matters sufficiently distinct; nor
can the one be more reasonably regarded as the other than a fish-
ing-hook as a fish. The definition, therefore, which is applicable
in the latter instance, *cannot*, in the former, be true. Grammar
in general is the analysis of language; English Grammar of the
English.

But to return to Versification as defined in our extract above.
"It is the art," says the extract, "of arranging words into lines *of
correspondent length*." Not so:—a correspondence in the length of
lines is by no means essential. Pindaric odes are, surely, instances of versification, yet these compositions are noted for extreme
diversity in the length of their lines.

The arrangement is moreover said to be for the purpose of producing "*harmony* by the regular alternation," &c. But *harmony*
is not the sole aim—not even the principal one. In the construction of verse, *melody* should never be left out of view; yet this is
a point which all our Prosodies have most unaccountably forborne
to touch. Reasoned rules on this topic should form a portion of
all systems of rhythm.

"So as to produce harmony," says the definition, "by the *regular alternation*," &c. A *regular* alternation, as described, forms
no part of any principle of versification. The arrangement of
spondees and dactyls, for example, in the Greek hexameter, is an
arrangement which may be termed *at random*. At least it is
arbitrary. Without interference with the line as a whole, a dactyl
may be substituted for a spondee, or the converse, at any point
other than the ultimate and penultimate feet, of which the former
is always a spondee, the latter nearly always a dactyl. Here, it
is clear, we have no "*regular* alternation of syllables differing in
quantity."

"So as to produce harmony," proceeds the definition, "by the
regular alternation of *syllables differing in quantity*,"—in other
words by the alternation of long and short syllables; for in

rhythm all syllables are necessarily either short or long. But not only do I deny the necessity of any *regularity* in the succession of feet and, by consequence, of syllables, but dispute the essentiality of any *alternation*, regular or irregular, of syllables long and short. Our author, observe, is now engaged in a definition of versification in general, not of English versification in particular. But the Greek and Latin metres abound in the spondee and pyrrhic — the former consisting of two long syllables; the latter of two short; and there are innumerable instances of the immediate succession of many spondees and many pyrrhics.

Here is a passage from Silius Italicus:

> Fallis te mensas inter quod credis inermem
> Tot bellis quæsita viro, tot cædibus armat
> Majestas eterna ducem: si admoveris ora
> Cannas et Trebium ante oculos Trasymenaque busta,
> Et Pauli stare ingentem miraberis umbram.

Making the elisions demanded by the classic Prosodies, we should scan these Hexameters thus:

> Fāllĭs | tē mēn—sās ĭn | tēr qŭod | crēdĭs ĭn | ērmēm |
> Tōt bĕl—lĭs qŭæ | sītă vĭ | rō tŏt—cædĭbŭs | ārmăt |
> Mājĕs | tās ē | tērnă dŭ | cēm s'ăd | mōvĕrĭs | ōră |
> Cānnăs | ĕt Trēbĭ | ānt'ŏcŭ | lōs Trăsy | mĕnăquē | bŭstă |
> ĕt Pāu | lĭ stă | r'ĭngēn | tēm mĭ | răbĕrĭs | ŭmbrăm |

It will be seen that, in the first and last of these lines, we have only two short syllables in thirteen, with an uninterrupted succession of no less than *nine* long syllables. But how are we to reconcile all this with a definition of versification which describes it as "the art of arranging words into lines of correspondent length so as to produce harmony by the *regular alternation of syllables differing in quantity?*"

It may be urged, however, that our prosodist's *intention* was to speak of the English metres alone, and that, by omitting all mention of the spondee and pyrrhic, he has virtually avowed their exclusion from our rhythms. A grammarian is never excusable on the ground of good intentions. We demand from him, if from any one, rigorous precision of style. But grant the design.

Let us admit that our author, following the example of all authors on English Prosody, has, in defining versification at large, intended a definition merely of the English. All these prosodists, we will say, reject the spondee and pyrrhic. Still all admit the iambus, which consists of a short syllable followed by a long; the trochee, which is the converse of the iambus; the dactyl, formed of one long syllable followed by two short; and the anapæst—two short succeeded by a long. The spondee is improperly rejected, as I shall presently show. The pyrrhic is rightfully dismissed. Its existence in either ancient or modern rhythm is purely chimerical, and the insisting on so perplexing a nonentity as a foot of *two short* syllables, affords, perhaps, the best evidence of the gross irrationality and subservience to authority which characterize our Prosody. In the meantime the acknowledged dactyl and anapæst are enough to sustain my proposition about the " alternation," &c., without reference to feet which are assumed to exist in the Greek and Latin metres alone : for an anapæst and a dactyl may meet in the same line; when of course we shall have an uninterrupted succession of four short syllables. The meeting of these two feet, to be sure, is an accident not contemplated in the definition now discussed; for this definition, in demanding a "regular alternation of syllables differing in quantity," insists on a regular succession of similar *feet*. But here is an example :

Sing tŏ mĕ | Isăbĕlle.

This is the opening line of a little ballad now before me, which proceeds in the same rhythm—a peculiarly beautiful one. More than all this :—English lines are often well composed, entirely, of a regular succession of syllables *all of the same quantity* :—the first lines, for instance, of the following quatrain by Arthur C. Coxe :

March ! march ! march !
Making sounds as they tread,
Ho ! ho ! how they step,
Going down to the dead !

The line italicised is formed of three cæsuras. The cæsura, of which I have much to say hereafter, is rejected by the English

Prosodies and grossly misrepresented in the classic. It *is* a perfect foot—the most important in all verse—and consists of a single *long* syllable ; *but the length of this syllable varies.*

It has thus been made evident that there is *not one* point of the definition in question which does not involve an error. And for anything more satisfactory or more intelligible we shall look in vain to any published treatise on the topic.

So general and so total a failure can be referred only to radical misconception. In fact the English Prosodists have blindly followed the pedants. These latter, like *les moutons de Panurge*, have been occupied in incessant tumbling into ditches, for the excellent reason that their leaders have so tumbled before. The Iliad, being taken as a starting point, was made to stand in stead of Nature and common sense. Upon this poem, in place of facts and deduction from fact, or from natural law, were built systems of feet, metres, rhythms, rules,—rules that contradict each other every five minutes, and for nearly all of which there may be found twice as many exceptions as examples. If any one has a fancy to be thoroughly confounded—to see how far the infatuation of what is termed "classical scholarship" can lead a book-worm in the manufacture of darkness out of sunshine, let him turn over, for a few moments, any of the German Greek Prosodies. The only thing clearly made out in them is a very magnificent contempt for Liebnitz's principle of " a sufficient reason."

To divert attention from the real matter in hand by any farther reference to these works, is unnecessary, and would be weak. I cannot call to mind, at this moment, one essential particular of information that is to be gleaned from them ; and I will drop them here with merely this one observation : that, employing from among the numerous " *ancient*" feet the spondee, the trochee, the iambus, the anapaest, the dactyl, and the caesura alone, I will engage to scan *correctly* any of the Horatian rhythms, or any true rhythm that human ingenuity can conceive. And this excess of chimerical feet is, perhaps, the very beast of the scholastic supererogations. *Ex uno disce omnia.* The fact is that *Quantity* is a point in whose investigation the lumber of mere learning may be dispensed with, if ever in any. Its appreciation is universal. It appertains to no region, nor race, nor æra in especial. To melody and to harmony the Greeks hearkened with ears precisely similar to those which we employ for similar purposes at present; and I should not be condemned for heresy in asserting that a pendulum at Athens would have vibrated much after the same fashion as does a pendulum in the city of Penn.

Verse originates in the human enjoyment of equality, fitness. To this enjoyment, also, all the moods of verse—rhythm, metre, stanza, rhyme, alliteration, the *refrain*, and other analogous effects —are to be referred. As there are some readers who habitually confound rhythm and metre, it may be as well here to say that the former concerns the *character* of feet (that is, the arrangements of syllables) while the latter has to do with the *number* of these feet. Thus by "a dactylic *rhythm*" we express a sequence of dactyls. By "a dactylic hexa*meter*" we imply a line or measure consisting of six of these dactyls.

To return to *equality*. Its idea embraces those of similarity, proportion, identity, repetition, and adaptation or fitness. It might not be very difficult to go even behind the idea of equality, and show both how and why it is that the human nature takes pleasure in it, but such an investigation would, for any purpose now in view, be supererogatory. It is sufficient that the *fact* is undeniable—the fact that man derives enjoyment from his perception of equality. Let us examine a crystal. We are at once interested by the equality between the sides and between the angles of one of its faces: the equality of the sides pleases us; that of the angles doubles the pleasure. On bringing to view a second face in all respects similar to the first, this pleasure seems to be squared; on bringing to view a third it appears to be cubed, and so on. I have no doubt, indeed, that the delight experienced, if measurable, would be found to have exact mathematical relations such as I suggest; that is to say, as far as a certain point, beyond which there would be a decrease in similar relations.

The perception of pleasure in the equality of *sounds* is the principle of *Music*. Unpractised ears can appreciate only simple equalities, such as are found in ballad airs. While comparing one simple sound with another they are too much occupied to be capable of comparing the equality subsisting between these two simple sounds, taken conjointly, and two other similar simple sounds taken conjointly.   Practised ears, on the other hand, appreciate both equalities at the same instant—although it is absurd to suppose that both are *heard* at the same instant.   One is heard and appreciated from itself: the other is heard by the memory; and the instant glides into and is confounded with the secondary, appreciation.   Highly cultivated musical taste in this manner enjoys not only these double equalities, all appreciated at once, but takes pleasurable cognizance, through memory, of equalities the members of which occur at intervals so great that the uncultivated taste loses them altogether.   That this latter can properly estimate or decide on the merits of what is called scientific music, is of course impossible.   But scientific music has no claim to intrinsic excellence—it is fit for scientific ears alone.   In its excess it is the triumph of the *physique* over the *morale* of music.   The sentiment is overwhelmed by the sense.   On the whole, the advocates of the simpler melody and harmony have infinitely the best of the argument;—although there has been very little of real argument on the subject.

In *verse*, which cannot be better designated than as an inferior or less capable Music, there is, happily, little chance for complexity. Its rigidly simple character not even Science—not even Pedantry can greatly pervert.

The rudiment of verse may, possibly, be found in the *spondee*. The very germ of a thought seeking satisfaction in equality of sound, would result in the construction of words of two syllables, equally accented.   In corroboration of this idea we find that spondees most abound in the most ancient tongues.   The second step we can easily suppose to be the comparison, that is to say, the collocation, of two spondees—of two words composed each of a spondee.   The third step would be the juxta-position of three of these words.   By this time the perception of monotone would induce farther consideration : and thus arises what Leigh Hunt so flounders in discussing under the title of "The *Principle* of Variety in Uniformity."   Of course there is no principle in the case—nor in maintaining it.   The "Uniformity" is the principle :—the "Variety" is but the principle's natural safeguard from self-destruction by excess of self.   "Uniformity," besides, is the very worst word that could have been chosen for the expression of the *general* idea at which it aims.

The perception of monotone having given rise to an attempt as its relief, the first thought in this new direction would be that of collating two or more words formed each of two syllables differently accented (that is to say, short and long) but having the same order in each word :—in other terms, of collating two or more iambuses, or two or more trochees. And here let me pause to assert that more pitiable nonsense has been written on the topic of *long* and *short* syllables than on any other subject under the sun. In general, a syllable is long or short, just as it is difficult or easy of enunciation. The *natural* long syllables are those encumbered—the *natural* short syllables are those *unencumbered*, with consonants; all the rest is mere artificiality and jargon. The Latin Prosodies have a rule that " a vowel before two consonants is long." This rule is deduced from " authority"—that is, from the observation that vowels so circumstanced, in the ancient poems, are always in syllables long by the laws of scansion. The philosophy of the rule is untouched, and lies simply in the physical difficulty of giving voice to such syllables—of performing the lingual evolutions necessary for their utterance. Of course, it is not the *vowel* that is long, (although the rule says so) but the syllable of which the vowel is a part. It will be seen that the length of a syllable, depending on the facility or difficulty of its enunciation, must have great variation in various syllables ; but for the purposes of verse we suppose a long syllable equal to two short ones :—and the natural deviation from this relativeness we correct in perusal. The more closely our long syllables approach this relation with our short ones, the better, *ceteris paribus*, will be our verse : but if the relation does not exist of itself, we force it by emphasis, which can, of course, make any syllable as long as desired ;—or, by an effort we can pronounce with unnatural brevity a syllable that is naturally too long. *Accented* syllables are of course always long—but, where *unencumbered* with consonants, must be classed among the *unnatural-y* long. Mere custom has declared that we shall accent them—that is to say, dwell upon them ; but no inevitable lingual difficulty forces us to do so. In fine, every long syllable must of its own accord occupy in its utterance, or must be *made* to occupy, precisely the time demanded for two short ones. The only exception to this rule is found in the cæsura—of which more anon.

The success of the experiment with the trochees or iambuses (the one would have suggested the other) must have led to a trial of dactyls or anapæsts—natural dactyls or anapæsts—dactylic or anapæstic *words*. And now some degree of complexity has been attained. There is an appreciation, first, of the equality between the several dactyls, or anapæsts, and, secondly, of that between the long syllable and the two short conjointly. But here it may be said, that step after step would have been taken, in continuation of this routine, until all the feet of the Greek Prosodies became exhausted. Not so:—these remaining feet have no existence except in the brains of the scholiasts. It is needless to imagine men inventing these things, and folly to explain how and why they invented them, until it shall be first shown that they are actually invented. All other "feet" than those which I have specified, are, if not impossible at first view, merely combinations of the specified; and, although this assertion is rigidly true, I will, to avoid misunderstanding, put it in a somewhat different shape. I will say, then, that at present I am aware of no *rhythm*—nor do I believe that any one can be constructed—which, in its last analysis, will not be found to consist altogether of the feet I have mentioned, either existing in their individual and obvious condition, or interwoven with each other in accordance with simple natural laws which I will endeavor to point out hereafter.

We have now gone so far as to suppose men constructing indefinite sequences of spondaic, iambic, trochaic, dactylic, or anapæstic words. In *extending* these sequences, they would be again arrested by the sense of monotone. A succession of spondees would *immediately* have displeased; one of iambuses or of trochees, on account of the variety included within the foot itself, would have taken longer to displease; one of dactyls or anapæsts, still longer: but even the last, if extended very far, must have become wearisome. The idea, first, of curtailing, and, secondly, of defining the length of, a sequence, would thus at once have arisen. Here then is the *line*, or verse proper.* The principle of equality being constantly at the bottom of the whole process, lines would naturally be made, in the first instance, equal in the number of their feet; in the second instance, there would be variation in the mere number; one line would be twice as long as another; then one would be some less obvious multiple of another; then still less obvious proportions would be adopted:—nevertheless there would be *pro*·*portion*, that is to say, a phase of equality, still.

Lines being once introduced, the necessity of distinctly defining these lines *to the ear*, (as yet written verse does not exist,) would lead to a scrutiny of their capabilities *at their terminations :*—and now would spring up the idea of equality in sound between the final syllables—in other words, of *rhyme.* First, it would be used only in the iambic, anapæstic, and spondaic rhythms, (granting that the latter had not been thrown aside, long since, on account of its tameness ;) because in these rhythms, the concluding syllable being long, could best sustain the necessary protraction of the voice. No great while could elapse, however, before the effect, found pleasant as well as useful, would be applied to the two remaining rhythms. But as the chief force of rhyme must lie in the accented syllable, the attempt to create rhyme at all in these two remaining rhythms, the trochaic and dactylic, would necessarily result in double and triple rhymes, such as *beauty* with *duty* (trochaic,) and *beautiful* with *dutiful* (dactylic.)

It must be observed, that in suggesting these processes, I assign them no date; nor do I even insist upon their order. Rhyme is supposed to be of modern origin, and were this proved, my positions remain untouched. I may say, however, in passing, that several instances of rhyme occur in the the "Clouds" of Aristophanes, and that the Roman poets occasionally employ it. There is an effective species of ancient rhyming which has never descend-

* Verse, from the Latin *vertere*, to turn, is so called on account of the turning or re-commencement of the series of feet. Thus a verse, strictly speaking, is a line. In this sense, however, I have preferred using the latter word alone ; employing the former in the general acceptation given it in the heading of this paper.

ed to the moderns: that in which the ultimate and penultimate syllables rhyme with each other.   For example :

Parturiunt montes et nascitur ridiculus mus.

And again :

Litoreis ingens inventa sub ilicibus sus.

The terminations of Hebrew verse, (as far as understood,) show no signs of rhyme; but what thinking person can doubt that it did actually exist?   That men have so obstinately and blindly insisted, *in general*, even up to the present day, in confining rhyme to the *ends* of lines, when its effect is even better applicable elsewhere, intimates, in my opinion, the sense of some *necessity* in the connexion of the end with the rhyme—hints that the origin of rhyme lay in a necessity which connected it with the end—shows that neither mere accident nor mere fancy gave rise to the connexion—points, in a word, at the very necessity which I have suggested, (that of some mode of defining lines *to the ear*,) as the true origin of rhyme.   Admit this, and we throw the origin far back in the night of Time—beyond the origin of written verse.

But, to resume.   The amount of complexity I have now supposed to be attained, is very considerable.   Various systems of equalization are appreciated at once (or nearly so) in their respective values and in the value of each system with reference to all the others.   As our present *ultimatum* of complexity, we have arrived at triple-rhymed, natural-dactylic lines, existing proportionally as well as equally with regard to other triple-rhymed, natural-dactylic lines.   For example :

Virginal Lilian, rigidly, humblily dutiful;
  Saintlily, lowlily,
  Thrillingly, holily
Beautiful !

Here we appreciate, first, the absolute equality between the long syllable of each dactyl and the two short conjointly; secondly, the absolute equality between each dactyl and any other dactyl—in other words, among all the dactyls; thirdly, the absolute equality between the two middle lines; fourthly, the absolute equality between the first line and the three others taken conjointly; fifthly, the absolute equality between the last two syllables of the respective words "dutiful" and "beautiful;" sixthly, the absolute equality between the two last syllables of the respective words "lowlily" and "holily;" seventhly, the proximate equality between the first syllable of "dutiful" and the first syllable of "beautiful;" eighthly, the proximate equality between the first syllable of "lowlily" and that of "holily;" ninthly, the proportional equality (that of five to one,) between the first line and each of its members, the dactyls; tenthly, the proportional equality (that of two to one,) between each of the middle lines and its members, the dactyls; eleventhly, the proportional equality between the first line and each of the two middle—that of five to two; twelfthly, the proportional equality between the first line and the last—that of five to one; thirteenthly, the proportional equality between each of the middle lines and the last—that of two to one; lastly, the proportional equality, as concerns number, between all the lines, taken collectively and any individual line—that of four to one.

The consideration of this last equality would give birth immediately to the idea of *stanza**—that is to say, the insulation of lines into equal or obviously proportional masses. In its primitive (which was also its best) form, the stanza would most probably have had absolute unity. In other words, the removal of any one of its lines would have rendered it imperfect; as in the case above, where, if the last line, for example, be taken away, there is left no rhyme to the "dutiful" of the first. Modern stanza is excessively loose—and where so, ineffective, as a matter of course.

Now, although in the deliberate written statement which I have here given of these various systems of equalities, there seems to be an infinity of complexity—so much that it is hard to conceive the mind taking cognizance of them all in the brief period occupied by the perusal or recital of the stanza—yet the difficulty is in fact apparent only when we will it to become so. Any one fond of mental experiment may satisfy himself, by trial, that, in listening to the lines, he does actually (although with a seeming unconsciousness, on account of the rapid evolutions of sensation,) recog-

* A stanza is often vulgarly, and with gross impropriety, called a *verse*.

nise and instantaneously appreciate (more or less intensely as his ear is cultivated,) each and all of the equalizations detailed. The pleasure received, or receivable, has very much such progressive increase, and in very nearly such mathematical relations, as those which I have suggested in the case of the crystal.

It will be observed that I speak of merely a proximate equality between the first syllable of "dutiful" and that of "beautiful;" and it may be asked why we cannot imagine the earliest rhymes to have had absolute instead of proximate equality of sound. But absolute equality would have involved the use of identical words; and it is the duplicate sameness or monotony—that of sense as well as that of sound—which would have caused these rhymes to be rejected in the very first instance.

The narrowness of the limits within which verse composed of natural feet alone, must necessarily have been confined, would have led, after a *very* brief interval, to the trial and immediate adoption of artificial feet—that is to say, of feet *not* constituted each of a single word, but two or even three words; or of parts of words. These feet would be intermingled with natural ones. For example:

ă brĕath | căn māke | thĕm ăs | ă brĕath | hăs māde.

This is an iambic line in which each iambus is formed of two words. Again:

Thĕ ūn | īmă | gīnă | blĕ mīght | ŏf Jōve.

This is an iambic line in which the first foot is formed of a word and a part of a word; the second and third, of parts taken from the body or interior of a word; the fourth, of a part and a whole; the fifth, of two complete words. There are no *natural* feet in either lines. Again:

ɯ
Căn ĭt bĕ | fāncĭĕd thăt | Dēĭty | ĕvĕr vĭn | dĭctīvely
Māde ĭn hĭs | īmăge ă | mānnĭkĭn | mĕrely tŏ | māddĕn ĭt !

These are two dactylic lines in which we find natural feet, ("Deity," "mannikin;") feet composed of two words ("fancied that," "image a," "merely to," "madden it;") feet composed of three words ("can it be," "made in his;") a foot composed of a part of a-word ("dictively;") and a foot composed of a word and a part of a word ("ever vin.")

And now, in our supposititious progress, we have gone so far as to exhaust all the *essentialities* of verse. What follows may, strictly speaking, be regarded as embellishment merely—but even in this embellishment, the rudimental sense of *equality* would have been the never-ceasing impulse. It would, for example, be simply in seeking farther administration to this sense that men would come, in time, to think of the *refrain*, or burden, where, at the closes of the several stanzas of a poem, one word or phrase is *repeated ;* and of alliteration, in whose simplest form a consonant is *repeated* in the commencements of various words. This effect would be extended so as to embrace repetitions both of vowels and of consonants, in the bodies as well as in the beginnings of words; and, at a later period, would be made to infringe on the province of rhyme, by the introduction of general similarity of sound between whole feet occurring in the body of a line :—all of which modifications I have exemplified in the line above,

*M*ade in his image a *mannikin* merely to *madden it.*

Farther cultivation would improve also the *refrain* by relieving its monotone in slightly varying the phrase at each repetition, or, (as I have attempted to do in "The Raven,") in retaining the phrase and varying its application—although this latter point is not strictly a rhythmical effect *alone.* Finally, poets when fairly wearied with following precedent—following it the more closely the less they perceived it in company with Reason—would adventure so far as to indulge in positive rhyme at other points than the ends of lines. First, they would put it in the middle of the line ; then at some point where the multiple would be less obvious; then, alarmed at their own audacity, they would undo all their work by cutting these lines in two. And here is the fruitful source of the infinity of "short metre," by which modern poetry, if not distinguished, is at least disgraced. It would require a high degree, indeed, both of cultivation and of courage, on the part of any versifier, to enable him to place his rhymes—and let them remain—at unquestionably their best position, that of unusual and *unanticipated* intervals.

On account of the stupidity of some people, or, (if talent be a more respectable word,) on account of their talent for misconception—I think it necessary to add here, first, that I believe the " processes" above detailed to be nearly if not accurately those which *did* occur in the gradual creation of what we now call verse; secondly, that, although I so believe, I yet urge neither the assumed fact nor my belief in it, as a part of the true propositions of this paper; thirdly, that in regard to the aim of this paper, it is of no consequence whether these processes did occur either in the order I have assigned them, or at all; my design being simply, in presenting a general type of what such processes *might* have been and *must* have resembled, to help *them*, the "some people," to an easy understanding of what I have farther to say on the topic of Verse.

There is one point which, in my summary of the processes, I have purposely forborne to touch; because this point, being the most important of all, on account of the immensity of error usually involved in its consideration, would have led me into a series of detail inconsistent with the object of a summary.

Every reader of verse must have observed how seldom it happens that even any one line proceeds uniformly with a succession, such as I have supposed, of absolutely equal feet; that is to say, with a succession of iambuses only, or of trochees only, or of dactyls only, or of anapæsts only, or of spondees only. Even in the most musical lines we find the succession interrupted. The iambic pentameters of Pope, for example, will be found on examination, frequently varied by trochees in the beginning, or by (what seem to be) anapæsts in the body, of the line.

ŏh thŏu | whătĕ | vĕr tī | tlĕ please | thīne ĕar |
Dĕan Drā | pĭer Bĭck | ĕr-stăff | ŏr Gŭl | ĭvĕr
Whĕthĕr | thŏu choŏse | Cĕrvān | tĕs' sĕ | rĭŏŭs āir |
ŏr laŭgh | ănd shăke | ĭn Răb | ĕlais' ĕā | sy chair. |

Were any one weak enough to refer to the Prosodies for the solution of the difficulty here, he would find it *solved* as usual by a *rule*, stating the fact, (or what it, the rule, supposes to be the fact,) but without the slightest attempt at the *rationale*. "By a *synæresis* of the two short syllables," say the books, " an anapæst may sometimes be employed for an iambus, or a dactyl for a trochee. . . . In the beginning of a line a trochee is often used for an iambus."

Blending is the plain English for *synæresis*—but there should be *no* blending; neither is an anapæst *ever* employed for an iambus, or a dactyl for a trochee. These feet differ in time ; and *no* feet so differing can ever be legitimately used in the same line. An anapæst is equal to four short syllables—an iambus only to three. Dactyls and trochees hold the same relation. The principle of *equality*, in verse, admits, it is true, of variation at certain points, for the relief of monotone, as I have already shown, but the point of *time* is that point which, being the rudimental one, must never be tampered with at all.

To explain :—In farther efforts for the relief of monotone than those to which I have alluded in the summary, men soon came to see that there was no absolute necessity for adhering to the precise number of syllables, provided the time required for the whole foot was preserved inviolate. They saw, for instance, that in such a line as

ŏr lăugh | ănd shăke | ĭn Răb | ĕlăis' ĕa | sy chăir, |

the equalization of the three syllables *elais ea* with the two syllables composing any of the other feet, could be readily effected by pronouncing the two syllables *elais* in double quick time. By pronouncing each of the syllables *e* and *lais* twice as rapidly as the syllable *sy*, or the syllable *in*, or any other short syllable, they could bring the two of them, taken together, to the length, that is to say to the time, of any one short syllable. This consideration enabled them to affect the agreeable variation of three syllables in place of the uniform two. And variation was the object—variation to the ear. What sense is there, then, in supposing this object rendered null by the *blending* of the two syllables so as to render them, in absolute effect, one ? Of course, there must be *no* blending. Each syllable must be pronounced as distinctly as possible, (or the variation is lost,) but with twice the rapidity in which the ordinary short syllable is enunciated. That the syllables *elais aa* do not compose an *anapæst* is evident, and the signs (ăăă) of their accentuation are erroneous. The foot might be written thus (ᵥᵥᵥ) the inverted crescents expressing double quick time ; and might be called a bastard iambus.

Here is a trochaic line :

Sēe thĕ dĕlĭcăte | fŏotĕd | rāin-deĕr. |

The prosodies—that is to say the most considerate of them— would here decide that " *delicate* " is a dactyl used in place of a trochee, and would refer to what they call their " rule," for justification. Others, varying the stupidity, would insist upon a Procrustean adjustment thus (del'cate)—an adjustment recommended to all such words as *silvery, murmuring,* etc., which, it is said, should be not only pronounced, but written *silv'ry, murm'ring,* and so on, whenever they find themselves in trochaic predicament. I have only to say that " delicate," when circumstanced as above, is neither a dactyl nor a dactyl's equivalent ; that I would suggest for it this (ᵥᵥᵥ) accentuation ; that I think it as well to call it a bastard trochee ; and that all words, at all events, should be written and pronounced *in full*, and as nearly as possible as nature intended them.

About eleven years ago, there appeared in " The American Monthly Magazine," (then edited, I believe, by Mess. Hoffman and Benjamin,) a review of Mr. Willis' Poems ; the critic putting forth his strength, or his weakness, in an endeavor to show that the poet was either absurdly affected, or grossly ignorant of the laws of verse ; the accusation being based altogether on the fact that Mr. W. made occasional use of this very word " delicate," and other similar words, in " the Heroic measure which every one knew consisted of feet of two syllables." Mr. W. has often, for example, such lines as

That binds him to a woman's *delicate* love—
In the gay sunshine, *reverent* in the storm—
With its *invisible* fingers my loose hair.

Here, of course, the feet *licate love, verent in,* and *sible fin,* are bastard iambuses ; are *not* anapæsts ; and are *not* improperly used.

Their employment, on the contrary, by Mr. Willis, is but one of the innumerable instances he has given of keen sensibility in all those matters of taste which may be classed under the general head of *fanciful embellishment.*

It is also about eleven years ago, if I am not mistaken, since Mr. Horne, (of England,) the author of "Orion," one of the noblest epics in any language, thought it necessary to preface his "Chaucer Modernized" by a very long and evidently a very elaborate essay, of which the greater portion was occupied in a discussion of the seemingly anomalous foot of which we have been speaking. Mr. Horne upholds Chaucer in its frequent use ; maintains his superiority, *on account* of his so frequently using it, over all English versifiers ; and, indignantly repelling the common idea of those who make verse on their fingers—that the superfluous syllable is a roughness and an error—very chivalrously makes battle for it as "a grace." That a grace it *is*, there can be no doubt ; and what I complain of is, that the author of the most happily versified long poem in existence, should have been under the necessity of discussing this grace merely *as* a grace, through forty or fifty vague pages, solely because of his inability to show *how* and *why* it is a grace—by which showing the question would have been settled in an instant.

About the trochee used for an iambus, as we see in the beginning of the line,

> Whĕthĕr thou choose Cervantes' serious air,

there is little that need be said. It brings me to the general proposition that, in all rhythms, the prevalent or distinctive feet may be varied at will, and nearly at random, by the *occasional* introduction of equivalent feet—that is to say, feet the sum of whose syllabic times is equal to the sum of the syllabic times of the distinctive feet. Thus the trochee, *whĕthĕr*, is equal, in the sum of the times of its syllables, to the iambus, *thŏu choōse*, in the sum of the times of *its* syllables ; each foot being, in time, equal to three short syllables. Good versifiers who happen to be, also, good poets, contrive to relieve the monotone of a series of feet, by the use of equivalent feet only at rare intervals, and at such points of their subject as seem in accordance with the *startling* character of the variation. Nothing of this care is seen in the line quoted above—although Pope has some fine instances of the duplicate effect. Where vehemence is to be strongly expressed, I am not sure that we should be wrong in venturing on *two consecutive* equivalent feet—although I cannot say that I have ever known the adventure made, except in the following passage, which occurs in " Al Aaraaf," a boyish poem, written by myself when a boy. I am referring to the sudden and rapid advent of a star.

> Dim was its little disk, and angel eyes
> Alone could see the phantom in the skies,
> Whĕn fĭrst thĕ phantŏm's cŏurse wăs fŏund tŏ bĕ
> *Hĕadlŏng hĭthĕrward o'er the starry sea.*

In the " general proposition" above, I speak of the *occasional* introduction of equivalent feet. It sometimes happens that unskilful versifiers, without knowing what they do, or why they do it, introduce so many " variations" as to exceed in number the " distinctive" feet ; when the ear becomes at once balked by the *bouleversement* of the rhythm. Too many trochees, for example, inserted in an iambic rhythm, would convert the latter to a trochaic. I may note here, that, in all cases, the rhythm designed should be commenced and continued, *without* variation, until the ear has had full time to comprehend what *is* the rhythm. In violation of a rule so obviously founded in common sense, many even of our best poets, do not scruple to begin an iambic rhythm with a trochee, or the converse ; or a dactylic with an anapæst, or the converse ; and so on.

A somewhat less objectionable error, although still a decided one, is that of commencing a rhythm, not with a different equivalent foot, but with a " bastard" foot of the rhythm intended. For example :

> Mănu ă | thŏught wĭll | cŏme tŏ | mĕmŏry. |

Here *many a* is what I have explained to be a bastard trochee, and to be understood should be accented with inverted crescents. It is objectionable solely on account of its position as the *opening* foot of a trochaic rhythm. *Memory*, similarly accented, is also a bastard trochee, but unobjectionable, although by no means demanded.

The farther illustration of this point will enable me to take an important step.

One of our finest poets, Mr. Christopher Pease Cranch, begins a very beautiful poem thus :

> Many are the thoughts that come to me
> In my lonely musing ;
> And they drift so strange and swift
> There's no time for choosing
> Which to follow ; for to leave
> Any, seems a losing.

" A losing" to Mr. Cranch, of course—but this *en passant*. It will be seen here that the intention is trochaic ;—although we do *not* see this intention by the opening foot, as we should do—or even by the opening line. Reading the whole stanza, however, we perceive the trochaic rhythm as the general design, and so, after some reflection, we divide the first line thus :

> Many are the | thŏughts thăt | cŏme tŏ | mă. |

Thus scanned, the line will seem musical. It *is*—highly so. And it is because there is no end to instances of just such lines of apparently incomprehensible music, that Coleridge thought proper to invent his nonsensical *system* of what he calls " scanning by accents"—as if " scanning by accents" were anything more than a phrase. Whenever " Christabel" is really *not rough*, it can be as readily scanned by the true *laws* (not the supposititious *rules*) of verse, as can the simplest pentameter of Pope ; and where it *is* rough (*passim*) these same laws will enable any one of common sense to show *why* it is rough and to point out, instantaneously, the remedy for the roughness.

A reads and re-reads a certain line, and pronounces it false in rhythm—unmusical. *B*, however, reads it *to A*, and *A* is at once struck with the perfection of the rhythm, and wonders at his dulness in not " catching" it before. Henceforward he admits the line to be musical. *B*, triumphant, asserts that, to be sure, the line is musical—for ' is the work of Coleridge—and that it is *A* who is *not* ; the fault being in *A's* false reading. Now here *A* is right and *B* wrong. *That* rhythm is erroneous, (at some point or other more or less obvious,) which *any* ordinary reader *can*, without design, read improperly. It is the business of the poet so to construct his line that the intention *must* be caught *at once*. Even when these men have precisely the same understanding of a sentence, they differ and often widely, in their modes of enunciating it. Any one who has taken the trouble to examine the topic of emphasis, (by which I here mean not *accent* of particular syllables, but the dwelling on entire words,) must have seen that men emphasize in the most singularly arbitrary manner. There are certain large classes of people, for example, who persist in emphasizing their monosyllables. Little uniformity of emphasis prevails; because the thing itself—the idea, emphasis—is referable to no natural—at least, to no well comprehended and therefore uniform law. Beyond a very narrow and vague limit, the whole matter is conventionality. And if we differ in emphasis even when we agree in comprehension, how much more so in the former when in the latter too! Apart, however, from the consideration of natural disagreement, is it not clear that, by tripping here and mouthing there, any sequence of words may be twisted into any species of rhythm? But are we thence to deduce that all sequences of words are rhythmical in a rational understanding of the term?—for this is the deduction, precisely to which the *reductio ad absurdum* will, in the end, bring all the propositions of Coleridge. Out of a hundred readers of "Christabel," fifty will be able to make nothing of its rhythm, while forty-nine of the remaining fifty will, with some ado, fancy they comprehend it, after the fourth or fifth perusal. The one out of the whole hundred who shall both comprehend and admire it at first sight —must be an unaccountably clever person—and I am by far too modest to assume, for a moment, that that very clever person is myself.

In illustration of what is here advanced I cannot do better than quote a poem :

> Pease porridge hot—pease porridge cold—
> Pease porridge   the pot—nine days old.

Now those of my readers who have never *heard* this poem pronounced according to the nursery conventionality, will find its rhythm as obscure as an explanatory note ; while those who *have* heard it, will divide it thus, declare it musical, and wonder how there can be any doubt about it.

Pease | porridge | hot | pease | porridge | cold |
Pease | porridge | in the | pot | nine | days | old. |

The chief thing in the way of this species of rhythm, is the necessity which it imposes upon the poet of travelling in constant company with his compositions, so as to be ready at a moment's notice, to avail himself of a well understood poetical license—that of reading aloud one's own doggrel.

In Mr. Cranch's line,

Many are the | thoughts that | come to | me, |

the general error of which I speak is, of course, very partially exemplified, and the purpose for which, chiefly, I cite it, lies yet further on in our topic.

The two divisions (*thoughts that*) and (*come to*) are ordinary trochees. Of the last division (*me*) we will talk hereafter. The first division (many are the) would be thus accented by the Greek Prosodies (mány ăre thĕ) and would be called by them ασστρολογος. The Latin books would style the foot *Pæon Primus*, and both Greek and Latin would swear that it was composed of a trochee and what they term a pyrrhic—that is to say, a foot of two *short* syllables—a thing that *cannot be*, as I shall presently show.

But now, there is an obvious difficulty. The *astrologos*, according to the Prosodies' own showing, is equal to *five* short syllables, and the trochee to *three*—yet, in the line quoted, these two feet are equal. They occupy *precisely* the same time. In fact, the whole music of the line depends upon their being *made* to occupy the same time. The Prosodies then, have demonstrated what all mathematicians have stupidly failed in demonstrating—that three and five are one and the same thing.

After what I have already said, however, about the bastard trochee and the bastard iambus, no one can have any trouble in understanding that *many are the* is of similar character. It is merely a bolder variation than usual from the routine of trochees, and introduces to the bastard trochee one additional syllable. But this syllable is not *short*. That is, it is not short in the sense of "*short*" as applied to the final syllable of the ordinary trochee, where the word means merely *the half of long*.

In this case, (that of the additional syllable) "short," if used at all, must be used in the sense of *the sixth of long*. And all the three final syllables can be called *short* only with the same understanding of the term. The three together are equal only to the one short syllable (whose place they supply) of the ordinary trochee. It follows that there is no sense in thus (˘) accenting these syllables. We must devise for them some new character which shall denote the sixth of long. Let it be (c)— the crescent placed with the curve to the left. The whole foot (many are the) might be called a *quick trochee*.

We come now to the final division (*me*) of Mr. Cranch's line. It is clear that this foot, short as it appears, is fully equal in time to each of the preceding. It is in fact the cæsura—the foot which, in the beginning of this paper, I called the most important in all verse. Its chief office is that of pause or termination; and here —at the end of a line— its use is easy, because there is no danger of misapprehending its value. We pause on it, by a seeming necessity, just so long as it has taken us to pronounce the preceding feet, whether iambuses, trochees, dactyls, or anapæsts. It is thus a *variable foot*, and, with some care, may be well introduced into the body of a line, as in a little poem of great beauty by Mrs. Welby :

I have | a lit | tle step | son | of on | ly three | years old. |

Here we dwell on the cæsura, *son*, just as long as it requires us to pronounce either of the preceding or succeeding iambuses. Its value, therefore, in this line, is that of three short syllables. In the following dactylic line its value is that of four short syllables.

Pale as a | lily was | Emily | Gray.

I have accented the cæsura with a (——) by way of expressing this variability of value.

I observed, just now that there could be no such foot as one

of two short syllables. What we start from in the very beginning of all idea on the topic of verse, is quantity, *length*. Thus
when we enunciate an independent syllable it is long, as a matter
of course. If we enunciate two, dwelling on both equally, we
express equality in the enumeration, or length, and have a right
to call them two long syllables. If we dwell on one more than
the other, we have also a right to call one short, because it is short
in relation to the other. But if we dwell on both equally and
with a tripping voice, saying to ourselves here are two short
syllables, the query might well be asked of us—"in relation to
what are they short?" Shortness is but the negation of length.
To say, then, that two syllables, placed independently of any
other syllable, are short, is merely to say that they have no positive length, or enunciation—in other words that they are no syllables—that they do not exist at all. And if, persisting, we add
anything about their equality, we are merely floundering in the
idea of an identical equation, where, x being equal to x, nothing
is shown to be equal to zero. In a word, we can form no conception of a pyrrhic as of an independent foot. It is a mere chimera
bred in the mad fancy of a pedant.

From what I have said about the equalization of the several
feet of a *line*, it must not be deduced that any *necessity* for equality in time exists between the rhythm of *several* lines. A poem,
or even a stanza, may begin with iambuses, in the first line, and
proceed with anapæsts in the second, or even with the less accor-
dant dactyls, as in the opening of quite a pretty specimen of
verse by Miss Mary A. S. Aldrich :

The wa | ter li | ly sleeps | in pride |
Down in thĕ | depths ŏf thĕ | azŭre | lăke. |

Here *azure* is a spondee, equivalent to a dactyl ; *lake* a cæsura.

I shall now best proceed in quoting the initial lines of Byron's
" Bride of Abydos :"

Know ye the land where the cypress and myrtle
   Are emblems of deeds that are done in their clime—
Where the rage of the vulture, the love of the turtle
   Now melt into softness, now madden to crime !
Know ye the land of the cedar and vine,

> Where the flowers ever blossom, the beams ever shine,
> And the light wings of Zephyr, oppressed with perfume,
> Wax faint o'er the gardens of Gul in their bloom!
> Where the citron and olive are fairest of fruit
> And the voice of the nightingale never is mute—
> Where the virgins are soft as the roses they twine,
> And all save the spirit of man is divine!
> 'Tis the land of the East—'tis the clime of the Sun—
> Can he smile on such deeds as his children have done?
> Oh, wild as the accents of lovers' farewell
> Are the hearts that they bear and the tales that they tell.

Now the flow of these lines, (as times go,) is very sweet and musical. They have been often admired, and justly—as times go—that is to say, it is a rare thing to find better versification of its kind. And where verse is pleasant to the ear, it is silly to find fault with it because it refuses to be scanned. Yet I have heard men, professing to be scholars, who made no scruple of abusing these lines of Byron's on the ground that they were musical in spite of *all law*. Other gentlemen, *not* scholars, abused "all law" for the same reason:—and it occurred neither to the one party nor to the other that the law about which they were disputing might possibly be no law at all—an ass of a law in the skin of a lion.

The Grammars said something about dactylic lines, and it was easily seen that *these* lines were at least meant for dactylic. The first one was, therefore, thus divided:

> Knŏw yĕ thĕ | lănd whĕre thĕ | cyprĕss ănd | myrtlĕ |

The concluding foot was a mystery; but the Prosodies said something about the dactylic "measure" calling now and then for a double rhyme; and the court of inquiry were content to rest in the double rhyme, without exactly perceiving what a double rhyme had to do with the question of an irregular foot. Quitting the first line, the second was thus scanned:

> Ăre ĕmblĕms | ŏf dĕĕds thăt | ăre dŏne ĭn | thĕir clĭme. |

It was immediately seen, however, that *this* would not do:—it was at war with the whole emphasis of the reading. It could not be supposed that Byron, or any one in his senses, intended to place stress upon such monosyllables as "are," "of," and "their," nor could "their clime," collated with "to crime," in the corresponding line below, be fairly twisted into anything like a "double rhyme," so as to bring everything within the category of the Grammars. But farther these Grammars spoke not. The inquirers, therefore, in spite of their sense of harmony in the lines, when considered without reference to scansion, fell back upon the idea that the "Are" was a blunder—an excess for which the poet should be sent to Coventry—and, striking it out, they scanned the remainder of the line as follows :

——ĕmblĕms ŏf | deĕds thăt ăre | dŏne ĭn thĕir clĭme. |

This answered pretty well; but the Grammars admitted no such foot as a foot of one syllable; and besides the rhythm was dactylic. In despair, the books are well searched, however, and at last the investigators are gratified by a full solution of the riddle in the profound "Observation" quoted in the beginning of this article:—" When a syllable is wanting, the verse is said to be catalectic; when the measure is exact, the line is acatalectic; when there is a redundant syllable it forms hypermeter." This is enough. The anomalous line is pronounced to be catalectic at the head and to form hypermeter at the tail :—and so on, and so on; it being soon discovered that nearly all the remaining lines are in a similar predicament, and that what flows so smoothly to the ear, although so roughly to the eye, is, after all, a mere jumble of catalecticism, acatalecticism, and hypermeter—not to say worse.

Now, had this court of inquiry been in possession of even the shadow of the *philosophy* of Verse, they would have had no trouble in reconciling this oil and water of the eye and ear, by merely scanning the passage without reference to lines, and, continuously, thus:

Know ye the | land where the | cypress and | myrtle Are | emblems of | deeds that are | done in their | clime Where the | rage of the | vulture the | love of the | turtle Now | melt into | softness now | madden to | *crime* | Know ye the | land of the | cedar and | vine Where the | flowers ever | blossom the | beams ever | shine Where the | light wings of | Zephyr op | pressed by per | *fume Wax* | faint o'er the | gardens of | Gul in their | bloom Where the | citron and | olive are | fairest of fruit

And the | voice of the | nightingale | never is | mute Where the | virgins
are | soft as the | roses they | *twine And* | all save the | spirit of | man
is di | vine 'Tis the | land of the | East 'tis the | clime of the | Sun Can
he | smile on such | deeds as his | children have | *done Oh* | wild as the |
accents of | lovers' fare | well Are the | hearts that they | bear and the |
tales that they | *tell.*

Here "crime" and "tell" (italicised) are cæsuras, each having the
value of a dactyl, four short syllables; while "fume Wax," "twine
and," and "done Oh," are spondees which, of course, being composed of two long syllables, are also equal to four short, and are
the dactyl's natural equivalent. The nicety of Byron's ear has
led him into a succession of feet which, with two trivial exceptions
as regards melody, are absolutely accurate—a very rare occurrence this in dactylic or anapæstic rhythms. The exceptions are
found in the spondee "*twine And,*" and the dactyl, "*smile on
such.*" Both feet are false in point of melody. In "*twine And,*"
to make out the rhythm, we must force "*And*" into a length
which it will not naturally bear. We are called on to sacrifice
either the proper length of the syllable as demanded by its position as a member of a spondee, or the customary accentuation of
the word in conversation. There is no hesitation, and should be
none. We at once give up the sound for the sense: and the
rhythm is imperfect. In this instance it is *very* slightly so;—not
one person in ten thousand could, by ear, detect the inaccuracy.
But the *perfection* of verse, as regards melody, consists in its
never demanding any such sacrifice as is here demanded. The
rhythmical must agree, *thoroughly*, with the reading, flow. This
perfection has in no instance been attained—but is unquestionably
attainable. "*Smile on such,*" the dactyl, is incorrect, because
"*such,*" from the character of the two consonants *ch*, cannot *easily*
be enunciated in the ordinary time of a short syllable, which its
position declares that it is. Almost every reader will be able to
appreciate the slight difficulty here; and yet the error is by no
means so important as that of the "*And*" in the spondee. By
dexterity we *may* pronounce "*such*" in the true time; but the
attempt to remedy the rhythmical deficiency of the And by drawing it out, merely aggravates the offense against natural enuncia
tion, by directing attention to the offence.

My main object, however, in quoting these lines, is to show that, in spite of the Prosodies, the length of a line is entirely an arbitrary matter. We might divide the commencement of Byron's poem thus:

> Know ye the | land where the. |

or thus:

> Know ye the | land where the | cypress and. |

or thus:

> Know ye the | land where the | cypress and | myrtle are. |

or thus:

> Know ye the | land where the | cypress and | myrtle are | emblems of. |

In short, we may give it any division we please, and the lines will be good—provided we have at least *two* feet in a line. As in mathematics two units are required to form number, so rhythm, (from the Greek αριθμος, number,) demands for its formation at least two feet. Beyond doubt, we often see such lines as

> Know ye the—
> Land where the—

lines of one foot; and our Prosodies admit such; but with impropriety; for common sense would dictate that every so obvious division of a poem as is made by a line, should include within itself all that is necessary for its own comprehension; but in a line of one foot we can have no appreciation of *rhythm*, which depends upon the equality between *two* or more pulsations. The false lines, consisting sometimes of a single cæsura, which are seen in mock Pindaric odes, are of course "rhythmical" only in connection with some other line; and it is this want of independent rhythm which adapts them to the purposes of burlesque alone. Their effect is that of incongruity (the principle of mirth;) for they include the blankness of prose amid the harmony of verse.

My second object in quoting Byron's lines, was that of showing how absurd it often is to cite a single line from amid the body of a poem, for the purpose of instancing the perfection or imperfection of the line's rhythm. Were we to see by itself

> Know ye the land where the cypress and myrtle,

we might justly condemn it as defective in the final foot, which is equal to only three, instead of being equal to four, short syllables.

In the foot (*flowers ever*) we shall find a further exemplification of the principle of the bastard iambus, bastard trochee, and quick trochee, as I have been at some pains in describing these feet above. All the Prosodies on English verse would insist upon making an elision in "flowers," thus (flow'rs,) but this is nonsense. In the quick trochee (mănȳ ăre thē) occurring in Mr. Cranch's *trochaic* line, we had to equalize the time of the three syllables (*ny, are, the,*) to that of the one *short* syllable whose position they usurp. Accordingly each of these syllables is equal to the third of a short syllable, that is to say, the *sixth of a long*. But in Byron's *dactylic* rhythm, we have to equalize the time of the three syllables (*ers, ev, er,*) to that of the one *long* syllable whose position they usurp, or, (which is the same thing,) of the *two short*. Therefore the value of each of the syllables (*ers, ev,* and *er*) is the *third of a long*. We enunciate them with only half the rapidity we employ in enunciating the three final syllables of the quick trochee—which latter is a rare foot. The "*flowers ever*," on the contrary, is as common in the dactylic rhythm as is the *bastard* trochee in the trochaic, or the bastard iambus in the iambic. We may as well accent it with the curve of the crescent to the right, and call it a *bastard dactyl*. A *bastard anapæst*, whose nature I now need be at no trouble in explaining, will of course occur, now and then, in an anapæstic rhythm.

In order to avoid any chance of that confusion which is apt to be introduced in an essay of this kind by too sudden and radical an alteration of the conventionalities to which the reader has been accustomed, I have thought it right to suggest for the accent marks of the bastard trochee, bastard iambus, etc., etc., certain characters which, in merely varying the direction of the ordinary short accent (˘) should imply, what is the fact, that the feet themselves are not *new* feet, in any proper sense, but simply modifications of the foot, respectively, from which they derive their names. Thus a bastard iambus is, in its essentiality, that is to say, in its time, an iambus. The variation lies only in the *distribution* of this time. The time, for example, occupied by the one short (or *half of long*) syllable, in the ordinary iambus, is, in the bastard, spread equally over two syllables, which are accordingly the *fourth of long*.

But this fact—the fact of the essentiality, or whole time, of the foot being unchanged, is now so fully before the reader, that I may venture to propose, finally, an accentuation which shall answer the real purpose—that is to say, what should be the real purpose of all accentuation—the purpose of expressing to the eye the exact relative value of every syllable employed in Verse.

I have already shown that enunciation, or *length*, is the point from which we start. In other words, we begin with a *long sylla-ble*. This then is our unit; and there will be no need of accent-ing it at all. An unaccented syllable, in a system of accentua-tion, is to be regarded always as a long syllable. Thus a spondee would be without accent. In an iambus, the first syllable being "short," or the *half* of long, should be accented with a small 2, placed *beneath* the syllable; the last syllable, being long, should be unaccented;—the whole would be thus (control.) In a trochee, these accents would be merely conversed, thus (manly.) In a dactyl, each of the two final syllables, being the half of long, should, also, be accented with a small 2 beneath the syllable; and, the first syllable left unaccented, the whole would be thus (happiness.) In an anapæst we should converse the dactyl thus, (in the land.) In the bastard dactyl, each of the three concluding syllables being the *third* of long, should be accented with a small 3 beneath the syllable and the whole foot would stand thus, (flowers ever.) In the bastard anapæst we should converse the bastard dactyl thus, (in the rebound.) In the bastard iambus, each of the two initial syllables, being the fourth of long, should be accented, below with a small 4; the whole foot would be thus, (in the rain.) In the bastard trochee, we should converse the bastard iambus thus, (many a.) In the quick trochee, each of the three concluding syllables, being the *sixth* of long, should be accented, below, with a small 6; the whole foot would be thus, (many are the.) The quick iambus is not yet created, and most probably never will be for it will be excessively useless, awkward, and liable to misconception—as I have already shown that even the quick trochee is:—but, should it appear, we must accent it by conversing the quick trochee. The cæsura, being variable in length, but always *longer than "long,"* should be accented, *above*, with a number expressing the length, or value, of the distinctive foot of the rhythm in which it occurs. Thus a cæsura, occurring in a spondaic rhythm, would be accented with a small 2 above the syllable, or, rather, foot. Occurring in a dactylic or anapæstic rhythm, we also accent it with the 2, above the foot. Occurring in an iambic rhythm, however, it must be accented, above, with $1\frac{1}{2}$: for this is the relative value of the iambus. Occurring in the trochaic rhythm, we give it, of course, the same accentuation. For the complex $1\frac{1}{4}$, however, it would be advisable to substitute the simpler expression $\frac{3}{2}$ which amounts to the same thing.

In this system of accentuation Mr. Cranch's lines, quoted above, would thus be written:

Many are the | thoughts that | come to | me
In my ! lonely | musing |

And they | drift so | strange and | swift
There's no | time for | choosing |

Which to | follow | for to | leave
Any, | seems a | losing. |

In the ordinary system the accentuation would be thus·

Mănÿ ărĕ thĕ | thŏughts thăt | cŏme tŏ | mē
In my | lŏnely | mūsĭng, |
ănd thĕy | drĭft sŏ | strănge ănd | swĭft |
Thĕrĕ's nŏ | tĭmĕ fŏr | chŏŏsĭng |
Whĭch tŏ | fŏllŏw, | fŏr tŏ | lĕave
ăny, | seĕms ă | lŏsĭng. |

It must be observed, here, that I do not grant this to be the "ordinary" *scansion*. On the contrary, I never yet met the man

who had the faintest comprehension of the true scanning of these
lines, or of such as these. But granting this to be the mode in
which our Prosodies would divide the feet, they would accentuate
the syllables as just above.

Now, let any reasonable person compare the two modes. The
first advantage seen in my mode is that of simplicity—of time
labor, and ink saved. Counting the fractions as *two* accents, even,
there will be found only *twenty-six* accents to the stanza. In the
common accentuation there are *forty-one*. But admit that all this
is a trifle, which it is *not*, and let us proceed to points of importance.
Does the common accentuation express the truth, in particular, in
general, or in any regard? Is it consistent with itself? Does it
convey either to the ignorant or to the scholar a just conception
of the rhythm of the lines? Each of these questions must be
answered in the negative. The crescents, being precisely similar,
must be understood as expressing, all of them, one and the same
thing: and so all prosodies have always understood them and
wished them to be understood. They express, indeed, "short"—
but this word has all kinds of meanings. It serves to represent
(the reader is left to guess *when*) sometimes the half, sometimes
the third, sometimes the fourth, sometimes the sixth, of "long"—
while "long" itself, in the books, is left undefined and undescribed.
On the other hand, the horizontal accent, it may be said, expresses
sufficiently well, and unvaryingly, the syllables which are meant to
be long. It does nothing of the kind. This horizontal accent is
placed over the cæsura (wherever, as in the Latin Prosodies, the
cæsura is recognised) as well as over the ordinary long syllable,
and implies anything and everything, just as the crescent. But
grant that it does express the ordinary long syllables, (leaving the
cæsura out of question,) have I not given the identical expression,
by not employing any expression at all? In a word, while the
Prosodies, with a certain number of accents, express *precisely nothing whatever*, I, with scarcely half the number, have expressed
everything which, in a system of accentuation, demands expression. In glancing at my mode in the lines of Mr. Cranch, it will
be seen that it conveys not only the exact relation of the syllables and feet, among themselves, in those particular lines,
but their precise value in relation to any other existing or con

ceivable feet or syllables, in any existing or conceivable system of rhythm.

The object of what we call *scansion* is the distinct marking of the rhythmical flow. Scansion with accents or perpendicular lines between the feet—that is to say scansion *by* the voice only—is scansion *to* the ear only; and all very good in its way. The written scansion addresses the ear through the eye. In either case the object is the distinct marking of the rhythmical, musical, or reading flow. There *can* be no other object and there is none. Of course, then, the scansion and the reading flow should go hand in hand. The former must agree with the latter. The former represents and expresses the latter; and is good or bad as it truly or falsely represents and expresses it. If by the written scansion of a line we are not enabled to perceive any rhythm or music in the line, then either the line is unrhythmical or the scansion false. Apply all this to the English lines which we have quoted, at various points, in the course of this article. It will be found that the scansion exactly conveys the rhythm, and thus thoroughly fulfils the only purpose for which scansion is required.

But let the scansion *of the schools* be applied to the Greek and Latin verse, and what result do we find?—that the verse is one thing and the scansion quite another. The ancient verse, *read* aloud, is in general musical, and occasionally *very* musical. *Scanned* by the Prosodial rules we can, for the most part, make nothing of it whatever. In the case of the English verse, the more emphatically we dwell on the divisions between the feet, the more distinct is our perception of the kind of rhythm intended. In the case of the Greek and Latin, the more we dwell the *less* distinct is this perception. To make this clear by an example:

Mæcenas, atavis edite regibus,
O, et præsidium et dulce decus meum,
Sunt quos curriculo pulverem Olympicum
Collegisse juvat, metaque fervidis
Evitata rotis, palmaque nobilis
Terrarum dominos evehit ad Deos.

Now in *reading* these lines, there is scarcely one person in a thousand who, if even ignorant of Latin, will not immediately *feel* and appreciate their flow—their music. A prosodist, however, informs the public that the *scansion* runs thus:

Mæce | nas ata | vis | edite | regibus |
O, et | præsidi' | et | dulce de | cus meum |
Sunt quos | curricu | lo | pulver' O | lympicum |
Colle | gisse ju | vat | metaque | fervidis |
Evi | tata ro | tis | palmaque | nobilis |
Terra | rum domi | nos | evehit | ad Deos. |

Now I do not deny that we get a *certain sort* of music from the lines if we read them according to this scansion, but I wish to call attention to the fact that this scansion and the certain sort of music which grows out of it, are entirely at war not only with the reading flow which any ordinary person would naturally give the lines, but with the reading flow universally given them, and never denied them, by even the most obstinate and stolid of scholars.

And now these questions are forced upon us—" Why exists this discrepancy between the modern verse with its scansion, and the ancient verse with its scansion ?"—" Why, in the former case, are there agreement and representation, while in the latter there is neither the one or the other !" or, to come to the point,—" How are we to reconcile the ancient verse with the scholastic scansion of it ?" This absolutely necessary conciliation—shall we bring it about by supposing the scholastic scansion wrong because the ancient verse is right, or by maintaining that the ancient verse is wrong because the scholastic scansion is not to be gainsayed !

Were we to adopt the latter mode of arranging the difficulty, we might, in some measure, at least simplify the expression of the arr   nent by putting it thus—Because the pedants have no   , therefore the old poets had no ears.

" But," say the gentlemen without the eyes, " the scholastic scansion, although certainly not handed down to us in form from the old poets themselves (the gentlemen without the ears,) is nevertheless deduced from certain facts which are supplied us by careful observation of the old poems.

And let us illustrate this strong position by an example from an American poet—who must be a poet of some eminence, or he will not answer the purpose. Let us take Mr. Alfred B. Street. I remember these two lines of his,

> His sinuous path, by blazes, wound
> Among trunks grouped in myriads round.

With the *sense* of these lines I have nothing to do. When a poet is in a "fine frenzy," he may as well imagine a large forest as a small one—and "by blazes!" is *not* intended for an oath. My concern is with the rhythm, which is iambic.

Now let us suppose that, a thousand years hence, when the "American language" is dead, a learned prosodist should be deducing from "careful observation" of our best poets, a system of scansion for our poetry. And let us suppose that this prosodist had so little dependence in the generality and immutability of the laws of Nature, as to assume in the outset, that, because we lived a thousand years before his time, and made use of steam-engines instead of mesmeric balloons, we must therefore have had a *very* singular fashion of mouthing our vowels, and altogether of hudsonizing our verse. And let us suppose that with these and other fundamental propositions carefully put away in his brain, he should arrive at the line,—

> Among | trunks grouped | in my | riads round.

Finding it an obviously iambic rhythm, he would divide it as above; and observing that "trunks" made the first member of an iambus, he would call it short, as Mr. Street intended it to be. Now farther:—if instead of admitting the possibility that Mr. Street, (who by that time would be called Street simply, just as we say Homer,)—that Mr. Street might have been in the habit of writing carelessly, as the poets of the prosodist's own era did, and as all poets will do (on account of being geniuses,)—instead of admitting this, suppose the learned scholar should make a "rule" and put it in a book, to the effect that, in the American verse, the vowel *u, when found imbedded among nine consonants, was short :* what, under such circumstances, would the sensible people of the scholar's day have a right not only to think, but to say of that scholar?—why, that he was "a fool—by blazes!"

I have put an extreme case, but it strikes at the root of the error. The "rules" are grounded in "authority;" and this "authority"—can any one tell us what it means? or can any one suggest anything that it may *not* mean? Is it not clear that the "scholar" above referred to, might as readily have deduced from authority a totally false system as a partially true one? To deduce from authority a consistent prosody of the ancient metres would indeed have been within the limits of the barest possibility; and the task has *not* been accomplished, for the reason that it demands a species of ratiocination altogether out of keeping with the brain of a bookworm. A rigid scrutiny will show that the very few "rules" which have not as many exceptions as examples, are those which have, by accident, their true bases not in authority, but in the omniprevalent laws of syllabification; such, for example, as the rule which declares a vowel before two consonants to be long.

In a word, the gross confusion and antagonism of the scholastic prosody, as well as its marked inapplicability to the reading flow of the rhythms it pretends to illustrate, are attributable, first, to the utter absence of natural principle as a guide in the investigations which have been undertaken by inadequate men; and secondly, to the neglect of the obvious consideration that the ancient poems, which have been the *criteria* throughout, were the work of men who must have written as loosely, and with as little definitive system, as ourselves.

Were Horace alive to-day, he would divide for us his first Ode thus, and "make great eyes" when assured by the prosodists that he had no business to make any such division!

> Mæcenas | atavis | edite | regibus |
> O et præ | sidium et | dulce de | cus meum |
> Sunt quos cur | riculo | pulverem O | lympicum |
> Collegisse | juvat | metaque | fervidis |
> Evitata | rotis | palmaque | nobilis |
> Terrarum | dominos | evehit | ad Deos. |

Read by this scansion, the flow is preserved; and the more we dwell on the divisions, the more the intended rhythm becomes apparent. Moreover, the feet have all the same time; while, in the scholastic scansion, trochees—admitted trochees—are absurdly employed as equivalents to spondees and dactyls. The books declare, for instance, that *Colle*, which begins the fourth line, is a trochee, and seem to be gloriously unconscious that to put a trochee in opposition with a longer foot, is to violate the inviolable principle of all music, *time*.

It will be said, however, by "some people," that I have no business to make a dactyl out of such obviously long syllables as *sunt, quos, cur*. Certainly I have no business to do so. I *never* do so. And Horace should not have done so. But he did. Mr. Bryant and Mr. Longfellow do the same thing every day. And merely because these gentlemen, now and then, forget themselves in this way, it would be hard if some future prosodist should insist upon twisting the "Thanatopsis," or the "Spanish Student," into a jumble of trochees, spondees, and dactyls.

It may be said, also, by some other people, that in the word *decus*, I have succeeded no better than the books, in making the scansional agree with the reading flow; and that *decus* was not pronounced *decus*. I reply, that there can be no doubt of the word having been pronounced, in this case, *decus*. It must be observed, that the Latin inflection, or variation of a word in its terminating syllables, caused the Romans —*must* have caused them, to pay greater attention to the termination of a word than to its commencement, or than we do to the terminations of our words. The end of the Latin word established that relation of the word with other words which we establish by prepositions or auxiliary verbs. Therefore, it would seem infinitely less odd to them than it does to us, to dwell at any time, for any slight purpose, abnormally, on a terminating syllable. In verse, this license —scarcely a license —would be frequently admitted. These ideas unlock the secret of such lines as the

> Litoreis ingens inventa sub ilici*bus sus*,

and the

> Parturiunt montes et nascitur ridicu*lus mus*,

which I quoted, some time ago, while speaking of rhyme.

As regards the prosodial elisions, such as that of *rem* before *&*

n *pulverem Olympicum,* it is really difficult to understand how so dismally silly a notion could have entered the brain even : a pedant. Were it demanded of me why the books cut off one *vowel* before another, I might say—It is, perhaps, because the books think that, since a bad reader is so apt to slide the one vowel into the other at any rate, it is just as well to print them *ready-slided.* But in the case of the terminating *m,* which is the most readily pronounced of all consonants, (as the infantile *mamma* will testify,) and the most impossible to cheat the ear of by any system of sliding—in the case of the *m,* I should be driven to reply that, to the best of my belief, the prosodists did the thing, because they had a fancy for doing it, and wished to see how funny it would look after it was done. The thinking reader will perceive that, from the great facility with which *em* may be enunciated, it is admirably suited to form one of the rapid short syllables in the bastard dactyl (pulverem O ;) but because the books had no conception of a bastard dactyl, they knocked it in the head at once—by cutting off its tail !

Let me now give a specimen of the true scansion of another Horatian measure—embodying an instance of proper elision.

$$\text{Integer} \mid \text{vitæ} \mid \text{scelerisque} \mid \text{purus} \mid$$
$$\text{Non eget} \mid \text{Mauri} \mid \text{jaculis ne} \mid \text{que arcu} \mid$$
$$\text{Nec vene} \mid \text{natis} \mid \text{gravida sa} \mid \text{gittis,}$$
$$\text{Fusce, pha} \mid \text{retrâ.}$$

Here the regular recurrence of the bastard dactyl, gives great animation to the rhythm. The *e* before the *a* in *que arcu,* is, almost of sheer necessity, cut off—that is to say, run into the *a* so as to preserve the spondee. But even this license it would have been better not to take.

Had I space, nothing would afford me greater pleasure than to proceed with the scansion of *all* the ancient rhythms, and to show how easily, by the help of common sense, the intended music of each and all can be rendered instantaneously apparent. But I have already overstepped my limits, and must bring this paper to an end.

It will never do, however, to omit all mention of the heroic hexameter.

I began the "processes" by a suggestion of the spondee as the first step towards verse. But the innate monotony of the spondee has caused its disappearance, as the basis of rhythm, from all modern poetry. We *may* say, indeed, that the French heroic—the most wretchedly monotonous verse in existence—is, to all intents and purposes, spondaic. But it is not designedly spondaic—and if the French were ever to examine it at all, they would no doubt pronounce it iambic. It must be observed, that the French language is strangely peculiar in this point—*that it is without accentuation, and consequently without verse.* The genius of the people, rather than the structure of the tongue, declares that their words are, for the most part, enunciated with an uniform dwelling on each syllable. For example—*we* say, "syl*l*abification." A Frenchman would say, syl-la-bi-fi-ca-ti-on; dwelling on no one of the syllables with any noticeable particularity. Here again I put an extreme case, in order to be well understood; but the general fact is as I give it—that, comparatively, the French have *no* accentuation. And there can be nothing worth the name of verse, without. Therefore, the French have no verse worth the name—which is the fact, put in sufficiently plain terms. Their iambic rhythm so superabounds in absolute spondees, as to warrant me in calling its basis spondaic; but French is the *only* modern tongue which has any rhythm with such basis; and even in the French, it is, as I have said, unintentional.

Admitting, however, the validity of my suggestion, that the spondee was the first approach to verse, we should expect to find, first, natural spondees (words each forming just a spondee,) most abundant in the most ancient languages; and, secondly, we should expect to find spondees forming the basis of the most ancient rhythms. These expectations are in both cases confirmed.

Of the Greek hexameter, the intentional basis is spondaic. The dactyls are the *variation* of the theme. It will be observed that there is no absolute certainty about *their* points of interposition. The penultimate foot, it is true, is usually a dactyl; but not uniformly so; while the ultimate, on which the ear *lingers* is always a spondee. Even that the penultimate is usually a dactyl may be clearly referred to the necessity of winding up with the *distinctive* spondee. In corrob.-ation of this idea, again, we should look to find the penultimate spondee most usual in the most ancient verse; and, accordingly, we find it more frequent in the Greek than in the Latin hexameter.

But besides all this, spondees are not only more prevalent in the heroic hexameter than dactyls, but occur to such an extent as is even unpleasant to modern ears, on account of monotony. What the modern chiefly appreciates and admires in the Greek hexameter, is the *melody of the abundant vowel sounds.* The Latin hexameters *really* please very few moderns—although so many pretend to fall into ecstasies about them. In the hexameters quoted, several pages ago, from Silius Italicus, the preponderance of the spondee is strikingly manifest. Besides the natural spondees of the Greek and Latin, numerous artificial ones arise in the verse of these tongues on account of the tendency which inflection has to throw full accentuation on terminal syllables; and the preponderance of the spondee is farther ensured by the comparative infrequency of the small prepositions which *we* have to serve us *instead* of case, and also the absence of the diminutive auxiliary verbs with which *we* have to eke out the expression of our primary ones. These are the monosyllables whose abundance serve to stamp the poetic genius of a language as tripping or dactylic.

Now paying no attention to these facts, Sir Philip Sidney, Professor Longfellow, and innumerable other persons more or less modern, have busied themselves in constructing what they supposed to be "English hexameters on the model of the Greek." The only difficulty was that (even leaving out of question the melodious masses of vowel,) these gentlemen never could get their English hexameters to *sound* Greek. Did they *look* Greek?—that should have been the query; and the reply might have led to a solution of the riddle. In placing a copy of ancient hexameters side by side with a copy (in similar type) of such hexameters as Professor Longfellow, or Professor Felton, or the Frogpondian Professors collectively, are in the shameful practice of composing "on the model of the Greek," it will be seen that the latter (hexameters, not professors) are about one third longer *to the eye*, on an average, than the former. The more abundant dactyls make the difference. And it is the greater number of spondees in the Greek than in the English—in the ancient than in the modern tongue—which has caused it to fall out that while these eminent scholars were groping about in the dark for a Greek hexameter, which is a spondaic rhythm varied now and then by dactyls, they merely stumbled, to the lasting scandal of scholarship, over something which, on account of its long-leggedness, we may as well term a Feltonian hexameter, and which is a dactylic rhythm, interrupted, rarely, by artificial spondees which are no spondees at all, and which are curiously thrown in by the heels at all kinds of improper and impertinent points.

Here is a specimen of the Longfellownian hexameter.

Also the | church with | in was a | dorned for | this was the | season |
In which the | young their | parents' | hope and the | loved ones of | Heaven |
Should at the | foot of the | altar re | new the | vows of their | baptism |
Therefore each | nook and | corner was | swept and | cleaned and the | dust was |
Blown from the | walls and | ceiling and | from the | oil-painted | benches. |

Mr. Longfellow is a man of imagination—but *can* he imagine that any individual, with a proper understanding of the danger of lockjaw, would make the attempt of twisting his mouth into the shape necessary for the emission of such spondees as "parents," and "from the," or such dactyls as "cleaned and the" and "loved ones of?" "Baptism" is by no means a bad spondee—perhaps because it happens to be a dactyl;—of all the rest, however, I am dreadfully ashamed.

But these feet—dactyls and spondees, all together,—should thus be put at once into their proper position:

"Also, the church within was adorned; for this was the season in which the young, their parents' hope, and the loved ones of Heaven, should, at the feet of the altar, renew the vows of their baptism. Therefore, each nook and corner was swept and cleaned; and the dust was blown from the walls and ceiling, and from the oil-painted benches."

There!—That is respectable prose; and it will incur no danger of ever getting its character ruined by any body's mistaking it for verse.

But even when we let these modern hexameters go, as Greek, and merely hold them fast in their proper character of Longfellownian, or Feltonian, or Frogpondian, we must still condemn them as having been committed in a radical misconception of the philosophy of verse. The spondee, as I observed, is the *theme* of the Greek line. Most of the ancient hexameters *begin* with spondees, for the reason that the spondee *is* the theme ; and the ear is filled with it as with a burden. Now the Feltonian dactylics have, in the same way, dactyls for the theme, and most of them begin with dactyls—which is all very proper if not very Greek—but, unhappily, the one point at which they *are* very Greek is that point, precisely, at which they should be nothing but Feltonian. They always *close* with what is meant for a spondee. To be consistently silly, they should die off in a dactyl.

That a truly Greek hexameter *cannot*, however, be readily composed in English, is a proposition which I am by no means inclined to admit. I think I could manage the point myself. For example :

Do tell ! | when may we | hope to make | men of sense | out of the | Pundits |
Born and brought | up with their | snouts deep | down in the | mud of the | Frog-pond !
Why ask ! | who ever | yet saw | money made | out of a | fat old |
Jew, or | downright | upright | nutmegs | out of a | pine-knot ! |

The proper spondee predominance is here preserved. Some of the dactyls are not so good as I could wish—but, upon the whole, the rhythm is very decent—to say nothing of its excellent sense.

THE PHILOSOPHY OF COMPOSITION.

CHARLES DICKENS, in a note now lying before me, alluding to an examination I once made of the mechanism of " Barnaby Rudge," says—" By the way, are you aware that Godwin wrote his ' Caleb Williams' backwards ? He first involved his hero in a web of difficulties, forming the second volume, and then, for the first, cast about him for some mode of accounting for what had been done."

I cannot think this the *precise* mode of procedure on the part of Godwin—and indeed what he himself acknowledges, is not altogether in accordance with Mr. Dickens' idea—but the author of " Caleb Williams " was too good an artist not to perceive the advantage derivable from at least a somewhat similar process. Nothing is more clear than that every plot, worth the name, must be elaborated to its *dénouement* before any thing be attempted with the pen. It is only with the *dénouement* constantly in view that we can give a plot its indispensable air of consequence, or causation, by making the incidents, and especially the tone at all points, tend to the development of the intention.

There is a radical error, I think, in the usual mode of constructing a story. Either history affords a thesis—or one is suggested by an incident of the day—or, at best, the author sets himself to work in the combination of striking events to form merely the basis of his narrative—designing, generally, to fill in with description, dialogue, or autorial comment, whatever crevices of fact, or action, may, from page to page, render themselves apparent.

I prefer commencing with the consideration of an *effect*. Keeping originality *always* in view—for he is false to himself who ventures to dispense with so obvious and so easily attainable a source of interest—I say to myself, in the first place, " Of the innumerable effects, or impressions, of which the heart, the intellect, or (more generally) the soul is susceptible, what one shall I, on the present occasion, select ?" Having chosen a novel, first, and secondly a vivid effect, I consider whether it can be best wrought by incident or tone—whether by ordinary incidents and peculiar tone, or the converse, or by peculiarity both of incident and tone—afterward looking about me (or rather within) for such combinations of event, or tone, as shall best aid me in the construction of the effect.

I have often thought how interesting a magazine paper might be written by any author who would—that is to say, who could—detail, step by step, the processes by which any one of his compositions attained its ultimate point of completion. Why such a paper has never been given to the world, I am much at a loss to say—but, perhaps, the autorial vanity has had more to do with the omission than any one other cause. Most writers—poets in especial—prefer having it understood that they compose by a species of fine frenzy—an ecstatic intuition—and would positively shudder at letting the public take a peep behind the scenes, at the elaborate and vacillating crudities of thought—at the true purposes seized only at the last moment—at the innumerable glimpses of idea that arrived not at the maturity of full view—at the fully matured fancies discarded in despair as unmanageable—at the cautious selections and rejections—at the painful erasures and interpolations—in a word, at the wheels and pinions—the tackle for scene-shifting—the step-ladders and demon-traps—the cock's feathers, the red paint and the black patches, which, in ninety-nine cases out of the hundred, constitute the properties of the literary *histrio.*

I am aware, on the other hand, that the case is by no means common, in which an author is at all in condition to retrace the steps by which his conclusions have been attained. In general, suggestions, having arisen pell-mell, are pursued and forgotten in a similar manner.

For my own part, I have neither sympathy with the repugnance alluded to, nor at any time, the least difficulty in recalling to mind the progressive steps of any of my compositions; and, since the interest of an analysis, or reconstruction, such as I have considered a *desideratum*, is quite independent of any real or fancied interest in the thing analyzed, it will not be regarded as a breach of decorum on my part to show the *modus operandi* by which some one of my own works.was put together. I select "The Raven" as most generally known. It is my design to render-it manifest that no one point in its composition is referible either to accident or intuition—that the work proceeded, step by step, to its completion with the precision and rigid consequence of a mathematical problem.

Let us dismiss, as irrelevant to the poem, *per se*, the circumstance—or say the necessity—which, in the first place, gave rise to the intention of composing *a* poem that should suit at once the popular and the critical taste.

We commence, then, with this intention.

The initial consideration was that of extent. If any literary work is too long to be read at one sitting, we must be content to dispense with the immensely important effect derivable from unity of impression—for, if two sittings be required, the affairs of the world interfere, and every thing like totality is at once destroyed. But since, *ceteris paribus*, no poet can afford to dispense with *any thing* that may advance his design, it but remains to be seen whether there is, in extent, any advantage to counterbalance the loss of unity which attends it. Here I say no, at once. What we term a long poem is, in fact, merely a succession of brief ones—that is to say, of brief poetical effects. It is needless to demonstrate that a poem is such, only inasmuch as it intensely excites, by elevating, the soul; and all intense excitements are, through a psychal necessity, brief. For this reason, at least one half of the "Paradise Lost" is essentially prose—a succession of poetical excitements interspersed, *inevitably*, with corresponding depressions—the whole being deprived, through the extremeness of its length, of the vastly important artistic element, totality, or unity, of effect.

It appears evident, then, that there is a distinct limit, as regards length, to all works of literary art—the limit of a single sitting—and that, although in certain classes of prose composition, such as "Robinson Crusoe," (demanding no unity,) this limit may be advantageously overpassed, it can never properly be overpassed in a poem. Within this limit, the extent of a poem may be made to bear mathematical relation to its merit—in other words, to the excitement or elevation—again, in other words, to the degree of the true poetical effect which it is capable of inducing; for it is clear that the brevity must be in direct ratio of the intensity of the intended effect:—this, with one proviso—that a certain degree of duration is absolutely requisite for the production of any effect at all.

Holding in view these considerations, as well as that degree of excitement which I deemed not above the popular, while not below the critical, taste, I reached at once what I conceived the proper *length* for my intended poem—a length of about one hundred lines. It is, in fact, a hundred and eight.

My next thought concerned the choice of an impression, or effect, to be conveyed: and here I may as well observe that, throughout the construction, I kept steadily in view the design of rendering the work *universally* appreciable. I should be carried too far out of my immediate topic were I to demonstrate a point upon which I have repeatedly insisted, and which, with the poetical, stands not in the slightest need of demonstration—the point, I mean, that Beauty is the sole legitimate province of the poem. A few words, however, in elucidation of my real meaning, which some of my friends have evinced a disposition to misrepresent. That pleasure which is at once the most intense, the most elevating, and the most pure, is, I believe, found in the contemplation of the beautiful. When, indeed, men speak of Beauty, they mean, precisely, not a quality, as is supposed, but an effect—they refer, in short, just to that intense and pure elevation of *soul*—*not* of intellect, or of heart—upon which I have commented, and which is experienced in consequence of contemplating "the beautiful." Now I designate Beauty as the province of the poem, merely because it is an obvious rule of Art that effects should be made to spring from direct causes—that objects should be attained through means best adapted for their attainment—no one as yet having been weak enough to deny that the peculiar elevation alluded to, is *most readily* attained in the poem. Now the object, Truth, or the satisfaction of the intellect, and the object Passion, or the excitement of the heart, are, although attainable, to a certain extent, in poetry, far more readily attainable in prose. Truth, in fact, demands a precision, and Passion a *homeliness* (the truly passionate will comprehend me) which are absolutely antagonistic to that Beauty which, I maintain, is the excitement, or pleasurable elevation, of the soul. It by no means follows from any thing here said, that passion, or even truth, may not be introduced, and even profitably introduced, into a poem— for they may serve in elucidation, or aid the general effect, as do discords in music, by contrast—but the true artist will always contrive, first, to tone them into proper subservience to the predominant aim, and, secondly, to enveil them, as far as possible, in that Beauty which is the atmosphere and the essence of the poem.

Regarding, then, Beauty as my province, my next question referred to the *tone* of its highest manifestation—and all experience has shown that this tone is one of *sadness*. Beauty of whatever kind, in its supreme development, invariably excites the sensitive soul to tears. Melancholy is thus the most legitimate of all the poetical tones.

The length, the province, and the tone, being thus determined, I betook myself to ordinary induction, with the view of obtaining some artistic piquancy which might serve me as a key-note in the construction of the poem—some pivot upon which the whole structure might turn. In carefully thinking over all the usual artistic effects—or more properly *points*, in the theatrical sense—I did not fail to perceive immediately that no one had been so universally employed as that of the *refrain*. The universality of its employment sufficed to assure me of its intrinsic value, and spared me the necessity of submitting it to analysis. I considered it, however, with regard to its susceptibility of improvement, and soon saw it to be in a primitive condition. As commonly used, the *refrain*, or burden, not only is limited to lyric verse, but depends for its impression upon the force of monotone—both in sound and thought. The pleasure is deduced solely from the sense of identity—of repetition. I resolved to diversify, and so heighten, the effect, by adhering, in general, to the monotone of sound, while I continually varied that of thought: that is to say, I determined to produce continuously novel effects, by the variation *of the application* of the *refrain*— the *refrain* itself remaining, for the most part, unvaried.

These points being settled, I next bethought me of the *nature* of my *refrain*. Since its application was to be repeatedly varied, it was clear that the *refrain* itself must be brief, for there would have been an insurmountable difficulty in frequent variations of application in any sentence of length. In proportion to the brevity of the sentence, would, of course, be the facility of the variation. This led me at once to a single word as the best *refrain*.

The question now arose as to the *character* of the word. Having made up my mind to a *refrain*, the division of the poem into stanzas was, of course, a corollary: the *refrain* forming the close to each stanza. That such a close, to have force, must be sonorous and susceptible of protracted emphasis, admitted no doubt: and these considerations inevitably led me to the long *o* as the most sonorous vowel, in connection with *r* as the most producible consonant.

The sound of the *refrain* being thus determined, it became necessary to select a word embodying this sound, and at the same time in the fullest possible keeping with that melancholy which I had predetermined as the tone of the poem. In such a search it would have been absolutely impossible to overlook the word "Nevermore." In fact, it was the very first which presented itself.

The next *desideratum* was a pretext for the continuous use of the one word "nevermore." In observing the difficulty which I at once found in inventing a sufficiently plausible reason for its continuous repetition, I did not fail to perceive that this difficulty arose solely from the pre-assumption that the word was to be so continuously or monotonously spoken by *a human* being—I did not fail to perceive, in short, that the difficulty lay in the reconciliation of this monotony with the exercise of reason on the part of the creature repeating the word. Here, then, immediately arose the idea of a *non*-reasoning creature capable of speech; and, very naturally, a parrot, in the first instance, suggested itself, but was superseded forthwith by a Raven, as equally capable of speech, and infinitely more in keeping with the intended *tone*.

I had now gone so far as the conception of a Raven—the bird of ill omen—monotonously repeating the one word, "Nevermore," at the conclusion of each stanza, in a poem of melancholy tone, and in length about one hundred lines. Now, never losing sight of the object *supremeness*, or perfection, at all points, I asked myself—"Of all melancholy topics, what, according to the *universal* understanding of mankind, is the *most* melancholy?" Death — was the obvious reply. "And when," I said, "is this most melancholy of topics most poetical?" From what I have already explained at some length, the answer, here also, is obvious—"When it most closely allies itself to *Beauty*: the death, then, of a beautiful woman is, unquestionably, the most poetical topic in the world —and equally is it beyond doubt that the lips best suited for such topic are those of a bereaved lover."

I had now to combine the two ideas, of a lover lamenting his deceased mistress and a Raven continuously repeating the word "Nevermore."—I had to combine these, bearing in mind my design of varying, at every turn, the *application* of the word repeated; but the only intelligible mode of such combination is that of imagining the Raven employing the word in answer to the queries of the lover. And here it was that I saw at once the opportunity afforded for the effect on which I had been depending—that is to say, the effect of the *variation of application*. I saw that I could make the first query propounded by the lover—the first query to which the Raven should reply "Nevermore"—that I could make this first query a commonplace one—the second less so—the third still less, and so on—until at length the lover, startled from his original *nonchalance* by the melancholy character of the word itself—by its frequent repetition—and by a consideration of the ominous reputation of the fowl that uttered it—is at length excited to superstition, and wildly propounds queries of a far different character—queries whose solution he has passionately at heart— propounds them half in superstition and half in that species of despair which delights in self-torture—propounds them not altogether because he believes in the prophetic or demoniac character of the bird (which, reason assures him, is merely repeating a lesson learned by rote) but because he experiences a frenzied pleasure in so modelling his questions as to receive from the *expected* "Nevermore" the most delicious because the most intolerable of sorrow. Perceiving the opportunity thus afforded me—or, more strictly, thus forced upon me in the progress of the construction—

I first established in mind the climax, or concluding query—that query to which "Nevermore" should be in the last place an answer—that query in reply to which this word "Nevermore" should involve the utmost conceivable amount of sorrow and despair.

Here then the poem may be said to have its beginning—at the end, where all works of art should begin—for it was here, at this point of my preconsiderations, that I first put pen to paper in the composition of the stanza:

> "Prophet," said I, "thing of evil! prophet still if bird or devil!
> By that heaven that bends above us—by that God we both adore,
> Tell this soul with sorrow laden, if within the distant Aidenn,
> It shall clasp a sainted maiden whom the angels name Lenore—
> Clasp a rare and radiant maiden whom the angels name Lenore."
> Quoth the raven "Nevermore."

I composed this stanza, at this point, first that, by establishing the climax, I might the better vary and graduate, as regards seriousness and importance, the preceding queries of the lover—and, secondly, that I might definitely settle the rhythm, the metre, and the length and general arrangement of the stanza—as well as graduate the stanzas which were to precede, so that none of them might surpass this in rhythmical effect. Had I been able, in the subsequent composition, to construct more vigorous stanzas, I should, without scruple, have purposely enfeebled them, so as not to interfere with the climacteric effect.

And here I may as well say a few words of the versification. My first object (as usual) was originality. The extent to which this has been neglected, in versification, is one of the most unaccountable things in the world. Admitting that there is little possibility of variety in mere *rhythm*, it is still clear that the possible varieties of metre and stanza are absolutely infinite—and yet, *for centuries, no man, in verse, has ever done, or ever seemed to think of doing, an original thing*. The fact is, that originality (unless in minds of very unusual force) is by no means a matter, as some suppose, of impulse or intuition. In general, to be found, it must be elaborately sought, and although a positive merit of the highest class, demands in its attainment less of invention than negation.

Of course, I pretend to no originality in either the rhythm or metre of the "Raven." The former is trochaic—the latter is octa-meter acatalectic, alternating with heptameter catalectic repeated in the *refrain* of the fifth verse, and terminating with tetrameter catalectic. Less pedantically—the feet employed throughout (trochees) consist of a long syllable followed by a short: the first line of the stanza consists of eight of these feet—the second of seven and a half (in effect two-thirds)—the third of eight—the fourth of seven and a half—the fifth the same—the sixth three and a half. Now, each of these lines, taken individually, has been employed before, and what originality the "Raven" has, is in their *combination into stanza*; nothing even remotely approaching this combination has ever been attempted. The effect of this originality of combination is aided by other unusual, and some altogether novel effects, arising from an extension of the application of the principles of rhyme and alliteration.

The next point to be considered was the mode of bringing together the lover and the Raven—and the first branch of this consideration was the *locale*. For this the most natural suggestion might seem to be a forest, or the fields—but it has always appeared to me that a close *circumscription of space* is absolutely necessary to the effect of insulated incident:—it has the force of a frame to a picture. It has an indisputable moral power in keeping concentrated the attention, and, of course, must not be confounded with mere unity of place.

I determined, then, to place the lover in his chamber—in a chamber rendered sacred to him by memories of her who had frequented it. The room is represented as richly furnished—this in mere pursuance of the ideas I have already explained on the subject of Beauty, as the sole true poetical thesis.

The *locale* being thus determined, I had now to introduce the bird—and the thought of introducing him through the window, was inevitable. The idea of making the lover suppose, in the first instance, that the flapping of the wings of the bird against the shutter, is a "tapping" at the door, originated in a wish to increase, by prolonging, the reader's curiosity, and in a desire to admit the incidental effect arising from the lover's throwing open the door, finding all dark, and thence adopting the half-fancy that it was the spirit of his mistress that knocked.

I made the night tempestuous, first, to account for the Raven's seeking admission, and secondly, for the effect of contrast with the (physical) serenity within the chamber.

I made the bird alight on the bust of Pallas, also for the effect of contrast between the marble and the plumage—it being understood that the bust was absolutely *suggested* by the bird—the bust of *Pallas* being chosen, first, as most in keeping with the scholarship of the lover, and, secondly, for the sonorousness of the word, Pallas, itself.

About the middle of the poem, also, I have availed myself of the force of contrast, with a view of deepening the ultimate impression. For example, an air of the fantastic—approaching as nearly to the ludicrous as was admissible—is given to the Raven's entrance. He comes in " with many a flirt and flutter."

Not the *least obeisance made he*—not a moment stopped or stayed he,
But with mien of lord or lady, perched above my chamber door.

In the two stanzas which follow, the design is more obviously carried out:—

Then this ebony bird beguiling my sad fancy into smiling
By the *grave and stern decorum of the countenance it wore*,
" Though thy *crest be shorn and shaven* thou," I said, " art sure no craven
Ghastly grim and ancient Raven wandering from the nightly shore-
Tell me what thy lordly name is on the Night's Plutonian shore !"
        Quoth the Raven " Nevermore."

—

Much I marvelled *this ungainly fowl* to hear discourse so plainly,
Though its answer little meaning—little relevancy bore ;
For we cannot help agreeing that no living human being
Ever yet was blessed with seeing bird above his chamber door—
Bird or beast upon the sculptured bust above his chamber door,
        With such name as " Nevermore."

—

The effect of the *dénouement* being thus provided for, I immediately drop the fantastic for a tone of the most profound seriousness :—this tone commencing in the stanza directly following the one last quoted, with the line,

But the Raven, sitting lonely on that placid bust, spoke only, etc.

From this epoch the lover no longer jests—no longer sees any thing even of the fantastic in the Raven's demeanor. He speaks of him as a "grim, ungainly, guastly, gaunt, and ominous bird of yore," and feels the "fiery eyes" burning into his "bosom's core." This revolution of thought, or fancy, on the lover's part, is intended to induce a similar one on the part of the reader—to bring the mind into a proper frame for the *dénouement*—which is now brought about as rapidly and as *directly* as possible.

With the *dénouement* proper—with the Raven's reply, "Nevermore," to the lover's final demand if he shall meet his mistress in another world—the poem, in its obvious phase, that of a simple narrative, may be said to have its completion. So far, every thing is within the limits of the accountable—of the real. A raven, having learned by rote the single word "Nevermore," and having escaped from the custody of its owner, is driven at midnight, through the violence of a storm, to seek admission at a window from which a light still gleams—the chamber-window of a student, occupied half in poring over a volume, half in dreaming of a beloved mistress deceased. The casement being thrown open at the fluttering of the bird's wings, the bird itself perches on the most convenient seat out of the immediate reach of the student, who, amused by the incident and the oddity of the visiter's demeanor, demands of it, in jest and without looking for a reply, its name. The raven addressed, answers with its customary word, "Nevermore"—a word which finds immediate echo in the melancholy heart of the student, who, giving utterance aloud to certain thoughts suggested by the occasion, is again startled by the fowl's repetition of "Nevermore." The student now guesses the state of the case, but is impelled, as I have before explained, by the human thirst for self-torture, and in part by superstition, to propound such queries to the bird as will bring him, the lover, the most of the luxury of sorrow, through the anticipated answer "Nevermore." With the indulgence, to the extreme, of this self-torture, the narration, in what I have termed its first or obvious phase, has a natural termination, and so far there has been no overstepping of the limits of the real.

But in subjects so handled, however skilfully, or with however vivid an array of incident, there is always a certain hardness or nakedness, which repels the artistical eye. Two things are invariably required—first, some amount of complexity, or more properly, adaptation; and, secondly, some amount of suggestiveness—some under current, however indefinite, of meaning. It is this latter, in especial, which imparts to a work of art so much of that *richness* (to borrow from colloquy a forcible term) which we are too fond of confounding with *the ideal*. It is the *excess* of the suggested meaning—it is the rendering this the upper instead of the under current of the theme—which turns into prose (and that of the very flattest kind) the so called poetry of the so called transcendentalists.

Holding these opinions, I added the two concluding stanzas of the poem—their suggestiveness being thus made to pervade all the narrative which has preceded them. The under-current of meaning is rendered first apparent in the lines—

> "Take thy beak from out *my heart*, and take thy form from off my door!"
> Quoth the Raven "Nevermore!"

It will be observed that the words, "from out my heart," involve the first metaphorical expression in the poem. They, with the answer, "Nevermore," dispose the mind to seek a moral in all that has been previously narrated. The reader begins now to regard the Raven as emblematical—but it is not until the very last line of the very last stanza, that the intention of making him emblematical of *Mournful and Never-ending Remembrance* is permitted distinctly to be seen:

> And the Raven, never flitting, still is sitting, still is sitting,
> On the pallid bust of Pallas just above my chamber door;
> And his eyes have all the seeming of a demon's that is dreaming,
> And the lamplight o'er him streaming throws his shadow on the floor
> And my soul *from out that shadow* that lies floating on the floor
> Shall be lifted—nevermore.

THE POWER OF WORDS.

Oinos.—Pardon, Agathos, the weakness of a spirit new-fledged with immortality!

Agathos.—You have spoken nothing, my Oinos, for which pardon is to be demanded. Not even here is knowledge a thing of intuition. For wisdom, ask of the angels freely, that it may be given!

Oinos.—But in this existence, I dreamed that I should be at once cognizant of all things, and thus at once happy in being cognizant of all.

Agathos.—Ah, not in knowledge is happiness, but in the acquisition of knowledge! In for ever knowing, we are for ever blessed; but to know all, were the curse of a fiend.

Oinos.—But does not The Most High know all?

Agathos.—*That* (since he is The Most Happy) must be still the *one* thing unknown even to HIM.

Oinos.—But, since we grow hourly in knowledge, must not *at last* all things be known?

Agathos.—Look down into the abysmal distances!—attempt to force the gaze down the multitudinous vistas of the stars, as we sweep slowly through them thus—and thus—and thus! Even the spiritual vision, is it not at all points arrested by the continuous golden walls of the universe?—the walls of the myriads of the shining bodies that mere number has appeared to blend into unity!

Oinos.—I clearly perceive that the infinity of matter is no dream.

Agathos.—There are *no* dreams in Aidenn—but it is here whispered that, of this infinity of matter, the *sole* purpose is to afford infinite springs, at which the soul may allay the thirst *to know* which is for ever unquenchable within it—since to quench it, would be to extinguish the soul's self. Question me then, my Oinos, freely and without fear. Come! we will leave to the left the loud harmony of the Pleiades, and swoop outward from the throne into the starry meadows beyond Orion, where, for pansies and violets, and heart's-ease, are the beds of the triplicate and triple-tinted suns.

Oinos.—And now, Agathos, as we proceed, instruct me!—speak to me in the earth's familiar tones! I understood not what you hinted to me, just now, of the modes or of the methods of what, during mortality, we were accustomed to call Creation. Do you mean to say that the Creator is not God?

Agathos.—I mean to say that the Deity does not create.

Oinos.—Explain!

Agathos.—In the beginning *only*, he created. The seeming creatures which are now, throughout the universe, so perpetually springing into being, can only be considered as the mediate or indirect, not as the direct or immediate results of the Divine creative power.

Oinos.—Among men, my Agathos, this idea would be considered heretical in the extreme.

Agathos.—Among angels, my Oinos, it is seen to be simply true.

Oinos.—I can comprehend you thus far—that certain operations of what we term Nature, or the natural laws, will, under certain conditions, give rise to that which has all the *appearance* of creation. Shortly before the final overthrow of the earth, there were, I well remember, many very successful experiments in what some philosophers were weak enough to denominate the creation of animalculæ.

Agathos.—The cases of which you speak were, in fact, instances of the secondary creation—and of the *only* species of creation which has ever been, since the first word spoke into existence the first law.

Oinos.—Are not the starry worlds that, from the abyss of non-entity, burst hourly forth into the heavens—are not these stars, Agathos, the immediate handiwork of the King?

Agathos.—Let me endeavor, my Oinos, to lead you, step by step, to the conception I intend. You are well aware that, as no thought can perish, so no act is without infinite result. We moved our hands, for example, when we were dwellers on the earth, and, in so doing, we gave vibration to the atmosphere which engirdled it. This vibration was indefinitely extended, till it gave impulse to every particle of the earth's air, which thenceforward, *and for ever,* was actuated by the one movement of the hand. This fact the mathematicians of our globe well knew. They made the special effects, indeed, wrought in the fluid by special impulses, the subject of exact calculation—so that it became easy to determine in what precise period an impulse of given extent would engirdle the orb, and impress (for ever) every atom of the atmosphere circumambient. Retrograding, they found no difficulty, from a given effect, under given conditions, in determining the value of the original impulse. Now the mathematicians who saw that the results of any given impulse were absolutely endless—and who saw that a portion of these results were accurately traceable through the agency of algebraic analysis—who saw, too, the facility of the retrogradation—these men saw, at the same time, that this species of analysis itself, had within itself a capacity for indefinite progress—that there were no bounds conceivable to its advancement and applicability, except within the intellect of him who advanced or applied it. But at this point our mathematicians paused.

Oinos.—And why, Agathos, should they have proceeded?

Agathos.—Because there were some considerations of deep interest beyond. It was deducible from what they knew, that to a being of infinite understanding—one to whom the *perfection* of the algebraic analysis lay unfolded—there could be no difficulty in tracing every impulse given the air—and the ether through the air—to the remotest consequences at any even infinitely remote epoch of time. It is indeed demonstrable that every such impulse *given the air,* must, *in the end,* impress every individual thing that exists *within the universe;*—and the being of infinite understanding—the being whom we have imagined—might trace the remote undulations of the impulse—trace them upward and onward in their influences upon all particles of all matter—upward and onward for ever in their modifications of old forms—or, in other words, *in their creation of new*—until he found them reflected—unimpressive *at last*—back from the throne of the Godhead. And not only could such a being do this, but at any epoch, should a given result be afforded him—should one of these numberless comets, for example, be presented to his inspection—he could have no difficulty in determining, by the analytic retrogradation, to what original impulse it was due. This power of retrogradation in its absolute fulness and perfection—this faculty of referring at *all* epochs, *all* effects to *all* causes—is of course the prerogative of the Deity alone—but in every variety of degree, short of the absolute perfection, is the power itself exercised by the whole host of the Angelic Intelligences.

Oinos.—But you speak merely of impulses upon the air.

Agathos.—In speaking of the air, I referred only to the earth : but the general proposition has reference to impulses upon the ether—which, since it pervades, and alone pervades all space, is thus the great medium of *creation*.

Oinos.—Then all motion, of whatever nature, creates ?

Agathos.—It must : but a true philosophy has long taught that the source of all motion is thought—and the source of all thought is——

Oinos.—God.

Agathos.—I have spoken to you, Oinos, as to a child of the fair Earth which lately perished—of impulses upon the atmosphere of the Earth.

Oinos.—You did.

Agathos.—And while I thus spoke, did there not cross your mind some thought of the *physical power of words* ? Is not every word an impulse on the air ?

Oinos.—But why, Agathos, do you weep—and why, oh why do your wings droop as we hover above this fair star—which is the greenest and yet most terrible of all we have encountered in our flight ? Its brilliant flowers look like a fairy dream—but its fierce volcanoes like the passions of a turbulent heart.

Agathos.—They *are !*—they *are !* This wild star—it is now three centuries since, with clasped hands, and with streaming eyes, at the feet of my beloved—I spoke it—with a few passionate sentences—into birth. Its brilliant flowers *are* the dearest of all unfulfilled dreams, and its raging volcanoes *are* the passions of the most turbulent and unhallowed of hearts.

THE COLLOQUY OF MONOS AND UNA.

Μέλλοντα ταυτα·

Sophocles—Antig :

These things are in the future.

Una. "Born again ?"

Monos. Yes, fairest and best beloved Una, "born again." These were the words upon whose mystical meaning I had so long pondered, rejecting the explanations of the priesthood, until Death himself resolved for me the secret.

Una. Death !

Monos. How strangely, sweet Una, you echo my words! I observe, too, a vacillation in your step—a joyous inquietude in your eyes. You are confused and oppressed by the majestic novelty of the Life Eternal. Yes, it was of Death I spoke. And here how singularly sounds that word which of old was wont to bring terror to all hearts—throwing a mildew upon all pleasures !

Una. Ah, Death, the spectre which sate at all feasts ! How often, Monos, did we lose ourselves in speculations upon its nature ! How mysteriously did it act as a check to human bliss—saying unto it "thus far, and no farther !" That earnest mutual love, my own Monos, which burned within our bosoms—how vainly did we flatter ourselves, feeling happy in its first up-springing, that our happiness would strengthen with its strength! Alas! as it grew, so grew in our hearts the dread of that evil hour which was hurrying to separate us forever ! Thus, in time, became painful to love. Hate would have been mercy then

Monos. Speak not here of these griefs, dear Una—mine, mine forever now!

Una. But the memory of past sorrow—is it not present joy? I have much to say yet of the things which have been. Above all, I burn to know the incidents of your own passage through the dark Valley and Shadow.

Monos. And when did the radiant Una ask anything of her Monos in vain? I will be minute in relating all—but at what point shall the weird narrative begin?

Una. At what point?

Monos. You have said.

Una. Monos, I comprehend you. In Death we have both learned the propensity of man to define the indefinable. I will not say, then, commence with the moment of life's cessation—but commence with that sad, sad instant when, the fever having abandoned you, you sank into a breathless and motionless torpor, and I pressed down your pallid eyelids with the passionate fingers of love.

Monos. One word first, my Una, in regard to man's general condition at this epoch. You will remember that one or two of the wise among our forefathers—wise in fact, although not in the world's esteem—had ventured to doubt the propriety of the term "improvement," as applied to the progress of our civilization. There were periods in each of the five or six centuries immediately preceding our dissolution, when arose some vigorous intellect, boldly contending for those principles whose truth appears now, to our disenfranchised reason, so utterly obvious—principles which should have taught our race to submit to the guidance of the natural laws, rather than attempt their control. At long intervals some master-minds appeared, looking upon each advance in practical science as a retro-gradation in the true utility. Occasionally the poetic intellect—that intellect which we now feel to have been the most exalted of all—since those truths which to us were of the most enduring importance could only be reached by that *analogy* which speaks in proof-tones to the imagination alone, and to the unaided reason bears no weight—occasionally did this poetic intellect proceed a step farther in the evolving of the vague idea of the philosophic, and find in the mystic parable that tells of the tree of knowledge, and of its forbidden fruit, death-producing, a distinct intimation that knowledge was not meet for man in the infant condition of his soul. And these men—the poets—living and perishing amid the scorn of the "utilitarians"—of rough pedants, who arrogated to themselves a title which could have been properly applied only to the scorned—these men, the poets, pondered piningly, yet not unwisely, upon the ancient days when our wants were not more simple than our enjoyments were keen—days when *mirth* was a word unknown, so solomnly deep-toned was happiness—holy, august and blissful days, when blue rivers an undammed, between hills unhewn, into far forest solitudes, primæval, odorous, and unexplored.

Yet these noble exceptions from the general misrule served but to strengthen it by opposition. Alas! we had fallen upon the most evil of all our evil days. The great "movement"—that was the cant term—went on: a diseased commotion, moral and physical. Art—the Arts—arose supreme, and, once enthroneu, cast chains upon the intellect which had elevated them to power. Man, because he could not but acknowledge the majesty of Nature, fell into childish exultation at his acquired and still-increasing dominion over her elements. Even while he stalked a God in his own fancy, an infantine imbecility came over him. As might be supposed from the origin of his disorder, he grew infected with system, and with abstraction. He enwrapped himself in generalities. Among other odd ideas, that of universal equality gained ground; and in the face of analogy and of God—in despite of the loud warning voice of the laws of *gradation* so visibly pervading all things in Earth and Heaven—wild attempts at an omni-prevalent Democracy were made. Yet this evil sprang necessarily from the leading evil, Knowledge. Man could not both know and succumb. Meantime huge smoking cities arose, innumerable. Green leaves shrank before the hot breath of furnaces. The fair face of Nature was deformed as with the ravages of some loathsome disease. And methinks, sweet Una, even our slumbering sense of the forced and of the far-fetched might have arrested us here. But now it appears that we had worked out our own destruction in the perversion of our *taste*, or rather in the blind neglect of its culture in the schools. For, in truth, it was at this crisis that taste alone—that faculty which, holding a middle position between the pure intellect and the moral sense, could never safely have been disregarded—it was now that taste alone could have led us gently back to Beauty, to Nature, and to Life. But alas for the pure contemplative spirit and majestic intuition of Plato! Alas for the μουσική which he justly regarded as an all-sufficient education for the soul! Alas for him and for it!—since both were most desperately needed when both were most entirely forgotten or despised.*

Pascal, a philosopher whom we both love, has said, how truly!—"que tout notre raisonnement se réduit à céder au sentiment;" and it is not impossible that the sentiment of the natural, had time permitted it, would have regained its old ascendancy over the harsh mathematical reason of the schools. But this thing was not to be. Prematurely induced by intemperance of knowledge, the old age of the world drew on. This the mass of mankind saw not, or, living lustily although unhappily, affected not to see. But, for myself, the Earth's records had taught me to look for widest ruin as the price of highest civilization. I had imbibed a prescience of our Fate from comparison of China the simple and enduring, with Assyria the architect, with Egypt the astrologer, with Nubia, more crafty than either, the turbulent mother of all Arts. In history† of these regions I met with a ray from the Fu-

---

* "It will be hard to discover a better [method of education] than that which the experience of so many ages has already discovered; and this may be summed up as consisting in gymnastics for the body, and *music* for the soul."—Repub. lib. 2. "For this reason is a musical education most essential; since it causes Rhythm and Harmony to penetrate most intimately into the soul, taking the strongest hold upon it, filling it with *beauty* and making the man *beautiful-minded*. . . . . He will praise and admire *the beautiful;* will receive it with joy into his soul, will feed upon it, and *assimilate his own condition with it*."—Ibid. lib. 3. Music (μουσική) had, however, among the Athenians, a far more comprehensive signification than with us. It included not only the harmonies of time and of tune, but the poetic diction, sentiment and creation, each in its widest sense. The study of *music* was with them, in fact, the general cultivation of the taste—of that which recognizes the beautiful—in contra-distinction from reason, which deals only with the true.

† "History" from ιστορειν, to contemplate.

13*

ture. The individual artificialities of the three latter were local diseases of the Earth, and in their individual overthrows we had seen local remedies applied ; but for the infected world at large I could anticipate no regeneration save in death. That man, as a race, should not become extinct, I saw that he must be " *born again.*"

And now it was, fairest and dearest, that we wrapped our spirits, daily, in dreams. Now it was that, in twilight, we discoursed of the days to come, when the Art-scarred surface of the Earth, having undergone that purification* which alone could efface its rectangular obscenities, should clothe itself anew in the verdure and the mountain-slopes and the smiling waters of Paradise, and be rendered at length a fit dwelling-place for man :—for man the Death-purged—for man to whose now exalted intellect there should be poison in knowledge no more—for the redeemed, regenerated, blissful, and now immortal, but still for the *material*, man.

Una. Well do I remember these conversations, dear Monos ; but the epoch of the fiery overthrow was not so near at hand as we believed, and as the corruption you indicate did surely warrant us in believing. Men lived ; and died individually. You yourself sickened, and passed into the grave ; and thither your constant Una speedily followed you. And though the century which has since elapsed, and whose conclusion brings us thus together once more, tortured our slumbering senses with no impatience of duration, yet, my Monos, it was a century still.

Monos. Say, rather, a point in the vague infinity. Unquestionably, it was in the Earth's dotage that I died. Wearied at neart with anxieties which had their origin in the general turmoil and decay, I succumbed to the fierce fever. After some few days of pain, and many of dreamy delirium replete with ecstasy, the manifestations of which you mistook for pain, while I longed but was impotent to undeceive you—after some days there came upon ne, as you have said, a breathless and motionless torpor ; and his was termed *Death* by those who stood around me.

Words are vague things. My condition did not deprive me of

---

* The word " *purification* ' seems here to be used with reference to its root n the Greek πυρ, fire.

sentience. It appeared to me not greatly dissimilar to the extreme quiescence of him, who, having slumbered long and profoundly, lying motionless and fully prostrate in a midsummer noon, begins to steal slowly back into consciousness, through the mere sufficiency of his sleep, and without being awakened by external disturbances.

I breathed no longer. The pulses were still. The heart had ceased to beat. Volition had not departed, but was powerless. The senses were unusually active, although eccentrically so—assuming often each other's functions at random. The taste and the smell were inextricably confounded, and became one sentiment, abnormal and intense. The rose-water with which your tenderness had moistened my lips to the last, affected me with sweet fancies of flowers—fantastic flowers, far more lovely than any of the old Earth, but whose prototypes we have here blooming around us. The eyelids, transparent and bloodless, offered no complete impediment to vision. As volition was in abeyance, the balls could not roll in their sockets—but all objects within the range of the visual hemisphere were seen with more or less distinctness; the rays which fell upon the external retina, or into the corner of the eye, producing a more vivid effect than those which struck the front or interior surface. Yet, in the former instance, this effect was so far anomalous that I appreciated it only as *sound*—sound sweet or discordant as the matters presenting themselves at my side were light or dark in shade—curved or angular in outline. The hearing, at the same time, although excited in degree, was not irregular in action—estimating real sounds with an extravagance of precision, not less than of sensibility. Touch had undergone a modification more peculiar. Its impressions were tardily received, but pertinaciously retained, and resulted always in the highest physical pleasure. Thus the pressure of your sweet fingers upon my eyelids, at first only recognised through vision, at length, long after their removal, filled my whole being with a sensual delight immeasurable. I say with a sensual delight. *All* my perceptions were purely sensual. The materials furnished the passive brain by the senses were not in the least degree wrought into shape by the deceased understanding. Of pain there was some little; of pleasure there was much ; but of moral pain or pleasure none at all. Thus your wild sobs floated into my ear with all their mournful cadences, and were appreciated in their every variation of sad tone ; but they were soft musical sounds and no more ; they conveyed to the extinct reason no intimation of the sorrows which gave them birth ; while the large and constant tears which fell upon my face, telling the bystanders of a heart which broke, thrilled every fibre of my frame with ecstasy alone. And this was in truth the *Death* of which these bystanders spoke reverently, in low whispers—you, sweet Una, gaspingly, with loud cries.

They attired me for the coffin—three or four dark figures which flitted busily to and fro. As these crossed the direct line of my vision they affected me as *forms ;* but upon passing to my side their images impressed me with the idea of shrieks, groans, and other dismal expressions of terror, of horror, or of wo. You alone, habited in a white robe, passed in all directions musically about me.

The day waned ; and, as its light faded away, I became possessed by a vague uneasiness—an anxiety such as the sleeper feels when sad real sounds fall continuously within his ear—low distant bell-tones, solemn, at long but equal intervals, and commingling with melancholy dreams. Night arrived ; and with its shadows a heavy discomfort. It oppressed my limbs with the oppression of some dull weight, and was palpable. There was also a moaning sound, not unlike the distant reverberation of surf, but more continuous, which, beginning with the first twilight, had grown in strength with the darkness. Suddenly lights were brought into the room, and this reverberation became forthwith interrupted into frequent unequal bursts of the same sound, but less dreary and less distinct. The ponderous oppression was in a great measure relieved ; and, issuing from the flame of each lamp, (for there were many,) there flowed unbrokenly into my ears a strain of melodious monotone. And when now, dear Una, approaching the bed upon which I lay outstretched, you sat gently by my side, breathing odor from your sweet lips, and pressing them upon my brow, there arose tremulously within my bosom, and mingling with the merely physical sensations which circumstances had called forth, a something akin to sentiment itself—a feeling that, half appreciating, half responded to your earnest love and sorrow; but this feeling took no root in the pulseless heart, and seemed indeed rather a shadow than a reality, and faded quickly away, first into extreme quiescence, and then into a purely sensual pleasure as before.

And now, from the wreck and the chaos of the usual senses, there appeared to have arisen within me a sixth, all perfect. In its exercise I found a wild delight—yet a delight still physical, inasmuch as the understanding had in it no part. Motion in the animal frame had fully ceased. No muscle quivered; no nerve thrilled; no artery throbbed. But there seemed to have sprung up in the brain, *that* of which no words could convey to the merely human intelligence even an indistinct conception. Let me term it a mental pendulous pulsation. It was the moral embodiment of man's abstract idea of *Time*. By the absolute equalization of this movement—or of such as this—had the cycles of the firmamental orbs themselves, been adjusted. By its aid I measured the irregularities of the clock upon the mantel, and of the watches of the attendants. Their tickings came sonorously to my ears. The slightest deviations from the true proportion—and these deviations were omni-prævalent—affected me just as violations of abstract truth were wont, on earth, to affect the moral sense. Although no two of the time-pieces in the chamber struck the individual seconds accurately together, yet I had no difficulty in holding steadily in mind the tones, and the respective momentary errors of each. And this—this keen, perfect, self-existing sentiment of *duration*—this sentiment existing (as man could not possibly have conceived it to exist) independently of any succession of events—this idea—this sixth sense, upspringing from the ashes of the rest, was the first obvious and certain step of the intemporal soul upon the threshold of the temporal Eternity.

It was midnight; and you still sat by my side. All others had departed from the chamber of Death. They had deposited me in the coffin. The lamps burned flickeringly; for this I knew by the tremulousness of the monotonous strains. But, suddenly these strains diminished in distinctness and in volume. Finally they ceased. The perfume in my nostrils died away. Forms affected my vision no longer. The oppression of the Darkness uplifted itself from my bosom. A dull shock like that of electricity pervaded my frame, and was followed by total loss of the idea of contact. All of what man has termed sense was merged in the sole consciousness of entity, and in the one abiding sentiment of duration. The mortal body had been at length stricken with the hand of the deadly *Decay*.

Yet had not all of sentience departed; for the consciousness and the sentiment remaining supplied some of its functions by a lethargic intuition. I appreciated the direful change now in operation upon the flesh, and, as the dreamer is sometimes aware of the bodily presence of one who leans over him, so, sweet Una, I still dully felt that you sat by my side. So, too, when the noon of the second day came, I was not unconscious of those movements which displaced you from my side, which confined me within the coffin, which deposited me within the hearse, which bore me to the grave, which lowered me within it, which heaped heavily the mould upon me, and which thus left me, in blackness and corruption, to my sad and solemn slumbers with the worm.

And here, in the prison-house which has few secrets to disclose, there rolled away days and weeks and months; and the soul watched narrowly each second as it flew, and, without effort, took record of its flight—without effort and without object.

A year passed. The consciousness of *being* had grown hourly more indistinct, and that of mere *locality* had, in great measure, usurped its position. The idea of entity was becoming merged in that of *place*. The narrow space immediately surrounding what had been the body, was now growing to be the body itself. At length, as often happens to the sleeper (by sleep and its world alone is *Death* imaged)—at length, as sometimes happened on Earth to the deep slumberer, when some flitting light half startled him into awaking, yet left him half enveloped in dreams—so to me, in the strict embrace of the *Shadow*, came *that* light which alone might have had power to startle—the light of enduring *Love*. Men toiled at the grave in which I lay darkling. They upthrew the damp earth. Upon my mouldering bones there descended the coffin of Una.

And now again all was void. That nebulous light had been extinguished. That feeble th'll had vibrated itself into quiescence. Many *lustra* had supervened. Dust had returned to dust. The worm had food no more. The sense of being had at length utterly departed, and there reigned in its stead—instead of all things—dominant and perpetual—the autocrats *Place* and *Time*. For *that* which *was not*—for that which had no form—for that which had no thought—for that which had no sentience—for that which was soulless, yet of which matter formed no portion—for all this nothingness, yet for all this immortality, the grave was still a home, and the corrosive hours, co-mates.

THE

CONVERSATION OF EIROS AND CHARMION.

Πυρ σοι προσοισω·
I will bring fire to thee.

Eui ipides—Androm :

EIROS.

WHY do you call me Eiros ?

CHARMION.

So henceforward will you always be called. You must forget, too, *my* earthly name, and speak to me as Charmion.

EIROS.

This is indeed no dream !

CHARMION.

Dreams are with us no more ;—but of these mysteries anon. I rejoice to see you looking life-like and rational. The film of the shadow has already passed from off your eyes. Be of heart, and fear nothing. Your allotted days of stupor have expired ; and, to-morrow, I will myself induct you into the full joys and wonders of your novel existence.

EIROS.

True—I feel no stupor—none at all. The wild sickness and the terrible darkness have left me, and I hear no longer that mad, rushing, horrible sound, like the " voice of many waters." Yet my senses are bewildered, Charmion, with the keenness of their perception of *the new*.

CHARMION.

A few days will remove all this ;—but I fully understand you, and 'eel for you. It is now ten earthly years since I underwent what you undergo—yet the remembrance of it hangs by me still. You have now suffered all of pain, however, which you will suffer in Aidenn.

EIROS.

In Aidenn ?

CHARMION.

In Aidenn.

EIROS.

Oh God !—pity me, Charmion !—I am overburthened with the majesty of all things—of the unknown now known—of the speculative Future merged in the august and certain Present.

CHARMION.

Grapple not now with such thoughts. To-morrow we will speak of this. Your mind wavers, and its agitation will find relief in the exercise of simple memories. Look not around, nor forward—but back. I am burning with anxiety to hear the details of that stupendous event which threw you among us. Tell me of it. Let us converse of familiar things, in the old familiar language of the world which has so fearfully perished.

EIROS.

Most fearfully, fearfully !—this is indeed no dream.

CHARMION.

Dreams are no more. Was I much mourned, my Eiros ?

EIROS.

Mourned, Charmion ?—oh deeply. To that last hour of all, there hung a cloud of intense gloom and devout sorrow over your household.

CHARMION.

And that last hour—speak of it. Remember that, beyond the naked fact of the catastrophe itself, I know nothing. When, coming out from among mankind, I passed into Night through the Grave—at that period, if I remember aright, the calamity which overwhelmed you was utterly unanticipated. But, indeed, I knew little of the speculative philosophy of the day.

EIROS.

The individual calamity was, as you say, entirely unanticipated; but analogous misfortunes had been long a subject of discussion with astronomers. I need scarce tell you, my friend, that, even when you left us, men had agreed to understand those passages in the most holy writings which speak of the final destruction of all things by fire, as having reference to the orb of the earth alone. But in regard to the immediate agency of the ruin, speculation had been at fault from that epoch in astronomical knowledge in which the comets were divested of the terrors of flame. The very moderate density of these bodies had been well established. They had been observed to pass among the satellites of Jupiter, without bringing about any sensible alteration either in the masses or in the orbits of these secondary planets. We had long regarded the wanderers as vapory creations of inconceivable tenuity, and as altogether incapable of doing injury to our substantial globe, even in the event of contact. But contact was not in any degree dreaded; for the elements of all the comets were accurately known. That among *them* we should look for the agency of the threatened fiery destruction had been for many years considered an inadmissible idea. But wonders and wild fancies had been, of late days, strangely rife among mankind; and, although it was only with a few of the ignorant that actual apprehension prevailed, upon the announcement by astronomers of a *new* comet, yet this announce ment was generally received with I know not what of agitation and mistrust.

The elements of the strange orb were immediately calculated, and it was at once conceded by all observers, that its path, at perihelion, would bring it into very close proximity with the earth. There were two or three astronomers, of secondary note, who resolutely maintained that a contact was inevitable. I cannot very well express to you the effect of this intelligence upon the people. For a few short days they would not believe an assertion which their intellect, so long employed among worldly considerations, could not in any manner grasp. But the truth of a vitally important fact soon makes its way into the understanding of even the most stolid. Finally, all men saw that astronomical knowledge lied not, and they awaited the comet. Its approach was not, at first, seemingly rapid; nor was its appearance of very unusual character. It was of a dull red, and had little per ceptible train. For seven or eight days we saw no material in crease in its apparent diameter, and but a partial alteration in its color. Meantime, the ordinary affairs of men were discarded, and all interests absorbed in a growing discussion, instituted by the philosophic, in respect to the cometary nature. Even the grossly ignorant aroused their sluggish capacities to such considerations. The learned *now* gave their intellect—their soul—to no such points as the allaying of fear, or to the sustenance of loved theory. They sought—they panted for right views They groaned for perfected knowledge. *Truth* arose in the purity of her strength and exceeding majesty, and the wise bowed down and adored.

That material injury to our globe or to its inhabitants would result from the apprehended contact, was an opinion which hourly lost ground among the wise; and the wise were now freely permitted to rule the reason and the fancy of the crowd. It was demonstrated, that the density of the comet's *nucleus* was far less than that of our rarest gas; and the harmless passage of a similar visitor among the satellites of Jupiter was a point strongly insisted upon, and which served greatly to allay terror. Theologists, with an earnestness fear-enkindled, dwelt upon the biblical prophecies, and expounded them to the people with a directness and simplicity of which no previous instance had been known. That the final destruction of the earth must be brought about by the agency of fire, was urged with a spirit that enforced every where conviction; and that the comets were of no fiery nature (as all men now knew) was a truth which relieved all, in a great measure, from the apprehension of the great calamity foretold. It is noticeable that the popular prejudices and vulgar errors in regard to pestilences and wars—errors which were wont to prevail upon every appearance of a comet—were now altogether unknown. As if by some sudden convulsive exertion, reason had at once hurled superstition from her throne. The feeblest intellect had derived vigor from excessive interest.

What minor evils might arise from the contact were points of elaborate question. The learned spoke of slight geological disturbances, of probable alterations in climate, and consequently in vegetation; of possible magnetic and electric influences. Many held that no visible or perceptible effect would in any manner be produced. While such discussions were going on, their subject gradually approached, growing larger in apparent diameter, and of a more brilliant lustre. Mankind grew paler as it came. All human operations were suspended.

There was an epoch in the course of the general sentiment when the comet had attained, at length, a size surpassing that of any previously recorded visitation. The people now, dismissing any lingering hope that the astronomers were wrong, experienced all the certainty of evil. The chimerical aspect of their terror was gone. The hearts of the stoutest of our race beat violently within their bosoms. A very few days sufficed, however, to merge even such feelings in sentiments more unendurable. We could no longer apply to the strange orb any *accustomed* thoughts. Its *historical* attributes had disappeared. It oppressed us with a hideous *novelty* of emotion. We saw it not as an astronomical phenomenon in the heavens, but as an incubus upon our hearts, and a shadow upon our brains. It had taken, with inconceivable rapidity, the character of a gigantic mantle of rare flame, extending from horizon to horizon.

Yet a day, and men breathed with greater freedom. It was clear that we were already within the influence of the comet; yet we lived. We even felt an unusual elasticity of frame and vivacity of mind. The exceeding tenuity of the object of our dread was apparent; for all heavenly objects were plainly visible through it. Meantime, our vegetation had perceptibly altered; and we gained faith, from this predicted circumstance, in the foresight of the wise. A wild luxuriance of foliage, utterly unknown before, burst out upon every vegetable thing.

Yet another day—and the evil was not altogether upon us. It was now evident that its nucleus would first reach us. A wild change had come over all men; and the first sense of *pain* was the wild signal for general lamentation and horror. This first sense of pain lay in a rigorous constriction of the breast and lungs, and an insufferable dryness of the skin. It could not be denied that our atmosphere was radically affected; the conformation of this atmosphere and the possible modifications to which it might be subjected, were now the topics of discussion. The result of investigation sent an electric thrill of the intensest terror through the universal heart of man.

It had been long known that the air which encircled us was a compound of oxygen and nitrogen gases, in the proportion of twenty-one measures of oxygen, and seventy-nine of nitrogen, in every one hundred of the atmosphere. Oxygen, which was the principle of combustion, and the vehicle of heat, was absolutely necessary to the support of animal life, and was the most powerful and energetic agent in nature. Nitrogen, on the contrary, was incapable of supporting either animal life or flame. An unnatural excess of oxygen would result, it had been ascertained, in just such an elevation of the animal spirits as we had latterly experienced. It was the pursuit, the extension of the idea, which had engendered awe. What would be the result of *a total extraction of the nitrogen?* A combustion irresistible, all-devouring, omni-prevalent, immediate;—the entire fulfilment, in all their minute and terrible details, of the fiery and horror-inspiring denunciations of the prophecies of the Holy Book.

Why need I paint, Charmion, the now disenchained frenzy of mankind? That tenuity in the comet which had previously inspired us with hope, was now the source of the bitterness of despair. In its impalpable gaseous character we clearly perceived the consummation of Fate. Meantime a day again passed—bearing away with it the last shadow of Hope. We gasped in the rapid modification of the air. The red blood bounded tumultuously through its strict channels. A furious delirium possessed all men; and, with arms rigidly outstretched towards the threatening heavens, they trembled and shrieked aloud. But the nucleus of the destroyer was now upon us;—even here in Aidenn, I shudder while I speak. Let me be brief—brief as the ruin that overwhelmed. For a moment there was a wild lurid light alone, visiting and penetrating all things. Then—let us bow down, Charmion, before the excessive majesty of the great God!—then, there came a shouting and pervading sound, as if from the mouth itself of HIM; while the whole incumbent mass of ether in which we existed, burst at once into a species of intense flame, for whose surpassing brilliancy and all-fervid heat even the angels in the high Heaven of pure knowledge have no name. Thus ended all

SHADOW.—A PARABLE.

Yea! though I walk through the valley of the *Shadow*:—*Psalm of David.*

`Ye who read are still among the living: but I who write shall have long since gone my way into the region of shadows. For indeed strange things shall happen, and secret things be known, and many centuries shall pass away, ere these memorials be seen of men. And, when seen, there will be some to disbelieve, and some to doubt, and yet a few who will find much to ponder upon in the characters here graven with a stylus of iron.

The year had been a year of terror, and of feelings more intense than terror for which there is no name upon the earth. For many prodigies and signs had taken place, and far and wide, over sea and land, the black wings of the Pestilence were spread abroad. To those, nevertheless, cunning in the stars, it was not unknown that the heavens wore an aspect of ill; and to me, the Greek Oinos, among others, it was evident that now had arrived the alternation of that seven hundred and ninety-fourth year when, at the entrance of Aries, the planet Jupiter is conjoined with the red ring of the terrible Saturnus. The peculiar spirit of the skies, if I mistake not greatly, made itself manifest, not only in the physical orb of the earth, but in the souls, imaginations, and meditations of mankind.

Over some flasks of the red Chian wine, within the walls of a noble hall, in a dim city called Ptolemais, we sat, at night, a company of seven. And to our chamber there was no entrance save by a lofty door of brass: and the door was fashioned by the artisan Corinnos, and, being of rare workmansh p, was fastened from within.   Black draperies, likewise, in the gloomy room, shut out from our view the moon, the lurid stars, and the peopleless streets— but the boding and the memory of Evil, they would not be so excluded.   There were things around us and about of which I can render no distinct account—things material and spiritual—heaviness in the atmosphere—a sense of suffocation—anxiety—and, above all, that terrible state of existence which the nervous experience when the senses are keenly living and awake, and meanwhile the powers of thought lie dormant.   A dead weight hung upon us.   It hung upon our limbs—upon the household furniture— upon the goblets from which we drank; and all things were depressed, and borne down thereby—all things save only the flames of the seven iron lamps which illumined our revel.   Uprearing themselves in tall slender lines of light, they thus remained burning all pallid and motionless; and in the mirror which their lustre formed upon the round table of ebony at which we sat, each of us there assembled beheld the pallor of his own countenance, and the unquiet glare in the downcast eyes of his companions. Yet we laughed and were merry in our proper way—which was hysterical; and sang the songs of Anacreon—which are madness; and drank deeply—although the purple wine reminded us of blood. For there was yet another tenant of our chamber in the person of young Zoilus.   Dead, and at full length he lay, enshrouded;—the genius and the demon of the scene.   Alas! he bore no portion in our mirth, save that his countenance, distorted with the plague, and his eyes in which Death had but half extinguished the fire of the pestilence, seemed to take such interest in our merriment as the dead may haply take in the merriment of those who are to die. But although I, Oinos, felt that the eyes of the departed were upon me, still I forced myself not to perceive the bitterness of their expression, and, gazing down steadily into the depths of the ebony mirror, sang with a loud and sonorous voice the songs of the son of Teios.   But gradually my songs they ceased, and their echoes, rolling afar off among the sable draperies of the chamber, became weak, and undistinguishable, and so faded away.   And lo! from among those sable draperies where the sounds of the song departed, there came forth a dark and undefined shadow— a shadow such as the moon, when low in heaven, might fashion from the figure of a man : but it was the shadow neither of man, nor of God, nor of any familiar thing. And quivering awhile among the draperies of the room, it at length rested in full view upon the surface of the door of brass. But the shadow was vague, and formless, and indefinite, and was the shadow neither of man nor God—neither God of Greece, nor God of Chaldea, nor any Egyptian God. And the shadow rested upon the brazen doorway, and under the arch of the entablature of the door, and moved not, nor spoke any word, but there became stationary and remained. And the door whereupon the shadow rested was, if I remember aright, over against the feet of the young Zoilus enshrouded. But we, the seven there assembled, having seen the shadow as it came out from among the draperies, dared not steadily behold it, but cast down our eyes, and gazed continually into the depths of the mirror of ebony. And at length I, Oinos, speaking some low words, demanded of the shadow its dwelling and its appellation. And the shadow answered, "I am SHADOW, and my dwelling is near to the Catacombs of Ptolemais, and hard by those dim plains of Helusion which border upon the foul Charonian canal." And then did we, the seven, start from our seats in horror, and stand trembling, and shuddering, and aghast: for the tones in the voice of the shadow were not the tones of any one being, but of a multitude of beings, and, varying in their cadences from syllable to syllable, fell duskily upon our ears in the well remembered and familiar accents of many thousand departed friends.

SILENCE.—A FABLE.

'Ευδουσιν δ'ορεων κορυφαι τε και φαραγγες
Πρωνες τε και χαραδραι.   ALCMAN.

The mountain pinnacles slumber; valleys, crags and caves are silent.

"LISTEN to *me*," said the Demon, as he placed his hand upon my head. "The region of which I speak is a dreary region in Libya, by the borders of the river Zäire. And there is no quiet there, nor silence.

"The waters of the river have a saffron and sickly hue; and they flow not onward to the sea, but palpitate forever and forever beneath the red eye of the sun with a tumultuous and convulsive motion. For many miles on either side of the river's oozy bed is a pale desert of gigantic water-lilies. They sigh one unto the other in that solitude, and stretch towards the heaven their long and ghastly necks, and nod to and fro their everlasting heads. And there is an indistinct murmur which cometh out from among them like the rushing of subterrene water. And they sigh one unto the other.

"But there is a boundary to their realm—the boundary of the dark, horrible, lofty forest. There, like the waves about the Hebrides, the low underwood is agitated continually. But there is no wind throughout the heaven. And the tall primeval trees rock eternally hither and thither with a crashing and mighty sound. And from their high summits, one by one, drop everlasting dews. And at the roots strange poisonous flowers lie writhing in perturbed slumber. And overhead, with a rustling and loud noise, the gray

VOL. II.—14.

clouds rush westwardly forever, until they roll, a cataract, over the fiery wall of the horizon. But there is no wind throughout the heaven. And by the shores of the river Zäire there is neither quiet nor silence.

"It was night, and the rain fell; and, falling, it was rain, but, having fallen, it was blood. And I stood in the morass among the tall lilies, and the rain fell upon my head—and the lilies sighed one unto the other in the solemnity of their desolation.

"And, all at once, the moon arose through the thin ghastly mist, and was crimson in color. And mine eyes fell upon a huge gray rock which stood by the shore of the river, and was lighted by the light of the moon. And the rock was gray, and ghastly, and tall,—and the rock was gray. Upon its front were characters engraven in the stone; and I walked through the morass of water-lilies, until I came close unto the shore, that I might read the characters upon the stone. But I could not decypher them. And I was going back into the morass, when the moon shone with a fuller red, and I turned and looked again upon the rock, and upon the characters;—and the characters were DESOLATION.

"And I looked upwards, and there stood a man upon the summit of the rock; and I hid myself among the water-lilies that I might discover the actions of the man. And the man was tall and stately in form, and was wrapped up from his shoulders to his feet in the toga of old Rome. And the outlines of his figure were indistinct—but his features were the features of a deity; for the mantle of the night, and of the mist, and of the moon, and of the dew, had left uncovered the features of his face. And his brow was lofty with thought, and his eye wild with care; and, in the few furrows upon his cheek I read the fables of sorrow, and weariness, and disgust with mankind, and a longing after solitude.

"And the man sat upon the rock, and leaned his head upon his hand, and looked out upon the desolation. He looked down into the low unquiet shrubbery, and up into the tall primeval trees, and up higher at the rustling heaven, and into the crimson moon. And I lay close within shelter of the lilies, and observed the actions of the man. And the man trembled in the solitude;—but the night waned, and he sat upon the rock.

"And the man turned his attention from the heaven, and looked out upon the dreary river Zäire, and upon the yellow ghastly waters, and upon the pale legions of the water-lilies. And the man listened to the sighs of the water-lilies, and to the murmur that came up from among them. And I lay close within my covert and observed the actions of the man. And the man trembled in the solitude ;—but the night waned and he sat upon the rock.

" Then I went down into the recesses of the morass, and waded afar in among the wilderness of the lilies, and called unto the hippopotami which dwelt among the fens in the recesses of the morass. And the hippopotami heard my call, and came, with the behemoth, unto the foot of the rock, and roared loudly and fearfully beneath the moon. And I lay close within my covert and observed the actions of the man. And the man trembled in the solitude ;—but the night waned and he sat upon the rock.

" Then I cursed the elements with the curse of tumult ; and a frightful tempest gathered in the heaven, where, before, there had been no wind. And the heaven became livid with the violence of the tempest—and the rain beat upon the head of the man—and the floods of the river came down—and the river was tormented into foam—and the water-lilies shrieked within their beds—and the forest crumbled before the wind—and the thunder rolled—and the lightning fell—and the rock rocked to its foundation. And I lay close within my covert and observed the actions of the man. And the man trembled in the solitude ;—but the night waned and he sat upon the rock.

" Then I grew angry and cursed, with the curse of *silence*, the river, and the lilies, and the wind, and the forest, and the heaven, and the thunder, and the sighs of the water-lilies. And they became accursed, and *were still*. And the moon ceased to totter up its pathway to heaven—and the thunder died away—and the lightning did not flash—and the clouds hung motionless —and the waters sunk to their level and remained—and the trees ceased to rock—and the water-lilies sighed no more—and the murmur was heard no longer from among them, nor any shadow of sound throughout the vast illimitable desert. And I looked upon the characters of the rock, and they were changed ;—and the characters were SILENCE.

"And mine eyes fell upon the countenance of the man, and his countenance was wan with terror. And, hurriedly, he raised his head from his hand, and stood forth upon the rock and listened. But there was no voice throughout the vast illimitable desert, and the characters upon the rock were SILENCE. And the man shuddered, and turned his face away, and fled afar off, in haste, so that I beheld him no more."

*   *   *   *   *   *   *

Now there are fine tales in the volumes of the Magi—in the iron-bound, melancholy volumes of the Magi. Therein, I say, are glorious histories of the Heaven, and of the Earth, and of the mighty sea—and of the Genii that overruled the sea, and the earth, and the lofty heaven. There was much lore too in the sayings which were said by the Sybils; and holy, holy things were heard of old by the dim leaves that trembled around Dodona—but, as Allah liveth, that fable which the demon told me as he sat by my side in the shadow of the tomb, I hold to be the most wonderful of all! And as the Demon made an end of his story, he fell back within the cavity of the tomb and laughed. And I could not laugh with the Demon, and he cursed me because I could not laugh. And the lynx which dwelleth forever in the tomb, came out therefrom, and lay down at the feet of the Demon, and looked at him steadily in the face.

PHILOSOPHY OF FURNITURE.

In the internal decoration, if not in the external architecture of their residences, the English are supreme. The Italians have but little sentiment beyond marbles and colors. In France, *meliora probant, deteriora sequuntur*—the people are too much a race of gad-abouts to maintain those household proprieties of which, indeed, they have a delicate appreciation, or at least the elements of a proper sense. The Chinese and most of the eastern races have a warm but inappropriate fancy. The Scotch are *poor* decorists. The Dutch have, perhaps, an indeterminate idea that a curtain is not a cabbage. In Spain they are *all* curtains—a nation of hangmen. The Russians do not furnish. The Hottentots and Kickapoos are very well in their way. The Yankees alone are preposterous.

How this happens, it is not difficult to see. We have no aristocracy of blood, and having therefore as a natural, and indeed as an inevitable thing, fashioned for ourselves an aristocracy of dollars, the *display of wealth* has here to take the place and perform the office of the heraldic display in monarchical countries. By a transition readily understood, and which might have been as readily foreseen, we have been brought to merge in simple *show* our notions of taste itself.

To speak less abstractly. In England, for example, no mere parade of costly appurtenances would be so likely as with us, to create an impression of the beautiful in respect to the appurtenances themselves—or of taste as regards the proprietor :—this for the reason, first, that wealth is not, in England, the loftiest object of ambition as constituting a nobility; and secondly, that there, the true nobility of blood, confining itself within the strict limits of legitimate taste, rather avoids than affects that mere costliness in which a *parvenu* rivalry may at any time be successfully attempted. The people *will* imitate the nobles, and the result is a thorough diffusion of the proper feeling. But in America, the coins current being the sole arms of the aristocracy, their display may be said, in general, to be the sole means of aristocratic distinction; and the populace, looking always upward for models, are insensibly led to confound the two entirely separate ideas of magnificence and beauty. In short, the cost of an article of furniture has at length come to be, with us, nearly the sole test of its merit in a decorative point of view—and this test, once established, has led the way to many analogous errors, readily traceable to the one primitive folly.

There could be nothing more directly offensive to the eye of an artist than the interior of what is termed in the United States— that is to say, in Appallachia—a well-furnished apartment. Its most usual defect is a want of keeping. We speak of the keeping of a room as we would of the keeping of a picture—for both the picture and the room are amenable to those undeviating principles which regulate all varieties of art; and very nearly the same laws by which we decide on the higher merits of a painting, suffice for decision on the adjustment of a chamber.

A want of keeping is observable sometimes in the character of the several pieces of furniture, but generally in their colors or modes of adaptation to use. *Very* often the eye is offended by their inartistical arrangement. Straight lines are too prevalent—too uninterruptedly continued—or clumsily interrupted at right angles. If curved lines occur, they are repeated into unpleasant uniformity. By undue precision, the appearance of many a fine apartment is utterly spoiled.

Curtains are rarely well disposed, or well chosen in respect to other decorations. With formal furniture, curtains are out of place; and an extensive volume of drapery of any kind is, under any circumstances, irreconcilable with good taste—the proper quantum, as well as the proper adjustment, depending upon the character of the general effect.

Carpets are better understood of late than of ancient days, but we still very frequently err in their patterns and colors. The soul of the apartment is the carpet. From it are deduced not only the hues but the forms of all objects incumbent. A judge at common law may be an ordinary man; a good judge of a carpet *must be* a genius. Yet we have heard discoursing of carpets, with the air *"d'un mouton qui rêve,"* fellows who should not and who could not be entrusted with the management of their own *moustaches.* Every one knows that a large floor *may* have a covering of large figures, and that a small one *must* have a covering of small—yet this is not all the knowledge in the world. As regards texture, the Saxony is alone admissible. Brussels is the preterpluperfect tense of fashion, and Turkey is taste in its dying agonies. Touching pattern—a carpet should *not* be bedizzened out like a Riccaree Indian—all red chalk, yellow ochre, and cock's feathers. In brief—distinct grounds, and vivid circular or cycloid figures, *of no meaning,* are here Median laws. The abomination of flowers, or representations of well-known objects of any kind, should not be endured within the limits of Christendom. Indeed, whether on carpets, or curtains, or tapestry, or ottoman coverings, all upholstery of this nature should be rigidly Arabesque. As for those antique floor-cloths still occasionally seen in the dwellings of the rabble—cloths of huge, sprawling, and radiating devises, stripe-interspersed, and glorious with all hues, among which no ground is intelligible—these are but the wicked invention of a race of time-servers and money-lovers—children of Baal and worshippers of Mammon—Benthams, who, to spare thought and economize fancy, first cruelly invented the Kaleidoscope, and then established joint-stock companies to twirl it by steam.

Glare is a leading error in the philosophy of American household decoration—an error easily recognised as deduced from the perversion of taste just specified. We are violently enamored of gas and of glass. The former is totally inadmissible within doors. Its harsh and unsteady light offends. No one having both brains and eyes will use it. A mild, or what artists term a cool light, with its consequent warm shadows, will do wonders for even an ill-furnished apartment. Never was a more lovely thought than that of the astral lamp. We mean, of course, the astral lamp proper—the lamp of Argand, with its original plain ground-glass shade, and its tempered and uniform moonlight rays. The cut-glass shade is a weak invention of the enemy. The eagerness with which we have adopted it, partly on account of its *flashis.ess*, but principally on account of its *greater cost*, is a good commentary on the proposition with which we began. It is not too much to say, that the deliberate employer of a cut-glass shade, is either radically deficient in taste, or blindly subservient to the caprices of fashion. The light proceeding from one of these gaudy abominations is unequal, broken, and painful. It alone is sufficient to mar a world of good effect in the furniture subjected to its influence. Female loveliness, in especial, is more than one-half disenchanted beneath its evil eye.

In the matter of glass, generally, we proceed upon false principles. Its leading feature is *glitter*—and in that one word how much of all that is detestable do we express! Flickering, unquiet lights, are *sometimes* pleasing—to children and idiots always so—but in the embellishment of a room they should be scrupulously avoided. In truth, even strong *steady* lights are inadmissible. The huge and unmeaning glass chandeliers, prism-cut, gas-lighted, and without shade, which dangle in our most fashionable drawing-rooms, may be cited as the quintessence of all that is false in taste or preposterous in folly.

The rage for *glitter*—because its idea has become, as we before observed, confounded with that of magnificence in the abstract—has led us, also, to the exaggerated employment of mirrors. We line our dwellings with great British plates, and then imagine we have done a fine thing. Now the slightest thought will be sufficient to convince any one who has an eye at all, of the ill effect of numerous looking-glasses, and especially of large ones. Regarded apart from its reflection, the mirror presents a continuous, flat, colorless, unrelieved surface,—a thing always and obviously unpleasant. Considered as a reflector, it is potent in producing a monstrous and odious uniformity: and the evil is here aggravated, not in merely direct proportion with the augmentation of its sources, but in a ratio constantly increasing. In fact, a room with four or five mirrors arranged at random, is, for all purposes of artistic show, a room of no shape at all. If we add to this evil, the attendant glitter upon glitter, we have a perfect farrago of discordant and displeasing effects. The veriest bumpkin, on entering an apartment so bedizzened, would be instantly aware of something wrong, although he might be altogether unable to assign a cause for his dissatisfaction. But let the same person be led into a room tastefully furnished, and he would be startled into an exclamation of pleasure and surprise.

It is an evil growing out of our republican institutions, that here a man of large purse has usually a very little soul which he keeps in it. The corruption of taste is a portion or a pendant of the dollar-manufacture. As we grow rich, our ideas grow rusty. It is, therefore, not among *our* aristocracy that we must look (if at all, in Appallachia,) for the spirituality of a British *boudoir*. But we have seen apartments in the tenure of Americans of modern means, which, in negative merit at least, might vie with any of the *or-molu'd* cabinets of our friends across the water. Even *now*, there is present to our mind's eye a small and not ostentatious chamber with whose decorations no fault can be found. The proprietor lies asleep on a sofa—the weather is cool—the time is near midnight: we will make a sketch of the room during his slumber.

It is oblong—some thirty feet in length and twenty-five in breadth—a shape affording the best (ordinary) opportunities for the adjustment of furniture. It has but one door—by no means a wide one—which is at one end of the parallelogram, and but two windows, which are at the other. These latter are large, reaching down to the floor—have deep recesses—and open on an Italian *veranda*. Their panes are of a crimson-tinted glass, set in rose-wood framings, more massive than usual. They are curtained within the recess, by a thick silver tissue adapted to the shape of the window, and hanging loosely in small volumes. Without the recess are curtains of an exceedingly rich crimson silk, fringed with a deep network of gold, and lined with the silver tissue, which is the material of the exterior blind. There are no cornices; but the folds of the whole fabric (which are sharp rather than massive, and have an airy appearance,) issue from beneath a broad entablature of rich giltwork, which encircles the room at the junction of the ceiling and walls. The drapery is thrown open also, or

14*

closed, by means of a thick rope of gold loosely enveloping it, and resolving itself readily into a knot; no pins or other such devices are apparent. The colors of the curtains and their fringe—the tints of crimson and gold—appear everywhere in profusion, and determine the *character* of the room. The carpet—of Saxony material—is quite half an inch thick, and is of the same crimson ground, relieved simply by the appearance of a gold cord (like that festooning the curtains) slightly relieved above the surface of the *ground*, and thrown upon it in such a manner as to form a succession of short irregular curves—one occasionally overlaying the other. The walls are prepared with a glossy paper of a silver gray tint, spotted with small Arabesque devices of a fainter hue of the prevalent crimson. Many paintings relieve the expanse of the paper. These are chiefly landscapes of an imaginative cast—such as the fairy grottoes of Stanfield, or the lake of the Dismal Swamp of Chapman. There are, nevertheless, three or four female heads, of an ethereal beauty—portraits in the manner of Sully. The tone of each picture is warm, but dark. There are no " brilliant effects." *Repose* speaks in all. Not one is of small size. Diminutive paintings give that *spotty* look to a room, which is the blemish of so many a fine work of Art overtouched. The frames are broad but not deep, and richly carved, without being *dulled* or filagreed. They have the whole lustre of burnished gold. They lie flat on the walls, and do not hang off with cords. The designs themselves are often seen to better advantage in this latter position, but the general appearance of the chamber is injured. But one mirror—and this not a very large one—is visible. In shape it is nearly circular—and it is hung so that a reflection of the person can be obtained from it in none of the ordinary sitting-places of the room. Two large low sofas of rosewood and crimson silk, gold-flowered, form the only seats, with the exception of two light conversation chairs, also of rose-wood. There is a pianoforte, (rose-wood, also,) without cover, and thrown open. An octagonal table, formed altogether of the richest gold-threaded marble, is placed near one of the sofas. This is also without cover—the drapery of the curtains has been thought sufficient. Four large and gorgeous Sèvres vases, in which bloom a profusior of sweet and vivid flowers, occupy the slightly rounded angles of the room. A tall candelabrum, bearing a small antique lamp with highly perfumed oil, is standing near the head of my sleeping friend. Some light and graceful hanging shelves, with golden edges and crimson silk cords with gold tassels, sustain two or three hundred magnificently bound books. Beyond these things, there is no furniture, if we except an Argand lamp, with a plain crimson-tinted ground-glass shade, which depends from the lofty vaulted ceiling by a single slender gold chain, and throws a tranquil but magical radiance over all.

A TALE OF JERUSALEM

Intensos rigidam in frontem ascendere canos
Passus erat ——————

LUCAN—*De Catone.*

——————a bristly *bore.*

Translation.

"LET us hurry to the walls," said Abel-Phittim to Buzi-Ben-Levi and Simeon the Pharisee, on the tenth day of the month Thammuz, in the year of the world three thousand nine hundred and forty-one—"let us hasten to the ramparts adjoining the gates of Benjamin, which is in the city of David, and overlooking the camp of the uncircumcised; for it is the last hour of the fourth watch, being sunrise; and the idolaters, in fulfilment of the promise of Pompey, should be awaiting us with the lambs for the sacrifices."

Simeon, Abel-Phittim, and Buzi-Ben-Levi, were the Gizbarim, or sub-collectors of the offering, in the holy city of Jerusalem.

"Verily," replied the Pharisee, "let us hasten: for this generosity in the heathen is unwonted; and fickle-mindedness has ever been an attribute of the worshippers of Baal."

"That they are fickle-minded and treacherous is as true as the Pentateuch," said Buzi-Ben-Levi, "but that is only towards the people of Adonai. When was it ever known that the Ammonites proved wanting to their own interests? Methinks it is no great stretch of generosity to allow us lambs for the altar of the Lord, receiving in lieu thereof thirty silver shekels per head!"

"Thou forgettest, however, Ben-Levi," replied Abel-Phittim, "that the Roman Pompey, who is now impiously besieging the city of the Most High, has no assurity that we apply not the lambs thus purchased for the altar, to the sustenance of the body, rather than of the spirit."

"Now, by the five corners of my beard," shouted the Pharisee, who belonged to the sect called The Dashers (that little knot of saints whose manner of *dashing* and lacerating the feet against the pavement was long a thorn and a reproach to less zealous devotees—a stumbling block to less gifted perambulators)—"by the five corners of that beard which as a priest I am forbidden to shave!—have we lived to see the day when a blaspheming and idolatrous upstart of Rome shall accuse us of appropriating to the appetites of the flesh the most holy and consecrated elements! Have we lived to see the day when"——

"Let us not question the motives of the Philistine," interrupted Abel-Phittem, "for to-day we profit for the first time by his avarice or by his generosity; but rather let us hurry to the ramparts, lest offerings should be wanting for that altar whose fire the rains of heaven cannot extinguish, and whose pillars of smoke no tempest can turn aside."

That part of the city to which our worthy Gizbarim now hastened, and which bore the name of its architect King David, was esteemed the most strongly fortified district of Jerusalem; being situated upon the steep and lofty hill of Zion. Here a broad, deep, circumvallatory trench, hewn from the solid rock, was defended by a wall of great strength erected upon its inner edge. This wall was adorned, at regular interspaces, by square towers of white marble; the lowest sixty, and the highest one hundred and twenty cubits in height. But, in the vicinity of the gate of Benjamin, the wall arose by no means from the margin of the fosse. On the contrary, between the level of the ditch and the basement of the rampart, sprang up a perpendicular cliff of two hundred and fifty cubits; forming part of the precipitous Mount Moriah. So that when Simeon and his associates arrived on the Summit of the tower called Adoni-Bezek—the loftiest of all the turrets around about Jerusalem, and the usual place of conference with the besieging army—they looked down upon the camp of the enemy from an eminence excelling by many feet, that of the Pyramid of Cheops, and, by several, that of the temple of Belus.

"Verily," sighed the Pharisee, as he peered dizzily over the precipice, "the uncircumcised are as the sands by the sea-shore— as the locusts in the wilderness! The valley of The King hath become the vally of Adommin."

"And yet," added Ben-Levi, "thou canst not point me out a Philistine—no, not one—from Aleph to Tau—from the wilderness to the battlements—who seemeth any bigger than the letter Jod!"

"Lower away the basket with the shekels of silver!" here shouted a Roman soldier in a hoarse, rough voice, which appeared to issue from the regions of Pluto—"lower away the basket with the accursed coin which it has broken the jaw of a noble Roman to pronounce! Is it thus you evince your gratitude to our master Pompeius, who, in his condescension, has thought fit to listen to your idolatrous importunities? The god Phœbus, who is a true god, has been charioted for an hour—and were you not to be on the ramparts by sunrise? Ædepol! do you think that we, the conquerors of the world, have nothing better to do than stand waiting by the walls of every kennel, to traffic with the dogs of the earth? Lower away! I say—and see that your trumpery be bright in color, and just in weight!"

"El Elohim!" ejaculated the Pharisee, as the discordant tones of the centurion rattled up the crags of the precipice, and fainted away against the temple—"El Elohim!—who is the God Phœbus?—whom doth the blasphemer invoke? Thou, Buzi-Ben-Levi! who art read in the laws of the Gentiles, and hast sojourned among them who dabble with the Teraphim!—is it Nergal of whom the idolater speaketh?—or Ashimah?—or Nibhaz?—or Tartak?—or Adramalech?—or Anamalech?—or Succoth-Benith?—or Dagon? —or Belial?—or Baal-Perith?—or Baal-Peor?—or Baal-Zebub?"

"Verily it is neither—but beware how thou lettest the rope slip too rapidly through thy fingers; for should the wicker-work chance to hang on the projection of yonder crag, there will be a woful outpouring of the holy things of the santuary."

By the assistance of some rudely constructed machinery, the heavily laden basket was now carefully lowered down among the multitude; and, from the giddy pinnacle, the Romans were seen gathering confusedly round it; but owing to the vast height and the prevalence of a fog, no distinct view of their operations could be obtained.

Half an hour had already elapsed.

"We shall be too late," sighed the Pharisee, as at the expiration of this period, he looked over into the abyss—"we shall be too late! we shall be turned out of office by the Katholim."

"No more," responded Abel-Phittim, "no more shall we feast upon the fat of the land—no longer shall our beards be odorous with frankincense—our loins girded up with fine linen from the Temple."

"Raca!" swore Ben-Levi, "Raca! do they mean to defraud us of the purchase money? or, Holy Moses! are they weighing the shekels of the tabernacle?"

"They have given the signal at last," cried the Pharisee, "they have given the signal at last!—pull away, Abel-Phittim!—and thou, Buzi-Ben-Levi, pull away!—for verily the Philistines have either still hold upon the basket, or the Lord hath softened their hearts to place therein a beast of good weight!" And the Gizbarim pulled away, while their burthen swung heavily upwards through the still increasing mist.

*   *   *   *   *   *   *   *   *

"Booshoh he!"—as, at the conclusion of an hour, some object at the extremity of the rope became indistinctly visible—"Booshoh he!" was the exclamation which burst from the lips of Ben-Levi.

"Booshoh he!—for shame!—it is a ram from the thickets of Engedi, and as rugged as the valley of Jehosaphat!"

"It is a firstling of the flock," said Abel-Phittim, "I know him by the bleating of his lips, and the innocent folding of his limbs. His eyes are more beautiful than the jewels of the Pectoral, and his flesh is like the honey of Hebron."

"It is a fatted calf from the pastures of Bashan," said the Pharisee, "the heathen have dealt wonderfully with us!—let us raise up our voices in a psalm!—let us give thanks on the shawm and on the psaltery—on the harp and on the huggab—on the cythern and on the sackbut!"

It was not until the basket had arrived within a few feet of the

Gizbarim, that a low grunt betrayed to their perception a *hog* of no common size.

" Now El Emanu !" slowly, and with upturned eyes ejaculated the trio, as, letting go their hold, the emancipated porker tumbled headlong among the Philistines, "El Emanu !—God be with us! —*it is the unutterable flesh !"*

A TALE OF THE RAGGED MOUNTAINS

DURING the fall of the year 1827, while residing near Charlottesville, Virginia, I casually made the acquaintance of Mr. Augustus Bedloe. This young gentleman was remarkable in every respect, and excited in me a profound interest and curiosity. I found it impossible to comprehend him either in his moral or his physical relations. Of his family I could obtain no satisfactory account. Whence he came, I never ascertained. Even about his age—although I call him a young gentleman—there was something which perplexed me in no little degree. He certainly *seemed* young—and he made a point of speaking about his youth —yet there were moments when I should have had little trouble in imagining him a hundred years of age. But in no regard was he more peculiar than in his personal appearance. He was singularly tall and thin. He stooped much. His limbs were exceedingly long and emaciated. His forehead was broad and low. His complexion was absolutely bloodless. His mouth was large and flexible, and his teeth were more wildly uneven, although sound, than I had ever before seen teeth in a human head. The expression of his smile, however, was by no means unpleasing, as might be supposed; but it had no variation whatever. It was one of profound melancholy—of a phaseless and unceasing gloom. His eyes were abnormally large, and round like those of a cat. The pupils, too, upon any accession or diminution of light, underwent contraction or dilation, just such as is observed in the feline tribe. In moments of excitement the orbs grew bright to a degree almost inconceivable; seeming to emit luminous rays, not of a reflected, but of an intrinsic lustre, as does a candle or the sun; yet their ordinary condition was so totally vapid, filmy and dull, as to convey the idea of the eyes of a long-interred corpse.

These peculiarities of person appeared to cause him much annoyance, and he was continually alluding to them in a sort of half explanatory, half apologetic strain, which, when I first heard it, impressed me very painfully. I soon, however, grew accustomed to it, and my uneasiness wore off. It seemed to be his design rather to insinuate than directly to assert that, physically, he had not always been what he was—that a long series of neuralgic attacks had reduced him from a condition of more than usual personal beauty, to that which I saw. For many years past he had been attended by a physician, named Templeton—an old gentleman, perhaps seventy years of age—whom he had first encountered at Saratoga, and from whose attention, while there, he either received, or fancied that he received, great benefit. The result was that Bedloe, who was wealthy, had made an arrangement with Doctor Templeton, by which the latter, in consideration of a liberal annual allowance, had consented to devote his time and medical experience exclusively to the care of the invalid.

Doctor Templeton had been a traveller in his younger days, and, at Paris, had become a convert, in great measure, to the doctrines of Mesmer. It was altogether by means of magnetic remedies that he had succeeded in alleviating the acute pains of his patient; and this success had very naturally inspired the latter with a certain degree of confidence in the opinions from which the remedies had been educed. The Doctor, however, like all enthusiasts, had struggled hard to make a thorough convert of his pupil, and finally so far gained his point as to induce the sufferer to submit to numerous experiments.—By a frequent repetition of these, a result had arisen, which of late days has become so common as to attract little or no attention, but which, at the period of which I write, had very rarely been known in America. I mean to say, that between Doctor Templeton and Bedloe there had grown up, little by little, a very distinct and strongly marked *rapport*, or magnetic relation. I am not prepared to assert, however, that this *rapport* extended beyond the limits of the simple sleep-producing power; but this power itself had attained great intensity. At the first attempt to induce the magnetic somnolency, the mesmerist entirely failed. In the fifth or sixth he succeeded very partially, and after long continued effort. Only at the twelfth was the triumph complete. After this the will of the patient succumbed rapidly to that of the physician, so that, when I first became acquainted with the two, sleep was brought about almost instantaneously, by the mere volition of the operator, even when the invalid was unaware of his presence. It is only now, in the year 1845, when similar miracles are witnessed daily by thousands, that I dare venture to record this apparent impossibility as a matter of serious fact.

The temperature of Bedloe was, in the highest degree, sensitive, excitable, enthusiastic. His imagination was singularly vigorous and creative; and no doubt it derived additional force from the habitual use of morphine, which he swallowed in great quantity, and without which he would have found it impossible to exist. It was his practice to take a very large dose of it immediately after breakfast, each morning—or rather immediately after a cup of strong coffee, for he ate nothing in the forenoon—and then set forth alone, or attended only by a dog, upon a long ramble among the chain of wild and dreary hills that lie westward and southward of Charlottesville, and are there dignified by the title of the Ragged Mountains.

Upon a dim, warm, misty day, towards the close of November, and during the strange *interregnum* of the seasons which in America is termed the Indian Summer, Mr. Bedloe departed as usual, for the hills. The day passed, and still he did not return.

About eight o'clock at night, having become seriously alarmed as his protracted absence, we were about setting out in search of him, when he unexpectedly made his appearance, in health no worse than usual, and in rather more than ordinary spirits. The account which he gave of his expedition, and of the events which had detained him, was a singular one indeed.

" You will remember," said he, " that it was about nine in the morning when I left Charlottesville. I bent my steps immediately to the mountains, and, about ten, entered a gorge which was entirely new to me. I followed the windings of this pass with much interest.—The scenery which presented itself on all sides, although scarcely entitled to be called grand, had about it an indescribable, and to me, a delicious aspect of dreary desolation The solitude seemed absolutely virgin. I could not help believing that the green sods and the gray rocks upon which I trod, had been trodden never before by the foot of a human being. So entirely secluded, and in fact inaccessible, except through a series of accidents, is the entrance of the ravine, that it is by no means impossible that I was indeed the first adventurer—the very first and sole adventurer who had ever penetrated its recesses

"The thick and peculiar mist, or smoke, which distinguishes the Indian Summer, and which now hung heavily over all objects, served, no doubt, to deepen the vague impressions which these objects created. So dense was this pleasant fog, that I could at no time see more than a dozen yards of the path before me. This path was excessively sinuous, and as the sun could not be seen, I soon lost all idea of the direction in which I journeyed. In the meantime the morphine had its customary effect—that of enduing all the external world with an intensity of interest. In the quivering of a leaf—in the hue of a blade of grass—in the shape of a trefoil—in the humming of a bee—in the gleaming of a dew-drop —in the breathing of the wind—in the faint odors that came from the forest—there came a whole universe of suggestion—a gay and motly train of rhapsodical and immethodical thought.

" Busied in this, I walked on for several hours, during which the mist deepened around me to so great an extent, that at length I was reduced to an absolute groping of the way. And now an indescribable uneasiness possessed me—a species of nervous hesitation and tremor.—I feared to tread, lest I should be precipitated into some abyss. I remembered, too, strange stories told about these Ragged Hills, and of the uncouth and fierce races of men who tenanted their groves and caverns. A thousand vague fancies oppressed and disconcerted me—fancies the more distressing because vague. Very suddenly my attention was arrested by the loud beating of a drum.

"My amazement was, of course, extreme. A drum in these hills was a thing unknown. I could not have been more surprised at the sound of the trump of the Archangel. But a new and still more astounding source of interest and perplexity arose. There came a wild rattling or jingling sound, as if of a bunch of large keys—and upon the instant a dusky-visaged and half-naked man rushed past me with a shriek. He came so close to my person that I felt his hot breath upon my face. He bore in one hand an instrument composed of an assemblage of steel rings, and shook them vigorously as he ran. Scarcely had he disappeared in the mist, before, panting after him, with open mouth and glaring eyes, there darted a huge beast. I could not be mistaken in its character. It was a hyena.

"The sight of this monster rather relieved than heightened my terrors—for I now made sure that I dreamed, and endeavored to arouse myself to waking consciousness. I stepped boldly and briskly forward. I rubbed my eyes. I called aloud. I pinched my limbs. A small spring of water presented itself to my view, and here, stooping, I bathed my hands and my head and neck. This seemed to dissipate the equivocal sensations which had hitherto annoyed me. I arose, as I thought, a new man, and proceeded steadily and complacently on my unknown way.

"At length, quite overcome by exertion, and by a certain oppressive closeness of the atmosphere, I seated myself beneath a tree. Presently there came a feeble gleam of sunshine, and the shadow of the leaves of the tree fell faintly but definitely upon the grass. At this shadow I gazed wonderingly for many minutes. Its character stupified me with astonishment. I looked upward. The tree was a palm.

"I now arose hurriedly, and in a state of fearful agitation—for the fancy that I dreamed would serve me no longer. I saw—I felt that I had perfect command of my senses—and these senses now brought to my soul a world of novel and singular sensation. The heat became all at once intolerable. A strange odor loaded the breeze.—A low continuous murmur, like that arising from a full, but gently flowing river, came to my ears, intermingled with the peculiar hum of multitudinous human voices.

"While I listened in an extremity of astonishment which I need not attempt to describe, a strong and brief gust of wind bore off the incumbent fog as if by the wand of an enchanter.

"I found myself at the foot of a high mountain, and looking down into a vast plain, through which wound a majestic river. On the margin of this river stood an Eastern-looking city, such as

we read of in the Arabian Tales, but of a character even more singular than any there described. From my position, which was
far above the level of the town, I could perceive its every nook
and corner, as if delineated on a map. The streets seemed innumerable, and crossed each other irregularly in all directions, but
were rather long winding alleys than streets, and absolutely
swarmed with inhabitants. The houses were wildly picturesque.
On every hand was a wilderness of balconies, of verandahs, of minarets, of shrines, and fantastically carved oriels. Bazaars abound-
ed ; and in these were displayed rich wares in infinite variety and
profusion—silks, muslins, the most dazzling cutlery, the most magnificent jewels and gems. Besides these things, were seen, on all
sides, banners and palanquins, litters with stately dames close
veiled, elephants gorgeously caparisoned, idols grotesquely hewn,
drums, banners and gongs, spears, silver and gilded maces. And
amid the crowd, and the clamor, and the general intricacy and
confusion—amid the million of black and yellow men, turbaned
and robed, and of flowing beard, there roamed a countless multitude of holy filleted bulls, while vast legions of the filthy but sacred ape clambered, chattering and shrieking, about the cornices
of the mosques, or clung to the minarets and oriels. From the
swarming streets to the banks of the river, there descended innumerable flights of steps leading to bathing places, while the river
itself seemed to force a passage with difficulty through the vast
fleets of deeply-burthened ships that far and wide encountered its
surface. Beyond the limits of the city arose, in frequent majestic
groups, the palm and the cocoa, with other gigantic and wierd
trees of vast age; and here and there might be seen a field of rice,
the thatched hut of a peasant, a tank, a stray temple, a gypsy
camp, or a solitary graceful maiden taking her way, with a pitcher
upon her head, to the banks of the magnificent river.

   "You will say now, of course, that I dreamed ; but not so.
What I saw—what I heard—what I felt—what I thought—had
about it nothing of the unmistakeable idiosyncrasy of the dream.
All was rigorously self-consistent. At first, doubting that I was
really awake, I entered into a series of tests, which soon convinced
me that I really was. Now, when one dreams, and, in the dream,
suspects that he dreams, the suspicion *never fails to confirm itself,*

and the sleeper is almost immediately aroused. Thus Novalis errs not in saying that 'we are near waking when we dream that we dream.' Had the vision occurred to me as I describe it, without my suspecting it as a dream, then a dream it might absolutely have been, but, occurring as it did, and suspected and tested as it was, I am forced to class it among other phenomena."

"In this I am not sure that you are wrong," observed Dr Templeton, "but proceed. You arose and descended into the city."

"I arose," continued Bedloe, regarding the Doctor with an air of profound astonishment, "I arose, as you say, and descended into the city. On my way, I fell in with an immense populace, crowding through every avenue, all in the same direction, and exhibiting in every action the wildest excitement. Very suddenly, and by some inconceivable impulse, I became intensely imbued with personal interest in what was going on. I seemed to feel that I had an important part to play, without exactly understanding what it was. Against the crowd which environed me, however, I experienced a deep sentiment of animosity. I shrank from amid them, and, swiftly, by a circuitous path, reached and entered the city. Here all was the wildest tumult and contention. A small party of men, clad in garments half Indian, half European, and officered by gentlemen in a uniform partly British, were engaged, at great odds, with the swarming rabble of the alleys. I joined the weaker party, arming myself with the weapons of a fallen officer, and fighting I knew not whom with the nervous ferocity of despair. We were soon overpowered by numbers, and driven to seek refuge in a species of kiosk. Here we barricaded ourselves, and, for the present, were secure. From a loop-hole near the summit of the kiosk, I perceived a vast crowd, in furious agitation, surrounding and assaulting a gay palace that overhung the river. Presently, from an upper window of this palace, there descended an effeminate-looking person, by means of a string made of the turbans of his attendants. A boat was at hand, in which he escaped to the opposite bank of the river.

"And now a new object took possession of my soul. I spoke a few hurried but energetic words to my companions, and, having succeeded in gaining over a few of them to my purpose, made a frantic sally from the kiosk. We rushed amid the crowd that surrounded it. They retreated, at first, before us. They rallied, fought madly, and retreated again. In the meantime we were borne far from the kiosk, and became bewildered and entangled among the narrow streets of tall overhanging houses, into the recesses of which the sun had never been able to chine. The rabble pressed impetuously upon us, harassing us with their spears, and overwhelming us with flights of arrows. These latter were very remarkable, and resembled in some respects the writhing creese of the Malay. They were made to imitate the body of a creeping serpent, and were long and black, with a poisoned barb. One of them struck me upon the right temple. I reeled and fell. An instantaneous and dreadful sickness seized me. I struggled—I gasped—I died.

" You will hardly persist *now*," said I, smiling, " that the whole of your adventure was not a dream. You are not prepared to maintain that you are dead ?"

When I said these words, I of course expected some lively sally from Bedloe in reply ; but, to my astonishment, he hesitated, trembled, became fearfully pallid, and remained silent. I looked towards Templeton. He sat erect and rigid in his chair—his teeth chattered, and his eyes were starting from their sockets. " Proceed !" he at length said hoarsely to Bedloe.

" For many minutes," continued the latter, " my sole sentiment —my sole feeling—was that of darkness and nonentity, with the consciousness of death. At length, there seemed to pass a violent and sudden shock through my soul, as if of electricity. With it came the sense of elasticity and of light. This latter I felt—not saw. In an instant I seemed to rise from the ground. But I had no bodily, no visible, audible, or palpable presence. The crowd had departed. The tumult had ceased. The city was in comparative repose. Beneath me lay my corpse, with the arrow in my temple, the whole head greatly swollen and disfigured. But all these things I felt—not saw. I took interest in nothing. Even the corpse seemed a matter in which I had no concern. Volition I had none, but appeared to be impelled into motion, and flitted buoyantly out of the city, retracing the circuitous path by which I had entered it. When I had attained that point of the ravine in the mountains, at which I had encountered the hyena, I again experienced a shock as of a galvanic battery; the sense of weight, of volition, of substance, returned. I became my original self, and bent my steps eagerly homewards—but the past had not lost the vividness of the real—and not now, even for an instant, can I compel my understanding to regard it as a dream."

"Nor was it," said Templeton, with an air of deep solemnity, "yet it would be difficult to say how otherwise it should be termed. Let us suppose only, that the soul of the man of to-day is upon the verge of some stupendous psychal discoveries. Let us content ourselves with this supposition. For the rest I have some explanation to make. Here is a water-color drawing, which I should have shown you before, but which an unaccountable sentiment of horror has hitherto prevented me from showing."

We looked at the picture which he presented. I saw nothing in it of an extraordinary character; but its effect upon Bedloe was prodigious. He nearly fainted as he gazed. And yet it was but a miniature portrait—a miraculously accurate one, to be sure—of his own very remarkable features. At least this was my thought as I regarded it.

"You will perceive," said Templeton, "the date of this picture —it is here, scarcely visible, in this corner—1780. In this year was the portrait taken. It is the likeness of a dead friend—a Mr. Oldeb—to whom I became much attached at Calcutta, during the administration of Warren Hastings. I was then only twenty years old. When I first saw you, Mr. Bedloe, at Saratoga, it was the miraculous similarity which existed between yourself and the painting, which induced me to accost you, to seek your friendship, and to bring about those arrangements which resulted in my becoming your constant companion. In accomplishing this point, I was urged partly, and perhaps principally, by a regretful memory of the deceased, but also, in part, by an uneasy, and not altogether horrorless curiosity respecting yourself.

"In your detail of the vision which presented itself to you amid the hills, you have described, with the minutest accuracy, the Indian city of Benares, upon the Holy River. The riots, the combats, the massacre, were the actual events of the insurrection of Cheyte Sing, which took place in 1780, when Hastings was put in imminent peril of his life. The man escaping by the string of turbans, was Cheyte Sing himself. The party in the kiosk were sepoys and British officers, headed by Hastings. Of this party I was one, and did all I could to prevent the rash and fatal sally of the officer who fell, in the crowded alleys, by the poisoned arrow of a Bengalee. That officer was my dearest friend. It was Oldeb. You will perceive by these manuscripts," (here the speaker produced a note-book in which several pages appeared to have been freshly written) " that at the very period in which you fancied these things amid the hills, I was engaged in detailing them upon paper here at home."

In about a week after this conversation, the following paragraphs appeared in a Charlottesville paper:

" We have the painful duty of announcing the death of Mr. AUGUSTUS BEDLO, a gentleman whose amiable manners many virtues have long endeared him to the citizens of Charlottesville.

" Mr. B., for some years past, has been subject to neuralgia, which has often threatened to terminate fatally ; but this can be regarded only as the mediate cause of his decease. The proximate cause was one of especial singularity. In an excursion to the Ragged Mountains, a few days since, a slight cold and fever were contracted, attended with great determination of blood to the head. To relieve this, Dr. Templeton resorted to topical bleeding. Leeches were applied to the temples. In a fearfully brief period the patient died, when it appeared that, in the jar containing the leeches, had been introduced, by accident, one of the venomous vermicular sangsues which are now and then found in the neighboring ponds. This creature fastened itself upon a small artery in the right temple. Its close resemblance to the medicinal leech caused the mistake to be overlooked until too late.

" N. B. The poisonous sangsue of Charlottesville may always be distinguished from the medicinal leech by its blackness, and especially by its writhing or vermicular motions, which very nearly resemble those of a snake."

I was speaking with the editor of the paper in question, upon the topic of this remarkable accident, when it occurred to me to ask how it happened that the name of th deceased had been given as Bedlo.

"I presume," said I, "you have authority for this spelling, but I have always supposed the name to be written with an *e* at the end."

"Authority?—no," he replied. "It is a mere typographical error. The name is Bedlo with an *e*, all the world over, and I never knew it to be spelt otherwise in my life."

"Then," said I mutteringly, as I turned upon my heel, "then indeed has it come to pass that one truth is stranger than any fiction—for Bedlo, without the *e*, what is it but Oldeb conversed! And this man tells me it is a typographical error."

THE SPECTACLES.

Many years ago, it was the fashion to ridicule the idea of
'love at first sight;" but those who think, not less than those
who feel deeply, have always advocated its existence. Modern
discoveries, indeed, in what may be termed ethical magnetism or
magnetœsthetics, render it probable that the most natural, and,
consequently, the truest and most intense of the human affections,
are those which arise in the heart as if by electric sympathy—in
a word, that the brightest and most enduring of the psychal fetters
are those which are riveted by a glance. The confession I am
about to make, will add another to the already almost innumerable instances of the truth of the position.

My story requires that I should be somewhat minute. I am
still a very young man—not yet twenty-two years of age. My
name, at present, is a very usual and rather plebeian one—Simpson. I say " at present;" for it is only lately that I have been so
called—having legislatively adopted this surname within the last
year, in order to receive a large inheritance left me by a distant
male relative, Adolphus Simpson, Esq. The bequest was con-
ditioned upon my taking the name of the testator;—the family,
not the Christian name; my Christian name is Napoleon Buona-
parte—or, more properly, these are my first and middle appel-
lations.

I assumed the name, Simpson, with some reluctance, as in my
true patronym, Froissart, I felt a very pardonable pride—believing

that I could trace a descent from the immortal author of the "Chronicles." While on the subject of names, by the by, I may mention a singular coincidence of sound attending the names of some of my immediate predecessors. My father was a Monsieur Froissart, of Paris. His wife—my mother, whom he married at fifteen—was a Mademoiselle Croissart, eldest daughter of Croissart the banker; whose wife, again, being only sixteen when married, was the eldest daughter of one Victor Voissart. Monsieur Voissart, very singularly, had married a lady of similar name—a Mademoiselle Moissart. She, too, was quite a child when married; and her mother, also, Madame Moissart, was only fourteen when led to the altar. These early marriages are usual in France. Here, however, are Moissart, Voissart, Croissart, and Froissart, all in the direct line of descent. My own name, though, as I say, became Simpson, by act of Legislature, and with so much repugnance on my part, that, at one period, I actually hesitated about accepting the legacy with the useless and annoying *proviso* attached.

As to personal endowments I am by no means deficient. On the contrary, I believe that I am well made, and possess what nine-tenths of the world would call a handsome face. In height I am five feet eleven. My hair is black and curling. My nose is sufficiently good. My eyes are large and gray; and although, in fact, they are weak to a very inconvenient degree, still no defect in this regard would be suspected from their appearance. The weakness itself, however, has always much annoyed me, and I have resorted to every remedy—short of wearing glasses. Being youthful and good-looking, I naturally dislike these, and have resolutely refused to employ them. I know nothing, indeed, which so disfigures the countenance of a young person, or so impresses every feature with an air of demureness, if not altogether of sanctimoniousness and of age. An eye-glass, on the other hand, has a savor of downright foppery and affectation. I have hitherto managed as well as I could without either. But something too much of these merely personal details, which, after all, are of little importance. I will content myself with saying, in addition, that my temperament is sanguine, rash, ardent, enthusiastic—and that all my life I have been a devoted admirer of the women.

One night last winter, I entered a box at the P—— Theatre, in company with a friend, Mr. Talbot. It was an opera night, and the bills presented a very rare attraction, so that the house was excessively crowded. We were in time, however, to obtain the front seats which had been reserved for us, and into which, with some little difficulty, we elbowed our way.

For two hours, my companion, who was a musical *fanatico*, gave his undivided attention to the stage; and, in the meantime, I amused myself by observing the audience, which consisted, in chief part, of the very *élite* of the city. Having satisfied myself upon this point, I was about turning my eyes to the *prima donna*, when they were arrested and riveted by a figure in one of the private boxes which had escaped my observation.

If I live a thousand years, I can never forget the intense emotion with which I regarded this figure. It was that of a female, the most exquisite I had ever beheld. The face was so far turned towards the stage, that, for some minutes, I could not obtain a view of it—but the form was *divine;* no other word can sufficiently express its magnificent proportion—and even the term "divine," seems ridiculously feeble as I write it.

The magic of a lovely form in woman—the necromancy of female gracefulness—was always a power which I had found it impossible to resist; but here was grace personified, incarnate, the *beau idéal* of my wildest and most enthusiastic visions. The figure, almost all of which the construction of the box permitted to be seen, was somewhat above the medium height, and nearly approached, without positively reaching, the majestic. Its perfect fulness and *tournure* were delicious. The head, of which only the back was visible, rivalled in outline that of the Greek Psyche, and was rather displayed than concealed by an elegant cap of *gaze aérienne*, which put me in mind of the *ventum textilem* of Apuleius. The right arm hung over the balustrade of the box, and thrilled every nerve of my frame with its exquisite symmetry. Its upper portion was draperied by one of the loose open sleeves now in fashion. This extended but little below the elbow. Beneath it was worn an under one of some frail material, close-fitting, and terminated by a cuff of rich lace which fell gracefully over the top of the hand, revealing only the delicate fingers, upon one of which sparkled a diamond ring, which I at once saw was of extraordinary value. The admirable roundness of the wrist was well set off by a bracelet which encircled it, and which also was ornamented and clasped by a magnificent *aigrette* of jewels—telling, in words that could not be mistaken, at once of the wealth and fastidious taste of the wearer.

I gazed at this queenly apparition for at least half an hour, as if I had been suddenly converted to stone; and, during this period, I felt the full force and truth of all that has been said or sung concerning "love at first sight." My feelings were totally different from any which I had hitherto experienced, in the presence of even the most celebrated specimens of female loveliness. An unaccountable, and what I am compelled to consider a *magnetic* sympathy of soul for soul, seemed to rivet, not only my vision, but my whole powers of thought and feeling upon the admirable object before me. I saw—I felt—I knew that I was deeply, madly, irrevocably in love—and this even before seeing the face of the person beloved. So intense, indeed, was the passion that consumed me, that I really believe it would have received little if any abatement had the features, yet unseen, proved of merely ordinary character; so anomalous is the nature of the only true love—of the love at first sight—and so little really dependent is it upon the external conditions which only seem to create and control it.

While I was thus wrapped in admiration of this lovely vision, a sudden disturbance among the audience caused her to turn her head partially towards me, so that I beheld the entire profile of the face. Its beauty even exceeded my anticipations—and yet there was something about it which disappointed me without my being able to tell exactly what it was. I said "disappointed," but this is not altogether the word. My sentiments were at once quieted and exalted. They partook less of transport and more of calm enthusiasm—of enthusiastic repose. This state of feeling arose, perhaps, from the Madonna-like and matronly air of the face; and yet I at once understood that it could not have arisen entirely from this. There was something else—some mystery which I could not develope—some expression about the countenance which slightly disturbed me while it greatly heightened my interest. In fact, I was just in that condition of mind which prepares a young and susceptible man for any act of extravagance. Had the lady been alone, I should undoubtedly have entered her box and accosted her at all hazards; but, fortunately, she was attended by two companions—a gentleman, and a strikingly beautiful woman, to all appearance a few years younger than herself.

I revolved in my mind a thousand schemes by which I might obtain, hereafter, an introduction to the elder lady, or, for the present, at all events, a more distinct view of her beauty. I would have removed my position to one nearer her own, but the crowded state of the theatre rendered this impossible; and the stern decrees of Fashion had, of late, imperatively prohibited the use of the opera-glass, in a case such as this, even had I been so fortunate as to have one with me—but I had not—and was thus in despair.

At length I bethought me of applying to my companion.

"Talbot," I said, "*you* have an opera-glass. Let me have it."

"An opera-glass!—no!—what do you suppose *I* would be doing with an opera-glass?" Here he turned impatiently towards the stage.

"But, Talbot," I continued, pulling him by the shoulder, "listen to me, will you? Do you see the stage-box?—there!—no, the next—Did you ever behold as lovely a woman?"

"She is very beautiful, no doubt," he said.

"I wonder who she can be?"

"Why, in the name of all that is angelic, don't you *know* who she is? 'Not to know her, argues yourself unknown.' She is the celebrated Madame Lalande—the beauty of the day *par excellence*, and the talk of the whole town. Immensely wealthy, too—a widow—and a great match—has just arrived from Paris."

"Do you know her?"

"Yes—I have the honor."

"Will you introduce me?"

"Assuredly—with the greatest pleasure; when shall it be?"

"To-morrow, at one, I will call upon you at B——'s."

"Very good; and now *do* hold your tongue, *if* you can."

In this latter respect I was forced to take Talbot's advice; for he remained obstinately deaf to every further question or suggestion, and occupied himself exclusively for the rest of the evening with what was transacting upon the stage.

In the mean time I kept my eyes riveted on Madame Lalande, and at length had the good fortune to obtain a full front view of her face. It was exquisitely lovely : this, of course, my heart had told me before, even had not Talbot fully satisfied me upon the point—but still the unintelligible something disturbed me. I finally concluded that my senses were impressed by a certain air of gravity, sadness, or, still more properly, of weariness, which took something from the youth and freshness of the countenance, only to endow it with a seraphic tenderness and majesty, and thus, of course, to my enthusiastic and romantic temperament, with an interest tenfold.

While I thus feasted my eyes, I perceived, at last, to my great trepidation, by an almost imperceptible start on the part of the lady, that she had become suddenly aware of the intensity of my gaze. Still, I was absolutely fascinated, and could not withdraw it, even for an instant. She turned aside her face, and again I saw only the chiselled contour of the back portion of the head. After some minutes, as if urged by curiosity to see if I was still looking, she gradually brought her face again around and again encountered my burning gaze. Her large dark eyes fell instantly, and a deep blush mantled her cheek. But what was my astonishment at perceiving that she not only did not a second time avert her head, but that she actually took from her girdle a double eye-glass — elevated it — adjusted it — and then regarded me through it, intently and deliberately, for the space of several minutes.

Had a thunderbolt fallen at my feet I could not have been more thoroughly astounded—astounded *only*—not offended or disgusted in the slightest degree ; although an action so bold in any other woman, would have been likely to offend or disgust. But the whole thing was done with so much quietude—so much *nonchalance*—so much repose—with so evident an air of the highest breeding, in short—that nothing of mere effrontery was perceptible, and my sole sentiments were those of admiration and surprise.

I observed that, upon her first elevation of the glass, she had seemed satisfied with a momentary inspection of my person, and

15*

was withdrawing the instrument, when, as if struck by a second thought, she resumed it, and so continued to regard me with fixed attention for the space of several minutes—for five minutes, at the very least, I am sure.

This action, so remarkable in an American theatre, attracted very general observation, and gave rise to an indefinite movement, or *buzz*, among the audience, which for a moment filled me with confusion, but produced no visible effect upon the countenance of Madame Lalande.

Having satisfied her curiosity—if such it was—she dropped the glass, and quietly gave her attention again to the stage; her profile now being turned toward myself, as before. I continued to watch her unremittingly, although I was fully conscious of my rudeness in so doing. Presently I saw the head slowly and slightly change its position; and soon I became convinced that the lady, while pretending to look at the stage was, in fact, attentively regarding myself. It is needless to say what effect this conduct, on the part of so fascinating a woman, had upon my excitable mind.

Having thus scrutinized me for perhaps a quarter of an hour, the fair object of my passion addressed the gentleman who attended her, and, while she spoke, I saw distinctly, by the glances of both, that the conversation had reference to myself.

Upon its conclusion, Madame Lalande again turned towards the stage, and, for a few minutes, seemed absorbed in the performances. At the expiration of this period, however, I was thrown into an extremity of agitation by seeing her unfold, for the second time, the eye-glass which hung at her side, fully confront me as before, and, disregarding the renewed buzz of the audience, survey me, from head to foot, with the same miraculous composure which had previously so delighted and confounded my soul.

This extraordinary behavior, by throwing me into a perfect fever of excitement—into an absolute delirium of love—served rather to embolden than to disconcert me. In the mad intensity of my devotion, I forgot everything but the presence and the majestic loveliness of the vision which confronted my gaze. Watching my opportunity, when I thought the audience were fully engaged with the opera, I at length caught the eyes of Madame Lalande, and, upon the instant, made a slight but unmistakeable bow.

She blushed very deeply—then averted her eyes—then slowly and cautiously looked around, apparently to see if my rash action had been noticed—then leaned over towards the gentleman who sat by her side.

I now felt a burning sense of the impropriety I had committed, and expected nothing less than instant exposure; while a vision of pistols upon the morrow floated rapidly and uncomfortably through my brain. I was greatly and immediately relieved, however, when I saw the lady merely hand the gentleman a playbil, without speaking; but the reader may form some feeble conception of my astonishment—of my *profound* amazement—my delirious bewilderment of heart and soul—when, instantly afterwards, having again glanced furtively around, she allowed her bright eyes to settle fully and steadily upon my own, and then, with a faint smile, disclosing a bright line of her pearly teeth, made two distinct, pointed and unequivocal affirmative inclinations of the head.

It is useless, of course, to dwell upon my joy—upon my transport—upon my illimitable ecstasy of heart. If ever man was mad with excess of happiness, it was myself at that moment. I loved. This was my *first* love—so I felt it to be. It was love supreme—indescribable. It was "love at first sight;" and at first sight too, it had been appreciated and *returned*.

Yes, returned. How and why should I doubt it for an instant? What other construction could I possibly put upon such conduct, on the part of a lady so beautiful—so wealthy—evidently so accomplished—of so high breeding—of so lofty a position in society—in every regard so entirely respectable as I felt assured was Madame Lalande? Yes, she loved me—she returned the enthusiasm of my love, with an enthusiasm as blind—as uncompromising—as uncalculating—as abandoned—and as utterly unbounded as my own! These delicious fancies and reflections, however, were now interrupted by the falling of the drop-curtain. The audience arose; and the usual tumult immediately supervened. Quitting Talbot abruptly, I made every effort to force my way into closer proximity with Madame Lalande. Having failed in this, on account of the crowd, I at length gave up the chase, and bent my steps homewards; consoling myself for my disappointment in not having been able to touch even the hem of her robe, by the reflection that I should be introduced by Talbot, in due form upon the morrow.

This morrow at last came; that is to say, a day finally dawned upon a long and weary night of impatience; and then the hours until "one," were snail-paced, dreary and innumerable. But even Stamboul, it is said, shall have an end, and there came an end to this long delay. The clock struck. As the last echo ceased, I stepped into B——'s and inquired for Talbot.

"Out," said the footman—Talbot's own.

"Out!" I replied, staggering back half a dozen paces—"let me tell you, my fine fellow, that this thing is thoroughly impossible and impracticable; Mr. Talbot is *not* out. What do you mean!"

"Nothing, sir: only Mr. Talbot is not in. That's all. He rode over to S——, immediately after breakfast, and left word that he would not be in town again for a week."

I stood petrified with horror and rage. I endeavored to reply, but my tongue refused its office. At length I turned on my heel, livid with wrath, and inwardly consigning the whole tribe of the Talbots to the innermost regions of Erebus. It was evident that my considerate friend, *il fanatico*, had quite forgotten his appointment with myself—had forgotten it as soon as it was made. At no time was he a very scrupulous man of his word. There was no help for it; so smothering my vexation as well as I could, I strolled moodily up the street, propounding futile inquiries about Madame Lalande to every male acquaintance I met. By report she was known, I found, to all—to many by sight—but she had been in town only a few weeks, and there were very few, therefore, who claimed her personal acquaintance. These few, being still comparatively strangers, could not, or would not, take the liberty of introducing me through the formality of a morning call. While I stood thus, in despair, conversing with a trio of friends upon the all absorbing subject of my heart, it so happened that the subject itself passed by.

"As I live, there she is!" cried one.

"Surpassingly beautiful!" exclaimed a second.

"An angel upon earth!" ejaculated a third.

I looked; and, in an open carriage which approached us, passing slowly down the street, sat the enchanting vision of the opera, accompanied by the younger lady who had occupied a portion of her box.

"Her companion also wears remarkably well," said the one of my trio who had spoken first.

"Astonishingly," said the second; "still quite a brilliant air; but art will do wonders. Upon my word, she looks better than she did at Paris five years ago. A beautiful woman still;—don't you think so, Froissart?—Simpson, I mean."

"*Still!*" said I, "and why shouldn't she be? But compared with her friend she is as a rushlight to the evening star—a glow-worm to Antares."

"Ha! ha! ha!—why, Simpson, you have an astonishing tact at making discoveries—original ones, I mean." And here we separated, while one of the trio began humming a gay *vaudeville*, of which I caught only the lines—

> Ninon, Ninon, Ninon à bas—
> A bas Ninon De L'Enclos!

During this little scene, however, one thing had served greatly to console me, although it fed the passion by which I was consumed. As the carriage of Madame Lalande rolled by our group, I had observed that she recognised me; and more than this, she had blessed me, by the most seraphic of all imaginable smiles, with no equivocal mark of the recognition.

As for an introduction, I was obliged to abandon all hope of it, until such time as Talbot should think proper to return from the country. In the meantime I perseveringly frequented every reputable place of public amusement; and, at length, at the theatre, where I first saw her, I had the supreme bliss of meeting her, and of exchanging glances with her once again. This did not occur, however, until the lapse of a fortnight. Every day, in the *interim*, I had inquired for Talbot at his hotel, and every day had been thrown into a spasm of wrath by the everlasting "Not come home yet" of his footman.

Upon the evening in question, therefore, I was in a condition little short of madness. Madame Lalande, I had been told, was a Parisian—had lately arrived from Paris—might she not suddenly return ?—return before Talbot came back—and might she not be thus lost to me forever ? The thought was too terrible to bear. Since my future happiness was at issue, I resolved to act with a manly decision. In a word, upon the breaking up of the play, I traced the lady to her residence, noted the address, and the next morning sent her a full and elaborate letter, in which I poured out my whole heart.

I spoke boldly, freely—in a word, I spoke with passion. I concealed nothing—nothing even of my weakness. I alluded to the romantic circumstances of our first meeting—even to the glances which had passed between us. I went so far as to say that I felt assured of her love ; while I offered this assurance, and my own intensity of devotion, as two excuses for my otherwise unpardonable conduct. As a third, I spoke of my fear that she might quit the city before I could have the opportunity of a formal introduction. I concluded the most wildly enthusiastic epistle ever penned, with a frank declaration of my worldly circumstances—of my affluence—and with an offer of my heart and of my hand.

In an agony of expectation I awaited the reply. After what seemed the lapse of century it came.

Yes, *actually came*. Romantic as all this may appear, I really received a letter from Madame Lalande—the beautiful, the wealthy, the idolised Madame Lalande.—Her eyes—her magnificent eyes—had not belied her noble heart. Like a true Frenchwoman, as she was, she had obeyed the frank dictates of her reason—the generous impulses of her nature—despising the conventional pruderies of the world. She had *not* scorned my proposals. She had *not* sheltered herself in silence. She had *not* returned my letter unopened. She had even sent me, in reply, one penned by her own exquisite fingers. It ran thus :

Monsieur Simpson vill pardonne me for not compose de butefulle tong of his contrée so vell as might. It is only de late dat I am arrive, and not yet ave de opportunité for to—l'étudier.

Vid dis apologie for the manière, I vill now say dat, hélas !—Monsieur Simpson ave guess but de too true. Need I say de more ! Hélas ! am I not ready speak de too moahe !   EUGÉNIE LALANDE.

This noble-spirited note I kissed a million times, and committed, no doubt, on its account, a thousand other extravagances that have now escaped my memory. Still Talbot *would* not return. Alas! could he have formed even the vaguest idea of the suffering his absence occasioned his friend, would not his sympathising nature have flown immediately to my relief? Still, however, he came *not*. I wrote. He replied. He was detained by urgent business—but would shortly return. He begged me not to be impatient—to moderate my transports—to read soothing books—to drink nothing stronger than Hock—and to bring the consolations of philosophy to my aid. The fool! if he could not come himself, why, in the name of everything rational, could he not have enclosed me a letter of presentation? I wrote again, entreating him to forward one forthwith. My letter was returned by *that* footman, with the following endorsement in pencil. The scoundrel had joined his master in the country:

Left S—— yesterday, for parts unknown—did not say where—or when be back—so thought best to return letter, knowing your handwriting, and as how you is always, more or less, in a hurry.

Yours, sincerely, STUBBS.

After this, it is needless to say, that I devoted to the infernal deities both master and valet;—but there was little use in anger, and no consolation at all in complaint.

But I had yet a resource left, in my constitutional audacity. Hitherto it had served me well, and I now resolved to make it avail me to the end. Besides, after the correspondence which had passed between us, what act of mere informality *could* I commit, within bounds, that ought to be regarded as indecorous by Madame Lalande? Since the affair of the letter, I had been in the habit of watching her house, and thus discovered that, about twilight, it was her custom to promenade, attended only by a negro in livery, in a public square overlooked by her windows. Here, amid the luxuriant and shadowing groves, in the gray gloom of a sweet midsummer evening, I observed my opportunity and accosted her.

The better to deceive the servant in attendance, I did this with the assured air of an old and familiar acquaintance. With a presence of mind truly Parisian, she took the cue at once, and, to greet me, held out the most bewitchingly little of hands. The valet at once fell into the rear; and now, with hearts full to overflowing, we discoursed long and unreservedly of our love.

As Madame Lalande spoke English even less fluently than she wrote it, our conversation was necessarily in French. In this sweet tongue, so adapted to passion, I gave loose to the impetuous enthusiasm of my nature, and with all the eloquence I could command, besought her consent to an immediate marriage.

At this impatience she smiled. She urged the old story of decorum—that bug-bear which deters so many from bliss until the opportunity for bliss has forever gone by. I had most imprudently made it known among my friends, she observed, that I desired her acquaintance—thus that I did not possess it—thus, again, there was no possibility of concealing the date of our first knowledge of each other. And then she adverted, with a blush, to the extreme recency of this date. To wed immediately would be improper—would be indecorous—would be *outré*. All this she said with a charming air of *näiveté* which enraptured while it grieved and convinced me. She went even so far as to accuse me, laughingly, of rashness—of imprudence. She bade me remember that I really even knew not who she was—what were her prospects, her connections, her standing in society. She begged me, but with a sigh, to reconsider my proposal, and termed my love an infatuation—a will 'o the wisp—a fancy or fantasy of the moment—a baseless and unstable creation rather of the imagination than of the heart. These things she uttered as the shadows of the sweet twilight gathered darkly and more darkly around us—and then, with a gentle pressure of her fairy-like hand, overthrew, in a single sweet instant, all the argumentative fabric she had reared.

I replied as best I could—as only a true lover can. I spoke at length, and perseveringly of my devotion, of my passion—of her exceeding beauty, and of my own enthusiastic admiration. In conclusion, I dwelt, with a convincing energy, upon the perils that encompass the course of love—that course of true love that never did run smooth, and thus deduced the manifest danger of rendering that course unnecessarily long.

This latter argument seemed finally to soften the rigor of her determination. She relented; but there was yet an obstacle, she said, which she felt assured I had not properly considered. This was a delicate point—for a woman to urge, especially so; in mentioning it, she saw that she must make a sacrifice of her feelings; still, for *me*, every sacrifice should be made. She alluded to the topic of *age*. Was I aware—was I fully aware of the discrepancy between us? That the age of the husband should surpass by a few years—even by fifteen or twenty—the age of the wife, was regarded by the world as admissible, and, indeed, as even proper; but she had always entertained the belief that the years of the wife should *never* exceed in number those of the husband. A discrepancy of this unnatural kind gave rise, too frequently, alas! to a life of unhappiness. Now she was aware that my own age did not exceed two and twenty; and I, on the contrary, perhaps, was *not* aware that the years of my Eugènie extended very considerably beyond that sum.

About all this there was a nobility of soul—a dignity of candor—which delighted—which enchanted me—which eternally riveted my chains. I could scarcely restrain the excessive transport which possessed me.

"My sweetest Eugènie," I cried, "what is all this about which you are discoursing? Your years surpass in some measure my own. But what then? The customs of the world are so many conventional follies. To those who love as ourselves, in what respect differs a year from an hour? I am twenty-two, you say; granted: indeed you may as well call me, at once, twenty-three. Now you yourself, my dearest Eugènie, can have numbered no more than—can have numbered no more than—no more than—than—than—than—"

Here I paused for an instant, in the expectation that Madame Lalande would interrupt me by supplying her true age. But a French woman is seldom direct, and has always, by way of answer to an embarrassing query, some little practical reply of her own. In the present instance, Eugènie, who, for a few moments past, had seemed to be searching for something in her bosom, at length let fall upon the grass a miniature, which I immediately picked up and presented to her.

"Keep it!" she said, with one of her most ravishing smiles

" Keep it for my sake—for the sake of her whom it too flatteringly
represents. Besides, upon the back of the trinket, you may discover,
perhaps, the very information you seem to desire. It is now, to
be sure, growing rather dark—but you can examine it at your leisure in the morning. In the mean time, you shall be my escort
home to-night. My friends are about holding a little musical le-
vée. I can promise you, too, some good singing. We French are
not nearly so punctilious as you Americans, and I shall have no
difficulty in smuggling you in, in the character of an old acquaintance."

With this, she took my arm, and I attended her home. The
mansion was quite a fine one, and, I believe, furnished in good
taste. Of this latter point, however, I am scarcely qualified to
judge ; for it was just dark as we arrived ; and in American man-
sions of the better sort, lights seldom, during the heat of summer,
make their appearance at this, the most pleasant period of the day.
In about an hour after my arrival, to be sure, a single shaded solar lamp was lit in the principal drawing-room ; and this apartment, I could thus see, was arranged with unusual good taste and
even splendor ; but two other rooms of the suite, and in which
the company chiefly assembled, remained, during the whole evening, in a very agreeable shadow. This is a well conceived custom,
giving the party at least a choice of light or shade, and one which our
friends over the water could not do better than immediately adopt.

The evening thus spent was unquestionably the most delicious
of my life. Madame Lalande had not overrated the musical abilities of her friends ; and the singing I here heard I had never
heard excelled in any private circle out of Vienna. The instrumen-
tal performers were many and of superior talents. The vocalists
were chiefly ladies, and no individual sang less than well. At
length, upon a peremptory call for " Madame Lalande," she arose
at once, without affectation or demur, from the *chaise longue* upon
which she had sate by my side, and, accompanied by one or two
gentlemen and her female friend of the opera, repaired to the piano
in the main drawing-room. I would have escorted her myself ; but
felt that, under the circumstances of my introduction to the house,
I had better remain unobserved where I was. I was thus deprived of the pleasure of seeing, although not of hearing her, sing.

The impression she produced upon the company seemed electrical—but the effect upon myself was something even more. I know not how adequately to describe it. It arose in part, no doubt, from the sentiment of love with which I was imbued; but chiefly from my conviction of the extreme sensibility of the singer. It is beyond the reach of art to endow either air or recitative with more impassioned *expression* than was hers. Her utterance of the romance in Otello—the tone with which she gave the words "*Sul mio sasso*," in the Capuletti—is ringing in my memory yet. Her lower tones were absolutely miraculous. Her voice embraced three complete octaves, extending from the contralto D to the D upper soprano, and, though sufficiently powerful to have filled the San Carlos, executed, with the minutest precision, every difficulty of vocal composition—ascending and descending scales, cadences, or *fiorituri*. In the finale of the Sonnambula, she brought about a most remarkable effect at the words—

> Ah ! non guinge uman pensiero
> Al contento ond 'io son piena.

Here, in imitation of Malibran, she modified the original phrase of Bellini, so as to let her voice descend to the tenor G, when by a rapid transition, she struck the G above the treble stave, springing over an interval of two octaves.

Upon rising from the piano after these miracles of vocal execution, she resumed her seat by my side; when I expressed to her, in terms of the deepest enthusiasm, my delight at her performance. Of my surprise I said nothing, and yet was I most unfeignedly surprised; for a certain feebleness, or rather a certain tremulous indecision of voice in ordinary conversation, had prepared me to anticipate that, in singing, she would not acquit herself with any remarkable ability.

Our conversation was now long, earnest, uninterrupted, and totally unreserved. She made me relate many of the earlier passages of my life, and listened with breathless attention, to every word of the narrative. I concealed nothing—I felt that I had a right to conceal nothing from her confiding affection. Encouraged by her candor upon the delicate point of her age, I entered, with perfect frankness, not only into a detail of my many minor vices, but made full confession of those moral and even of those physical infirmities, the disclosure of which, in demanding so much higher a degree of courage, is so much surer an evidence of love. I touched upon my college indiscretions—upon my extravagances upon my carousals—upon my debts—upon my flirtations. I even went so far as to speak of a slightly hectic cough with which, at one time, I had been troubled—of a chronic rheumatism—of a twinge of hereditary gout—and, in conclusion, of the disagreeable and inconvenient, but hitherto carefully concealed, weakness of my eyes.

"Upon this latter point," said Madame Lalande, laughingly, "you have been surely injudicious in coming to confession; for, without the confession, I take it for granted that no one would have accused you of the crime. By the by," she continued, "have you any recollection"—and here I fancied that a blush, even through the gloom of the apartment, became distinctly visible upon her cheek—"have you any recollection, *mon cher ami*, of this little ocular assistant which now depends from my neck?"

As she spoke she twirled in her fingers the identical double eyeglass, which had so overwhelmed me with confusion at the opera.

"Full well—alas! do I remember it," I exclaimed, pressing passionately the delicate hand which offered the glasses for my inspection. They formed a complex and magnificent toy, richly chased and filagreed, and gleaming with jewels, which, even in the deficient light, I could not help perceiving were of high value.

"*Eh bien! mon ami,*" she resumed with a certain *empressement* of manner that rather surprised me—"*Eh bien, mon ami,* you have earnestly besought of me a favor which you have been pleased to denominate priceless. You have demanded of me my hand upon the morrow. Should I yield to your entreaties—and, I may add, to the pleadings of my own bosom—would I not be entitled to demand of you a very—a very little boon in return?"

"Name it!" I exclaimed with an energy that had nearly drawn upon us the observation of the company, and restrained by their presence alone from throwing myself impetuously at her feet. "Name it, my beloved, my Eugènie, my own!—name it!—but alas, it is already yielded ere named."

"You shall conquer then, *mon amie*," said she, "for the sake of the Eugénie whom you love, this little weakness which you have last confessed—this weakness more moral than physical—and which, let me assure you, is so unbecoming the nobility of your real nature—so inconsistent with the candor of your usual character—and which, if permitted farther control, will assuredly involve you, sooner or later, in some very disagreeable scrape. You shall conquer, for my sake, this affectation which leads you, as you yourself acknowledge, to the tacit or implied denial of your infirmity of vision. For, this infirmity you virtually deny, in refusing to employ the customary means for its relief. You will understand me to say, then, that I wish you to wear spectacles:—ah, hush!—you have already consented to wear them, *for my sake*. You shall accept the little toy which I now hold in my hand, and which, though admirable as an aid to vision, is really of no very immense value as a gem. You perceive that, by a trifling modification thus—or thus—it can be adapted to the eyes in the form of spectacles, or worn in the waistcoat pocket as an eye-glass. It is in the former mode, however, and habitually, that you have already consented to wear it *for my sake*."

This request—must I confess it?—confused me in no little degree. But the condition with which it was coupled rendered hesitation, of course, a matter altogether out of the question.

"It is done!" I cried, with all the enthusiasm that I could muster at the moment. "It is done—it is most cheerfully agreed. I sacrifice every feeling for your sake. To-night I wear this dear eye-glass, *as an eye-glass*, and upon my heart; but with the earliest dawn of that morning which gives me the pleasure of calling you wife, I will place it upon my—upon my nose—and there wear it ever afterwards, in the less romantic, and less fashionable, but certainly in the more serviceable form which you desire."

Our conversation now turned upon the details of our arrangements for the morrow. Talbot, I learned from my betrothed, had just arrived in town. I was to see him at once, and procure a carriage. The *soirée* would scarcely break up before two; and by this hour the vehicle was to be at the door: when, in the confusion occasioned by the departure of the company, Madame L. could easily enter it unobserved. We were then to call at the house of a clergyman who would be in waiting; there be married, drop Talbot, and proceed on a short tour to the East; leaving the fashionable world at home to make whatever comments upon the matter it thought best.

Having planned all this, I immediately took leave, and went in search of Talbot, but, on the way, I could not refrain from stepping into a hotel, for the purpose of inspecting the miniature and this I did by the powerful aid of the glasses. The countenance was a surpassingly beautiful one! Those large luminous eyes!—that proud Grecian nose!—those dark luxuriant curls!— "Ah!" said I exultingly to myself, "this is indeed the speaking image of my beloved!" I turned the reverse, and discovered the words—"Eugènie Lalande—aged twenty-seven years and seven months."

I found Talbot at home, and proceeded at once to acquaint him with my good fortune. He professed excessive astonishment, of course, but congratulated me most cordially, and proffered every assistance in his power. In a word, we carried out our arrangement to the letter; and, at two in the morning, just ten minutes after the ceremony, I found myself in a close carriage with Madame Lalande—with Mrs. Simpson, I should say—and driving at a great rate out of town, in a direction North-east by North, half-North.

It had been determined for us by Talbot, that, as we were to be up all night, we should make our first stop at C——, a village about twenty miles from the city, and there get an early breakfast and some repose, before proceeding upon our route. At four precisely, therefore, the carriage drew up at the door of the principal inn. I handed my adored wife out, and ordered breakfast forthwith. In the mean time we were shown into a small parlor, and sat down.

It was now nearly if not altogether daylight; and, as I gazed, enraptured, at the angel by my side, the singular idea came, all at once, into my head, that this was really the very first moment since my acquaintance with the celebrated loveliness of Madame Lalande, that I had enjoyed a near inspection of that loveliness by daylight at all.

"And now, *mon ami*," said she, taking my hand, and so interrupting this train of reflection, "and now, *mon cher ami*, since we are indissolubly one—since I have yielded to your passionate entreaties, and performed my portion of our agreement—I presume you have not forgotten that you also have a little favor to bestow—a little promise which it is your intention to keep. Ah!—let me see! Let me remember! Yes; full easily do I call to mind the precise words of the dear promise you made to Eugénie last night. Listen! You spoke thus: 'It is done!—it is most cheerfully agreed! I sacrifice every feeling for your sake. To-night I wear this dear eye-glass *as* an eye-glass, and upon my heart; but with the earliest dawn of that morning which gives me the privilege of calling you wife, I will place it upon my—upon my nose—and there wear it ever afterwards, in the less romantic, and less fashionable, but certainly in the more serviceable form which you desire.' These were the exact words, my beloved husband, were they not?"

"They were," I said; "you have an excellent memory; and assuredly, my beautiful Eugénie, there is no disposition on my part to evade the performance of the trivial promise they imply. See! Behold! They are becoming—rather—are they not?" And here, having arranged the glasses in the ordinary form of spectacles, I applied them gingerly in their proper position; while Madame Simpson, adjusting her cap, and folding her arms, sat bolt upright in her chair, in a somewhat stiff and prim, and indeed, in a somewhat undignified position.

"Goodness gracious me!" I exclaimed almost at the very instant that the rim of the spectacles had settled upon my nose—"*My!* goodness gracious me!—why what *can* be the matter with these glasses?" and taking them quickly off, I wiped them carefully with a silk handkerchief, and adjusted them again.

But if, in the first instance, there had occurred something which occasioned me surprise, in the second, this surprise became elevated into astonishment; and this astonishment was profound—was extreme—indeed I may say it was horrific. What, in the name of everything hideous, did this mean? Could I believe my eyes?—*could* I?—that was the question. Was that—was that—was that *rouge*? And were those—and were those—were those *wrinkles* upon the visage of Eugénie Lalande? And oh, Jupiter! an every one of the gods and goddesses, little and big!—what—what—what—*what* had become of her teeth. I dashed the spectacles violently to the ground, and, leaping to my feet, stood erect in the middle of the floor, confronting Mrs. Simpson, with my arms set a-kimbo, and grinning and foaming, but, at the same time utterly speechless and helpless with terror and with rage.

Now I have already said that Madame Eugénie Lalande—that is to say, Simpson—spoke the English language but very little better than she wrote it; and for this reason she very properly never attempted to speak it upon ordinary occasions. But rage will carry a lady to any extreme; and in the present case it carried Mrs. Simpson to the very extraordinary extreme of attempting to hold a conversation in a tongue that she did not altogether understand.

"Vell, Monsieur," said she, after surveying me, in great apparent astonishment, for some moments—"Vell, Monsieur!—and vat den?—vat de matter now? Is it de dance of de Saint Vitusse dat you ave? If not like me, vat for vy buy de pig in de poke?"

"You wretch!" said I, catching my breath—"you—you—you villainous old hag!"

"Ag?—ole?—me not so *ver* ole, after all! me not one single day more dan de eighty-doo."

"Eighty-two!" I ejaculated, staggering to the wall—"eighty-two hundred thousand baboons! The miniature said twenty-seven years and seven months!"

"To be sure!—dat is so!—ver true! but den de portraite has been take for dese fifty-five year. Ven I go marry my segonde usbande, Monsieur Lalande, at dat time I had de portraite take for my daughter by my first usbande, Monsieur Moissart!"

"Moissart!" said I.

"Yes, Moissart;" said she, mimicking my pronunciation, which, to speak the truth, was none of the best; "and vat den? Vat you know bout de Moissart?"

"Nothing, you old fright!—I know nothing about him at all; only I had an ancestor of that name, once upon a time."

"Dat name! and vat you ave for *sa* : to dat name? 'Tis ver

goot name ; and so is Voissart—*dat* is ver goot name too.   My daughter, Madamoiselle Moissart, she marry von Monsieur Voissart ; and de name is bote *ver* respectaable name."

" Moissart ?" I exclaimed, " and Voissart ! why what is it you mean ?"

" Vat I mean ?—I mean Moissart and Voissart ; and for de matter of dat, I mean Croissart and Froissart, too, if I only tink proper to mean it.   My daughter's daughter, Mademoiselle Voissart, she marry von Monsieur Croissart, and den agin, my daughter's grande daughter, Mademoiselle Croissart, she marry von Monsieur Froissart ; and I suppose you say dat *dat* is not von *ver* respectaable name."

" Froissart !" said I, beginning to faint, " why surely you don't say Moissart, and Voissart, and Croissart, and Froissart ?"

" Yes," she replied, leaning fully back in her chair, and stretching out her lower limbs at great length ; " yes, Moissart, and Voissart, and Croissart, and Froissart.   But Monsieur Froissart, he vas von *ver* big vat you call fool—he vas von ver great big donce like yourself—for he lef *la belle France* for come to dis stupide Amérique—and ven he get here he vent and ave von *ver* stupide, von *ver, ver* stupide sonn, so I hear, dough I not yet av ad de plaisir to meet vid him—neither me nor my companion, de Madame Stephanie Lalande.   He is name de Napoleon Bonaparte Froissart, and I suppose you say dat *dat*, too is not von *ver* respectaable name."

Either the length or the nature of this speech, had the effect of working up Mrs. Simpson into a very extraordinary passion indeed : and as she made an end of it, with great labor, she jumped up from her chair like somebody bewitched, dropping upon the floor an entire universe of bustle as she jumped.   Once upon her feet, she gnashed her gums, brandished her arms, rolled up her sleeves, shook her fist in my face, and concluded the performance by tearing the cap from her head, and with it an immense wig of the most valuable and beautiful black hair, the whole of which she dashed upon the ground with a yell, and there trampled and danced a fandango upon it, in an absolute ecstasy and agony of rage.

Meantime I sank aghast into the chair which she had vacated.

"Moissart and Voissart!" I repeated, thoughtfully, as she cut one of her pigeon-wings, and Croissart and Froissart!" as she completed another—"Moissart and Voissart and Croissart and Napolean Bonaparte Froissart!—why, you ineffable old serpent, that's me—that's me—d'ye hear?—that's me"—here I screamed at the top of my voice—"that's me e e! _I_ am Napoleon Bonaparte Froissart! and if I hav'nt married my great, great, grandmother, I wish I may be everlastingly confounded!"

Madame Eugénie Lalande, *quasi* Simpson—formerly Moissart—was, in sober fact, my great, great, grandmother. In her youth she had been beautiful, and even at eighty-two, retained the majestic height, the sculptural contour of head, the fine eyes and the Grecian nose of her girlhood. By the aid of these, of pearl-powder, of rouge, of false hair, false teeth, and false *tournure*, as well as of the most skilful modistes of Paris, she contrived to hold a respectable footing among the beauties *en peu passées* of the French metropolis. In this respect, indeed, she might have been regarded as little less than the equal of the celebrated Ninon De L'Enclos.

She was immensely wealthy, and being left, for the second time, a widow without children, she bethought herself of my existence in America, and, for the purpose of making me her heir, paid a visit to the United States, in company with a distant and exceedingly lovely relative of her second husband's—a Madame Stephanie Lalande.

At the opera, my great, great, grandmother's attention was arrested by my notice; and, upon surveying me through her eye-glass, she was struck with a certain family resemblance to herself. Thus interested and knowing that the heir she sought was actually in the city, she made inquiries of her party respecting me. The gentleman who attended her knew my person, and told her who I was. The information thus obtained induced her to renew her scrutiny; and this scrutiny it was which so emboldened me that I behaved in the absurd manner already detailed. She returned my bow, however, under the impression that, by some odd accident, I had discovered her identity. When, deceived by my weakness of vision, and the arts of the toilet, in respect to the age and charms of the strange lady, I demanded so enthusiastically of Talbot who she was, he concluded that I meant the younger beauty, as a matter of course, and so informed me, with perfect truth, that she was " the celebrated widow, Madame Lalande."

In the street, next morning, my great, great, grandmother encountered Talbot, an old Parisian acquaintance; and the conversation, very naturally, turned upon myself. My deficiencies of vision were then explained; for these were notorious, although I was entirely ignorant of their notoriety; and my good old relative discovered much to her chagrin, that she had been deceived in supposing me aware of her identity, and that I had been merely making a fool of myself, in making open love, in a theatre, to an old woman unknown. By way of punishing me for this imprudence, she concocted with Talbot a plot. He purposely kept out of my way, to avoid giving me the introduction. My street inquiries about " the lovely widow, Madame Lalande," were supposed to refer to the younger lady, of course; and thus the conversation with the three gentlemen whom I encountered shortly after leaving Talbot's hotel, will be easily explained, as also their allusion to Ninon De L'Enclos. I had no opportunity of seeing Madame Lalande closely during daylight and, at her musical *soirée*, my silly weakness in refusing the aid of glasses, effectually prevented me from making a discovery of her age. When " Madame Lalande" was called upon to sing, the younger lady was intended; and it was she who arose to obey the call; my great, great, grandmother, to further the deception, arising at the same moment, and accompanying her to the piano in the main drawing-room. Had I decided upon escorting her thither, it had been her design to suggest the propriety of my remaining where I was; but my own prudential views rendered this unnecessary. The songs which I so much admired, and which so confirmed my impression of the youth of my mistress, were executed by Madame Stephanie Lalande. The eye-glass was presented by way of adding a reproof to the hoax—a sting to the epigram of the deception. Its presentation afforded an opportunity for the lecture upon affectation with which I was so especially edified. It is a'most superfluous to add that the glasses of the instrument, as worn by the old lady, had been exchanged by her for a pair better adapted to my years. They suited me, in fact to a T.

The clergyman, who merely pretended to tie the fatal knot, was a boon companion of Talbot's, and no priest. He was an excellent "whip," however; and having doffed his cassock to put on a great coat, he drove the hack which conveyed the "happy couple" out of town. Talbot took a seat at his side. The two scoundrels were thus "in at the death," and through a half open window of the back parlor of the inn, amused themselves in grinning at the *dénouement* of the drama. I believe I shall be forced to call them both out.

Nevertheless, I am *not* the husband of my great, great, grandmother; and this is a reflection which affords me infinite relief;—but I *am* the husband of Madame Lalande—of Madame Stephanie Lalande—with whom my good old relative, besides making me her sole heir when she dies—if she ever does—has been at the trouble of concocting me a match. In conclusion: I am done forever with *billets doux*, and am never to be met without SPECTACLES.

THE DUC DE L'OMELETTE.

And stepped at once into a cooler clime.——*Cowper.*

KEATS fell by a criticism. Who was it died of " *The Andromache?*"* Ignoble souls!—De L'Omelette perished of an ortolan. *L'histoire en est brève.* Assist me, Spirit of Apicius!

A golden cage bore the little winged wanderer, enamored, melting, indolent, to the *Chaussée D'Antin,* from its home in far Peru. From its queenly possessor La Bellissima, to the Duc De L'Omelette, six peers of the empire conveyed the happy bird.

That night the Duc was to sup alone. In the privacy of his bureau he reclined languidly on that ottoman for which he sacrificed his loyalty in outbidding his king,—the notorious ottoman of Cadét.

He buries his face in the pillow. The clock strikes! Unable to restrain his feelings, his Grace swallows an olive. At this moment the door gently opens to the sound of soft music, and lo! the most delicate of birds is before the most enamored of men! But what inexpressible dismay now overshadows the countenance of the Duc?——" *Horreur! — chien! — Baptiste! — l'oiseau! ah, bon Dieu! cet oiseau modeste que tu as deshabillé de ses plumes, et que tu as servi sans papier!*" It is superfluous to say more:— the Duc expired in a paroxysm of disgust. * * * * *

---

* Montfleury. The author of the *Parnasse Réformé* makes him speak in Hades:—" *L'homme donc qui voudrait savoir ce dont Je suis mort, qu'il ne demande pas s'il fût de fievre ou de podagre ou d'autre chose, mais qu'il entende que ce fut de 'l'Andromache'* "

"Ha! ha! ha!" said his Grace on the third day after his decease.

"He! he! he!" replied the Devil faintly, drawing himself up with an air of *hauteur.*

"Why, surely you are not serious," retorted De L'Omelette. "I have sinned—*c'est vrai*—but, my good sir, consider!—you have no actual intention of putting such—such—barbarous threats into execution."

"No *what?*" said his majesty—"come, sir, strip!"

"Strip, indeed!—very pretty i' faith!—no, sir, I shall *not* strip. Who are you, pray, that I, Duc De L'Omelette, Prince de Foie-Gras, just come of age, author of the 'Mazurkiad,' and Member of the Academy, should divest myself at your bidding of the sweetest pantaloons ever made by Bourdon, the daintiest *robe-de-chambre* ever put together by Rombêrt—to say nothing of the taking my hair out of paper—not to mention the trouble I should have in drawing off my gloves?"

"Who am I?—ah, true! I am Baal-Zebub, Prince of the Fly. I took thee, just now, from a rose-wood coffin inlaid with ivory. Thou wast curiously scented, and labelled as per invoice. Belial sent thee,—my Inspector of Cemeteries. The pantaloons, which thou sayest were made by Bourdon, are an excellent pair of linen drawers, and thy *robe-de-chambre* is a shroud of no scanty dimensions."

"Sir!" replied the Duc, "I am not to be insulted with impunity!—Sir! I shall take the earliest opportunity of avenging this insult!—Sir! you shall hear from me! In the meantime *au revoir!*"—and the Duc was bowing himself out of the Satanic presence, when he was interrupted and brought back by a gentleman in waiting. Hereupon his Grace rubbed his eyes, yawned, shrugged his shoulders, reflected. Having become satisfied of his identity, he took a bird's eye view of his whereabouts.

The apartment was superb. Even De L'Omelette pronounced it *bien comme il faut.* It was not its length nor its breadth,—but its height—ah, that was appalling!—There was no ceiling—certainly none—but a dense whirling mass of fiery-colored clouds. His Grace's brain reeled as he glanced upwards. From above, hung a chain of an unknown blood-red metal—its upper end lost, like the city of Boston, *parmi les nues*. From its nether extremity swung a large cresset. The Duc knew it to be a ruby; but from it there poured a light so intense, so still, so terrible, Persia never worshipped such—Gheber never imagined such—Mussulman never dreamed of such when, drugged with opium, he has tottered to a bed of poppies, his back to the flowers, and his face to the God Apollo. The Duc muttered a slight oath, decidedly approbatory.

The corners of the room were rounded into niches.—Three of these were filled with statues of gigantic proportions. Their beauty was Grecian, their deformity Egyptian, their *tout ensemble* French. In the fourth niche the statue was veiled; it was *not* colossal. But then there was a taper ankle, a sandalled foot. De L'Omelette pressed his hand upon his heart, closed his eyes, raised them, and caught his Satanic Majesty—in a blush.

But the paintings!—Kupris! Astarte! Astoreth!—a thousand and the same! And Rafaelle has beheld them! Yes, Rafaelle has been here; for did he not paint the——! and was he not consequently damned? The paintings!—the paintings! O luxury! O love!—who, gazing on those forbidden beauties, shall have eyes for the dainty devices of the golden frames that besprinkled, like stars, the hyacinth and the porphyry walls?

But the Duc's heart is fainting within him. He is not, however, as you suppose, dizzy with magnificence, nor drunk with the ecstatic breath of those innumerable censers. *C'est vrai que de toutes ces choses il a pensé beaucoup—mais!* The Duc De L'Omelette is terror-stricken; for, through the lurid vista which a single uncurtained window is affording, lo! gleams the most ghastly of all fires!

Le pauvre Duc! He could not help imagining that the glorious, the voluptuous, the never-dying melodies which pervaded that hall, as they passed filtered and transmuted through the alchemy of the enchanted window-panes, were the wailings and the howlings of the hopeless and the damned! And there, too!—there!—upon that ottoman!—who could *he* be?—he, the *petit-maitre*—no, the Deity—who sat as if carved in marble, *et qui sourit*, with his pale countenance, *si amérement?*

Mais il faut agir,—that is to say, a Frenchman never faints outright. Besides, his Grace hated a scene—De L'Omelette is himself again. There were some foils upon a table—some points also. The Duc had studied under B——; *il avait tué ses six hommes.* Now, then, *il peut s'échapper.* He measures two points," and, with a grace inimitable, offers his majesty the choice. *Horreur!* his majesty does not fence!

Mais il joue!—how happy a thought!—but his Grace had always an excellent memory. He had dipped in the "*Diable*" of the Abbé Gualtier. Therein it is said "*que le Diable n'ose pas refuser un jeu d'écarté.*"

But the chances—the chances! True—desperate: but scarcely more desperate than the Duc. Besides, was he not in the secret? —had he not skimmed over Père Le Brun?—was he not a member of the Club Vingt-un?—"*Si je perds,*" said he, "*je serai deux fois perdu*—I shall be doubly damned—*voila tout!* (Here his Grace shrugged his shoulders.) *Si je gagne, je reviendrai à mes ortolans—que les cartes soient préparées!*"

His Grace was all care, all attention—his Majesty all confidence. A spectator would have thought of Francis and Charles. His Grace thought of his game. His Majesty did not think; he shuffled. The Duc cut.

The cards are dealt. The trump is turned—it is—it is—the king! No—it was the queen. His Majesty cursed her masculine habiliments. De L'Omelette placed his hand upon his heart.

They play. The Duc counts. The hand is out. His Majesty counts heavily, smiles, and is taking wine. The Duc slips a card.

"*C'est à vous à faire,*" said his Majesty, cutting. His Grace bowed, dealt, and arose from the table *en presentant le Roi.*

His Majesty looked chagrined.

Had Alexander not been Alexander, he would have been Diogenes; and the Duc assured his antagonist in taking leave. "*que s'il n'eût pas été De L'Omelette il n'aurait point d'objection d'être le Diable.*"

THE OBLONG BOX.

SOME years ago, I engaged passage from Charleston, S. C., to the city of New York, in the fine packet-ship "Independence," Captain Hardy. We were to sail on the fifteenth of the month (June,) weather permitting; and, on the fourteenth, I went on board to arrange some matters in my state room.

I found that we were to have a great many passengers, including a more than usual number of ladies. On the list were several of my acquaintances; and among other names, I was rejoiced to see that of Mr. Cornelius Wyatt, a young artist, for whom I entertained feelings of warm friendship. He had been with me a fellow student at C—— University, where we were very much together. He had the ordinary temperament of genius, and was a compound of misanthropy, sensibility, and enthusiasm. To these qualities he united the warmest and truest heart which ever beat in a human bosom.

I observed that his name was carded upon *three* state rooms; and, upon again referring to the list of passengers, I found that he had engaged passage for himself, wife, and two sisters—his own. The state rooms were sufficiently roomy, and each had two berths, one above the other. These berths, to be sure, were so exceedingly narrow as to be insufficient for more than one person; still, I could not comprehend why there were *three* state-rooms for these four persons. I was, just at that epoch, in one of those moody frames of mind which make a man abnormally inquisitive about trifles: and I confess, with shame, that I busied myself in a variety of ill-bred and preposterous conjectures about this matter of

16*

the supernumerary state-room. It was no business of mine, to be sure; but with none the less pertinacity did I occupy myself in attempts to resolve the enigma. At last I reached a conclusion which wrought in me great wonder why I had not arrived at it before. "It is a servant, of course," I said; "what a fool I am, not sooner to have thought of so obvious a solution!" And then I again repaired to the list—but here I saw distinctly that *no* servant was to come with the party; although, in fact, it had been the original design to bring one—for the words "and servant" had been first written and then overscored. "Oh, extra baggage to be sure," I now said to myself—"something he wishes not to be put in the hold—something to be kept under his own eye—ah, I have it—a painting or so—and this is what he has been bargaining about with Nicolino, the Italian Jew." This idea satisfied me, and I dismissed my curiosity for the nonce.

Wyatt's two sisters I knew very well, and most amiable and clever girls they were. His wife he had newly married, and I had never yet seen her. He had often talked about her in my presence, however, and in his usual style of enthusiasm. He described her as of surpassing beauty, wit, and accomplishment. I was, therefore, quite anxious to make her acquaintance.

On the day in which I visited the ship, (the fourteenth,) Wyatt and party were also to visit it—so the captain informed me—and I waited on board an hour longer than I had designed, in hope of being presented to the bride; but then an apology came. "Mrs. W. was a little indisposed, and would decline coming on board until to-morrow, at the hour of sailing."

The morrow having arrived, I was going from my hotel to the wharf, when Captain Hardy met me and said that, "owing to circumstances," (a stupid but convenient phrase,) "he rather thought the 'Independence' would not sail for a day or two, and that when all was ready, he would send up and let me know." This I thought strange, for there was a stiff southerly breeze; but as "the circumstances" were not forthcoming, although I pumped for them with much perseverance, I had nothing to do but to return home and digest my impatience at leisure.

I did not receive the expected message from the captain for nearly a week. It came at length, however, and I immediately went on board the ship was crowded with passengers, and everything was in the bustle attendant upon making sail. Wyatt's party arrived in about ten minutes after myself. There were the two sisters, the bride, and the artist—the latter in one of his customary fits of moody misanthropy. I was too well used to these however, to pay them any special attention. He did not even introduce me to his wife;—this courtesy devolving, per force, upon his sister Marian—a very sweet and intelligent girl, who, in a few hurried words, made us acquainted.

Mrs. Wyatt had been closely veiled; and when she raised her veil, in acknowledging my bow, I confess that I was very profoundly astonished. I should have been much more so, however, had not long experience advised me not to trust, with too implicit a reliance, the enthusiastic descriptions of my friend, the artist, when indulging in comments upon the loveliness of woman. When beauty was the theme, I well knew with what facility he soared into the regions of the purely ideal.

The truth is, I could not help regarding Mrs. Wyatt as a decidedly plain-looking woman. If not positively ugly, she was not, I think, very far from it. She was dressed, however, in exquisite taste—and then I had no doubt that she had captivated my friend's heart by the more enduring graces of the intellect and soul. She said very few words, and passed at once into her stateroom with Mr. W.

My old inquisitiveness now returned. There was *no* servant—*that* was a settled point. I looked, therefore, for the extra baggage. After some delay, a cart arrived at the wharf, with an oblong pine box, which was everything that seemed to be expected. Immediately upon its arrival we made sail, and in a short time were safely over the bar and standing out to sea.

The box in question was, as I say, oblong. It was about six feet in length by two and a half in breadth;—I observed it attentively, and like to be precise. Now this shape was *peculiar*; and no sooner had I seen it, than I took credit to myself for the accuracy of my guessing. I had reached the conclusion, it will be remembered, that the extra baggage of my friend, the artist, would prove to be pictures, or at least a picture; for I knew he had been for several weeks in conference with Nicolino:—and now here was a box which, from its shape, *could* possibly contain nothing in the world but a copy of Leonardo's "Last Supper;" and a copy of this very "Last Supper," done by Rubini the younger, at Florence, I had known, for some time, to be in the possession of Nicolino. This point, therefore, I considered as sufficiently settled. I chuckled excessively when I thought of my acumen. It was the first time I had ever known Wyatt to keep from me any of his artistical secrets; but here he evidently intended to steal a march upon me, and smuggle a fine picture to New York, under my very nose; expecting me to know nothing of the matter. I resolved to quiz him *well*, now and hereafter.

One thing, however, annoyed me not a little. The box did *not* go into the extra state-room. It was deposited in Wyatt's own; and there, too, it remained, occupying very nearly the whole of the floor—no doubt to the exceeding discomfort of the artist and his wife;—this the more especially as the tar or paint with which it was lettered in sprawling capitals, emitted a strong, disagreeable, and, to *my* fancy, a peculiarly disgusting odor. On the lid were painted the words—"*Mrs. Adelaide Curtis, Albany, New York. Charge of Cornelius Wyatt, Esq. This side up. To be handled with care.*"

Now, I was aware that Mrs. Adelaide Curtis, of Albany, was the artist's wife's mother;—but then I looked upon the whole address as a mystification, intended especially for myself. I made up my mind, of course, that the box and contents would never get farther north than the studio of my misanthropic friend, in Chambers Street, New York.

For the first three or four days we had fine weather, although the wind was dead ahead; having chopped round to the northward, immediately upon our losing sight of the coast. The passengers were, consequently, in high spirits, and disposed to be social. I *must* except, however, Wyatt and his sisters, who behaved stiffly, and, I could not help thinking, uncourteously to the rest of the party. *Wyatt's* conduct I did not so much regard. He was gloomy, even beyond his usual habit—in fact he was *morose*—but in him I was prepared for eccentricity. For the sisters, however, I could make no excuse. They secluded themselves in their state-rooms during the greater part of the passage, and absolutely refu sed, although I repeatedly urged them, to hold com munication with any person on board.

Mrs. Wyatt herself was far more agreeable. That is to say, she was *chatty ;* and to be chatty is no slight recommendation at sea. She became *excessively* intimate with most of the ladies ; and, to my profound astonishment, evinced no equivocal disposition to coquet with the men. She amused us all very much. I say "*amused*"—and scarcely know how to explain myself. The truth is, I soon found that Mrs. W. was far oftener laughed *at* than *with.* The gentlemen said little about her ; but the ladies, in a little while, pronounced her " a good-hearted thing, rather indifferent-looking, totally uneducated, and decidedly vulgar." The great wonder was, how Wyatt had been entrapped into such a match. Wealth was the general solution—but this I knew to be no solution at all ; for Wyatt had told me that she neither brought him a dollar nor had any expectations from any source whatever. "He had married," he said, " for love, and for love only ; and his bride was far more than worthy of his love." When I thought of these expressions, on the part of my friend, I confess that I felt indescribably puzzled. Could it be possible that he was taking leave of his senses? What else could I think? *He*, so refined, so intellectual, so fastidious, with so exquisite a perception of the faulty, and so keen an appreciation of the beautiful ! To be sure, the lady seemed especially fond of *him*—particularly so in his absence—when she made herself ridiculous by frequent quotations of what had been said by her " beloved husband, Mr. Wyatt." The word " husband" seemed forever—to use one of her own delicate expressions—forever " on the tip of her tongue." In the meantime, it was observed by all on board, that he avoided *her* in the most pointed manner, and, for the most part, shut himself up alone in his state-room, where, in fact, he might have been said to live altogether, leaving his wife at full liberty to amuse herself as she thought best, in the public society of the main cabin.

My conclusion, from what I saw and heard, was, that the artist, by some unaccountable freak of fate, or perhaps in some fit of enthusiastic and fanciful passion, had been induced to unite himself with a person altogether beneath him, and that the natural result, entire and speedy disgust, had ensued. I pitied him from the

bottom of my heart—but could not, for that reason, quite forgive
his incommunicativeness in the matter of the "Last Supper."
For this I resolved to have my revenge.

One day he came upon deck, and, taking his arm as had been
my wont, I sauntered with him backwards and forwards. His
gloom, however, (which I considered quite natural under the circumstances,) seemed entirely unabated. He said little, and that
moodily, and with evident effort. I ventured a jest or two, and
he made a sickening attempt at a smile. Poor fellow!—as I
thought of *his wife*, I wondered that he could have heart to put
on even the semblance of mirth. At last I ventured a home
thrust. I determined to commence a series of covert insinuations,
or inuendoes, about the oblong box—just to let him perceive,
gradually, that I was *not* altogether the butt, or victim, of his little
bit of pleasant mystification. My first observation was by way of
opening a masked battery. I said something about the " peculiar shape of *that* box ;" and, as I spoke the words, I smiled knowingly, winked, and touched him gently with my fore-finger in the
ribs.

The manner in which Wyatt received this harmless pleasantry,
convinced me, at once, that he was mad. At first he stared at
me as if he found it impossible to comprehend the witticism of
my remark ; but as its point seemed slowly to make its way into
his brain, his eyes in the same proportion, seemed protruding
from their sockets. Then he grew very red—then hideously pale
—then, as if highly amused with what I had insinuated, he began
a loud and boisterous laugh, which, to my astonishment, he kept
up, with gradually increasing vigor, for ten minutes or more. In
conclusion, he fell flat and heavily upon the deck. When I ran
to uplift him, to all appearance he was *dead*.

I called assistance, and, with much difficulty, we brought him
to himself. Upon reviving he spoke incoherently for some time.
At length we bled him and put him to bed. The next morning
he was quite recovered, so far as regarded his mere bodily health.
Of his mind I say nothing, of course. I avoided him during the
rest of the passage, by advice of the captain, who seemed to coincide with me altogether in my views of his insanity, but cautioned
me to say nothing on this head to any person on board.

Several circumstances occurred immediately after this fit of Wyatt's, which contributed to heighten the curiosity with which I was already possessed. Among other things, this : I had been nervous—drank too much strong green tea, and slept ill at night —in fact, for two nights I could not be properly said to sleep at all. Now, my state-room opened into the main cabin, or dining-room, as did those of all the single men on board. Wyatt's three rooms were in the after-cabin, which was separated from the main one by a slight sliding door, never locked even at night. As we were almost constantly on a wind, and the breeze was not a little stiff, the ship heeled to leeward very considerably ; and whenever her starboard side was to leeward, the sliding door between the cabins slid open, and so remained, nobody taking the trouble to get up and shut it. But my berth was in such a position, that when my own state-room door was open, as well as the sliding door in question, (and my own door was *always* open on account of the heat,) I could see into the after cabin quite distinctly, and just at that portion of it, too, where were situated the state-rooms of Mr. Wyatt. Well, during two nights (*not* consecutive) while I lay awake, I clearly saw Mrs. W., about eleven o'clock upon each night, steal cautiously from the state-room of Mr. W., and enter the extra room, where she remained until day break, when she was called by her husband and went back. That they were virtually separated was clear. They had separate apartments—no doubt in contemplation of a more permanent divorce : and here, after all, I thought, was the mystery of the extra state-room.

There was another circumstance, too, which interested me much. During the two wakeful nights in question, and immediately after the disappearance of Mrs. Wyatt into the extra state-room, I was attracted by certain singular, cautious, subdued noises in that of her husband. After listening to them for some time, with thoughtful attention, I at length succeeded perfectly in translating their import. They were sounds occasioned by the artist in prying open the oblong box, by means of a chisel and mallet—the latter being apparently muffled, or deadened, by some soft woollen or cotton substance in which its head was enveloped.

In this manner I fancied I could distinguish the precise moment

when he fairly disengaged the lid—also, that I could determine
when he removed it altogether, and when he deposited it upon
the lower berth in his room; this latter point I knew, for example,
by certain slight taps which the lid made in striking against the
wooden edges of the berth, as he endeavored to lay it down *very*
gently—there being no room for it on the floor.   After this there
was a dead stillness, and I heard nothing more, upon either occasion, until nearly daybreak; unless, perhaps, I may mention a low
sobbing, or murmuring sound, so very much suppressed as to be
nearly inaudible—if, indeed, the whole of this latter noise were
not rather produced by my own imagination.   I say it seemed to
resemble sobbing or sighing—but, of course, it could not have been
either.   I rather think it was a ringing in my own ears.   Mr. Wyatt,
no doubt, according to custom, was merely giving the rein to one
of his hobbies—indulging in one of his fits of artistic enthusiasm.
He had opened his oblong box, in order to feast his eyes on the
pictorial treasure within.   There was nothing in this however, to
make him *sob*.   I repeat therefore, that it must have been simply
a freak of my own fancy, distempered by good Captain Hardy's
green tea.   Just before dawn, on each of the two nights of which
I speak, I distinctly heard Mr. Wyatt replace the lid upon the
oblong box, and force the nails into their old places, by means of
the muffled mallet.   Having done this, he issued from his state-
room, fully dressed, and proceeded to call Mrs. W. from hers.

We had been at sea seven days, and were now off Cape Hat-
teras, when there came a tremendously heavy blow from the
southwest.   We were, in a measure, prepared for it, however, as
the weather had been holding out threats for some time.   Everything was made snug, alow and aloft; and as the wind steadily
freshened, we lay to, at length, under spanker and foretopsail, both
double-reefed.

In this trim, we rode safely enough for forty-eight hours—the
ship proving herself an excellent sea boat, in many respects, and
shipping no water of any consequence.   At the end of this period,
however, the gale had freshened into a hurricane, and our after-
sail split into ribbons, bringing us so much in the trough of the
water that we shipped several prodigious seas, one immedi
after the other.   By this accident we lost three men over

with the caboose, and nearly the whole of the larboard bulwarks.
Scarcely had we recovered our senses, before the foretopsail went
into shreds, when we got up a storm stay-sail, and with this did
pretty well for some hours, the ship heading the sea much more
steadily than before.

The gale still held on, however, and we saw no signs of its
abating.   The rigging was found to be ill-fitted, and greatly
strained; and on the third day of the blow, about five in the
afternoon, our mizzen-mast, in a heavy lurch to windward, went
by the board.   For an hour or more, we tried in vain to get rid
of it, on account of the prodigious rolling of the ship; and, before
we had succeeded, the carpenter came aft and announced four feet
water in the hold.   To add to our dilemma, we found the pumps
choked and nearly useless.

All was now confusion and despair—but an effort was made to
lighten the ship by throwing overboard as much of her cargo as
could be reached, and by cutting away the two masts that remained.   This we at last accomplished—but we were still unable to do
anything at the pumps; and, in the meantime, the leak gained
on us very fast.

At sundown, the gale had sensibly diminished in violence, and,
as the sea went down with it, we still entertained faint hopes of
saving ourselves in the boats.   At eight, P. M., the clouds broke
away to windward, and we had the advantage of a full moon—a
piece of good fortune which served wonderfully to cheer our
drooping spirits.

After incredible labor we succeeded, at length, in getting the
long-boat over the side without material accident, and into this
we crowded the whole of the crew and most of the passengers.
This party made off immediately, and, after undergoing much
suffering, finally arrived, in safety, at Ocracoke Inlet, on the third
day after the wreck.

Fourteen passengers, with the Captain, remained on board,
resolving to trust their fortunes to the jolly-boat at the stern.   We
lowered it without difficulty, although it was only by a miracle that
we prevented it from swamping as it touched the water.   It contain-
ed, when afloat, the captain and his wife, Mr. Wyatt and party, a
Mexican officer, wife, four children, and myself, with a negro valet.

We had no room, of course, for anything except a few positively necessary instruments, some provision, and the clothes upon our backs. No one had thought of even attempting to save anything more. What must have been the astonishment of all then, when, having proceeded a few fathoms from the ship, Mr. Wyatt stood up in the stern-sheets, and coolly demanded of Captain Hardy that the boat should be put back for the purpose of taking in his oblong box !

"Sit down, Mr. Wyatt," replied the Captain, somewhat sternly; "you will capsize us if you do not sit quite still. Our gunwale is almost in the water now."

"The box !" vociferated Mr. Wyatt, still standing—"the box, I say ! Captain Hardy, you cannot, you *will* not refuse me. Its weight will be but a trifle—it is nothing—mere nothing. By the mother who bore you—for the love of Heaven—by your hope of salvation, I *implore* you to put back for the box !"

The Captain, for a moment, seemed touched by the earnest appeal of the artist, but he regained his stern composure, and merely said—

"Mr. Wyatt, you are *mad*. I cannot listen to you. Sit down, I say, or you will swamp the boat. Stay—hold him—seize him ! —he is about to spring overboard ! There—I knew it—he is over !"

As the Captain said this, Mr. Wyatt, in fact, sprang from the boat, and, as we were yet in the lee of the wreck, succeeded, by almost superhuman exertion, in getting hold of a rope which hung from the fore-chains. In another moment he was on board, and rushing frantically down into the cabin.

In the meantime, we had been swept astern of the ship, and being quite out of her lee, were at the mercy of the tremendous sea which was still running. We made a determined effort to put back, but our little boat was like a feather in the breath of the tempest. We saw at a glance that the doom of the unfortunate artist was sealed.

As our distance from the wreck rapidly increased, the madman (for as such only could we regard him) was seen to emerge from the companion-way, up which, by dint of a strength that appeared gigantic, he dragged, bodily, the oblong box. While we gazed in the extremity of astonishment, he passed, rapidly, several turns of a three-inch rope, first around the box and then around his body. In another instant both body and box were in the sea—disappearing suddenly, at once and forever.

We lingered awhile sadly upon our oars, with our eyes riveted upon the spot. At length we pulled away. The silence remained unbroken for an hour. Finally, I hazarded a remark.

"Did you observe, Captain, how suddenly they sank? Was not that an exceedingly singular thing? I confess that I entertained some feeble hope of his final deliverance, when I saw him lash himself to the box, and commit himself to the sea."

"They sank as a matter of course," replied the Captain, "and that like a shot. They will soon rise again, however—*but not till the salt melts*."

"The salt!" I ejaculated.

"Hush!" said the Captain, pointing to the wife and sisters of the deceased. "We must talk of these things at some more appropriate time."

We suffered much, and made a narrow escape; but fortune befriended *us*, as well as our mates in the long boat. We landed, in fine, more dead than alive, after four days of intense distress, upon the beach opposite Roanoke Island. We remained here a week, were not ill-treated by the wreckers, and at length obtained a passage to New York.

About a month after the loss of the "Independence," I happened to meet Captain Hardy in Broadway. Our conversation turned, naturally, upon the disaster, and especially upon the sad fate of poor Wyatt. I thus learned the following particulars.

The artist had engaged passage for himself, wife, two sisters and a servant. His wife was, indeed, as she had been represented, a most lovely, and most accomplished woman. On the morning of the fourteenth of June, (the day in which I first visited the ship,) the lady suddenly sickened and died. The young husband was frantic with grief—but circumstances imperatively forbade the deferring his voyage to New York. It was necessary to take to her mother the corpse of his adored wife, and on the other hand, the universal prejudice which would prevent his doing so openly,

was well known. Nine-tenths of the passengers would have abandoned the ship rather than take passage with a dead body.

In this dilemma, Captain Hardy arranged that the corpse, being
first partially embalmed, and packed, with a large quantity of salt,
in a box of suitable dimensions, should be conveyed on board as
merchandise. Nothing was to be said of the lady's decease; and,
as it was well understood that Mr. Wyatt had engaged passage
for his wife, it became necessary that some person should person-
ate her during the voyage. This the deceased's lady's-maid was
easily prevailed on to do. The extra state-room, originally engaged for this girl, during her mistress' life, was now merely
retained. In this state-room the pseudo wife slept, of course,
every night. In the day-time she performed, to the best of her
ability, the part of her mistress—whose person, it had been carefully ascertained, was unknown to any of the passengers on board.

My own mistakes arose, naturally enough, through too careless,
too inquisitive, and too impulsive a temperament. But of late, it
is a rare thing that I sleep soundly at night. There is a countenance which haunts me, turn as I will. There is an hysterical
laugh which will forever ring within my ears.

KING PEST.

A TALE CONTAINING AN ALLEGORY.

The gods do bear and well allow in kings
The things which they abhor in rascal routes.
Buckhurst's Tragedy of Ferrex and Porrex

ABOUT twelve o'clock, one night in the month of October, and during the chivalrous reign of the third Edward, two seamen belonging to the crew of the "Free and Easy," a trading schooner plying between Sluys and the Thames, and then at anchor in that river, were much astonished to find themselves seated in the taproom of an ale-house in the parish of St. Andrews, London—which ale-house bore for sign the portraiture of a "Jolly Tar."

The room, although ill-contrived, smoke-blackened, low-pitched, and in every other respect agreeing with the general character of such places at the period—was, nevertheless, in the opinion of the grotesque groups scattered here and there within it, sufficiently well adapted to its purpose.

Of these groups our two seamen formed, I think, the most interesting, if not the most conspicuous.

The one who appeared to be the elder, and whom his companion addressed by the characteristic appellation of "Legs," was at the same time much the taller of the two. He might have measured six feet and a half, and an habitual stoop in the shoulders seemed to have been the necessary consequence of an altitude so enormous. —Superfluities in height were, however, more than accounted for by deficiencies in other respects. He was exceedingly thin; and might, as his associates asserted, have answered, when drunk, for a pennant at the mast-head, or, when sober, have served for a jibboom. But these jests, and others of a similar nature, had evidently produced, at no time, any effect upon the cachinnatory muscles of the tar. With high cheek-bones, a large hawk-nose, retreating chin, fallen under-jaw, and huge protruding white eyes, the expression of his countenance, although tinged with a species of dogged indifference to matters and things in general, was not the less utterly solemn and serious beyond all attempts at imitation or description.

The younger seaman was, in all outward appearance, the converse of his companion. His stature could not have exceeded four feet. A pair of stumpy bow-legs supported his squat, unwieldly figure, while his unusually short and thick arms, with no ordinary fists at their extremities, swung off dangling from his sides like the fins of a sea-turtle. Small eyes, of no particular color, twinkled far back in his head. His nose remained buried in the mass of flesh which enveloped his round, full, and purple face; and his thick upper-lip rested upon the still thicker one beneath with an air of complacent self-satisfaction, much heightened by the owner's habit of licking them at intervals. He evidently regarded his tall shipmate with a feeling half-wondrous, half-quizzical; and stared up occasionally in his face as the red setting sun stares up at the crags of Ben Nevis.

Various and eventful, however, had been the peregrinations of the worthy couple in and about the different tap-houses of the neighborhood during the earlier hours of the night. Funds even the most ample, are not always everlasting: and it was with empty pockets our friends had ventured upon the present hostelrie.

At the precise period, then, when this history properly commences, Legs, and his fellow, Hugh Tarpaulin, sat, each with both elbows resting upon the large oaken table in the middle of the floor, and with a hand upon either cheek. They were eyeing, from behind a huge flagon of unpaid-for "humming-stuff," the portentous words, "No Chalk," which to their indignation and astonishment were scored over the doorway by means of that very mineral whose presence they purported to deny. Not that the gift of deciphering written characters—a gift among the commonalty of that day considered little less cabalistical than the art of

inditing—could, in strict justice, have been laid to the charge of
either disciple of the sea; but there was, to say the truth, a certain twist in the formation of the letters—an indescribable lee-
lurch about the whole—which foreboded, in the opinion of both
seamen, a long run of dirty weather; and determined them at
once, in the allegorical words of Legs himself, to "pump ship,
clew up all sail, and scud before the wind."

Having accordingly disposed of what remained of the ale, and
looped up the points of their short doublets, they finally made a
bolt for the street. Although Tarpaulin rolled twice into the fire-
place, mistaking it for the door, yet their escape was at length
happily effected—and half after twelve o'clock found our heroes
ripe for mischief, and running for life down a dark alley in the
direction of St. Andrew's Stair, hotly pursued by the landlady
of the "Jolly Tar."

At the epoch of this eventful tale, and periodically, for many
years before and after, all England, but more especially the metropolis, resounded with the fearful cry of "Plague!" The city was
in a great measure depopulated—and in those horrible regions, in
the vicinity of the Thames, where amid the dark, narrow, and
filthy lanes and alleys, the Demon of Disease was supposed to
have had his nativity, Awe, Terror, and Superstition were alone
to be found stalking abroad.

By authority of the king such districts were placed *under ban*,
and all persons forbidden, under pain of death, to intrude upon
their dismal solitude. Yet neither the mandate of the monarch,
nor the huge barriers erected at the entrances of the streets, nor
the prospect of that loathsome death which, with almost absolute
certainty, overwhelmed the wretch whom no peril could deter
from the adventure, prevented the unfurnished and untenanted
dwellings from being stripped, by the hand of nightly rapine, of
every article, such as iron, brass, or lead-work, which could in any
manner be turned to a profitable account.

Above all, it was usually found, upon the annual winter opening
of the barriers, that locks, bolts, and secret cellars, had proved but
slender protection to those rich stores of wines and liquors which,
in consideration of the risk and trouble of removal, many of the
numerous dealers having shops in the neighborhood had consent

ed to trust, during the period of exile, to so insufficient a security.

But there were very few of the terror-stricken people who attributed these doings to the agency of human hands. Pest-spirits, plague-goblins, and fever-demons, were the popular imps of mischief; and tales so blood-chilling were hourly told, that the whole mass of forbidden buildings was, at length, enveloped in terror as in a shroud, and the plunderer himself was often scared away by the horrors his own depredations had created; leaving the entire vast circuit of prohibited district to gloom, silence, pestilence, and death.

It was by one of the terrific barriers already mentioned, and which indicated the region beyond to be under the Pest-ban, that, in scrambling down an alley, Legs and the worthy Hugh Tarpaulin found their progress suddenly impeded. To return was out of the question, and no time was to be lost, as their pursuers were close upon their heels. With thorough-bred seamen to clamber up the roughly fashioned plank-work was a trifle; and, maddened with the twofold excitement of exercise and liquor, they leaped unhesitatingly down within the enclosure, and holding on their drunken course with shouts and yellings, were soon bewildered in its noisome and intricate recesses.

Had they not, indeed, been intoxicated beyond moral sense, their reeling footsteps must have been palsied by the horrors of their situation. The air was cold and misty. The paving-stones, loosened from their beds, lay in wild disorder amid the tall, rank grass, which sprang up around the feet and ankles. Fallen houses choked up the streets. The most fetid and poisonous smells everywhere prevailed;—and by the aid of that ghastly light which, even at midnight, never fails to emanate from a vapory and pestilential atmosphere, might be discerned lying in the by-paths and alleys, or rotting in the windowless habitations, the carcass of many a nocturnal plunderer arrested by the hand of the plague in the very perpetration of his robbery.

But it lay not in the power of images, or sensations, or impediments such as these, to stay the course of men who, naturally brave, and at that time especially, brimful of courage and of " humming-stuff !" would have reeled, as straight as their condition might have permitted, undauntedly into the very jaws of

Death. Onward—still onward stalked the grim Legs, making the desolate solemnity echo and re-echo with yells like the terrific war-whoop of the Indian : and onward, still onward rolled the dumpy Tarpaulin, hanging on to the doublet of his more active companion, and far surpassing the latter's most strenuous exertions in the way of vocal music, by bull-roarings *in basso,* from the profundity of his stentorian lungs.

They had now evidently reached the strong hold of the pestilence. Their way at every step or plunge grew more noisome and more horrible—the paths more narrow and more intricate. Huge stones and beams falling momently from the decaying roofs above them, gave evidence, by their sullen and heavy descent, of the vast height of the surrounding houses ; and while actual exertion became necessary to force a passage through frequent heaps of rubbish, it was by no means seldom that the hand fell upon a skeleton or rested upon a more fleshy corpse.

Suddenly, as the seamen stumbled against the entrance of a tall and ghastly-looking building, a yell more than usually shrill from the throat of the excited Legs, was replied to from within, in a rapid succession of wild, laughter-like, and fiendish shrieks. Nothing daunted at sounds which, of such a nature, at such a time, and in such a place, might have curdled the very blood in hearts less irrevocably on fire, the drunken couple rushed headlong against the door, burst it open, and staggered into the midst of things with a volley of curses.

The room within which they found themselves proved to be the shop of an undertaker ; but an open trap-door, in a corner of the floor near the entrance, looked down upon a long range of wine-cellars, whose depths the occasional sound of bursting bottles proclaimed to be well stored with their appropriate contents. In the middle of the room stood a table—in the centre of which again arose a huge tub of what appeared to be punch. Bottles of various wines and cordials, together with jugs, pitchers, and flagons of every shape and quality, were scattered profusely upon the board. Around it, upon coffin-tressels, was seated a company of six. This company I will endeavor to delineate one by one.

Fronting the entrance, and elevated a little above his companions, sat a personage who appeared to be the president of the table. His stature was gaunt and tall, and Legs was confounded to behold in him a figure more emaciated than himself. His face was as yellow as saffron—but no feature excepting one alone, was sufficiently marked to merit a particular description. This one consisted in a forehead so unusually and hideously lofty, as to have the appearance of a bonnet or crown of flesh superadded upon the natural head. His mouth was puckered and dimpled into an expression of ghastly affability, and his eyes, as indeed the eyes of all at table, were glazed over with the fumes of intoxication. This gentleman was clothed from head to foot in a richly-embroidered black silk-velvet pall, wrapped negligently around his form after the fashion of a Spanish cloak. His head was stuck full of sable hearse-plumes, which he nodded to and fro with a jaunty and knowing air; and, in his right hand, he held a huge human thigh-bone, with which he appeared to have been just knocking down some member of the company for a song.

Opposite him, and with her back to the door, was a lady of no whit the less extraordinary character. Although quite as tall as the person just described, she had no right to complain of his unnatural emaciation. She was evidently in the last stage of a dropsy; and her figure resembled nearly that of the huge puncheon of October beer which stood, with the head driven in, close by her side, in a corner of the chamber. Her face was exceedingly round, red, and full; and the same peculiarity, or rather want of peculiarity, attached itself to her countenance, which I before mentioned in the case of the president—that is to say, only one feature of her face was sufficiently distinguished to need a separate characterization: indeed the acute Tarpaulin immediately observed that the same remark might have applied to each individual person of the party; every one of whom seemed to possess a monopoly of some particular portion of physiognomy. With the lady in question this portion proved to be the mouth. Commencing at the right ear, it swept with a terrific chasm to the left—the short pendants which she wore in either auricle continually bobbing into the aperture. She made, however, every exertion to keep her mouth closed and look dignified, in a dress consisting of a newly starched and ironed shroud coming up close under her chin, with a crimpled ruffle of cambric muslin.

At her right hand sat a diminutive young lady whom she appeared to patronise. This delicate little creature, in the trembling of her wasted fingers, in the livid hue of her lips, and in the slight hectic spot which tinged her otherwise leaden complexion, gave evident indications of a galloping consumption. An air of extreme *haut ton*, however, pervaded her whole appearance; she wore in a graceful and *degagé* manner, a large and beautiful winding-sheet of the finest India lawn; her hair hung in ringlets over her neck; a soft smile played about her mouth; but her nose, extremely long, thin, sinuous, flexible and pimpled, hung down far below her under lip, and in spite of the delicate manner in which she now and then moved it to one side or the other with her tongue, gave to her countenance a somewhat equivocal expression.

Over against her, and upon the left of the dropsical lady, was seated a little puffy, wheezing, and gouty old man, whose cheeks reposed upon the shoulders of their owner, like two huge bladders of Oporto wine. With his arms folded, and with one bandaged leg deposited upon the table, he seemed to think himself entitled to some consideration. He evidently prided himself much upon every inch of his personal appearance, but took more especial delight in calling attention to his gaudy-colored surtout. This, to say the truth, must have cost him no little money, and was made to fit him exceedingly well—being fashioned from one of the curiously embroidered silken covers appertaining to those glorious escutcheons which, in England and elsewhere, are customarily hung up, in some conspicuous place, upon the dwellings of departed aristocracy.

Next to him, and at the right hand of the president, was a gentleman in long white hose and cotton drawers. His frame shook, in a ridiculous manner, with a fit of what Tarpaulin called "the horrors." His jaws, which had been newly shaved, were tightly tied up by a bandage of muslin; and his arms being fastened in a similar way at the wrists, prevented him from helping himself too freely to the liquors upon the table; a precaution rendered necessary, in the opinion of Legs, by the peculiarly sottish and wine-bibbing cast of his visage. A pair of prodigious ears, nevertheless, which it was no doubt found impossible to confine, towered away into the atmosphere of the apartment, and were occasionally pricked up in a spasm, at the sound of the drawing of a cork.

Fronting him, sixthly and lastly, was situated a singularly stiff-looking personage, who, being afflicted with paralysis, must, to speak seriously, have felt very ill at ease in his unaccommodating habiliments. He was habited, somewhat uniquely, in a new and handsome mahogany coffin. Its top or head-piece pressed upon the skull of the wearer, and extended over it in the fashion of a hood, giving to the entire face an air of indescribable interest. Arm-holes had been cut in the sides, for the sake not more of elegance than of convenience; but the dress, nevertheless, prevented its proprietor from sitting as erect as his associates; and as he lay reclining against his tressel, at an angle of forty-five degrees, a pair of huge goggle eyes rolled up their awful whites towards the ceiling in absolute amazement at their own enormity.

Before each of the party lay a portion of a skull, which was used as a drinking cup. Overhead was suspended a human skele-ton, by means of a rope tied round one of the legs and fastened to a ring in the ceiling. The other limb confined by no such fetter, stuck off from the body at right angles, causing the whole loose and rattling frame to dangle and twirl about at the caprice of every occasional puff of wind which found its way into the apart-ment. In the cranium of this hideous thing lay a quantity of ignited charcoal, which threw a fitful but vivid light over the entire scene; while coffins, and other wares appertaining to the shop of an undertaker, were piled high up around the room, and against the windows, preventing any ray from escaping into the street.

At sight of this extraordinary assembly, and of their still more extraordinary paraphernalia, our two seamen did not conduct themselves with that degree of decorum which might have been expected. Legs, leaning against the wall near which he happened to be standing, dropped his lower jaw still lower than usual, and spread open his eyes to their fullest extent: while Hugh Tarpau-lin, stooping down so as to bring his nose upon a level with the table, and spreading out a palm upon either knee, burst into a long, loud, and obstreperous roar of very ill-timed and immoderate laughter.

Without, however, taking offence at behavior so excessively

rude, the tall president smiled very graciously upon the intruders
—nodded to them in a dignified manner with his head of sable
plumes—and, arising, took each by an arm, and led him to a seat
which some others of the company had placed in the meantime
for his accommodation. Legs to all this offered not the slightest
resistance, but sat down as he was directed; while the gallant
Hugh, removing his coffin trestel from its station near the head
of the table, to the vicinity of the little consumptive lady in the
winding sheet, plumped down by her side in high glee, and pouring out a skull of red wine, quaffed it to their better acquaintance.
But at this presumption the stiff gentleman in the coffin seemed
exceedingly nettled; and serious consequences might have ensued
had not the president, rapping upon the table with his truncheon
diverted the attention of all present to the following speech:

" It becomes our duty upon the present happy occasion"———

" Avast there!" interrupted Legs, looking very serious, " avast
there a bit, I say, and tell us who the devil ye all are, and what
business ye have here, rigged off like the foul fiends, and swilling
the snug blue ruin stowed away for the winter by my honest shipmate, Will Wimble the undertaker!"

At this unpardonable piece of ill-breeding, all the original company half started to their feet, and uttered the same rapid succession of wild fiendish shrieks which had before caught the
attention of the seamen. The president, however, was the first to
recover his composure, and at length, turning to Legs with great
dignity, recommenced:

" Most willingly will we gratify any reasonable curiosity on the
part of guests so illustrious, unbidden though they be. Know
then that in these dominions I am monarch, and here rule with
undivided empire under the title of ' King Pest the First.'

" This apartment, which you no doubt profanely suppose to be
the shop of Will Wimble the undertaker —a man whom we know
not, and whose plebeian appellation has never before this night
thwarted our royal ears—this apartment, I say, is the Dais-Cham-
ber of our Palace, devoted to the councils of our kingdom, and to
other sacred and lofty purposes.

" The noble lady who sits opposite is Queen Pest, our Serene
Consort. The other exalted personages whom you behold are all

of our family, and wear the insignia of the blood royal under the respective titles of ' His Grace the Arch Duke Pest-Iferous'—' His Grace the Duke Pest-Ilential'—' His Grace the Duke Tem-Pest'—and ' Her Serene Highness the Arch Duchess Ana-Pest.'

" As regards," continued ne, " your demand of the business upon which we sit here in council, we might be pardoned for replying that it concerns, and concerns *alone*, our own private and regal interest, and is in no manner important to any other than ourself. But in consideration of those rights to which as guests and strangers you may feel yourselves entitled, we will furthermore explain that we are here this night, prepared by deep research and accurate investigation, to examine, analyze, and thoroughly determine the indefinable spirit—the incomprehensible qualities and nature—of those inestimable treasures of the palate, the wines, ales, and liqueurs of this goodly metropolis : by so doing to advance not more our own designs than the true welfare of that unearthly sovereign whose reign is over us all, whose dominions are unlimited, and whose name is ' Death.' "

" Whose name is Davy Jones !" ejaculated Tarpaulin, helping the lady by his side to a skull of liqueur, and pouring out a second for himself.

" Profane varlet !" said the president, now turning his attention to the worthy Hugh, " profane and execrable wretch !—we have said, that in consideration of those rights which, even in thy filthy person, we feel no inclination to violate, we have condescended to make reply to thy rude and unseasonable inquiries. We nevertheless, for your unhallowed intrusion upon our councils, believe it our duty to mulct thee and thy companion in each a gallon of Black Strap—having imbibed which to the prosperity of our kingdom—at a single draught—and upon your bended knees—ye shall be forthwith free either to proceed upon your way, or remain and be admitted to the privileges of our table, according to your respective and individual pleasures."

" It would be a matter of utter unpossibility," replied Legs, whom the assumptions and dignity of King Pest the First had evidently inspired with some feelings of respect, and who arose and steadied himself by the table as he spoke—" it would, please your majesty, be a matter of utter unpossibility to stow away in my bold even one-fourth part of that same liquor which your majesty has just mentioned. To say nothing of the stuffs placed on board in the forenoon by way of ballast, and not to mention the various ales and liqueurs shipped this evening at various seaports, I have, at present, a full cargo of 'humming stuff' taken in and duly paid for at the sign of the 'Jolly Tar.' You will, therefore, please your majesty, be so good as to take the will for the deed—for by no manner of means either can I or will I swallow another drop—least of all a drop of that villanous bilge-water that answers to the hail of 'Black Strap.'"

"Belay that!" interrupted Tarpaulin, astonished not more at the length of his companion's speech than at the nature of his refusal—"Belay that, you lubber!—and I say, Legs, none of your palaver! _My_ hull is still light, although I confess you yourself seem to be a little top-heavy; and as for the matter of your share of the cargo, why rather than raise a squall I would find stowage-room for it myself, but"——

"This proceeding," interposed the president, "is by no means in accordance with the terms of the mulct or sentence, which is in its nature Median, and not to be altered or recalled. The conditions we have imposed must be fulfilled to the letter, and that without a moment's hesitation—in failure of which fulfilment we decree that you do here be tied neck and heels together, and duly drowned as rebels in yon hogshead of October beer!"

"A sentence!—a sentence!—a righteous and just sentence!— a glorious decree!—a most worthy and upright, and holy condemnation!" shouted the Pest family altogether. The king elevated his forehead into innumerable wrinkles; the gouty little old man puffed like a pair of bellows; the lady of the winding sheet waved her nose to and fro; the gentleman in the cotton drawers pricked up his ears; she of the shroud gasped like a dying fish; and he of the coffin looked stiff and rolled up his eyes.

"Ugh! ugh! ugh!" chuckled Tarpaulin, without heeding the general excitation, "ugh! ugh! ugh!—ugh! ugh! ugh! ugh! —ugh! ugh! ugh!—I was saying," said he, "I was saying when Mr. King Pest poked in his marlin-spike, that as for the matter of two or three gallons more or less of Black Strap, it was a trifle to a tight sea-boat like myself not overstowed—but when it comes to drinking the health of the Devil (whom God assoilzie) and going down upon my marrow bones to his ill-favored majesty there, whom I know, as well as I know myself to be a sinner, to be nobody in the whole world, but Tim Hurlygurly the stage-player!—why! its quite another guess sort of a thing, and utterly and altogether past my comprehension."

He was not allowed to finish this speech in tranquillity. At the name of Tim Hurlygurly the whole assembly leaped from their seats.

"Treason!" shouted his Majesty King Pest the First.

"Treason!" said the little man with the gout.

"Treason!" screamed the Arch Duchess Ana-Pest.

"Treason!" muttered the gentleman with his jaws tied up.

"Treason!" growled he of the coffin.

"Treason!" treason!" shrieked her majesty of the mouth; and, seizing by the hinder part of his breeches the unfortunate Tarpaulin, who had just commenced pouring out for himself a skull of liqueur, she lifted him high into the air, and let him fall without ceremony into the huge open puncheon of his beloved ale. Bobbing up and down, for a few seconds, like an apple in a bowl of toddy, he, at length, finally disappeared amid the whirlpool of foam which, in the already effervescent liquor, his struggles easily succeeded in creating.

Not tamely, however, did the tall seaman behold the discomfiture of his companion. Jostling King Pest through the open trap, the valiant Legs slammed the door down upon him with an oath, and strode towards the centre of the room. Here tearing down the skeleton which swung over the table, he laid it about him with so much energy and good will, that, as the last glimpses of light died away within the apartment, he succeeded in knocking out the brains of the little gentleman with the gout. Rushing then with all his force against the fatal hogshead full of October ale and Hugh Tarpaulin, he rolled it over and over in an instant. Out burst a deluge of liquor so fierce—so impetuous—so overwhelming—that the room was flooded from wall to wall—the loaded table was overturned—the tressels were thrown upon their backs—the tub of punch into the fire-place—and the ladies into hysterics. Piles of death-furniture floundered about. Jugs, pitchers, and carboys mingled promiscuously in the *melée*, and wicker flagons encountered desperately with bottles of junk. The man with the horrors was drowned upon the spot—the little stiff gentleman floated off in his coffin—and the victorious Legs, seizing by the waist the fat lady in the shroud, rushed out with her into the street, and made a bee-line for the "Free and Easy," followed under easy sail by the redoubtable Hugh Tarpaulin, who, having sneezed three or four times, panted and puffed after him with the Arch Duchess Ana-Pest.

17*

THREE SUNDAYS IN A WEEK.

"You hard-hearted, dunder-headed, obstinate, rusty, crusty, musty, fusty, old savage!" said I, in fancy, one afternoon, to my grand uncle Rumgudgeon—shaking my first at him in imagination.

Only in imagination. The fact is, some trivial discrepancy *did* exist, just then, between what I said and what I had not the courage to say—between what I did and what I had half a mind to do.

The old porpoise, as I opened the drawing-room door, was sitting with his feet upon the mantel-piece, and a bumper of port in his paw, making strenuous efforts to accomplish the ditty

Remplis ton verre vide!
Vide ton verre plein!

"My *dear* uncle," said I, closing the door gently, and approaching him with the blandest of smiles, "you are always so *very* kind and considerate, and have evinced your benevolence in so many—so *very* many ways—that—that I feel I have only to suggest this little point to you once more to make sure of your full acquiescence."

"Hem!" said he, "good boy! go on!"

"I am sure, my dearest uncle, [you confounded old rascal!] that you have no design really, seriously, to oppose my union with Kate. This is merely a joke of yours, I know—ha! ha! ha!—how *very* pleasant you are at times."

"Ha! ha! ha!" said he, "curse you! yes!"

"To be sure—of course! I *knew* you were jesting. Now, uncle, all that Kate and myself wish at present, is that you would oblige us with your advice as—as regards the *time—you* know, uncle—in short, when will it be most convenient for yourself, that the wedding shall—shall—come off, you know?"

"Come off, you scoundrel!—what do you mean by that?—Better wait till it goes on."

"Ha! ha! ha!—he! he! he!—hi! hi! hi!—ho! ho! ho!—hu! hu! hu!—oh, that's good!—oh, that's capital—*such* a wit! But all we want just *now*, you know, uncle, is that you would indicate the time precisely."

"Ah!—precisely?"

"Yes, uncle—that is, if it would be quite agreeable to yourself."

"Would'nt it answer, Bobby, if I were to leave it at random—some time within a year or so, for example?—*must* I say precisely?"

"*If* you please, uncle—precisely."

"Well, then, Bobby, my boy—you're a fine fellow, aren't you?—since you *will* have the exact time, I'll—why I'll oblige you for once."

"Dear uncle!"

"Hush, sir!" [drowning my voice]—"I'll oblige you for once. You shall have my consent—and the *plum*, we mus'nt forget the plum—let me see! when shall it be? To-day's Sunday—is'nt it? Well, then, you shall be married precisely—*precisely*, now mind!—*when three Sundays come together in a week!* Do you hear me, sir! *What* are you gaping at? I say, you shall have Kate and her plum when three Sundays come together in a week—but not *till* then—you young scapegrace—not *till* then, if I die for it. You know me—*I'm a man of my word*—now be off!" Here he swallowed his bumper of port, while I rushed from the room in despair.

A very "fine old English gentleman," was my grand-uncle Rumgudgeon, but unlike him of the song, he had his weak points. He was a little, pursy, pompous, passionate, semicircular somebody, with a red nose, a thick skull, a long purse, and a strong sense of his own consequence. With the best heart in the world, he contrived, through a predominant whim of *contradiction*, to earn for himself, among those who only knew him superficially, the character of a curmudgeon. Like many excellent people, he seemed possessed with a spirit of *tantalization*, which might easily, at a casual glance, have been mistaken for malevolence. To every request, a positive "No!" was his immediate answer; but in the end—in the long, long end—there were exceedingly few requests which he refused. Against all attacks upon his purse he made the most sturdy defence; but the amount extorted from him, at last was, generally, in direct ratio with the length of the siege and the stubbornness of the resistance. In charity no one gave more liberally or with a worse grace.

For the fine arts, and especially for the belles lettres, he entertained a profound contempt. With this he had been inspired by Casimir Perier, whose pert little query "*A quoi un poete est il bon?*" he was in the habit of quoting, with a very droll pronunciation, as the *ne plus ultra* of logical wit. Thus my own inkling for the Muses had excited his entire displeasure. He assured me one day, when I asked him for a new copy of Horace, that the translation of "*Poeta nascitur non fit*" was "a nasty poet for nothing fit"—a remark which I took in high dudgeon. His repugnance to "the humanities" had, also, much increased of late, by an accidental bias in favor of what he supposed to be natural science. Somebody had accosted him in the street, mistaking him for no less a personage than Doctor Dubble L. Dee, the lecturer upon quack physics. This set him off at a tangent; and just at the epoch of this story—for story it is getting to be after all—my grand uncle Rumgudgeon was accessible and pacific only upon points which happened to chime in with the caprioles of the hobby he was riding. For the rest, he laughed with his arms and legs, and his politics were stubborn and easily understood. He thought, with Horsley, that "the people have nothing to do with the laws but to obey them."

I had lived with the old gentleman all my life. My parents, in dying, had bequeathed me to him as a rich legacy. I believe the old villain loved me as his own child—nearly if not quite as well as he loved Kate—but it was a dog's existence that he led me, after all. From my first year until my fifth, he obliged me with very regular floggings. From five to fifteen, he threatened me, hourly, with the House of Correction. From fifteen to twenty, not a day passed in which he did not promise to cut me off with a shilling. I was a sad dog, it is true—but then it was a part of my nature—a point of my faith. In Kate, however, I had a firm friend, and I knew it. She was a good girl, and told me very sweetly that I might have her (plum and all) whenever I could badger my grand uncle Rumgudgeon, into the necessary consent. Poor girl!—she was barely fifteen, and without this consent, her little amount in the funds was not come-at-able until five immeasurable summers had "dragged their slow length along." What then, to do? At fifteen, or even at twenty-one (for I had now passed my fifth olympiad) five years in prospect are very much the same as five hundred. In vain we besieged the old gentleman with importunities. Here was a *piece de resistance* (as Messieurs Ude and Carene would say) which suited his perverse fancy to a T. It would have stirred the indignation of Job himself, to see how much like an old mouser he behaved to us two poor wretched little mice. In his heart he wished for nothing more ardently than our union. He had made up his mind to this all along. In fact, he would have given ten thousand pounds from his own pocket (Kate's plum was *her own*) if he could have invented anything like an excuse for complying with our very natural wishes. But then we had been so imprudent as to broach the subject *ourselves*. Not to oppose it under such circumstances, I sincerely believe was not in his power.

I have said already that he had his weak points; but, in speaking of these, I must not be understood as referring to his obstinacy: which was one of his strong points—" *assurement ce n'etait pas sa foible.*" When I mention his weakness I have allusion to a *bizarre* old-womanish superstition which beset him. He was great in dreams, portents, *et id genus omne* of rigmarole. He was excessively punctilious, too, upon small points of honor, and, after his own fashion, was a man of his word, beyond doubt. This was, in fact, one of his hobbies. The *spirit* of his vows he made no scruple of setting at naught, but the *letter* was a bond inviolable. Now it was this latter peculiarity in his disposition, of which

Kate's ingenuity enabled us one fine day, not long after our inter
view in the dining-room, to take a very unexpected advantage ;
and, having thus, in the fashion of all modern bards and orators,
exhausted in *prolegomena*, all the time at my command, and nearly
all the room at my disposal, I will sum up in a few words what
constitutes the whole pith of the story.

It happened then—so the Fates ordered it—that among the
naval acquaintances of my betrothed, were two gentlemen who
had just set foot upon the shores of England, after a year's
absence, each, in foreign travel. In company with these gentlemen, my cousin and I, preconcertedly, paid uncle Rumgudgeon a
visit on the afternoon of Sunday, October the tenth,—just three
weeks after the memorable decision which had so cruelly defeated
our hopes. For about half an hour the conversation ran upon
ordinary topics ; but at last, we contrived, quite naturally, to give
it the following turn :

Capt. Pratt. "Well, I have been absent just one year. Just
one year to-day, as I live—let me see ! yes !—this is October the
tenth. You remember, Mr. Rumgudgeon, I called, this day year,
to bid you good-bye. And by the way, it *does* seem something
like a coincidence, does it not—that our friend, Captain Smitherton, here, has been absent exactly a year also—a year to-day ?"

Smitherton. "Yes ! just one year to a fraction. You will
remember, Mr. Rumgudgeon, that I called with Capt. Pratol on
this very day, last year, to pay my parting respects."

Uncle. "Yes, yes, yes—I remember it very well—very queer
indeed ! Both of you gone just one year. A very strange coincidence, indeed ! Just what Doctor Dubble L. Dee would denominate an extraordinary concurrence of events. Doctor Dub—"

Kate. [Interrupting.] "To be sure, papa, it *is* something
strange ; but then Captain Pratt and Captain Smitherton didn't
go altogether the same route, and that makes a difference you
know."

Uncle. "I don't know any such thing, you huzzy ! How
should I ? I think it only makes the matter more remarkable.
Doctor Dubble L. Dee"—

Kate. "Why, papa, Captain Pratt went round Cape Horn,
and Captain Smitherton doubled the Cape of Good Hope."

Uncle. " Precisely !—the one went east and the other went west, you jade, and they both have gone quite round the world. By the by, Doctor Dubble L. Dee"—

Myself, [*hurriedly.*] " Captain Pratt, you must come and spend the evening with us to-morrow—you and Smitherton—you can tell us all about your voyage, and we'll have a game of whist, and"—

Pratt. " Whist, my dear fellow—you forget. To-morrow will be Sunday. Some other evening"—

Kate. " Oh, no, fie ' -Robert's not *quite* so bad as that. To-day's Sunday."

Uncle. " To be sure—to be sure !"

Pratt. " I beg both your pardons—but I can't be so much mistaken. I know to-morrow's Sunday, because"—

Smitherton, (much surprised.) " What *are* you all thinking about ! Was'nt *yesterday* Sunday, I should like to know ?"

All. " Yesterday, indeed ! you *are* out !"

Uncle. " To-day's Sunday, I say—don't *I* know ?"

Pratt. " Oh no !—to-morrow's Sunday."

Smitherton. " You are *all* mad—every one of you. I am as positive that yesterday was Sunday, as I am that I sit upon this chair."

Kate, (jumping up eagerly.) " I see it—I see it all. Papa, this is a judgment upon you, about—about you know what. Let me alone, and I'll explain it all in a minute. It's a very simple thing, indeed. Captain Smitherton says that yesterday was Sunday : so it was ; he is right. Cousin Bobby, and uncle and I, say that to-day is Sunday : so it is ; we are right. Captain Pratt maintains that to-morrow will be Sunday : so it will ; he is right, too. The fact is, we are all right, and thus *three Sundays have come together in a week.*"

Smitherton, (after a pause.) " By the by, Pratt, Kate has us completely. What fools we two are ! Mr. Rumgudgeon, the matter stands thus : the earth you know is twenty-four thousand miles in circumference. Now this globe of the earth turns upon its own axis—revolves—spins round—these twenty-four thousand miles of extent, going from west to east, in precisely twenty-four hours. Do you understand, Mr. Rumgudgeon ?"

Uncle. "To be sure—to be sure—Doctor Dub"—

Smitherton, (drowning his voice.) "Well, sir ; that is at the rate of one thousand miles per hour. Now, suppose that I sail from this position a thousand miles east. Of course, I anticipate the rising of the sun here at London, by just one hour. I see the sun rise one hour before you do. Proceeding, in the same direction, yet another thousand miles, I anticipate the rising by two hours—another thousand, and I anticipate it by three hours, and so on, until I go entirely round the globe, and back to this spot, when, having gone twenty-four thousand miles east, I antici‧ pate the rising of the London sun by no less than twenty-four hours ; that is to say, I am a day *in advance* of your time. Understand, eh ?"

Uncle. "But Dubble L. Dee"—

Smitherton, (speaking very loud.) Captain Pratt, on the contrary, when he had sailed a thousand miles west of this position, was an hour, and when he had sailed twenty-four thousand miles west, was twenty-four hours, or one day, *behind* the time at London. Thus, with me, yesterday was Sunday—thus, with you, to-day is Sunday—and thus, with Pratt, to-morrow will be Sunday. And what is more, Mr. Rumgudgeon, it is positively clear that we are *all right* ; for there can be no philosophical reason assigned why the idea of one of us should have preference over that of the other."

Uncle. "My eyes !—well, Kate—well, Bobby !—this *is* a judgment upon me, as you say. But I am a man of my word— *mark that !* you shall have her, boy (plum and all,) when you please. Done up, by Jove ! Three Sundays all in a row ! I'll go, and take Dubble L. Dee's opinion upon *that.*"

THE DEVIL IN THE BELFRY.

What o'clock is it !—*Old Saying.*

EVERYBODY knows, in a general way, that the finest place in the world is—or, alas, *was*—the Dutch borough of Vondervottei-mittiss. Yet, as it lies some distance from any of the main roads, being in a somewhat out-of-the-way situation, there are, perhaps, very few of my readers who have ever paid it a visit. For the benefit of those who have *not*, therefore, it will be only proper that I should enter into some account of it. And this is, indeed, the more necessary, as with the hope of enlisting public sympathy in behalf of the inhabitants, I design here to give a history of the calamitous events which have so lately occurred within its limits. No one who knows me will doubt that the duty thus self-imposed will be executed to the best of my ability, with all that rigid impartiality, all that cautious examination into facts, and diligent collation of authorities, which should ever distinguish him who aspires to the title of historian.

By the united aid of medals, manuscripts, and inscriptions, I am enabled to say, positively, that the borough of Vondervottei-mittiss has existed, from its origin, in precisely the same condition which it at present preserves. Of the date of this origin, however, I grieve that I can only speak with that species of indefinite definiteness which mathematicians are, at times, forced to put up with in certain algebraic formulæ. The date, I may thus say, in regard to the remoteness of its antiquity, cannot be less than any assignable quantity whatsoever.

Touching the derivation of the name Vondervotteimittiss, I confess myself, with sorrow, equally at fault. Among a multitude of opinions upon this delicate point—some acute, some learned, some sufficiently the reverse—I am able to select nothing which ought to be considered satisfactory. Perhaps the idea of Grogswigg—nearly coincident with that of Kroutaplenttey—is to be cautiously preferred:—It runs:—"*Vondervotteimittiss—Vonder, lege Donder—Votteimittiss, quasi und Bleitziz—Bleitziz obsol: pro Blitzen.*" This derivation, to say the truth, is still countenanced by some traces of the electric fluid evident on the summit of the steeple of the House of the Town-Council. I do not choose, however, to commit myself on a theme of such importance, and must refer the reader desirous of information, to the "*Oratiunculæ de Rebus Præter-Veteris*," of Dundergutz. See, also, Blunderbuzzard "*De Derivationibus*," pp. 27 to 5010, Folio, Gothic edit., Red and Black character, Catch-word and No Cypher;—wherein consult, also, marginal notes in the autograph of Stuffundpuff, with the Sub-Commentaries of Gruntundguzzell.

Notwithstanding the obscurity which thus envelopes the date of the foundation of Vondervotteimittiss, and the derivation of its name, there can be no doubt, as I said before, that it has always existed as we find it at this epoch. The oldest man in the borough can remember not the slightest difference in the appearance of any portion of it; and, indeed, the very suggestion of such a possibility is considered an insult. The site of the village is in a perfectly circular valley, about a quarter of a mile in circumference, and entirely surrounded by gentle hills, over whose summit the people have never yet ventured to pass. For this they assign the very good reason that they do not believe there is anything at all on the other side.

Round the skirts of the valley, (which is quite level, and paved throughout with flat tiles,) extends a continuous row of sixty little houses. These, having their backs on the hills, must look, of course, to the centre of the plain, which is just sixty yards from the front door of each dwelling. Every house has a small garden before it, with a circular path, a sun-dial, and twenty-four cabbages. The buildings themselves are so precisely alike, that one can in no manner be distinguished from the other. Owing to the vast antiquity, the style of architecture is somewhat odd, but it is not for that reason the less strikingly picturesque. They are fashioned of hard-burned little bricks, red, with black ends, so that the walls look like a chess-board upon a great scale. The gables are turned to the front, and there are cornices, as big as all the rest of the house, over the eaves and over the main doors. The windows are narrow and deep, with very tiny panes and a great deal of sash. On the roof is a vast quantity of tiles with long curly ears. The woodwork, throughout, is of a dark hue, and there is much carving about it, with but a trifling variety of pattern; for, time out of mind, the carvers of Vondervotteimittiss have never been able to carve more than two objects—a timepiece and a cabbage. But these they do exceedingly well, and intersperse them, with singular ingenuity, wherever they find room for the chisel.

The dwellings are as much alike inside as out, and the furniture is all upon one plan. The floors are of square tiles, the chairs and tables of black-looking wood with thin crooked legs and puppy feet. The mantel-pieces are wide and high, and have not only time-pieces and cabbages sculptured over the front, but a real time-piece, which makes a prodigious ticking, on the top in the middle, with a flower-pot containing a cabbage standing on each extremity by way of outrider. Between each cabbage and the time-piece, again, is a little China man having a large stomach with a great round hole in it, through which is seen the dial-plate of a watch.

The fire-places are large and deep, with fierce crooked-looking fire-dogs. There is constantly a rousing fire, and a huge pot over it, full of sauer-kraut and pork, to which the good woman of the house is always busy in attending. She is a little fat old lady, with blue eyes and a red face, and wears a huge cap like a sugar-loaf, ornamented with purple and yellow ribbons. Her dress is of orange-colored linsey-woolsey, made very full behind and very short in the waist—and indeed very short in other respects, not reaching below the middle of her leg. This is somewhat thick, and so are her ankles, but she has a fine pair of green stockings to cover them. Her shoes—of pink leather—are fastened each with a bunch of yellow ribbons puckered up in the shape of a cabbage. In her left hand she has a little heavy Dutch watch; in her right she wields a ladle for the sauer-kraut and pork. By her side there stands a fat tabby cat, with a gilt toy repeater tied to its tail, which "the boys" have there fastened by way of a quiz.

The boys themselves are, all three of them, in the garden attending the pig. They are each two feet in height. They have three-cornered cocked hats, purple waistcoats reaching down to their thighs, buckskin knee-breeches, red woollen stockings, heavy shoes with big silver buckles, and long surtout coats with large buttons of mother-of-pearl. Each, too, has a pipe in his mouth, and a little dumpy watch in his right hand. He takes a puff and a look, and then a look and a puff. The pig—which is corpulent and lazy—is occupied now in picking up the stray leaves that fall from the cabbages, and now in giving a kick behind at the gilt repeater, which the urchins have also tied to *his* tail, in order to make him look as handsome as the cat.

Right at the front door, in a high-backed leather-bottomed armed chair, with crooked legs and puppy feet like the tables, is seated the old man of the house himself. He is an exceedingly puffy little old gentleman, with big circular eyes and a huge double chin. His dress resembles that of the boys—and I need say nothing farther about it. All the difference is, that his pipe is somewhat bigger than theirs, and he can make a greater smoke. Like them, he has a watch, but he carries his watch in his pocket. To say the truth, he has something of more importance than a watch to attend to—and what that is, I shall presently explain. He sits with his right leg upon his left knee, wears a grave countenance, and always keeps one of his eyes, at least, resolutely bent upon a certain remarkable object in the centre of the plain.

This object is situated in the steeple of the House of the Town-Council. The Town-Council are all very little, round, oily, intelligent men, with big saucer eyes and fat double chins, and have their coats much longer and their shoe-buckles much bigger than the ordinary inhabitants of Vondervotteimittiss. Since my sojourn in the borough, they have had several special meetings, and have adopted these three important resolutions :—

"That it is wrong to alter the good old course of things :"

"That there is nothing tolerable out of Vondervotteimittiss :" and—

"That we will stick by our clocks and our cabbages." ·

Above the session-room of the Council is the steeple, and in the steeple is the belfry, where exists, and has existed time out of mind, the pride and wonder of the village—the great clock of the borough of Vondervotteimittiss. And this is the object to which the eyes of the old gentlemen are turned who sit in the leather-bottomed arm chairs.

The great clock has seven faces—one in each of the seven sides of the steeples—so that it can be readily seen from all quarters. Its faces are large and white, and its hands heavy and black. There is a belfry-man whose sole duty is to attend to it ; but this duty is the most perfect of sinecures—for the clock of Vondervotteimittiss was never yet known to have anything the matter with it. Until lately, the bare supposition of such a thing was considered heretical. From the remotest period of antiquity to which the archives have reference, the hours have been regularly struck by the big bell. And, indeed, the case was just the same with all the other clocks and watches in the borough. Never was such a place for keeping the true time. When the large clapper thought proper to say "Twelve o'clock !" all its obedient followers opened their throats simultaneously, and responded like a very echo. In short, the good burghers were fond of their sauer-kraut, but then they were proud of their clocks.

All people who hold sinecure offices are held in more or less respect, and as the belfry-man of Vondervotteimittiss has the most perfect of sinecures, he is the most perfectly respected of any man in the world. He is the chief dignitary of the borough, and the very pigs look up to him with a sentiment of reverence. His coat-tail is *very* far longer—his pipe, his shoe-buckles, his eyes, and his stomach, *very* far bigger—than those of any other old gentleman in the village ; and as to his chin, it is not only double, but triple.

I have thus painted the happy estate of Vondervotteimittiss : alas, that so fair a picture should ever experience a reverse !

There has been long a saying among the wisest inhabitants,

that "no good can come from over the hills ;" and it really seemed that the words had in them something of the spirit of prophecy.
It wanted five minutes of noon, on the day before yesterday, when
there appeared a very odd-looking object on the summit of the
ridge to the eastward. Such an occurrence, of course, attracted
universal attention, and every little old gentleman who sat in a
leather-bottomed arm-chair, turned one of his eyes with a stare of
dismay upon the phenomenon, still keeping the other upon the
clock in the steeple.

By the time that it wanted only three minutes to noon, the
droll object in question was perceived to be a very diminutive
foreign-looking young man. He descended the hills at a great
rate, so that everybody had soon a good look at him. He was
really the most finnicky little personage that had ever been seen
in Vondervotteimittiss. His countenance was of a dark snuff-
color, and he had a long hooked nose, pea eyes, a wide mouth, and
an excellent set of teeth, which latter he seemed anxious of displaying, as he was grinning from ear to ear. What with mus-
tachios and whiskers, there was none of the rest of his face to be
seen. His head was uncovered, and his hair neatly done up in
papillotes. His dress was a tight-fitting swallow-tailed black coat,
(from one of whose pockets dangled a vast length of white handkerchief,) black kerseymere knee-breeches, black stockings, and
stumpy-looking pumps, with huge bunches of black satin ribbon
for bows. Under one arm he carried a huge *chapeau-de-bras,*
and under the other a fiddle nearly five times as big as himself.
In his left hand was a gold snuff-box, from which, as he capered
down the hill, cutting all manner of fantastical steps, he took snuff
incessantly with an air of the greatest possible self-satisfaction.
God bless me!—here was a sight for the honest burghers of Vondervotteimittiss !

To speak plainly, the fellow had, in spite of his grinning, an
audacious and sinister kind of face ; and as he curvetted right into
the village, the odd stumpy appearance of his pumps excited no
little suspicion ; and many a burgher who beheld him that day,
would have given a trifle for a peep beneath the white cambric
handkerchief which hung so obtrusively from the pocket of his
swallow-tailed coat. But what mainly occasioned a righteous in-

dignation was, that the scoundrelly popinjay, while he cut a fandango here, and a whirligig there, did not seem to have the remotest idea in the world of such a thing as *keeping time* in his steps.

The good people of the borough had scarcely a chance, however, to get their eyes thoroughly open, when, just as it wanted half a minute of noon, the rascal bounced, as I say, right into the midst of them; gave a *chassez* here, and a *balancez* there; and then, after a *pirouette* and a *pas-de-zephyr*, pigeon-winged himself right up into the belfry of the House of the Town-Council, where the wonder-stricken belfry-man sat smoking in a state of dignity and dismay. But the little chap seized him at once by the nose; gave it a swing and a pull; clapped the big *chapeau-de-bras* upon his head; knocked it down over his eyes and mouth; and then, lifting up the big fiddle, beat him with it so long and so soundly, that what with the belfry-man being so fat, and the fiddle being so hollow, you would have sworn that there was a regiment of double-bass drummers all beating the devil's tattoo up in the belfry of the steeple of Vondervotteimittiss.

There is no knowing to what desperate act of vengeance this unprincipled attack might have aroused the inhabitants, but for the important fact that it now wanted only half a second of noon. The bell was about to strike, and it was a matter of absolute and pre-eminent necessity that every body should look well at his watch. It was evident, however, that just at this moment, the fellow in the steeple was doing something that he had no business to do with the clock. But as it now began to strike, nobody had any time to attend to his manœuvres, for they had all to count the strokes of the bell as it sounded.

"One!" said the clock.

"Von!" echoed every little old gentleman in every leather-bottomed arm-chair in Vondervotteimittiss. "Von!" said his watch also; "von!" said the watch of his vrow, and "von!" said the watches of the boys, and the little gilt repeaters on the tails of the cat and pig.

"Two!" continued the big bell; and

"Doo!" repeated all the repeaters.

"Three! Four! Five! Six! Seven! Eight! Nine! Ten!" said the bell.

"Dree! Vour! Fibe Sax! Seben! Aight! Noin! Den!" answered the others.

"Eleven!" said the big one.

"Eleben!" assented the little fellows.

"Twelve!" said the bell.

"Dvelf!" they replied, perfectly satisfied, and dropping their voices.

"Und dvelf it iss!" said all the little old gentlemen, putting up their watches. But the big bell had not done with them yet.

"*Thirteen!*" said he.

"Der Teufel!" gasped the little old gentlemen, turning pale, dropping their pipes, and putting down all their right legs from over their left knees.

"Der Teufel!" groaned they, "Dirteen! Dirteen!!—Mein Gott, it is Dirteen o'clock!!"

Why attempt to describe the terrible scene which ensued! All Vondervotteimittiss flew at once into a lamentable state of uproar.

"Vot is cum'd to mein pelly?" roared all the boys,—"I've been ongry for dis hour!"

"Vot is cum'd to mein kraut?" screamed all the vrows, "It has been done to rags for dis hour!"

"Vot is cum'd to mein pipe?" swore all the little old gentlemen, "Donder and Blitzen! it has been smoked out for dis hour!" —and they filled them up again in a great rage, and, sinking back in their arm chairs, puffed away so fast and so fiercely that the whole valley was immediately filled with impenetrable smoke.

Meantime the cabbages all turned very red in the face, and it seemed as if old Nick himself had taken possession of everything in the shape of a time-piece. The clocks carved upon the furniture took to dancing as if bewitched, while those upon the mantel-pieces could scarcely contain themselves for fury, and kept such a continual striking of thirteen, and such a frisking and wriggling of their pendulums as was really horrible to see.—But, worse than all, neither the cats nor the pigs could put up any longer with the behavior of the little repeaters tied to their tails, and resented it by scampering all over the place, scratching and poking, and squeaking and screeching, and caterwauling and squalling, and flying into the faces, and running under the petticoats of the people, and creating altogether the most abominable din and confusion which it is possible for a reasonable person to conceive. And to make matters still more distressing, the rascally little scape-grace in the steeple was evidently exerting himself to the utmost. Every now and then one might catch a glimpse of the scoundrel through the smoke. There he sat in the belfry upon the belfry-man, who was lying flat upon his back. In his teeth the villain held the bell-rope, which he kept jerking about with his head, raising such a clatter that my ears ring again even to think of it. On his lap lay the big fiddle at which he was scraping out of all time and tune, with both hands, making a great show, the nincompoop! of playing "Judy O'Flannagan and Paddy O'Raferty."

Affairs being thus miserably situated, I left the place in disgust, and now appeal for aid to all lovers of correct time and fine kraut. Let us proceed in a body to the borough, and restore the ancient order of things in Vondervotteimittiss by ejecting that little fellow from the steeple.

VOL. II.—18.

LIONIZING.

――――――――― all people went
Upon their ton toes in wild wonderment.
                    Bishop Hall's Soirees.

I AM—that is to say I *was*—a great man ; but I am neither the author of Junius nor the man in the mask ; for my name, I believe, is Robert Jones, and I was born somewhere in the city of Fum-Fudge.

The first action of my life was the taking hold of my nose with both hands. My mother saw this and called me a genius :—my father wept for joy and presented me with a treatise on Nosology. This I mastered before I was breeched.

I now began to feel my way in the science, and soon came to understand that, provided a man had a nose sufficiently conspicuous, he might, by merely following it, arrive at a Lionship. But my attention was not confined to theories alone. Every morning I gave my proboscis a couple of pulls and swallowed a half dozen of drams.

When I came of age my father asked me, one day, if I would step with him into his study.

"My son," said he, when we were seated, "what is the chief end of your existence ?"

"My father," I answered, "it is the study of Nosology."   -

"And what, Robert," he inquired, "is Nosology ?"

"Sir," I said, "it is the Science of Noses."

"And can you tell me," he demanded, "what is the meaning of a nose ?"

"A nose, my father," I replied, greatly softened, "has been variously defined by about a thousand different authors." [Here

I pulled out my watch.] "It is now noon or thereabouts—we shall have time enough to get through with them all before midnight. To commence then:—The nose, according to Bartholinus, is that protuberance — that bump — that excrescence— that——"

"Will do, Robert," interrupted the good old gentleman. "I am thunderstruck at the extent of your information—I am positively—upon my soul." [Here he closed his eyes and placed his hand upon his heart.] "Come here!" [Here he took me by the arm.] "Your education may now be considered as finished —it is high time you should scuffle for yourself—and you cannot do a better thing than merely follow your nose—so—so—so—" [Here he kicked me down stairs and out of the door]—"so get out of my house, and God bless you!"

As I felt within me the divine *afflatus*, I considered this accident rather fortunate than otherwise. I resolved to be guided by the paternal advice. I determined to follow my nose. I gave it a pull or two upon the spot, and wrote a pamphlet on Nosology forthwith.

All Fum-Fudge was in an uproar.

"Wonderful genius!" said the Quarterly.

"Superb physiologist!" said the Westminster.

"Clever fellow!" said the Foreign.

"Fine writer!" said the Edinburgh.

"Profound thinker!" said the Dublin.

"Great man!" said Bentley.

"Divine soul!" said Fraser.

"One of us!" said Blackwood.

"Who can he be?" said Mrs. Bas-Bleu.

"What can he be?" said big Miss Bas-Bleu.

"Where can he be?" said little Miss Bas-Bleu.—But I paid these people no attention whatever—I just stepped into the shop of an artist.

The Duchess of Bless-my-Soul was sitting for her portrait; the Marquis of So-and-So was holding the Duchess' poodle; the Earl of This-and-That was flirting with her salts; and his Royal Highness of Touch-me-Not was leaning upon the back of her chair.

I approached the artist and turned up my nose.

"Oh, beautiful!" sighed her Grace.

"Oh my!" lisped the Marquis.

"Oh, shocking!" groaned the Earl.

"Oh, abominable!" growled his Royal Highness.

"What will you take for it?" asked the artist.

"For his *nose!*" shouted her Grace.

"A thousand pounds," said I, sitting down.

"A thousand pounds?" inquired the artist, musingly.

"A thousand pounds," said I.

"Beautiful!" said he, entranced.

"A thousand pounds," said I.

"Do you warrant it?" he asked, turning the nose to the light.

"I do," said I, blowing it well.

"Is it *quite* original?" he inquired, touching it with reverence.

"Humph!" said I, twisting it to one side.

"Has *no* copy been taken?" he demanded, surveying it through a microscope.

"None," said I, turning it up.

"*Admirable!*" he ejaculated, thrown quite off his guard by the beauty of the manœuvre.

"A thousand pounds," said I.

"A *thousand* pounds?" said he.

"Precisely," said I.

"A thousand *pounds?*" said he.

"Just so," said I.

"You shall have them," said he. "What a piece of *virtu!*" So he drew me a check upon the spot, and took a sketch of my nose. I engaged rooms in Jermyn street, and sent her Majesty the ninety-ninth edition of the "Nosology," with a portrait of the proboscis.—That sad little rake, the Prince of Wales, invited me to dinner.

We were all lions and *recherchés*.

There was a modern Platonist. He quoted Porphyry, Iamblicus, Plotinus, Proclus, Hierocles, Maximus Tyrius, and Syrianus.

There was a human-perfectibility man. He quoted Turgòt,

Price, Priestly, Condorcêt, De Staël, and the "Ambitious Student in Ill Health."

There was Sir Positive Paradox. He observed that all fools were philosophers, and that all philosophers were fools.

There was Æstheticus Ethix. He spoke of fire, unity, and atoms; bi-part and pre-existent soul; affinity and discord; primitive intelligence and homöomeria.

There was Theologos Theology. He talked of Eusebius and Arianus; heresy and the Council of Nice; Puseyism and consubstantialism; Homousios and Homouioisios.

There was Fricassée from the Rocher de Cancale. He mentioned Muriton of red tongue; cauliflowers with *velouté* sauce; veal *à la* St. Menehoult; marinade *à la* St. Florentin; and orange jellies *en mosaïques*.

There was Bibulus O'Bumper. He touched upon Latour and Markbrünnen; upon Mousseux and Chambertin; upon Richbourg and St. George; upon Haubrion, Leonville, and Medoc; upon Barac and Preignac; upon Grâve, upon Sauterne, upon Lafitte, and upon St. Peray. He shook his head at Clos de Vougeot, and told, with his eyes shut, the difference between Sherry and Amontillado.

There was Signor Tintontintino from Florence. He discoursed of Cimabué, Arpino, Carpaccio, and Argostino—of the gloom of Caravaggio, of the amenity of Albano, of the colors of Titian, of the frows of Rubens, and of the waggeries of Jan Steen.

There was the President of the Fum Fudge University. He was of opinion that the moon was called Bendis in Thrace, Bubastis in Egypt, Dian in Rome, and Artemis in Greece.

There was a Grand Turk from Stamboul. He could not help thinking that the angels were horses, cocks, and bulls; that somebody in the sixth heaven had seventy thousand heads; and that the earth was supported by a sky-blue cow with an incalculable number of green horns.

There was Delphinus Polyglott. He told us what had become of the eighty-three lost tragedies of Æschylus; of the fifty-four orations of Isæus; of the three hundred and ninety-one speeches of Lysias; of the hundred and eighty treatises of Theophrastus; of the eighth book of the conic sections of Apollonius; of Pindar's hymns and dithyrambics; and of the five and forty tragedies of Homer Junior.

There was Ferdinand Fitz-Fossillus Feltspar. He informed us all about internal fires and tertiary formations; about aeriforms, fluidiforms, and solidiforms; about quartz and marl; about schist and schorl; about gypsum and trap; about talc and calc; about blende and horn-blende; about mica-slate and pudding-stone; about cvanite and lepidolite; about hæmatite and tremolite; about anamony and calcedony; about manganese and whatever you please.

There was myself. I spoke of myself;—of myself, of myself, of myself;—of Nosology, of my pamphlet, and of myself. I turned up my nose, and I spoke of myself.

"Marvellous clever man!" said the Prince.

"Superb!" said his guests :—and next morning her Grace of Bless-my-Soul paid me a visit.

"Will you go to Almack's, pretty creature?" she said, tapping me under the cnin.

"Upon honor," said I.

"Nose and all?" she asked.

"As I live," I replied.

"Here then is a card, my life. Shall I say you *will* be there?"

"Dear Duchess, with all my heart."

"Pshaw, no!—but with all your nose?"

"Every bit of it, my love," said I :—so I gave it a twist or two, and found myself at Almack's.

The rooms were crowded to suffocation.

"He is coming!" said somebody on the staircase.

"He is coming!" said somebody farther up.

"He is coming!" said somebody farther still.

"He is come!" exclaimed the Duchess. "He is come, the little love!"—and, seizing me firmly by both hands, she kissed me thrice upon the nose.

A marked sensation immediately ensued.

"*Diavolo!*" cried Count Capricornutti.

"*Dios guarda!*" muttered Don Stiletto.

"*Mille tonnerres!*" ejaculated the Prince de Grenouille.

"*Tousand teufel !*" growled the Elector of Bluddennuff.

It was not to be borne. I grew angry. I turned short upon Bluddennuff.

"Sir !" said I to him, "you are a baboon."

"Sir," he replied, after a pause, "*Donner und Blitzen !*"

This was all that could be desired. We exchanged cards. At Chalk-Farm, the next morning, I shot off his nose—and then called upon my friends.

"*Bête !*" said the first.

"Fool !" said the second.

"Dolt !" said the third.

"Ass !" said the fourth.

"Ninny !" said the fifth.

"Noodle !" said the sixth.

"Be off !" said the seventh.

At all this I felt mortified, and so called upon my father.

"Father," I asked, "what is the chief end of my existence ?"

"My son," he replied, "it is still the study of Nosology ; but in hitting the Elector upon the nose you have overshot your mark. You have a fine nose, it is true ; but then Bluddennuff has none. You are damned, and he has become the hero of the day. I grant you that in Fum-Fudge the greatness of a lion is in proportion to the size of his proboscis—but, good heavens ! there is no competing with a lion who has no proboscis at all."

THE MAN OF THE CROWD.

Ce grand malheur, de ne pouvoir être seul.

La Bruyère.

IT was well said of a certain German book that *" er lasst sich nicht lesen"*—it does not permit itself to be read. There are some secrets which do not permit themselves to be told. Men die nightly in their beds, wringing the hands of ghostly confessors, and looking them piteously in the eyes—die with despair of heart and convulsion of throat, on account of the hideousness of mysteries which will not *suffer themselves* to be revealed. Now and then, alas, the conscience of man takes up a burthen so heavy in horror that it can be thrown down only into the grave. And thus the essence of all crime is undivulged.

Not long ago, about the closing in of an evening in autumn, I sat at the large bow window of the D—— Coffee-House in London. For some months I had been ill in health, but was now convalescent, and, with returning strength, found myself in one of those happy moods which are so precisely the converse of *ennui*—moods of the keenest appetency, when the film from the mental vision departs—the αχλυς ος πριν επηεν—and the intellect, electrified, surpasses as greatly its every-day condition, as does the vivid yet candid reason of Leibnitz, the mad and flimsy rhetoric of Gorgias. Merely to breathe was enjoyment; and I derived positive pleasure even from many of the legitimate sources of pain. I felt a calm but inquisitive interest in every thing. With a cigar in my mouth and a newspaper in my lap, I had been amusing myself for the greater part of the afternoon, now in poring over advertisements, now in observing the promiscuous company in the room, and now in peering through the smoky panes into the street.

This latter is one of the principal thoroughfares of the city, and had been very much crowded during the whole day. But, as the darkness came on, the throng momently increased; and, by the time the lamps were well lighted, two dense and continuous tides of population were rushing past the door. At this particular period of the evening I had never before been in a similar situation, and the tumultuous sea of human heads filled me, therefore, with a delicious novelty of emotion. I gave up, at length, all care of things within the hotel, and became absorbed in contemplation of the scene without.

At first my observations took an abstract and generalizing turn. I looked at the passengers in masses, and thought of them in their aggregate relations. Soon, however, I descended to details, and regarded with minute interest the innumerable varieties of figure, dress, air, gait, visage, and expression of countenance.

By far the greater number of those who went by had a satisfied business-like demeanor, and seemed to be thinking only of making their way through the press. Their brows were knit, and their eyes rolled quickly; when pushed against by fellow-wayfarers they evinced no symptom of impatience, but adjusted their clothes and hurried on. Others, still a numerous class, were restless in their movements, had flushed faces, and talked and gesticulated to themselves, as if feeling in solitude on account of the very denseness of the company around. When impeded in their progress, these people suddenly ceased muttering, but redoubled their gesticulations, and awaited, with an absent and overdone smile upon the lips, the course of the persons impeding them. If jostled, they bowed profusely to the jostlers, and appeared overwhelmed with confusion.—There was nothing very distinctive about these two large classes beyond what I have noted. Their habiliments belonged to that order which is pointedly termed the decent. They were undoubtedly noblemen, merchants, attorneys, tradesmen, stock-jobbers—the Eupatrids and the common-places of society—men of leisure and men actively engaged

18*

in affairs of their own—conducting business upon their own responsibility. They did not greatly excite my attention.

The tribe of clerks was an obvious one and here I discerned two remarkable divisions. There were the junior clerks of flash houses—young gentlemen with tight coats, bright boots, well-oiled hair, and supercilious lips. Setting aside a certain dapperness of carriage, which may be termed *deskism* for want of a better word, the manner of these persons seemed to me an exact fac-simile of what had been the perfection of *bon ton* about twelve or eighteen months before. They wore the cast-off graces of the gentry;—and this, I believe, involves the best definition of the class.

The division of the upper clerks of staunch firms, or of the " steady old fellows," it was not possible to mistake. These were known by their coats and pantaloons of black or brown, made to sit comfortably, with white cravats and waistcoats, broad solid-looking shoes, and thick hose or gaiters.—They had all slightly bald heads, from which the right ears, long used to pen-holding, had an odd habit of standing off on end. I observed that they always removed or settled their hats with both hands, and wore watches, with short gold chains of a substantial and ancient pattern. Theirs was the affectation of respectability ;— if indeed there be an affectation so honorable.

There were many individuals of dashing appearance, whom I easily understood as belonging to the race of swell pick-pockets, with which all great cities are infested. I watched these gentry with much inquisitiveness, and found it difficult to imagine how they should ever be mistaken for gentlemen by gentlemen themselves. Their voluminousness of wristband, with an air of excessive frankness, should betray them at once.

The gamblers, of whom I descried not a few, were still more easily recognisable. They wore every variety of dress, from that of the desperate thimble-rig bully, with velvet waistcoat, fancy neckerchief, gilt chains, and filagreed buttons, to that of the scrupulously inornate clergyman, than which nothing could be less liable to suspicion. Still all were distinguished by a certain sodden swarthiness of complexion, a filmy dimness of eye, and pallor and compression of lip. There were two other traits, moreover, by which I could always detect them ;—a guarded lowness of tone in conversation, and a more than ordinary extension of the thumb in a direction at right angles with the fingers. —Very often, in company with these sharpers, I observed an order of men somewhat different in habits, but still birds of a kindred feather. They may be defined as the gentlemen who live by their wits. They seem to prey upon the public in two battalions—that of the dandies and that of the military men. Of the first grade the leading features are long locks and smiles ; of the second frogged coats and frowns.

Descending in the scale of what is termed gentility, I found darker and deeper themes for speculation. I saw Jew pedlars, with hawk eyes flashing from countenances whose every other feature wore only an expression of abject humility ; sturdy professional street beggars scowling upon mendicants of a better stamp, whom despair alone had driven forth into the night for charity ; feeble and ghastly invalids, upon whom death had placed a sure hand, and who sidled and tottered through the mob, looking every one beseechingly in the face, as if in search of some chance consolation, some lost hope ; modest young girls returning from long and late labor to a cheerless home, and shrinking more tearfully than indignantly from the glances of ruffians, whose direct contact, even, could not be avoided ; women of the town of all kinds and of all ages—the unequivocal beauty in the prime of her womanhood, putting one in mind of the statue in Lucian, with the surface of Parian marble, and the interior filled with filth—the loathsome and utterly lost leper in rags—the wrinkled, bejewelled and paint-begrimed beldame, making a last effort at youth—the mere child of immature form, yet, from long association, an adept in the dreadful coquetries of her trade, and burning with a rabid ambition to be ranked the equal of her elders in vice ; drunkards innumerable and indescribable— some in shreds and patches, reeling, inarticulate, with bruised visage and lack-lustre eyes—some in whole although filthy garments, with a slightly unsteady swagger, thick sensual lips, and hearty-looking rubicund faces—others clothed in materials which had once been good, and which even now were scrupulously well brushed—men who walked with a more than natu-

rally firm and springy step, but whose countenances were fearfully pale, whose eyes hideously wild and red, and who clutched
with quivering fingers, as they strode through the crowd, at every
object which came within their reach; beside these, pie-men,
porters, coal-heavers, sweeps; organ-grinders, monkey-exhibiters
and ballad mongers, those who vended with those who sang;
ragged artizans and exhausted laborers of every description, and
all full of a noisy and inordinate vivacity which jarred discord-
antly upon the ear, and gave an aching sensation to the eye.

As the night deepened, so deepened to me the interest of the
scene; for not only did the general character of the crowd materially alter (its gentler features retiring in the gradual withdrawal of the more orderly portion of the people, and its harsher
ones coming out into bolder relief, as the late hour brought forth
every species of infamy from its den,) but the rays of the gas-
lamps, feeble at first in their struggle with the dying day, had now
at length gained ascendancy, and threw over every thing a fitful
and garish lustre. All was dark yet splendid—as that ebony to
which has been likened the style of Tertullian.

The wild effects of the light enchained me to an examination of
individual faces; and although the rapidity with which the world
of light flitted before the window, prevented me from casting
more than a glance upon each visage, still it seemed that, in my
then peculiar mental state, I could frequently read, even in that
brief interval of a glance, the history of long years.

With my brow to the glass, I was thus occupied in scrutinizing
the mob, when suddenly there came into view a countenance
(that of a decrepid old man, some sixty-five or seventy years of
age,)—a countenance which at once arrested and absorbed my
whole attention, on account of the absolute idiosyncracy of its
expression. Any thing even remotely resembling that expression
I had never seen before. I well remember that my first thought,
upon beholding it, was that Retzch, had he viewed it, would have
greatly preferred it to his own pictural incarnations of the fiend.
As I endeavored, during the brief minute of my original survey,
to form some analysis of the meaning conveyed, there arose confusedly and paradoxically within my mind, the ideas of vast mental power, of caution, of penuriousness, of avarice, of coolness,

of malice, of blood-thirstiness, of triumph, of merriment, of excessive terror, of intense—of supreme despair. I felt singularly aroused, startled, fascinated. "How wild a history," I said to myself, "is written within that bosom!" Then came a craving desire to keep the man in view—to know more of him. Hurriedly putting on an overcoat, and seizing my hat and cane, I made my way into the street, and pushed through the crowd in the direction which I had seen him take; for he had already disappeared. With some little difficulty I at length came within sight of him, approached, and followed him closely, yet cautiously, so as not to attract his attention.

I had now a good opportunity of examining his person. He was short in stature, very thin, and apparently very feeble. His clothes, generally, were filthy and ragged; but as he came, now and then, within the strong glare of a lamp, I perceived that his linen, although dirty, was of beautiful texture; and my vision deceived me, or, through a rent in a closely-buttoned and evidently second-handed *roquelaire* which enveloped him, I caught a glimpse both of a diamond and of a dagger. These observations heightened my curiosity, and I resolved to follow the stranger whithersoever he should go.

It was now fully night-fall, and a thick humid fog hung over the city, soon ending in a settled and heavy rain. This change of weather had an odd effect upon the crowd, the whole of which was at once put into new commotion, and overshadowed by a world of umbrellas. The waver, the jostle, and the hum increased in a tenfold degree. For my own part I did not much regard the rain—the lurking of an old fever in my system rendering the moisture somewhat too dangerously pleasant. Tying a handkerchief about my mouth, I kept on. For half an hour the old man held his way with difficulty along the great thoroughfare; and I here walked close at his elbow through fear of losing sight of him. Never once turning his head to look back, he did not observe me. By and bye he passed into a cross street, which, although densely filled with people, was not quite so much thronged as the main one he had quitted. Here a change in his demeanor became evident. He walked more slowly and with less object than before—more hesitatingly. He crossed and re-crossed the way repeatedly without apparent aim ; and the press was still so thick, that, at every such movement, I was obliged to follow him closely. The street was a narrow and long one, and his course lay within it for nearly an hour, during which the passengers had gradually diminished to about that number which is ordinarily seen at noon in Broadway near the park—so vast a difference is there between a London populace and that of the most frequented American city. A second turn brought us into a square, brilliantly lighted, and overflowing with life. The old manner of the stranger re-appeared. His chin fell upon his breast, while his eyes rolled wildly from under his knit brows, in every direction, upon those who hemmed him in. He urged his way steadily and perseveringly. I was surprised, however, to find, upon his having made the circuit of the square, that he turned and retraced his steps. Still more was I astonished to see him repeat the same walk several times—once nearly detecting me as he came round with a sudden movement.

In this exercise he spent another hour, at the end of which we met with far less interruption from passengers than at first. The rain fell fast ; the air grew cool ; and the people were retiring to their homes. With a gesture of impatience, the wanderer passed into a by-street comparatively deserted. Down this, some quarter of a mile long, he rushed with an activity I could not have dreamed of seeing in one so aged, and which put me to much trouble in pursuit. A few minutes brought us to a large and busy bazaar, with the localities of which the stranger appeared well acquainted, and where his original demeanor again became apparent, as he forced his way to and fro, without aim, among the host of buyers and sellers.

During the hour and a half, or thereabouts, which we passed in this place, it required much caution on my part to keep him within reach without attracting his observation. Luckily I wore a pair of caoutchouc over-shoes, and could move about in perfect silence. At no moment did he see that I watched him. He entered shop after shop, priced nothing, spoke no word, and looked at all objects with a wild and vacant stare. I was now utterly amazed at his behavior, and firmly resolved that we should not part until I had satisfied myself in some measure respecting him.

A loud-toned clock struck eleven, and the company were fast
deserting the bazaar. A shop-keeper, in putting up a shutter,
jostled the old man, and at the instant I saw a strong shudder
come over his frame. He hurried into the street, looked anxiously
around him for an instant, and then ran with incredible swiftness
through many crooked and peopleless lanes, until we emerged
once more upon the great thoroughfare whence we had started—
the street of the D—— Hotel. It no longer wore, however,
the same aspect. It was still brilliant with gas; but the rain
fell fiercely, and there were few persons to be seen. The stranger
grew pale. He walked moodily some paces up the once populous avenue, then, with a heavy sigh, turned in the direction
of the river, and, plunging through a great variety of devious
ways, came out, at length, in view of one of the principal thea-
tres. It was about being closed, and the audience were throng-
ing from the doors. I saw the old man gasp as if for breath
while he threw himself amid the crowd; but I thought that the
intense agony of his countenance had, in some measure, abated.
His head again fell upon his breast; he appeared as I had seen
him at first. I observed that he now took the course in which
had gone the greater number of the audience—but, upon the
whole, I was at a loss to comprehend the waywardness of his
actions.

As he proceeded, the company grew more scattered, and his
old uneasiness and vacillation were resumed. For some time he
followed closely a party of some ten or twelve roisterers; but
from this number one by one dropped off, until three only remained together, in a narrow and gloomy lane little frequented. The
stranger paused, and, for a moment, seemed lost in thought; then,
with every mark of agitation, pursued rapidly a route which
brought us to the verge of the city, amid regions very different
from those we had hitherto traversed. It was the most noisome
quarter of London, where everything wore the worst impress of
the most deplorable poverty, and of the most desperate crime.
By the dim light of an accidental lamp, tall, antique, worm-eaten,
wooden tenements were seen tottering to their fall, in directions
so many and capricious, that scarce the semblance of a passage
was discernible between them. The paving-stones lay at ran-

dom, displaced from their beds by the rankly-growing grass. Horrible filth festered in the dammed-up gutters. The whole atmosphere teemed with desolation. Yet, as we proceeded, the sounds of human life revived by sure degrees, and at length large bands of the most abandoned of a London populace were seen reeling to and fro. The spirits of the old man again flickered up, as a lamp which is near its death-hour. Once more he strode onward with elastic tread. Suddenly a corner was turned, a blaze of light burst upon our sight, and we stood before one of the huge suburban temples of Intemperance—one of the palaces of the fiend, Gin.

It was now nearly day-break; but a number of wretched inebriates still pressed in and out of the flaunting entrance. With a half shriek of joy the old man forced a passage within, resumed at once his original bearing, and stalked backward and forward, without apparent object, among the throng. He had not been thus long occupied, however, before a rush to the doors gave token that the host was closing them for the night. It was something even more intense than despair that I then observed upon the countenance of the singular being whom I had watched so pertinaciously. Yet he did not hesitate in his career, but, with a mad energy, retraced his steps at once, to the heart of the mighty London. Long and swiftly he fled, while I followed him in the wildest amazement, resolute not to abandon a scrutiny in which I now felt an interest all-absorbing. The sun arose while we proceeded, and, when we had once again reached that most thronged mart of the populous town, the street of the D—— Hotel, it presented an appearance of human bustle and activity scarcely inferior to what I had seen on the evening before. And here, long, amid the momently increasing confusion, did I persist in my pursuit of the stranger. But, as usual, he walked to and fro, and during the day did not pass from out the turmoil of that street. And, as the shades of the second evening came on, I grew wearied unto death, and, stopping fully in front of the wanderer, gazed at him steadfastly in the face. He noticed me not, but resumed his solemn walk, while I, ceasing to follow, remained absorbed in contemplation. "This old man," I said at length, "is the type and the genius of deep crime. He refuses to be alone.

He is the man of the crowd. It will be in vain to follow ; for I shall learn no more of him, nor of his deeds. The worst heart of the world is a grosser book than the 'Hortulus Animæ,'* and perhaps it is but one of the great mercies of God that ' *er lasst sich nicht lesen.*' "

* The " *Hortulus Animæ cum Oratiunculis Aliquibus Superadditis*" of Grünninger.

NEVER BET THE DEVIL YOUR HEAD.

A TALE WITH A MORAL.

"Con *tal que las costumbres de u ⊰ autor*," says Don Thomas De
Las Torres, in the preface to his "Amatory Poems" "*sean puras
y castas, importo muy poco que no sean igualmente severas sus
obras*"—meaning, in plain English, that, provided the morals of an
author are pure, personally, it signifies nothing what are the morals
of his books. We presume that Don Thomas is now in Purgatory
for the assertion. It would be a clever thing, too, in the way of
poetical justice, to keep him there until his "Amatory Poems" get
out of print, or are laid definitely upon the shelf through lack of
readers. Every fiction *should have* a moral; and, what is more
to the purpose, the critics have discovered that every fiction *has.*
Philip Melancthon, some time ago, wrote a commentary upon the
" Batrachomyomachia" and proved that the poet's object was to
excite a distaste for sedition. Pierre La Seine, going a step
farther, shows that the intention was to recommend to young men
temperance in eating and drinking. Just so, too, Jacobus Hugo
has satisfied himself that, by Euenis, Homer meant to insinuate
John Calvin; by Antinöus, Martin Luther; by the Lotophagi,
Protestants in general; and, by the Harpies, the Dutch. Our
more modern Scholiasts are equally acute. These fellows demonstrate a hidden meaning in " The Antediluvians," a parable in
" Powhatan," new views in " Cock Robin," and transcendentalism
in " Hop O' My Thumb." In short, it has been shown that no man
can sit down to write wi hout a very profound design. Thus to

authors in general much trouble is spared. A novelist, for example, need have no care of his moral. It is there—that is to say, it is somewhere—and the moral and the critics can take care of themselves. When the proper time arrives, all that the gentleman intended, and all that he did not intend, will be brought to light, in the "Dial," or the "Down-Easter," together with all that he ought to have intended, and the rest that he clearly meant to intend:—so that it will all come very straight in the end.

There is no just ground, therefore, for the charge brought against me by certain ignoramuses—that I have never written a moral tale, or, in more precise words, a tale with a moral. They are not the critics predestined to bring me out, and *develop* my morals:—that is the secret. By and by the "North American Quarterly Humdrum" will make them ashamed of their stupidity. In the meantime, by way of staying execution—by way of mitigating the accusations against me—I offer the sad history appended;—a history about whose obvious moral there can be no question whatever, since he who runs may read it in the large capitals which form the title of the tale. I should have credit for this arrangement—a far wiser one than that of La Fontaine and others, who reserve the impression to be conveyed until the last moment, and thus sneak it in at the fag end of their fables.

Defuncti injuriâ ne afficiantur was a law of the twelve tables, and *De mortuis nil nisi bonum* is an excellent injunction—even if the dead in question be nothing but dead small beer. It is not my design, therefore, to vituperate my deceased friend, Toby Dammit. He was a sad dog, it is true, and a dog's death it was that he died; but he himself was not to blame for his vices. They grew out of a personal defect in his mother. She did her best in the way of flogging him while an infant—for duties to her well-regulated mind were always pleasures, and babies, like tough steaks, or the modern Greek olive trees, are invariably the better for beating—but, poor woman! she had the misfortune to be left-handed, and a child flogged left-handedly had better be left unflogged. The world revolves from right to left. It will not do to whip a baby from left to right. If each blow in the proper direction drives an evil propensity out, it follows that every thump in an opposite one knocks its quota of wickedness in. I was often present at Toby's chastisements, and, even by the way in which he kicked, I could perceive that he was getting worse and worse every day. At last I saw, through the tears in my eyes, that there was no hope of the villain at all, and one day when he had been cuffed until he grew so black in the face that one might have mistaken him for a little African, and no effect had been produced beyond that of making him wriggle himself into a fit, I could stand it no longer, but went down upon my knees forthwith, and, uplifting my voice, made prophecy of his ruin.

The fact is that his precocity in vice was awful. At five months of age he used to get into such passions that he was unable to articulate. At six months, I caught him knawing a pack of cards. At seven months he was in the constant habit of catching and kissing the female babies. At eight months he peremptorily refused to put his signature to the Temperance pledge. Thus he went on increasing in iniquity, month after month, until, at the close of the first year, he not only insisted upon wearing *moustaches*, but had contracted a propensity for cursing and swearing, and for backing his assertions by bets.

Through this latter most ungentlemanly practice, the ruin which I had predicted to Toby Dammit overtook him at last. The fashion had " grown with his growth and strengthened with his strength," so that, when he came to be a man, he could scarcely utter a sentence without interlarding it with a proposition to gamble. Not that he actually *laid* wagers—no. I will do my friend the justice to say that he would as soon have laid eggs. With him the thing was a mere formula— nothing more. His expressions on this head had no meaning attached to them whatever. They were simple if not altogether innocent expletives—imaginative phrases wherewith to round off a sentence. When he said ' I'll bet you so and so," nobody ever thought of taking him up; but still I could not help thinking it my duty to put him down. The habit was an immoral one, and so I told him. It was a vulgar one—this I begged him to believe. It was discountenanced by society—here I said nothing but the truth. It was forbidden by act of Congress—here I had not the slightest intention of telling a lie. I remonstrated—but to no purpose. I demonstrated—in vain. I entreated—he smiled. I implored—he laughed. I preached—he sneered. I threatened—he swore. I kicked him—he called for the police. I pulled his nose—he blew it, and offered to bet the Devil his head that I would not venture to try that experiment again.

Poverty was another vice which the peculiar physical deficiency of Dammit's mother had entailed upon her son. He was detestably poor; and this was the reason, no doubt, that his expletive expressions about betting, seldom took a pecuniary turn. I will not be bound to say that I ever heard him make use of such a figure of speech as "I'll bet you a dollar." It was usually "I'll bet you what you please," or "I'll bet you what you dare," or "I'll bet you a trifle," or else, more significantly still, "*I'll bet the Devil my head.*"

This latter form seemed to please him best:—perhaps because it involved the least risk; for Dammit had become excessively parsimonious. Had any one taken him up, his head was small, and thus his loss would have been small too. But these are my own reflections, and I am by no means sure that I am right in attributing them to him. At all events the phrase in question grew daily in favor, notwithstanding the gross impropriety of a man betting his brains like bank-notes:—but this was a point which my friend's perversity of disposition would not permit him to comprehend. In the end, he abandoned all other forms of wager, and gave himself up to "*I'll bet the Devil my head,*" with a pertinacity and exclusiveness of devotion that displeased not less than it surprised me. I am always displeased by circumstances for which I cannot account. Mysteries force a man to think, and so injure his health. The truth is, there was something in *the air* with which Mr. Dammit was wont to give utterance to his offensive expression—something in his *manner* of enunciation—which at first interested, and afterwards made me very uneasy—something which, for want of a more definite term at present, I must be permitted to call *queer;* but which Mr. Coleridge would have called mystical, Mr. Kant pantheistical, Mr. Carlyle twistical, and Mr. Emerson hyperquizzitistical. I began not to like it at all. Mr. Dammit's soul was in a perilous state. I resolved to bring all my eloquence into play to save it. I vowed to serve him as St. Patrick, in the Irish chronicle. is said to have served the toad, that is to say, " awaken him to a sense of his situation." I addressed myself to the task forthwith. Once more I betook myself to remonstrance. Again I collected my energies for a final attempt at expostulation.

When I had made an end of my lecture, Mr. Dammit indulged himself in some very equivocal behavior. For some moments he remained silent, merely looking me inquisitively in the face. But presently he threw his head to one side, and elevated his eyebrows to great extent. Then he spread out the palms of his hands and shrugged up his shoulders. Then he winked with the right eye. Then he repeated the operation with the left. Then he shut them both up very tight. Then he opened them both so very wide that I became seriously alarmed for the consequences. Then, applying his thumb to his nose, he thought proper to make an indescribable movement with the rest of his fingers. Finally, setting his arms a-kimbo, he condescended to reply.

I can call to mind only the heads of his discourse. He would be obliged to me if I would hold my tongue. He wished none of my advice. He despised all my insinuations. He was old enough to take care of himself. Did I still think him baby Dammit? Did I mean to say anything against his character? Did I intend to insult him? Was I a fool? Was my maternal parent aware, in a word, of my absence from the domiciliary residence? He would put this latter question to me as to a man of veracity, and he would bind himself to abide by my reply. Once more he would demand explicitly if my mother knew that I was out. My confusion, he said, betrayed me, and he would be willing to bet the Devil his head that she did not.

Mr. Dammit did not pause for my rejoinder. Turning upon his heel, he left my presence with undignified precipitation. It was well for him that he did so. My feelings had been wounded. Even my anger had been aroused. For once I would have taken him up upon his insulting wager. I would have won for the Arch-Enemy Mr. Dammit's little head—for the fact is, my mamma *was* very well aware of my merely temporary absence from home.

But *Khoda shefa midêhed*—Heaven gives relief—as the Musselmen say when you tread upon their toes. It was in pursuance of my duty that I had been insulted, and I bore the insult like a man. It now seemed to me, however, that I had done all that could be required of me, in the case of this miserable individual, and I resolved to trouble him no longer with my counsel, but to leave him to his conscience and himself. But although I forebore to intrude with my advice, I could not bring myself to give up his society altogether. I even went so far as to humor some of his less reprehensible propensities; and there were times when I found myself lauding his wicked jokes, as epicures do mustard, with tears in my eyes:—so profoundly did it grieve me to hear his evil talk.

One fine day, having strolled out together, arm in arm, our route led us in the direction of a river. There was a bridge, and we resolved to cross it. It was roofed over, by way of protection from the weather, and the arch-way, having but few windows, was thus very uncomfortably dark. As we entered the passage, the contrast between the external glare, and the interior gloom, struck heavily upon my spirits. Not so upon those of the unhappy Dammit, who offered to bet the Devil his head that I was hipped. He seemed to be in an unusual good humor. He was excessively lively—so much so that I entertained I know not what of uneasy suspicion. It is not impossible that he was affected with the transcendentals. I am not well enough versed, however, in the diagnosis of this disease to speak with decision upon the point; and unhappily there were none of my friends of the "Dial" present. I suggest the idea, nevertheless, because of a certain species of austere Merry-Andrewism which seemed to beset my poor friend, and caused him to make quite a Tom-Fool of himself. Nothing would serve him but wriggling and skipping about under and over everything that came in his way; now shouting out, and now lisping out, all manner of odd little and big words, yet preserving the gravest face in the world all the time. I really could not make up my mind whether to kick or to pity him. At length, having passed nearly across the bridge, we approached the termination of the foot way, when our progress was impeded by a turn-stile of some height. Through this I made my way quietly, pushing it around as usual. But this turn would not serve the turn of Mr. Dammit. He insisted upon leaping the stile, and said he could cut a pigeon-wing over it in the air. Now this, conscientiously speaking, I did not think he could do. The best pigeon-winger over all kinds of style, was my friend Mr. Carlyle, and as I knew *he* could not do it, I would not believe that it could be done by Toby Dammit. I therefore told him, in so many words, that he was a braggadocio, and could not do what he said. For this, I had reason to be sorry afterwards ;—for he straightway offered to *bet the Devil his head* that he could.

I was about to reply, notwithstanding my previous resolutions, with some remonstrance against his impiety, when I heard, close at my elbow, a slight cough, which sounded very much like the ejaculation " *ahem !*" I started, and looked about me in surprise. My glance at length fell into a nook of the frame-work of the bridge, and upon the figure of a little lame old gentleman of venerable aspect. Nothing could be more reverend than his whole appearance ; for, he not only had on a full suit of black, but his shirt was perfectly clean and the collar turned very neatly down over a white cravat, while his hair was parted in front like a girl's. His hands were clasped pensively together over his stomach, and his two eyes were carefully rolled up into the top of his head.

Upon observing him more closely, I perceived that he wore a black silk apron over his small-clothes ; and this was a thing which I thought very odd. Before I had time to make any remark, however, upon so singular a circumstance, he interrupted me with a second " *ahem !*"

To this observation I was not immediately prepared to reply. The fact is, remarks of this laconic nature are nearly unanswerable. I have known a Quarterly Review *non-plused* by the word " *Fudge !*" I am not ashamed to say, therefore, that I turned to Mr. Dammit for assistance.

" Dammit," said I, " what are you about ! don't you hear !— the gentleman says ' *ahem !*'" I looked sternly at my friend while I thus addressed him ; for to say the truth, I felt particularly puzzled, and when a man is particularly puzzled he must knit his brows and look savage, or else he is pretty sure to look like a fool.

" Dammit," observed I—although this sounded very much like an oath, than which nothing was farther from my thoughts— " Dammit," I suggested—" the gentleman says ' *ahem !*'"

I do not attempt to defend my remark on the score of profundity; I did not think it profound myself; but I have noticed that the effect of our speeches is not always proportionate with their importance in our own eyes; and if I had shot Mr. D. through and through with a Paixhan bomb, or knocked him in the head with the "Poets and Poetry of America," he could hardly have been more discomfited than when I addressed him with those simple words—"Dammit, what are you about?—don't you hear?—the gentleman says '*ahem!*'"

"You don't say so?" gasped he at length, after turning more colors than a pirate runs up, one after the other, when chased by a man-of-war. "Are you quite sure he said *that?* Well, at all events I am in for it now, and may as well put a bold face upon the matter. Here goes, then—*ahem!*"

At this the little old gentleman seemed pleased—God only knows why. He left his station at the nook of the bridge, limped forward with a gracious air, took Dammit by the hand and shook it cordially, looking all the while straight up in his face with an air of the most unadulterated benignity which it is possible for the mind of man to imagine.

"I am quite sure you will win it, Dammit," said he, with the frankest of all smiles, "but we are obliged to have a trial you know, for the sake of mere form."

"Ahem!" replied my friend, taking off his coat with a deep sigh, tying a pocket-handkerchief around his waist, and producing an unaccountable alteration in his countenance by twisting up his eyes, and bringing down the corners of his mouth—"ahem!" And "ahem," said he again, after a pause; and not another word more than "ahem!" did I ever know him to say after that. "Aha!" thought I, without expressing myself aloud—"this is quite a remarkable silence on the part of Toby Dammit, and is no doubt a consequence of his verbosity upon a previous occasion. One extreme induces another. I wonder if he has forgotten the many unanswerable questions which he propounded to me so fluently on the day when I gave him my last lecture? At all events, he is cured of the transcendentals."

"Ahem!" here replied Toby, just as if he had been reading my thoughts, and looking like a very old sheep in a reverie.

The old gentleman now took him by the arm, and led him more

into the shade of the bridge—a few paces back from the turnstile.
" My good fellow," said he, " I make it a point of conscience to
allow you this much run.   Wait here, t.ll I take my place by the
stile, so that I may see whether you go over it handsomely, and
transcendentally, and don't omit any flourishes of the pigeon-wing.
A mere form, you know.   I will say ' one, two, three, and away.'
Mind you start at the word ' away.' "   Here he took his position
by the stile, paused a moment as if in profound reflection, then
looked up and, I thought, smiled very slightly, then tightened the
strings of his apron, then took a long look at Dammit, and finally
gave the word as agreed upon—

One—two—three—and away !

Punctually at the word " away," my poor friend set off in a
strong gallop.   The stile was not very high, like Mr. Lord's—nor
yet very low, like that of Mr. Lord's reviewers, but upon the whole
I made sure that he would clear it.   And then what if he did
not ?—ah, that was the question—what if he did not ?   " What
right," said I, " had the old gentleman to make any other gentleman jump ?   The little old dot-and-carry-one ! who is *he ?*   If he
asks *me* to jump, I won't do it, that's flat, and I don't care who
the devil he is."   The bridge, as I say, was arched and covered
in, in a very ridiculous manner, and there was a most uncomfort-
able echo about it at all times—an echo which I never before so
particularly observed as when I uttered the four last words of my
remark.
But what I said, or what I thought, or what I heard, occupied
only an instant.   In less than five seconds from his starting, my
poor Toby had taken the leap.   I saw him run nimbly, and spring
grandly from the floor of the bridge, cutting the most awful flourishes with his legs as he went up.   I saw him high in the air,
pigeon-winging it to admiration just over the top of the stile ; and
of course I thought it an unusually singular thing that he did not
continue to go over.   But the whole leap was the affair of a
moment, and, before I had a chance to make any profound reflections, down came Mr. Dammit on the flat of his back, on the same
side of the stile from which he had started.   At the same instant

I saw the old gentleman limping off at the top of his speed, having caught and wrapped up in his apron something that fell heavily into it from the darkness of the arch just over the turnstile. At all this I was much astonished; but I had no leisure to think, for Mr. Dammit lay particularly still, and I concluded that his feelings had been hurt, and that he stood in need of my assistance. I hurried up to him and found that he had received what might be termed a serious injury. The truth is, he had been deprived of his head, which after a close search I could not find anywhere;— so I determined to take him home, and send for the homœopathists. In the meantime a thought struck me, and I threw open an adjacent window of the bridge; when the sad truth flashed upon me at once. About five feet just above the top of the turnstile, and crossing the arch of the foot-path so as to constitute a brace, there extended a flat iron bar, lying with its breadth horizontally, and forming one of a series that served to strengthen the structure throughout its extent. With the edge of this brace it appeared evident that the neck of my unfortunate friend had come precisely in contact.

He did not long survive his terrible loss. The homœopathists did not give him little enough physic, and what little they did give him he hesitated to take. So in the end he grew worse, and at length died, a lesson to all riotous livers. I bedewed his grave with my tears, worked a *bar* sinister on his family escutcheon, and, for the general expenses of his funeral, sent in my very moderate bill to the transcendentalists. The scoundrels refused to pay it, so I had Mr. Dammit dug up at once, and sold him for dog's meat.

"THOU ART THE MAN."

I WILL now play the Œdipus to the Rattleborough enigma. I will expound to you—as I alone can—the secret of the enginery that effected the Rattleborough miracle—the one, the true, the admitted, the undisputed, the indisputable miracle, which put a definite end to infidelity among the Rattleburghers, and converted to the orthodoxy of the grandames all the carnal-minded who had ventured to be skeptical before.

This event—which I should be sorry to discuss in a tone of unsuitable levity—occurred in the summer of 18—. Mr. Barnabas Shuttleworthy—one of the wealthiest and most respectable citizens of the borough—had been missing for several days under circumstances which gave rise to suspicion of foul play. Mr. Shuttleworthy had set out from Rattleborough very early one Saturday morning, on horseback, with the avowed intention of proceeding to the city of ——, about fifteen miles distant, and of returning the night of the same day. Two hours after his departure, however, his horse returned without him, and without the saddle-bags which had been strapped on his back at starting. The animal was wounded, too, and covered with mud. These circumstances naturally gave rise to much alarm among the friends of the missing man; and when it was found, on Sunday morning, that he had not yet made his appearance, the whole borough arose *en masse* to go and look for his body.

The foremost and most energetic in instituting this search, was the bosom friend of Mr. Shuttleworthy—a Mr. Charles Goodfellow, or, as he was universally called, "Charley Goodfellow," or "Old Charley Goodfellow." Now, whether it is a marvellous coincidence, or whether i. is that the name itself has an imperceptible effect upon the character, I have never yet been able to ascertain; but the fact is unquestionable, that there never yet was any person named Charles who was not an open, manly, honest, good-natured, and frank-hearted fellow, with a rich, clear voice, that did you good to hear it, and an eye that looked you always straight in the face, as much as to say, "I have a clear conscience myself; am afraid of no man, and am altogether above doing a mean action." And thus all the hearty, careless, "walking gentlemen" of the stage are very certain to be called Charles.

Now, "Old Charley Goodfellow," although he had been in Rattleborough not longer than six months or thereabouts, and although nobody knew anything about him before he came to settle in the neighborhood, had experienced no difficulty in the world in making the acquaintance of all the respectable people in the borough. Not a man of them but would have taken his bare word for a thousand at any moment; and as for the women, there is no saying what they would not have done to oblige him. And all this came of his having been christened Charles, and of his possessing, in consequence, that ingenuous face which is proverbially the very "best letter of recommendation."

I have already said, that Mr. Shuttleworthy was one of the most respectable, and, undoubtedly, he was the most wealthy man in Rattleborough, while "Old Charley Goodfellow" was upon as intimate terms with him as if he had been his own brother. The two old gentlemen were next-door neighbors, and, although Mr. Shuttleworthy seldom, if ever, visited "Old Charley," and never was known to take a meal in his house, still this did not prevent the two friends from being exceedingly intimate, as I have just observed; for "Old Charley" never let a day pass without steping in three or four times to see how his neighbor came on, and very often he would stay to breakfast or tea, and almost always to dinner; and then the amount of wine that was made way with by the two cronies at a sitting, it would really be a difficult thing to ascertain. Old Charley's favorite beverage was *Chateau Margaux*, and it appeared to do Mr. Shuttleworthy's heart good to see the old fellow swallow it, as he did, quart after quart ; so that, one day, when the wine was *in* and the wit, as a natural consequence, somewhat *out*, he said to his crony, as he slapped him upon the back—" I tell you what it is, Old Charley, you are, by all odds, the heartiest old fellow I ever came across in all my born days ; and, since you love to guzzle the wine at that fashion, I'll be darned if I don't have to make thee a present of a big box of the Chateau Margaux. Od rot me,"—(Mr. Shuttleworthy had a sad habit of swearing, although he seldom went beyond " Od rot me," or " By gosh," or " By the jolly golly,")—" Od rot me," says he, " if I don't send an order to town this very afternoon for a double box of the best that can be got, and I'll make ye a present of it, I will!—ye needn't say a word now—I *will*, I tell ye, and there's an end of it ; so look out for it—it will come to hand some of these fine days, precisely when ye are looking for it the least!" I mention this little bit of liberality on the part of Mr. Shuttleworthy, just by way of showing you how *very* intimate an understanding existed between the two friends.

Well, on the Sunday morning in question, when it came to be fairly understood that Mr. Shuttleworthy had met with foul play, I never saw any one so profoundly affected as " Old Charley Good-fellow." When he first heard that the horse had come home without his master, and without his master's saddle-bags, and all bloody from a pistol-shot, that had gone clean through and through the poor animal's chest without quite killing him—when he heard all this, he turned as pale as if the missing man had been his own dear brother or father, and shivered and shook all over as if he had had a fit of the ague.

At first, he was too much overpowered with grief to be able to do anything at all, or to decide upon any plan of action ; so that for a long time he endeavored to dissuade Mr. Shuttleworthy's other friends from making a stir about the matter, thinking it best to wait awhile—say for a week or two, or a month or two—to see if something wouldn't turn up, or if Mr. Shuttleworthy wouldn't come in the natural way, and explain his reasons for sending his horse on before. I dare say you have often observed this disposition to temporize, or to procrastinate, in people who are laboring under any very poignant sorrow Their powers of mind seem to be rendered torpid, so that they have a horror of anything like action, and like nothing in the world so well as to lie quietly in bed and "nurse their grief," as the old ladies express it—that is to say, ruminate over their trouble.

The people of Rattleborough had, indeed, so high an opinion of the wisdom and discretion of "Old Charley," that the greater part of them felt disposed to agree with him, and not make a stir in the business "until something should turn up," as the honest old gentleman worded it; and I believe that, after all, this would have been the general determination, but for the very suspicious interference of Mr. Shuttleworthy's nephew, a young man of very dissipated habits, and otherwise of rather bad character. This nephew, whose name was Pennifeather, would listen to nothing like reason in the matter of "lying quiet," but insisted upon making immediate search for the "corpse of the murdered man." This was the expression he employed; and Mr. Goodfellow acutely remarked at the time, that it was "a *singular* expression, to say no more." This remark of Old Charley's, too, had great effect upon the crowd; and one of the party was heard to ask, very impressively, "how it happened that young Mr. Pennifeather was so intimately cognizant of all the circumstances connected with his wealthy uncle's disappearance, as to feel authorized to assert, distinctly and unequivocally, that his uncle *was* 'a murdered man.'" Hereupon some little squibbing and bickering occurred among various members of the crowd, and especially between "Old Charley" and Mr. Pennifeather—although this latter occurrence was, indeed, by no means a novelty, for little good will had subsisted between the parties for the last three or four months; and matters had even gone so far, that Mr. Pennifeather had actually knocked down his uncle's friend for some alleged excess of liberty that the latter had taken in the uncle's house, of which the nephew was an inmate. Upon this occasion, "Old Charley" is said to have behaved with exemplary moderation and Christian charity. He arose from the blow, adjusted his clothes, and made no attempt at retaliation at all—merely muttering a few words about "taking summary vengeance at the first convenient opportunity,"—a natural and very justifiable ebullition of anger, which meant nothing, however, and, beyond doubt, was no sooner given vent to than forgotten.

However these matters may be, (which have no reference to the point now at issue,) it is quite certain that the people of Rattleborough, principally through the persuasion of Mr. Pennifeather, came at length to the determination of dispersing over the adjacent country in search of the missing Mr. Shuttleworthy. I say they came to this determination in the first instance. After it had been fully resolved that a search should be made, it was considered almost a matter of course that the seekers should disperse— that is to say, distribute themselves in parties—for the more thorough examination of the region round about. I forget, however, by what ingenious train of reasoning it was that "Old Charley" finally convinced the assembly that this was the most injudicious plan that could be pursued. Convince them, however, he did—all except Mr. Pennifeather; and, in the end, it was arranged that a search should be instituted, carefully and very thoroughly, by the burghers *en masse*, "Old Charley" himself leading the way.

As for the matter of that, there could have been no better pioneer than "Old Charley," whom everybody knew to have the eye of a lynx; but, although he led them into all manner of out-of-the-way holes and corners, by routes that nobody had ever suspected of existing in the neighborhood, and although the search was incessantly kept up day and night for nearly a week, still no trace of Mr. Shuttleworthy could be discovered. When I say no trace, however, I must not be understood to speak literally; for trace, to some extent, there certainly was. The poor gentleman had been tracked, by his horse's shoes, (which were peculiar,) to a spot about three miles to the east of the borough, on the main road leading to the city. Here the track made off into a by-path through a piece of woodland—the path coming out again into the main road, and cutting off about half a mile of the regular distance. Following the shoe-marks down this lane, the party came at length to a pool of stagnant water, half hidden by the brambles to the right of the lane, and opposite this pool all vestige of the track was lost sight of. It appeared, however, that a struggle of some nature had here taken place, and it seemed as if some large and heavy body, much larger and heavier than a man, had been drawn from the by-path to the pool. This latter was carefully dragged twice, but nothing was found; and the party were upon the point of going away, in despair of coming to any result, when Providence suggested to Mr. Goodfellow the expediency of draining the water off altogether. This project was received with cheers, and many high compliments to "Old Charley" upon his sagacity and consideration. As many of the burghers had brought spades with them, supposing that they might possibly be called upon to disinter a corpse, the drain was easily and speedily effected; and no sooner was the bottom visible, than right in the middle of the mud that remained was discovered a black silk velvet waistcoat, which nearly every one present immediately recognised as the property of Mr. Pennifeather. This waistcoat was much torn and stained with blood, and there were several persons among the party who had a distinct remembrance of its having been worn by its owner on the very morning of Mr. Shuttleworthy's departure for the city; while there were others, again, ready to testify upon oath, if required, that Mr. P. did *not* wear the garment in question at any period during the *remainder* of that memorable day; nor could any one be found to say that he had seen it upon Mr. P.'s person at any period at all subsequent to Mr. Shuttleworthy's disappearance.

Matters now wore a very serious aspect for Mr. Pennifeather, and it was observed, as an indubitable confirmation of the suspicions which were excited against him, that he grew exceedingly pale, and when asked what he had to say for himself, was utterly incapable of saying a word. Hereupon, the few friends his riotous mode of living had left him deserted him at once to a man, and were even more clamorous than his ancient and avowed enemies for his instantaneous arrest. But, on the other hand, the magnanimity of Mr. Goodfellow shone forth with only the more brilliant lustre through contrast. He made a warm and intensely eloquent defence of Mr. Pennifeather, in which he alluded more than once to his own sincere forgiveness of that wild young gentleman—"the heir of the worthy Mr. Goodfellow,"—for the insult which he (the young gentleman) had, no doubt in the heat of passion, thought proper to put upon him (Mr. Goodfellow.) " He forgave him for it," he said, " from the very bottom of his heart ; and for himself (Mr. Goodfellow,) so far from pushing the suspicious circumstances to extremity, which, he was sorry to say, really *had* arisen against Mr. Pennifeather, he (Mr. Goodfellow) would make every exertion in his power, would employ all the little eloquence in his possession to—to—to—soften down, as much as he could conscientiously do so, the worst features of this really exceedingly perplexing piece of business."

Mr. Goodfellow went on for some half hour longer in this strain, very much to the credit both of his head and of his heart ; but your warm-hearted people are seldom apposite in their observations—they run into all sorts of blunders, *contre-temps* and *mal àpropos-isms*, in the hot-headedness of their zeal to serve a friend —thus, often with the kindest intentions in the world, doing infinitely more to prejudice his cause than to advance it.

So, in the present instance, it turned out with all the eloquence of " Old Charley ;" for, although he labored earnestly in behalf of the suspected, yet it so happened, somehow or other, that every syllable he uttered of which the direct but unwitting tendency was not to exalt the speaker in the good opinion of his audience, had the effect of deepening the suspicion already attached to the individual whose cause he plead, and of arousing against him the fury of the mob.

One of the most unaccountable errors committed by the orator was his allusion to the suspected as " the heir of the worthy old gentleman Mr. Goodfellow." The people had really never thought of this before. They had only remembered certain threats of disinheritance uttered a year or two previously by the uncle, (who had no living relative except the nephew ;) and they had, therefore, always looked upon this disinheritance as a matter that was settled—so single-minded a race of beings were the Rattleburghers ; but the remark of " Old Charley" brought them at once to a consideration of this point, and thus gave them to see the possibility of the threats having been nothing *more* than a threat. And straightway, hereupon, arose the natural question of *cui bono ?*—a question that tended even more than the waistcoat to fasten the terrible crime upon the young man. And here, lest I be misunderstood, permit me to digress for one moment merely to observe that the exceedingly brief and simple Latin phrase which I have employed, is invariably mistranslated and misconceived. "*Cui bono*," in all the crack novels and elsewhere,—in those of Mrs. Gore, for example, (the author of "*Cecil*,") a lady who quotes all tongues from the Chaldæan to Chickasaw, and is helped to her learning, "as needed," upon a systematic plan, by Mr. Beckford,—in *all* the crack novels, I say, from those of Bulwer and Dickens to those of Turnapenny and Ainsworth, the two little Latin words *cui bono* are rendered "to what purpose," or, (as if *quo bono*,) "to what good." Their true meaning, nevertheless, is "for whose advantage." *Cui*, to whom; *bono*, is it for a benefit. It is a purely legal phrase, and applicable precisely in cases such as we have now under consideration, where the probability of the doer of a deed hinges upon the probability of the benefit accruing to this individual or to that from the deed's accomplishment. Now, in the present instance, the question *cui bono* very pointedly implicated Mr. Pennifeather. His uncle had threatened him, after making a will in his favor, with disinheritance. But the threat had not been actually kept; the original will, it appeared, had not been altered. *Had* it been altered, the only supposable motive for murder on the part of the suspected would have been the ordinary one of revenge; and even this would have been counteracted by the hope of reinstation into the good graces of the uncle. But the will being unaltered, while the threat to alter remained suspended over the nephew's head, there appears at once the very strongest possible inducement for the atrocity: and so concluded, very sagaciously, the worthy citizens of the borough of Rattle.

Mr. Pennifeather was, accordingly, arrested upon the spot, and the crowd, after some farther search, proceeded homewards, having him in custody. On the route, however, another circumstance occurred tending to confirm the suspicion entertained. Mr. Goodfellow, whose zeal led him to be always a little in advance of the party, was seen suddenly to run forward a few paces, stoop, and then apparently to pick up some small object from the grass

Having quickly examined it, he was observed, too, to make a sort of half attempt at concealing it in his coat pocket; but this action was noticed, as I say, and consequently prevented, when the object picked up was found to be a Spanish knife which a dozen persons at once recognised as belonging to Mr. Pennifeather. Moreover, his initials were engraved upon the handle. The blade of this knife was open and bloody.

No doubt now remained of the guilt of the nephew, and immediately upon reaching Rattleborough he was taken before a magistrate for examination.

Here matters again took a most unfavorable turn. The prisoner, being questioned as to his whereabouts on the morning of Mr. Shuttleworthy's disappearance, had absolutely the audacity to acknowledge that on that very morning he had been out with his rifle deer-stalking, in the immediate neighborhood of the pool where the blood-stained waistcoat had been discovered through the sagacity of Mr. Goodfellow.

This latter now came forward, and, with tears in his eyes, asked permission to be examined. He said that a stern sense of the duty he owed his Maker, not less than his fellow-men, would permit him no longer to remain silent. Hitherto, the sincerest affection for the young man (notwithstanding the latter's ill treatment of himself, Mr. Goodfellow,) had induced him to make every hypothesis which imagination could suggest, by way of endeavoring to account for what appeared suspicious in the circumstances that told so seriously against Mr. Pennifeather; but these circumstances were now altogether *too* convincing—*too* damning; he would hesitate no longer—he would tell all he knew, although his heart (Mr. Goodfellow's) should absolutely burst asunder in the effort. He then went on to state that, on the afternoon of the day previous to Mr. Shuttleworthy's departure for the city, that worthy old gentleman had mentioned to his nephew, in *his* hearing, (Mr. Goodfellow's,) that his object in going to town on the morrow was to make a deposit of an unusually large sum of money in the "Farmers' and Mechanics' Bank," and that, then and there the said Mr. Shuttleworthy had distinctly avowed to the said nephew his irrevocable determination of rescinding the will originally made.

and of cutting him off with a shilling. He (the witness) now solemnly called upon the accused to state whether what he (the witness) had just stated was or was not the truth in every substantial particular. Much to the astonishment of every one present, Mr. Pennifeather frankly admitted that *it was.*

The magistrate now considered it his duty to send a couple of constables to search the chamber of the accused in the house of his uncle. From this search they almost immediately returned with the well known steel-bound, russet leather pocket-book which the old gentleman had been in the habit of carrying for years. Its valuable contents, however, had been abstracted, and the magistrate in vain endeavored to extort from the prisoner the use which had been made of them, or the place of their concealment. Indeed, he obstinately denied all knowledge of the matter. The constables, also, discovered, between the bed and sacking of the unhappy man, a shirt and neck-handkerchief both marked with the initials of his name, and both hideously besmeared with the blood of the victim.

At this juncture, it was announced that the horse of the murdered man had just expired in the stable from the effects of the wound he had received, and it was proposed by Mr. Goodfellow that a *post mortem* examination of the beast should be immediately made, with the view, if possible, of discovering the ball. This was accordingly done; and, as if to demonstrate beyond a question the guilt of the accused, Mr. Goodfellow, after considerable searching in the cavity of the chest, was enabled to detect and to pull forth a bullet of very extraordinary size, which, upon trial, was found to be exactly adapted to the bore of Mr. Pennifeather's rifle, while it was far too large for that of any other person in the borough or its vicinity. To render the matter even surer yet, however, this bullet was discovered to have a flaw or seam at right angles to the usual suture; and upon examination, this seam corresponded precisely with an accidental ridge or elevation in a pair of moulds acknowledged by the accused himself to be his own property. Upon the finding of this bullet, the examining magistrate refused to listen to any farther testimony, and immediately committed the prisoner for trial—declining resolutely to take any bail in the case, although against this severity Mr. Good-fellow very warmly remonstrated, and offered to become surety in whatever amount might be required. This generosity on the part of "Old Charley" was only in accordance with the whole tenor of his amiable and chivalrous conduct during the entire period of his sojourn in the borough of Rattle. In the present instance, the worthy man was so entirely carried away by the excessive warmth of his sympathy, that he seemed to have quite forgotten, when he offered to go bail for his young friend, that he himself (Mr. Good fellow) did not possess a single dollar's worth of property upon the face of the earth.

The result of the committal may be readily foreseen. Mr. Pen nifeather, amid the loud execrations of all Rattleborough, was brought to trial at the next criminal sessions, when the chair of circumstantial evidence (strengthened as it was by some additional damning facts, which Mr. Goodfellow's sensitive conscientiousness forbade him to withhold from the court,) was considered so unbroken and so thoroughly conclusive, that the jury, without leaving their seats, returned an immediate verdict of "*Guilty of murder in the first degree.*" Soon afterwards the unhappy wretch received sentence of death, and was remanded to the county jail to await the inexorable vengeance of the law.

In the mean time, the noble behavior of "Old Charley Goodfellow" had doubly endeared him to the honest citizens of the borough. He became ten times a greater favorite than ever; and, as a natural result of the hospitality with which he was treated, he relaxed, as it were, perforce, the extremely parsimonious habits which his poverty had hitherto impelled him to observe, and very frequently had little *réunions* at his own house, when wit and jollity reigned supreme—dampened a little, *of course*, by the occasional remembrance of the untoward and melancholy fate which impended over the nephew of the late lamented bosom friend of the generous host.

One fine day, this magnanimous old gentleman was agreeably surprised at the receipt of the following letter :—

Charles Goodfellow, Esq., Rattleborough. From H. F. B. & Co.

Chat. Mar. A—No. 1.—6 doz. bottles (½ Gross).

"Charles Goodfellow, Esquire—

"Dear Sir—In conformity with an order transmitted to our firm about two months since, by our esteemed correspondent, Mr. Barnabas Shuttleworthy, we have the honor of forwarding this morning, to your address, a double box of Chateau-Margaux, of the antelope brand, violet seal. Box numbered and marked as per margin.

'*We remain, sir,*

"*Your most ob'nt serv'ts,*

Horos, Froes, Boes & Co

"*City of* ——, *June* 21*st*, 18—.

"*P. S.—The box will reach you, by wagon, on the day after your receipt of this letter. Our respects to Mr. Shuttleworthy.*

H. F. B. & Co."

The fact is, that Mr. Goodfellow had, since the death of Mr. Shuttleworthy, given over all expectation of ever receiving the promised Chateau-Margaux ; and he, therefore, looked upon it *now* as a sort of especial dispensation of Providence in his behalf. He was highly delighted, of course, and in the exuberance of his joy, invited a large party of friends to a *petit souper* on the morrow, for the purpose of broaching the good old Mr. Shuttleworthy's present. Not that he *said* any thing about "the good old Mr. Shuttleworthy" when he issued the invitations. The fact is, he thought much and concluded to say nothing at all. He did *not* mention to any one—if I remember aright—that he had received a *present* of Chateau-Margaux. He merely asked his friends to come and help him drink some of a remarkably fine quality and rich flavor, that he had ordered up from the city a couple of months ago, and of which he would be in the receipt upon the morrow. I have often puzzled myself to imagine *why* it was that "Old Charley" came to the conclusion to say nothing about having received the wine from his old friend, but I could never precisely understand his reason for the silence, although he had *some* excellent and very magnanimous reason, no doubt.

The morrow at length arrived, and with it a very large and highly respectable company at Mr. Goodfellow's house. Indeed, half the borough was there—I myself among the number—but, much to the vexation of the host, the Chateau-Margaux did not arrive until a late hour, and when the sumptuous supper supplied by "Old Charley" had been done very ample justice by the guests. It came at length, however,—a monstrously big box of it there was, too,—and as the whole party were in excessively good humor, it was decided, *nem. con.*, that it should be lifted upon the table and its contents disemboweled forthwith.

No sooner said than done. I lent a helping hand; and, in a trice, we had the box upon the table, in the midst of all the bottles and glasses, not a few of which were demolished in the scuffle. "Old Charley," who was pretty much intoxicated, and excessively red in the face, now took a seat, with an air of mock dignity, at the head of the board, and thumped furiously upon it with a decanter, calling upon the company to keep order "during the ceremony of disinterring the treasure."

After some vociferation, quiet was at length fully restored, and, as very often happens in similar cases, a profound and remarkable silence ensued. Being then requested to force open the lid, I complied, of course, "with an infinite deal of pleasure." I inserted a chisel, and giving it a few slight taps with a hammer, the top of the box flew suddenly and violently off, and, at the same instant, there sprang up into a sitting position, directly facing the host, the bruised, bloody and nearly putrid corpse of the murdered Mr. Shuttleworthy himself. It gazed for a few moments, fixedly and sorrowfully, with its decaying and lack-lustre eyes, full into the countenance of Mr. Goodfellow; uttered slowly, but clearly and impressively, the words—"Thou art the man!" and then, falling over the side of the chest as if thoroughly satisfied, stretched out its limbs quiveringly upon the table.

The scene that ensued is altogether beyond description. The rush for the doors and windows was terrific, and many of the most robust men in the room fainted outright through sheer horror. But after the first wild, shrieking burst of affright, all eyes were directed to Mr. Goodfellow. If I live a thousand years, I can never forget the more than mortal agony which was depicted in that ghastly face of his, so lately rubicund with triumph and wine. For several minutes, he sat rigidly as a statue of marble; his eyes seeming, in the intense vacancy of their gaze, to be turned inwards and absorbed in the contemplation of his own miserable, murderous soul. At length, their expression appeared to flash suddenly out into the external world, when with a quick leap, he sprang from his chair, and falling heavily with his head and shoulders upon the table, and in contact with the corpse, poured out rapidly and vehemently a detailed confession of the hideous crime for which Mr. Pennifeather was then imprisoned and doomed to die.

What he recounted was in substance this:—He followed his victim to the vicinity of the pool; there shot his horse with a pistol; despatched the rider with its butt end; possessed himself of the pocket-book; and, supposing the horse dead, dragged it with great labor to the brambles by the pond. Upon his own beast he slung the corpse of Mr. Shuttleworthy, and thus bore it to a secure place of concealment a long distance off through the woods.

The waistcoat, the knife, the pocket-book and bullet, had been placed by himself where found, with the view of avenging himself upon Mr. Pennifeather. He had also contrived the discovery of the stained handkerchief and shirt.

Towards the end of the blood-chilling recital, the words of the guilty wretch faltered and grew hollow. When the record was finally exhausted, he arose, staggered backwards from the table, and fell—*dead*.

The means by which this happily-timed confession was extorted, although efficient, were simple indeed. Mr. Goodfellow's excess of frankness had disgusted me, and excited my suspicions from the first. I was present when Mr. Pennifeather had struck him, and the fiendish expression which then arose upon his countenance, although momentary, assured me that his threat of vengeance would, if possible, be rigidly fulfilled. I was thus prepared to view the *manœuvring* of "Old Charley" in a very different light from that in which it was regarded by the good citizens of Rattleborough. I saw at once that all the criminating discoveries arose, either directly, or indirectly, from himself. But the fact which clearly opened my eyes to the true state of the case, was the affair of the bullet, *found* by Mr. G. in the carcass of the horse. I had not forgotten, although the Rattleburghers *had*, that there was a hole where the ball had entered the horse, and another where it *went out*. If it were found in the animal then, after having made its exit I saw clearly that it must have been deposited by

the person who found it. The bloody shirt and handkerchief confirmed the idea suggested by the bullet; for the blood upon
examination proved to be capital claret, and no more. When I
came to think of these things, and also of the late increase of
liberality and expenditure on the part of Mr. Goodfellow, I entertained a suspicion which was none the less strong because I kept
it altogether to myself.

In the mean time, I instituted a rigorous private search for the
corpse of Mr. Shuttleworthy, and, for good reasons, searched in
quarters as divergent as possible from those to which Mr. Goodfellow conducted his party. The result was that, after some days,
I came across an old dry well, the mouth of which was nearly
hidden by brambles; and here, at the bottom, I discovered what
I sought.

Now it so happened that I had overheard the colloquy between
the two cronies, when Mr. Goodfellow had contrived to cajole his
host into the promise of a box of Chateau-Margaux. Upon this
hint I acted. I procured a stiff piece of whalebone, thrust it
down the throat of the corpse, and deposited the latter in an old
wine box—taking care so to double the body up as to double the
whalebone with it. In this manner I had to press forcibly upon
the lid to keep it down while I secured it with nails; and I anticipated, of course, that as soon as these latter were removed, the top
would fly *off* and the body *up*.

Having thus arranged the box, I marked, numbered and addressed it as already told; and then writing a letter in the name
of the wine merchants with whom Mr. Shuttleworthy dealt, I
gave instructions to my servant to wheel the box to Mr. Goodfel-
lows's door, in a barrow, at a given signal from myself. For the
words which I intended the corpse to speak, I confidently depended upon my ventriloquial abilities; for their effect, I counted upon
the conscience of the murderous wretch.

I believe there is nothing more to be explained. Mr. Pennifeather was released upon the spot, inherited the fortune of his
uncle, profited by the lessons of experience, turned over a new
leaf, and led happily ever afterwards a new life.

THE SPHINX.

DURING the dread reign of the Cholera in New-York, I had accepted the invitation of a relative to spend a fortnight with him in the retirement of his *cottage ornée* on the banks of the Hudson. We had here around us all the ordinary means of summer amusement ; and what with rambling in the woods, sketching, boating, fishing, bathing, music and books, we should have passed the time pleasantly enough, but for the fearful intelligence which reached us every morning from the populous city. Not a day elapsed which did not bring us news of the decease of some acquaintance. Then, as the fatality increased, we learned to expect daily the loss of some friend. At length we trembled at the approach of every messenger. The very air from the South seemed to us redolent with death. That palsying thought, indeed, took entire possession of my soul. I could neither speak, think, nor dream of anything else. My host was of a less excitable temperament, and, although greatly depressed in spirits, exerted himself to sustain my own. His richly philosophical intellect was not at any time affected by unrealities. To the substances of terror he was sufficiently alive, but of its shadows he had no apprehension.

His endeavors to arouse me from the condition of abnormal gloom into which I had fallen, were frustrated in great measure, by certain volumes which I had found in his library. These were of a character to force into germination whatever seeds of hereditary superstition lay latent in my bosom. I had been reading these books without his knowledge, and thus he was often at a loss to account for the forcible impressions which had been made upon my fancy.

A favorite topic with me was the popular belief in omens—a belief which, at this one epoch of my life, I was almost seriously disposed to defend. On this subject we had long and animated discussions—he maintaining the utter groundlessness of faith in such matters—I contending that a popular sentiment arising with absolute spontaneity—that is to say, without apparent traces of suggestion—had in itself the unmistakeable elements of truth, and was entitled to much respect.

The fact is, that soon after my arrival at the cottage, there had occurred to myself an incident so entirely inexplicable, and which had in it so much of the portentous character, that I might well have been excused for regarding it as an omen. It appalled, and at the same time so confounded and bewildered me, that many days elapsed before I could make up my mind to communicate the circumstance to my friend.

Near the close of an exceedingly warm day, I was sitting, book in hand, at an open window, commanding, through a long vista of the river banks, a view of a distant hill, the face of which nearest my position, had been denuded, by what is termed a land-slide, of the principal portion of its trees. My thoughts had been long wandering from the volume before me to the gloom and desolation of the neighboring city. Uplifting my eyes from the page, they fell upon the naked face of the hill, and upon an object—upon some living monster of hideous conformation, which very rapidly made its way from the summit to the bottom, disappearing finally in the dense forest below. As this creature first came in sight, I doubted my own sanity—or at least the evidence of my own eyes ; and many minutes passed before I succeeded in convincing myself that I was neither mad nor in a dream. Yet when I describe the monster, (which I distinctly saw, and calmly surveyed through the whole period of its progress,) my readers, I fear, will feel more difficulty in being convinced of these points than even I did myself.

Estimating the size of the creature by comparison with the diameter of the large trees near which it passed—the few giants of the forest which had escaped the fury of the land-slide—I concluded it to be far larger than any ship of the line in existence. I say ship of the line, because the shape of the monster suggested the idea—the hull of one of our seventy-fours might convey a very tolerable conception of the general outline. The mouth of the animal was situated at the extremity of a proboscis some sixty or seventy feet in length, and about as thick as the body of an ordinary elephant. Near the root of this trunk was an immense quantity of black shaggy hair—more than could have been supplied by the coats of a score of buffaloes; and projecting from this hair downwardly and laterally, sprang two gleaming tusks not unlike those of the wild boar, but of infinitely greater dimension. Extending forward, parallel with the proboscis, and on each side of it, was a gigantic staff, thirty or forty feet in length, formed seemingly of pure crystal, and in shape a perfect prism :—it reflected in the most gorgeous manner the rays of the declining sun. The trunk was fashioned like a wedge with the apex to the earth. From it there were outspread two pairs of wings—each wing nearly one hundred yards in length—one pair being placed above the other, and all thickly covered with metal scales; each scale apparently some ten or twelve feet in diameter. I observed that the upper and lower tiers of wings were connected by a strong chain. But the chief peculiarity of this horrible thing, was the representation of a *Death's Head*, which covered nearly the whole surface of its breast, and which was as accurately traced in glaring white, upon the dark ground of the body, as if it had been there carefully designed by an artist. While I regarded this terrific animal, and more especially the appearance on its breast, with a feeling of horror and awe—with a sentiment of forthcoming evil, which I found it impossible to quell by any effort of the reason, I perceived the huge jaws at the extremity of the proboscis, suddenly expand themselves, and from them there proceeded a sound so loud and so expressive of wo, that it struck upon my nerves like a knell, and as the monster disappeared at the foot of the hill, I fell at once, fainting, to the floor.

Upon recovering, my first impulse of course was, to inform my friend of what I had seen and heard—and I can scarcely explain what feeling of repugnance it was, which, in the end, operated to prevent me.

At length, one evening, some three or four days after the occurrence, we were sitting together in the room in which I had seen the apparition—I occupying the same seat at the same window, and he lounging on a sofa near at hand. The association of the place and time impelled me to give him an account of the phenomenon. He heard me to the end—at first laughed heartily—and then lapsed into an excessively grave demeanor, as if my insanity was a thing beyond suspicion. At this instant I again had a distinct view of the monster—to which, with a shout of absolute terror, I now directed his attention. He looked eagerly—but maintained that he saw nothing—although I designated minutely the course of the creature, as it made its way down the naked face of the hill.

I was now immeasurably alarmed, for I considered the vision either as an omen of my death, or, worse, as the forerunner of an attack of mania. I threw myself passionately back in my chair, and for some moments buried my face in my hands. When I uncovered my eyes, the apparition was no longer visible.

My host, however, had in some degree resumed the calmness of his demeanor, and questioned me very rigorously in respect to the conformation of the visionary creature. When I had fully satisfied him on this head, he sighed deeply, as if relieved of some intolerable burden, and went on to talk, with what I thought a cruel calmness, of various points of speculative philosophy, which had heretofore formed subject of discussion between us. I remember his insisting very especially (among other things) upon the idea that the principal source of error in all human investigations, lay in the liability of the understanding to under-rate or to over-value the importance of an object, through mere misadmeasurement of its propinquity. "To estimate properly, for example," he said, "the influence to be exercised on mankind at large by the thorough diffusion of Democracy, the distance of the epoch at which such diffusion may possibly be accomplished, should not fail to form an item in the estimate. Yet can you tell me one writer on the subject of government, who has ever thought this particular branch of the subject worthy of discussion at all?"

He here paused for a moment, stepped to a book-case, and brought forth one of the ordinary synopses of Natural History.

Requesting me then to exchange seats with him, that he might the better distinguish the fine print of the volume, he took my arm-chair at the window, and, opening the book, resumed his discourse very much in the same tone as before.

"But for your exceeding minuteness," he said, "in describing the monster, I might never have had it in my power to demonstrate to you what it was. In the first place, let me read to you a school-boy account of the genus *Sphinx*, of the family *Crepuscularia*, of the order *Lepidoptera*, of the class of *Insecta*—or insects. The account runs thus:

"'Four membranous wings covered with little colored scales of a metallic appearance; mouth forming a rolled proboscis, produced by an elongation of the jaws, upon the sides of which are found the rudiments of manibles and downy palpi; the inferior wings retained to the superior by a stiff hair; antennæ in the form of an elongated club, prismatic; abdomen pointed. The Death's-headed Sphinx has occasioned much terror among the vulgar, at times, by the melancholy kind of cry which it utters, and the insignia of death which it wears upon its corslet.'"

He here closed the book and leaned forward in the chair, placing himself accurately in the position which I had occupied at the moment of beholding "the monster."

"Ah, here it is!" he presently exclaimed—"it is reascending the face of the hill, and a very remarkable looking creature, I admit it to be. Still, it is by no means so large or so distant as you imagined it; for the fact is that, as it wriggles its way up this thread, which some spider has wrought along the window-sash, I find it to be about the sixteenth of an inch in its extreme length, and also about the sixteenth of an inch distant from the pupil of my eye."

SOME WORDS WITH A MUMMY.

THE *symposium* of the preceding evening had been a little too much for my nerves. I had a wretched head-ache, and was desperately drowsy. Instead of going out, therefore, to spend the evening, as I had proposed, it occurred to me that I could not do a wiser thing than just eat a mouthful of supper and go immediately to bed.

A *light* supper, of course. I am exceedingly fond of Welsh rabbit. More than a pound at once, however, may not at all times be advisable. Still, there can be no material objection to two. And really between two and three, there is merely a single unit of difference. I ventured, perhaps, upon four. My wife will have it five;—but, clearly, she has confounded two very distinct affairs. The abstract number, five, I am willing to admit; but, concretely, it has reference to bottles of Brown Stout, without which, in the way of condiment, Welsh rabbit is to be eschewed.

Having thus concluded a frugal meal, and donned my night-cap, with the serene hope of enjoying it till noon the next day, I placed my head upon the pillow, and, through the aid of a capital conscience, fell into a profound slumber forthwith.

But when were the hopes of humanity fulfilled? I could not have completed my third snore when there came a furious ringing at the street-door bell, and then an impatient thumping at the knocker, which awakened me at once. In a minute afterward, and while I was still rubbing my eyes, my wife thrust in my face a note, from my old friend, Doctor Ponnonner. It ran thus:

"Come to me, by all means, my dear good friend, as soon as you receive this. Come and help us to rejoice. At last, by long persevering diplomacy, I have gained the assent of the Directors of the City Museum, to my examination of the Mummy—you know the one I mean. I have permission to unswathe it and open it, if desirable. A few friends only will be present— you, of course. The Mummy is now at my house, and we shall begin to unroll it at eleven to-night.

"Yours, ever,

"PONNONNER."

By the time I had reached the "Ponnonner," it struck me that I was as wide awake as a man need be. I leaped out of bed in an ecstacy, overthrowing all in my way; dressed myself with a rapidity truly marvellous; and set off, at the top of my speed, for the Doctor's.

There I found a very eager company assembled. They had been awaiting me with much impatience; the Mummy was extended upon the dining-table; and the moment I entered, its examination was commenced.

It was one of a pair brought, several years previously, by Captain Arthur Sabretash, a cousin of Ponnonner's, from a tomb near Eleithias, in the Lybian Mountains, a considerable distance above Thebes on the Nile. The grottoes at this point, although less magnificent than the Theban sepulchres, are of higher interest, on account of affording more numerous illustrations of the private life of the Egyptians. The chamber from which our specimen was taken, was said to be very rich in such illustrations—the walls being completely covered with fresco paintings and bas-reliefs, while statues, vases, and Mosaic work of rich patterns, indicated the vast wealth of the deceased.

The treasure had been deposited in the Museum precisely in the same condition in which Captain Sabretash had found it ;— that is to say, the coffin had not been disturbed. For eight years it had thus stood, subject only externally to public inspection. We had now, therefore, the complete Mummy at our disposal; and to those who are aware how very rarely the unransacked antique reaches our shores, it will be evident, at once, that we had great reason to congratulate ourselves upon our good fortune.

Approaching the table, I saw on it a large box, or case, nearly seven feet long, and perhaps three feet wide, by two feet and a

half deep.   It was oblong—not coffin shaped.   The material was
at first supposed to be the wood of the sycamore (*platanus*,) but,
upon cutting into it, we found it to be pasteboard, or, more properly, *papier maché*, composed of papyrus.   It was thickly ornamented with paintings, representing funeral scenes, and other
mournful subjects—interspersed among which, in every variety of
position, were certain series of hieroglyphical characters, intended,
no doubt, for the name of the departed.   By good luck, Mr. Gliddon formed one of our party ; and he had no difficulty in translating the letters, which were simply phonetic, and represented
the word, *Allamistakeo.*

We had some difficulty in getting this case open without injury ;
but, having at length accomplished the task, we came to a second,
coffin-shaped, and very considerably less in size than the exterior
one, but resembling it precisely in every other respect.   The interval between the two was filled with resin, which had, in some degree, defaced the colors of the interior box.

Upon opening this latter, (which we did quite easily,) we arrived at a third case, also coffin-shaped, and varying from the
second one in no particular, except in that of its material, which
was cedar, and still emitted the peculiar and highly aromatic odor
of that wood.   Between the second and the third case there was
no interval—the one fitting accurately within the other.

Removing the third case, we discovered and took out the body
tself.   We had expected to find it, as usual, enveloped in frequent
rolls, or bandages, of linen ; but, in place of these, we found a sort
of sheath, made of papyrus, and coated with a layer of plaster,
thickly gilt and painted.   The paintings represented subjects connected with the various supposed duties of the soul, and its presentation to different divinities, with numerous identical human figures,
intended, very probably, as portraits of the persons embalmed.
Extending from head to foot, was a columnar, or perpendicular
inscription, in phonetic hieroglyphics, giving again his name and
titles, and the names and titles of his relations.

Around the neck thus unsheathed, was a collar of cylindrical
glass beads, diverse in color, and so arranged as to form images
of deities, of the scarabæus, etc., with the winged globe.   Around
the small of the waist was a similar collar or belt.

Stripping off the papyrus, we found the flesh in excellent preservation, with no perceptible odor. The color was reddish. The skin was hard, smooth, and glossy. The teeth and hair were in good condition. The eyes (it seemed) had been removed, and glass ones substituted, which were very beautiful and wonderfully life-like, with the exception of somewhat too determined a stare. The finger and the nails were brilliantly gilded.

Mr. Gliddon was of opinion, from the redness of the epidermis, that the embalment had been effected altogether by asphaltum; but, on scraping the surface with a steel instrument, and throwing into the fire some of the powder thus obtained, the flavor of camphor and other sweet-scented gums became apparent.

We searched the corpse very carefully for the usual openings through which the entrails are extracted, but, to our surprise, we could discover none. No member of the party was at that period aware that entire or unopened mummies are not unfrequently met. The brain it was customary to withdraw through the nose; the intestines through an incision in the side; the body was then shaved, washed, and salted; then laid aside for several weeks, when the operation of embalming, properly so called, began.

As no trace of an opening could be found, Doctor Ponnonner was preparing his instruments for dissection, when I observed that it was then past two o'clock. Hereupon it was agreed to postpone the internal examination until the next evening; and we were about to separate for the present, when some one suggested an experiment or two with the Voltaic pile.

The application of electricity to a Mummy three or four thousand years old at the least, was an idea, if not very sage, still sufficiently original, and we all caught it at once. About one-tenth in earnest and nine-tenths in jest, we arranged a battery in the Doctor's study, and conveyed thither the Egyptian.

It was only after much trouble that we succeeded in laying bare some portions of the temporal muscle which appeared of less stony rigidity than other parts of the frame, but which, as we had anticipated, of course, gave no indication of galvanic susceptibility when brought in contact with the wire. This, the first trial, indeed, seemed decisive, and, with a hearty laugh at our own absurdity, we were bidding each other good night, when my eyes, happening to fall upon those of the Mummy, were there immediately riveted in amazement. My brief glance, in fact, had sufficed to assure me that the orbs which we had all supposed to be glass, and which were originally noticeable for a certain wild stare, were now so far covered by the lids, that only a small portion of the *tunica albuginea* remained visible.

With a shout I called attention to the fact, and it became immediately obvious to all.

I cannot say that I was *alarmed* at the phenomenon, because "alarmed" is, in my case, not exactly the word. It is possible, however, that, but for the Brown Stout, I might have been a little nervous. As for the rest of the company, they really made no attempt at concealing the downright fright which possessed them. Doctor Ponnonner was a man to be pitied. Mr. Gliddon, by some peculiar process, rendered himself invisible. Mr. Silk Buckingham, I fancy, will scarcely be so bold as to deny that he made his way, upon all fours, under the table.

After the first shock of astonishment, however, we resolved, as a matter of course, upon farther experiment forthwith. Our operations were now directed against the great toe of the right foot. We made an incision over the outside of the exterior *os sesamoideum pollicis pedis*, and thus got at the root of the *abductor* muscle. Re-adjusting the battery, we now applied the fluid to the bisected nerves—when, with a movement of exceeding life-likeness, the Mummy first drew up its right knee so as to bring it nearly in contact with the abdomen, and then, straightening the limb with inconceivable force, bestowed a kick upon Doctor Ponnonner, which had the effect of discharging that gentleman, like an arrow from a catapult, through a window into the street below.

We rushed out *en masse* to bring in the mangled remains of the victim, but had the happiness to meet him upon the staircase, coming up in an unaccountable hurry, brimfull of the most ardent philosophy, and more than ever impressed with the necessity of prosecuting our experiments with rigor and with zeal.

It was by his advice, accordingly, that we made, upon the spot, a profound incision into the tip of the subject's nose, while the Doctor himself, laying violent hands upon it, pulled it into vehement contact with the wire.

Morally and physically—figuratively and literally—was the effect electric. In the first place, the corpse opened its eyes and winked very rapidly for several minutes, as does Mr. Barnes in the pantomime; in the second place, it sneezed; in the third, it sat upon end; in the fourth, it shook its fist in Doctor Ponnonner's face; in the fifth, turning to Messieurs Gliddon and Buckingham, it addressed them, in very capital Egyptian, thus:

"I must say, gentlemen, that I am as much surprised as I am mortified, at your behavior. Of Doctor Ponnonner nothing better was to be expected. He is a poor little fat fool who *knows* no better. I pity and forgive him. But you, Mr. Gliddon—and you, Silk—who have travelled and resided in Egypt until one might imagine you to the manor born—you, I say, who have been so much among us that you speak Egyptian fully as well, I think, as you write your mother tongue—you, whom I have always been led to regard as the firm friend of the mummies—I really did anticipate more gentlemanly conduct from *you*. What am I to think of your standing quietly by and seeing me thus unhandsomely used? What am I to suppose by your permitting Tom, Dick, and Harry to strip me of my coffins, and my clothes, in this wretchedly cold climate? In what light (to come to the point) am I to regard your aiding and abetting that miserable little villain, Doctor Ponnonner, in pulling me by the nose?"

It will be taken for granted, no doubt, that upon hearing this speech under the circumstances, we all either made for the door, or fell into violent hysterics, or went off in a general swoon. One of these three things was, I say, to be expected. Indeed each and all of these lines of conduct might have been very plausibly pursued. And, upon my word, I am at a loss to know how or why it was that we pursued neither the one or the other. But, perhaps, the true reason is to be sought in the spirit of the age, which proceeds by the rule of contraries altogether, and is now usually admitted as the solution of everything in the way of paradox and impossibility. Or, perhaps, after all, it was only the Mummy's exceedingly natural and matter-of-course air that divested his words of the terrible. However this may be, the facts are clear, and no member of our party betrayed any very particular trepidation, or seemed to consider that anything had gone very especially wrong.

For my part I was convinced it was all right, and merely stepped aside, out of the range of the Egyptian's fist.   Doctor Ponnonner thrust his hands into his breeches' pockets, looked hard at the Mummy, and grew excessively red in the face.   Mr. Gliddon stroked his whiskers and drew up the collar of his shirt.   Mr. Buckingham hung down his head, and put his right thumb into the left corner of his mouth.

The Egyptian regarded him with a severe countenance for some minutes, and at length, with a sneer, said :

" Why don't you speak, Mr. Buckingham ?   Did you hear what I asked you, or not ?   Do take your thumb out of your mouth !"

Mr. Buckingham, hereupon, gave a slight start, took his right thumb out of the left corner of his mouth, and, by way of indemnification, inserted his left thumb in the right corner of the aperture above-mentioned.

Not being able to get an answer from Mr. B., the figure turned peevishly to Mr. Gliddon, and, in a peremptory tone, demanded in general terms what we all meant.

Mr. Gliddon replied at great length, in phonetics ; and but for the deficiency of American printing-offices in hieroglyphical type, it would afford me much pleasure to record here, in the original, the whole of his very excellent speech.

I may as well take this occasion to remark, that all the subsequent conversation in which the Mummy took a part, was carried on in primitive Egyptian, through the medium (so far as concerned myself and other untravelled members of the company)—through the medium, I say, of Messieurs Gliddon and Buckingham, as interpreters.   These gentlemen spoke the mother-tongue of the mummy with inimitable fluency and grace ; but I could not help observing that (owing, no doubt, to the introduction of images entirely modern, and, of course, entirely novel to the stranger,) the two travellers were reduced, occasionally, to the employment of sensible forms for the purpose of conveying a particular meaning.   Mr. Gliddon, at one period, for example, could not make the Egyptian comprehend the term " politics," until he sketched upon the wall, with a bit of charcoal, a little carbuncle nosed gentleman, out at elbows, standing upon a stump, with his left leg drawn back, his right arm thrown forward, with his fist shut, the eyes rolled up toward Heaven, and the mouth open at an angle of ninety degrees. Just in the same way Mr. Buckingham failed to convey the absolutely modern idea, "whig," until, (at Doctor Ponnonner's suggestion,) he grew very pale in the face, and consented to take off his own.

It will be readily understood that Mr. Gliddon's discourse turned chiefly upon the vast benefits accruing to science from the unrolling and disemboweling of mummies; apologizing, upon this score, for any disturbance that might have been occasioned *him*, in particular, the individual Mummy called Allamistakeo; and concluding with a mere hint, (for it could scarcely be considered more,) that, as these little matters were now explained, it might be as well to proceed with the investigation intended. Here Doctor Ponnonner made ready his instruments.

In regard to the latter suggestions of the orator, it appears that Allamistakeo had certain scruples of conscience, the nature of which I did not distinctly learn; but he expressed himself satisfied with the apologies tendered, and, getting down from the table, shook hands with the company all round.

When this ceremony was at an end, we immediately busied ourselves in repairing the damages which our subject had sustained from the scalpel. We sewed up the wound in his temple, bandaged his foot, and applied a square inch of black plaster to the tip of his nose.

It was now observed that the Count, (this was the title, it seems, of Allamistakeo,) had a slight fit of shivering—no doubt from the cold. The doctor immediately repaired to his wardrobe, and soon returned with a black dress coat, made in Jennings' best manner, a pair of sky-blue plaid pantaloons with straps, a pink gingham *chemise*, a flapped vest of brocade, a white sack overcoat, a walking cane with a hook, a hat with no brim, patent-leather boots, straw-colored kid gloves, an eye-glass, a pair of whiskers, and a waterfall cravat. Owing to the disparity of size between the Count and the doctor, (the proportion being as two to one,) there was some little difficulty in adjusting these habiliments upon the person of the Egyptian; but when all was arranged, he might have been said to be dressed. Mr Gliddon, therefore, gave him

his arm, and led him to a comfortable chair by the fire, while the
doctor rang the bell upon the spot and ordered a supply of cigars
and wine.

The conversation soon grew animated. Much curiosity was, of
course, expressed in regard to the somewhat remarkable fact of
Allamistakeo's still remaining alive.

"I should have thought," observed Mr. Buckingham, "that it
is high time you were dead."

"Why," replied the Count, very much astonished, "I am little
more than seven hundred years old! My father lived a thousand,
and was by no means in his dotage when he died."

Here ensued a brisk series of questions and computations, by
means of which it became evident that the antiquity of the
Mummy had been grossly misjudged. It had been five thousand
and fifty years, and some months, since he had been consigned to
the catacombs at Eleithias.

"But my remark," resumed Mr. Buckingham, "had no reference to your age at the period of interment; (I am willing to
grant, in fact, that you are still a young man,) and my allusion
was to the immensity of time during which, by your own showing,
you must have been done up in asphaltum."

"In what?" said the Count.

"In asphaltum," persisted Mr. B.

"Ah, yes; I have some faint notion of what you mean; it
might be made to answer, no doubt,—but in my time we employed scarcely anything else than the Bichloride of Mercury."

"But what we are especially at a loss to understand," said
Doctor Ponnonner, "is how it happens that, having been dead
and buried in Egypt, five thousand years ago, you are here to-day
all alive, and looking so delightfully well."

"Had I been, as you say, *dead*," replied the Count, "it is more
than probable that dead I should still be; for I perceive you are
yet in the infancy of Galvanism, and cannot accomplish with it
what was a common thing among us in the old days. But the
fact is, I fell into catalepsy, and it was considered by my best
friends that I was either dead or should be; they accordingly embalmed me at once—I presume you are aware of the chief principle of the embalming process?"

"Why, not altogether."

"Ah, I perceive ;—a deplorable condition of ignorance! Well, I cannot enter into details just now : but it is necessary to explain that to embalm, (properly speaking,) in Egypt, was to arrest indefinitely *all* the animal functions subjected to the process. I use the word ' animal in its widest sense, as including the physical not more than the moral and *vital* being. I repeat that the leading principle of embalment consisted, with us, in the immediately arresting, and holding in perpetual *abeyance, all* the animal functions subjected to the process. To be brief, in whatever condition the individual was, at the period of embalment, in that condition he remained. Now, as it is my good fortune to be of the blood of the Scarabœus, I was embalmed *alive*, as you see me at present."

"The bloood of the Scarabœus !" exclaimed Doctor Ponnonner.

"Yes. The Scarabœus was the *insignium*, or the ' arms,' of a very distinguished and very rare patrician family. To be ' of the blood of the Scarabœus,' is merely to be one of that family of which the Scarabœus is the *insignium*. I speak figuratively."

"But what has this to do with your being alive ?"

"Why it is the general custom in Egypt, to deprive a corpse, before embalment, of its bowels and brains ; the race of Scarabœi alone did not coincide with the custom. Had I not been a Scarabœus, therefore, I should have been without bowels and brains; and without either it is inconvenient to live."

"I perceive that ;" said Mr. Buckingham, " and I presume that all the *entire* mummies that come to hand are of the race of Scarabœi."

"Beyond doubt."

"I thought," said Mr. Gliddon, very meekly, " that the Scarabœus was one of the Egyptian gods."

"One of the Egyptian *what* !" exclaimed the Mummy, starting to its feet.

"Gods !" repeated the traveller.

"Mr. Gliddon, I really am astonished to hear you talk in this style," said the Count, resuming his chair. " No nation upon the face of the earth has ever acknowledged more than *one god*. The Scarabœus, the Ibis, etc., were with us, (as similar creatures

20*

have been with others) the symbols, or *media*, through which we
offered worship to the Creator too august to be more directly approached."

There was here a pause. At length the colloquy was renewed
by Doctor Ponnonner.

" It is not improbable, then, from what you have explained,"
said he, "that among the catacombs near the Nile, there may exist
other mummies of the Scarabœus tribe, in a condition of vitality."

" There can be no question of it," replied the Count ; " all
the Scarabœi embalmed accidentally while alive, are alive. Even
some of those *purposely* so embalmed, may have been overlooked
by their executors, and still remain in the tombs."

" Will you be kind enough to explain," I said, " what you mean
by ' purposely so embalmed !' "

" With great pleasure," answered the Mummy, after surveying
me leisurely through his eye-glass—for it was the first time I had
ventured to address him a direct question.

" With great pleasure," he said. " The usual duration of man's
life, in my time, was about eight hundred years. Few men died,
unless by most extraordinary accident, before the age of six hundred ; few lived longer than a decade of centuries ; but eight
were considered the natural term. After the discovery of the
embalming principle, as I have already described it to you, it occurred to our philosophers that a laudable curiosity might be
gratified, and, at the same time, the interests of science much advanced, by living this natural term in instalments. In the case
of history, indeed, experience demonstrated that something of this
kind was indispensable. An historian, for example, having attained the age of five hundred, would write a book with great
labor and then get himself carefully embalmed ; leaving instructions to his executors *pro. tem.*, that they should cause him to be
revivified after the lapse of a certain period—say five or six hundred years. Resuming existence at the expiration of this time, he
would invariably find his great work converted into a species of
hap-hazard note-book—that is to say, into a kind of literary arena
for the conflicting guesses, riddles, and personal squabbles of whole
herds of exasperated commentators. These guesses, etc., which
passed under the name of annotations, or emendations, were found

so completely to have enveloped, distorted, and overwhelmed the text, that the author had to go about with a lantern to discover his own book. When discovered, it was never worth the trouble of the search. After re-writing it throughout, it was regarded as the bounden duty of the historian to set himself to work, immediately, in correcting from his own private knowledge and experience, the traditions of the day concerning the epoch at which he had originally lived. Now this process of re-scription and personal rectification, pursued by various individual sages, from time to time, had the effect of preventing our history from degenerating into absolute fable."

" I beg your pardon," said Doctor Ponnonner at this point, laying his hand gently upon the arm of the Egyptian—" I beg your pardon, sir, but may I presume to interrupt you for one moment ?"

" By all means, *sir*," replied the Count, drawing up.

" I merely wished to ask you a question," said the Doctor. " You mentioned the historian's personal correction of *traditions* respecting his own epoch. Pray, sir, upon an average, what proportion of these Kabbala were usually found to be right ?"

" The Kabbala, as you properly term them, sir, were generally discovered to be precisely on a par with the facts recorded in the un-re-written histories themselves ;—that is to say, not one individual iota of either, was ever known, under any circumstances, to be not totally and radically wrong."

" But since it is quite clear," resumed the Doctor, " that at least five thousand years have elapsed since your entombment, I take it for granted that your histories at that period, if not your traditions, were sufficiently explicit on that one topic of universal interest, the Creation, which took place, as I presume you are aware, only about ten centuries before."

" Sir !" said the Count Allamistakeo.

The Doctor repeated his remarks, but it was only after much additional explanation, that the foreigner could be made to comprehend them. The latter at length said, hesitatingly :

" The ideas you have suggested are to me, I confess, utterly novel. During my time I never knew any one to entertain so singular a fancy as that the universe (or this world if you will have it so,) ever had a beginning at all. I remember once, and once only, hearing something remotely hinted, by a man of many speculations, concerning the origin *of the human race ;* and by this individual, the very word *Adam*, (or Red Earth) which you make use of, was employed. He employed it, however, in a generical sense, with reference to the spontaneous germination from rank soil (just as a thousand of the lower *genera* of creatures are germinated)—the spontaneous germination, I say, of five vast hordes of men, simultaneously upspringing in five distinct and nearly equal divisions of the globe."

Here, in general, the company shrugged their shoulders, and one or two of us touched our foreheads with a very significant air. Mr. Silk Buckingham, first glancing slightly at the occiput and then at the siniciput of Allamistakeo, spoke as follows :

" The long duration of human life in your time, together with the occasional practice of passing it, as you have explained, in instalments, must have had, indeed, a strong tendency to the general development and conglomeration of knowledge. I presume, therefore, that we are to attribute the marked inferiority of the old Egyptians in all particulars of science, when compared with the moderns, and more especially, with the Yankees, altogether to the superior solidity of the Egyptian skull."

" I confess again," replied the Count, with much suavity, " that I am somewhat at a loss to comprehend you ; pray, to what particulars of science do you allude ?"

Here our whole party, joining voices, detailed, at great length, the assumptions of phrenology and the marvels of animal magnetism.

Having heard us to an end, the Count proceeded to relate a few anecdotes, which rendered it evident that prototypes of Gall and Spurzheim had flourished and faded in Egypt so long ago as to have been nearly forgotten, and that the manœuvres of Mesmer were really very contemptible tricks when put in collation with the positive miracles of the Theban *savans*, who created lice and a great many other similar things.

I here asked the Count if his people were able to calculate eclipses. He smiled rather contemptuously, and said they were. This put me a little out, but I began to make other inquiries in regard to his astronomical knowledge, when a member of the company, who had never as yet opened his mouth, whispered in my ear, that for information on this head, I had better consult Ptolemy, (whoever Ptolemy is,) as well as one Plutarch *de facie lunæ.*

I then questioned the Mummy about burning-glasses and lenses, and, in general, about the manufacture of glass; but I had not made an end of my queries before the silent member again touched me quietly on the elbow, and begged me for God's sake to take a peep at Diodorus Siculus. As for the Count, he merely asked me, in the way of reply, if we moderns possessed any such microscopes as would enable us to cut cameos in the style of the Egyptians. While I was thinking how I should answer this question, little Doctor Ponnonner committed himself in a very extraordinary way.

" Look at our architecture !" he exclaimed, greatly to the indignation of both the travellers, who pinched him black and blue to no purpose.

" Look," he cried with enthusiasm, " at the Bowling-Green Fountain in New-York ! or if this be too vast a contemplation, regard for a moment the Capitol at Washington, D. C. !"—and the good little medical man went on to detail, very minutely, the proportions of the fabric to which he referred. He explained that the portico alone was adorned with no less than four and twenty columns, five feet in diameter, and ten feet apart.

The Count said that he regretted not being able to remember, just at that moment, the precise dimensions of any one of the principal buildings of the city of Aznac, whose foundations were laid in the night of Time, but the ruins of which were still standing, at the epoch of his entombment, in a vast plain of sand to the westward of Thebes. He recollected, however, (talking of porticoes) that one affixed to an inferior palace in a kind of suburb called Carnac, consisted of a hundred and forty-four columns, thirty-seven feet each in circumference, and twenty-five feet apart. The approach of this portico, from the Nile, was through an avenue two miles long, composed of sphynxes, statues and obelisks, twenty, sixty, and a hundred feet in height. The palace itself (as well as he could remember) was, in one direction, two miles long, and might have been altogether, about seven in circuit. Its walls were richly painted all over, within and without, with hieroglyphics. He would not pretend to *assert* that even fifty or sixty of the Doctor's Capitols might have been built within these walls, but he was by no means sure that two or three hundred of them might not have been squeezed in with some trouble. That palace at Carnac was an insignificant little building after all. He, (the Count) however, could not conscientiously refuse to admit the ingenuity, magnificence, and superiority of the Fountain at the Bowling Green, as described by the Doctor. Nothing like it, he was forced to allow, had ever been seen in Egypt or elsewhere.

I here asked the Count what he had to say to our railroads.

"Nothing," he replied, "in particular." They were rather slight, rather ill-conceived, and clumsily put together. They could not be compared, of course, with the vast, level, direct, iron-grooved causeways, upon which the Egyptians conveyed entire temples and solid obelisks of a hundred and fifty feet in altitude.

I spoke of our gigantic mechanical forces.

He agreed that we knew something in that way, but inquired how I should have gone to work in getting up the imposts on the lintels of even the little palace at Carnac.

This question I concluded not to hear, and demanded if he had any idea of Artesian wells; but he simply raised his eye-brows; while Mr. Gliddon winked at me very hard and said, in a low tone, that one had been recently discovered by the engineers employed to bore for water in the Great Oasis.

I then mentioned our steel; but the foreigner elevated his nose, and asked me if our steel could have executed the sharp carved work seen on the obelisks, and which was wrought altogether by edge-tools of copper.

This disconcerted us so greatly that we thought it advisable to vary the attack to Metaphysics. We sent for a copy of a book called the "Dial," and read out of it a chapter or two about something which is not very clear, but which the Bostonians call the Great Movement or Progress.

The Count merely said that Great Movements were awfully common things in his day, and as for Progress, it was at one time quite a nuisance, but it never progressed.

We then spoke of the great beauty and importance of Demo-cracy, and were at much trouble in impressing the Count with a due sense of the advantages we enjoyed in living where there was suffrage *ad libitum*, and no king.

He listened with marked interest, and in fact seemed not a little amused. When we had done, he said that, a great while ago, there had occurred something of a very similar sort. Thirteen Egyptian provinces determined all at once to be free, and so set a magnificent example to the rest of mankind. They assembled their wise men, and concocted the most ingenious constitution it is possible to conceive. For a while they managed remarkably well; only their habit of bragging was prodigious. The thing ended, however, in the consolidation of the thirteen states, with some fifteen or twenty others, in the most odious and insupporta-ble despotism that ever was heard of upon the face of the Earth.

I asked what was the name of the usurping tyrant.

As well as the Count could recollect, it was *Mob*.

Not knowing what to say to this, I raised my voice, and de-plored the Egyptian ignorance of steam.

The Count looked at me with much astonishment, but made no answer. The silent gentleman, however, gave me a violent nudge in the ribs with his elbows—told me I had sufficiently exposed myself for once—and demanded if I was really such a fool as not to know that the modern steam engine is derived from the inven-tion of Hero, through Solomon de Caus.

We were now in imminent danger of being discomfited; but, as good luck would have it, Doctor Ponnonner, having rallied, re-turned to our rescue, and inquired if the people of Egypt would seriously pretend to rival the moderns in the all important partic-ular of dress.

The Count, at this, glanced downwards to the straps of his pan-taloons, and then taking hold of the end of one of his coat-tails, held it up close to his eyes for some minutes. Letting it fall, at last, his mouth extended itself very gradually from ear to ear; but I do not remember that he said anything in the way of reply.

Hereupon we recovered our spirits, and the Doctor, approach-ing the Mummy with great dignity, desired it to say candidly upon its hono' as a gentleman, if the Egyptians had comprehend-

ed, at *any* period, the manufacture of either Ponnonner's lozenges,
or Brandreth's pills.

We looked, with profound anxiety, for an answer;—but in vain.
It was not forthcoming.   The Egyptian blushed and hung down
his head.   Never was triumph more consummate; never was
defeat borne with so ill a grace.   Indeed, I could not endure the
spectacle of the poor Mummy's mortification.   I reached my hat,
bowed to him stiffly, and took leave.

Upon getting home I found it past four o'clock, and went immediately to-bed.   It is now ten, A. M.   I have been up since seven,
penning these memoranda for the benefit of my family and of
mankind.   The former I shall behold no more.   My wife is a
shrew.   The truth is, I am heartily sick of this life and of the
nineteenth century in general.   I am convinced that everything is
going wrong.   Besides, I am anxious to know who will be President in 2045.   As soon, therefore, as I shave and swallow a cup
of coffee, I shall just step over to Ponnonner's and get embalmed
for a couple of hundred years.

H O P · F R O G.

I NEVER knew any one so keenly alive to a joke as the king was. He seemed to live only for joking. To tell a good story of the joke kind, and to tell it well, was the surest road to his favor. Thus it happened that his seven ministers were all noted for their accomplishments as jokers. They all took after the king, too, in being large, corpulent, oily men, as well as inimitable jokers. Whether people grow fat by joking, or whether there is something in fat itself which predisposes to a joke, I have never been quite able to determine; but certain it is that a lean joker is a *rara avis in terris*.

About the refinements, or, as he called them, the "ghosts" of wit, the king troubled himself very little. He had an especial admiration for *breadth* in a jest, and would often put up with *length*, for the sake of it. Over-niceties wearied him. He would have preferred Rabelais's "Gargantua," to the "Zadig" of Voltaire : and, upon the whole, practical jokes suited his taste far better than verbal ones.

At the date of my narrative, professing jesters had not altogether gone out of fashion at court. Several of the great continental "powers" still retained their "fools," who wore motley, with caps and bells, and who were expected to be always ready with sharp witticisms, at a moment's notice, in consideration of the crumbs that fell from the royal table.

Our king, as a matter of course, retained his "fool." The fact is, he *required* something in the way of folly—if only to counterbalance the heavy wisdom of the seven wise men who were his ministers—not to mention himself.

His fool, or professional jester, was not *only* a fool, however. His value was trebled in the eyes of the king, by the fact of his being also a dwarf and a cripple. Dwarfs were as common at court, in those days, as fools ; and many monarchs would have found it difficult to get through their days (days are rather longer at court than elsewhere) without both a jester to laugh *with*, and a dwarf to laugh *at*. But, as I have already observed, your jesters, in ninety-nine cases out of a hundred, are fat, round and unwieldy—so that it was no small source of self-gratulation with our king that, in Hop-Frog (this was the fool's name,) he possessed a triplicate treasure in one person.

I believe the name "Hop-Frog" was *not* that given to the dwarf by his sponsors at baptism, but it was conferred upon him, by general consent of the seven ministers, on account of his inability to walk as other men do. In fact, Hop-Frog could only get along by a sort of interjectional gait—something between a leap and a wriggle—a movement that afforded illimitable amusement, and of course consolation, to the king , for (notwithstanding the protuberance of his stomach and a constitutional swelling of the head) the king, by his whole court, was accounted a capital figure.

But although Hop-Frog, through the distortion of his legs, could move only with great pain and difficulty along a road or floor, the prodigious muscular power which nature seemed to have bestowed upon his arms, by way of compensation for deficiency in the lower limbs, enabled him to perform many feats of wonderful dexterity, where trees or ropes were in question, or anything else to climb. At such exercises he certainly much more resembled a squirrel, or a small monkey, than a frog.

I am not able to say, with precision, from what country Hop-Frog originally came. It was from some barbarous region, however, that no person ever heard of—a vast distance from the court of our king. Hop-Frog, and a young girl very little less dwarfish than himself (although of exquisite proportions, and a marvellous dancer,) had been forcibly carried off from their respective homes in adjoining provinces, and sent as presents to the king, by one of his ever-victorious generals.

Under these circumstances, it is not to be wondered at that a close intimacy arose between the two little captives. Indeed, they soon became sworn friends. Hop-Frog, who, although he made a great deal of sport, was by no means popular, had it not in his power to render Trippetta many services; but *she*, on account of her grace and exquisite beauty (although a dwarf,) was universally admired and petted : so she possessed much influence; and never failed to use it, whenever she could, for the benefit of Hop-Frog.

On some grand state occasion—I forget what—the king determined to have a masquerade; and whenever a masquerade, or anything of that kind, occurred at our court, then the talents both of Hop-Frog and Trippetta were sure to be called in play. Hop-Frog, in especial, was so inventive in the way of getting up pageants, suggesting novel characters, and arranging costume, for masked balls, that nothing could be done, it seems, without his assistance.

The night appointed for the *fête* had arrived. A gorgeous hall had been fitted up, under Trippetta's eye, with every kind of device which could possibly give *éclat* to a masquerade. The whole court was in a fever of expectation. As for costumes and characters, it might well be supposed that everybody had come to a decision on such points. Many had made up their minds (as to what *rôles* they should assume) a week, or even a month, in advance; and, in fact, there was not a particle of indecision anywhere—except in the case of the king and his seven ministers. Why *they* hesitated I never could tell, unless they did it by way of a joke. More probably, they found it difficult, on account of being so fat, to make up their minds. At all events, time flew; and, as a last resource, they sent for Trippetta and Hop-Frog.

When the two little friends obeyed the summons of the king, they found him sitting at his wine with the seven members of his cabinet council; but the monarch appeared to be in a very ill humor. He knew that Hop-Frog was not fond of wine; for it excited the poor cripple almost to madness; and madness is no comfortable feeling. But the king loved his practical jokes, and took pleasure in forcing Hop-Frog to drink and (as the king called it) "to be merry."

"Come here, Hop-Frog," said he, as the jester and his friend entered the room : " swallow this bumper to the health of your absent friends [here Hop-Frog sighed,] and then let us have the benefit of your invention. We want characters—*characters*, man—something novel—out of the way. We are wearied with this everlasting sameness. Come, drink ! the wine will brighten your wits."

Hop-Frog endeavored, as usual, to get up a jest in reply to these advances from the king ; but the effort was too much. It happened to be the poor dwarf's birthday, and the command to drink to his " absent friends" forced the tears to his eyes. Many large, bitter drops fell into the goblet as he took it, humbly, from the hand of the tyrant.

"Ah ! ha ! ha ! ha !" roared the latter, as the dwarf reluctantly drained the beaker. "See what a glass of good wine can do ! Why, your eyes are shining already !"

Poor fellow ! his large eyes *gleamed*, rather than shone ; for the effect of wine on his excitable brain was not more powerful than instantaneous. He placed the goblet nervously on the table, and looked round upon the company with a half-insane stare. They all seemed highly amused at the success of the king's "*joke.*"

"And now to business," said the prime minister, a *very fat* man.

"Yes," said the king ; " come, Hop-Frog, lend us your assistance. Characters, my fine fellow ; we stand in need of characters—all of us—ha ! ha ! ha !" and as this was seriously meant for a joke, his laugh was chorused by the seven.

"Hop-Frog also laughed, although feebly and somewhat vacantly.

"Come, come," said the king, impatiently, " have you nothing to suggest ?"

"I am endeavoring to think of something *novel*," replied the dwarf, abstractedly, for he was quite bewildered by the wine.

"Endeavoring !" cried the tyrant, fiercely ; " what do you mean by *that !* Ah, I perceive. You are sulky, and want more wine. Here, drink this !" and he poured out another goblet full and offered it to the cripple, who merely gazed at it, gasping for breath.

" Drink, I say !" shouted the monster, " or by the fiends—"

The dwarf hesitated. The king grew purple with rage. The courtiers smirked. Trippetta, pale as a corpse, advanced to the monarch's seat, and, falling on her knees before him, implored him to spare her friend.

The tyrant regarded her, for some moments, in evident wonder at her audacity. He seemed quite at a loss what to do or say—how most becomingly to express his indignation. At last, without uttering a syllable, he pushed her violently from him, and threw the contents of the brimming goblet in her face.

The poor girl got up as best she could, and, not daring even to sigh, resumed her position at the foot of the table.

There was a dead silence for about a half a minute, during which the falling of a leaf, or of a feather, might have been heard. It was interrupted by a low, but harsh and protracted *grating* sound which seemed to come at once from every corner of the room.

" What—what—*what* are you making that noise for ?" demanded the king, turning furiously to the dwarf.

The latter seemed to have recovered, in great measure, from his intoxication, and looking fixedly but quietly into the tyrant's face, merely ejaculated :

" I—I ! How could it have been me ?"

" The sound appeared to come from without," observed one of the courtiers. " I fancy it was the parrot at the window, whetting his bill upon his cage-wires."

" True," replied the monarch, as if much relieved by the suggestion ; " but, on the honor of a knight, I could have sworn that it was the gritting of this vagabond's teeth."

Hereupon the dwarf laughed (the king was too confirmed a joker to object to any one's laughing), and displayed a set of large, powerful, and very repulsive teeth. Moreover, he avowed his perfect willingness to swallow as much wine as desired. The monarch was pacified ; and having drained another bumper with no very perceptible ill effect, Hop-Frog entered at once, and with spirit, into the plans for the masquerade.

" I cannot tell what was the association of idea," observed he, very tranquilly, and as if he had never tasted wine in his life, " but *just after* your majesty had struck the girl and thrown the wine in her face—*just after* your majesty had done this, and while the parrot was making that odd noise outside the window, there came into my mind a capital diversion—one of my own country frolics —often enacted among us, at our masquerades : but here it will be new altogether. Unfortunately, however, it requires a company of eight persons, and—"

" Here we *are !*" cried the king, laughing at his acute discovery of the coincidence ; " eight to a fraction—I and my seven ministers. Come ! what is the diversion ?"

" We call it," replied the cripple, " the Eight Chained Ourang-Outangs, and it really is excellent sport if well enacted."

" *We* will enact it," remarked the king, drawing himself up, and lowering his eyelids.

" The beauty of the game," continued Hop-Frog, " lies in the fright it occasions among the women."

" Capital !" roared in chorus the monarch and his ministry.

" *I* will equip you as ourang-outangs," proceeded the dwarf ; " leave all that to me. The resemblance shall be so striking, that the company of masqueraders will take you for real beasts—and of course, they will be as much terrified as astonished."

" O, this is exquisite !" exclaimed the king. " Hop-Frog ! I will make a man of you."

" The chains are for the purpose of increasing the confusion by their jangling. You are supposed to have escaped, *en masse*, from your keepers. Your majesty cannot conceive the *effect* produced, at a masquerade, by eight chained ourang-outangs, imagined to be real ones by most of the company ; and rushing in with savage cries, among the crowd of delicately and gorgeously habited men and women. The *contrast* is inimitable."

" It *must* be," said the king : and the council arose hurriedly (as it was growing late), to put in execution the scheme of Hop-Frog.

His mode of equipping the party as ourang-outangs was very simple, but effective enough for his purposes. The animals in question had, at the epoch of my story, very rarely been seen in any part of the civilized world ; and as the imitations made by the dwarf were sufficiently beast-like and more than sufficiently hideous, their truthfulness to nature was thus thought to be secured.

The king and his ministers were first encased in tight-fitting stockinet shirts and drawers. They were then saturated with tar. At this stage of the process, some one of the party suggested feathers; but the suggestion was at once overruled by the dwarf, who soon convinced the eight, by ocular demonstration, that the hair of such a brute as the ourang-outang was much more efficiently represented by *flax*. A thick coating of the latter was accordingly plastered upon the coating of tar. A long chain was now procured. First, it was passed about the waist of the king, *and tied ;* then about another of the party, and also tied; then about all successively, in the same manner. When this chaining arrangement was complete, and the party stood as far apart from each other as possible, they formed a circle; and to make all things appear natural, Hop-Frog passed the residue of the chain, in two diameters, at right angles, across the circle, after the fashion adopted, at the present day, by those who capture Chimpanzees, or other large apes, in Borneo.

The grand saloon in which the masquerade was to take place, was a circular room, very lofty, and receiving the light of the sun only through a single window at top. At night (the season for which the apartment was especially designed,) it was illuminated principally by a large chandelier, depending by a chain from the centre of the sky-light, and lowered, or elevated, by means of a counter-balance as usual ; but (in order not to look unsightly) this latter passed outside the cupola and over the roof.

The arrangements of the room had been left to Trippetta's superintendance ; but, in some particulars, it seems, she had been guided by the calmer judgment of her friend the dwarf. At his suggestion it was that, on this occasion, the chandelier was removed. Its waxen drippings (which, in weather so warm, it was quite impossible to prevent,) would have been seriously detrimental to the rich dresses of the guests, who, on account of the crowded state of the saloon, could not *all* be expected to keep from out its centre—that is to say, from under the chandelier. Additional sconces were set in various parts of the hall, out of the way ; and

a flambeau, emitting sweet odor, was placed in the right hand of
each of the Caryaides that stood against the wall—some fifty or
sixty altogether.

The eight ourang-outangs, taking Hop-Frog's advice, waited
patiently until midnight (when the room was thoroughly filled
with masqueraders) before making their appearance. No sooner
had the clock ceased striking, however, than they rushed, or rather rolled in, all together—for the impediment of their chains
caused most of the party to fall, and all to stumble as they entered.

The excitement among the masqueraders was prodigious, and
filled the heart of the king with glee. As had been anticipated,
there were not a few of the guests who supposed the ferocious-
looking creatures to be beasts of *some* kind in reality, if not precisely ourang-outangs. Many of the women swooned with affright;
and had not the king taken the precaution to exclude all weapons
from the saloon, his party might soon have expiated their frolic
in their blood. As it was, a general rush was made for the doors;
but the king had ordered them to be locked immediately upon
his entrance; and, at the dwarf's suggestion, the keys had been
deposited with *him*.

While the tumult was at its height, and each masquerader
attentive only to his own safety—(for, in fact, there was much
real danger from the pressure of the excited crowd,)—the chain
by which the chandelier ordinarily hung, and which had been
drawn up on its removal, might have been seen very gradually
to descend, until its hooked extremity came within three feet of
the floor.

Soon after this, the king and his seven friends, having reeled
about the hall in all directions, found themselves, at length, in
its centre, and, of course, in immediate contact with the chain.
While they were thus situated, the dwarf, who had followed
closely at their heels, inciting them to keep up the commotion,
took hold of their own chain at the intersection of the two portions which crossed the circle diametrically and at right angles.
Here, with the rapidity of thought, he inserted the hook from
which the chandelier had been wont to depend; and, in an instant,

by some unseen agency, the chandelier-chain was drawn so far upward as to take the hook out of reach, and, as an inevitable consequence, to drag the ourang-outangs together in close connection, and face to face.

The masqueraders, by this time, had recovered, in some measure, from their alarm; and, beginning to regard the whole matter as a well-contrived pleasantry, set up a loud shout of laughter at the predicament of the apes.

"Leave them to *me!*" now screamed Hop-Frog, his shrill voice making itself easily heard through all the din. "Leave them to *me.* I fancy *I* know them. If I can only get a good look at them, *I* can soon tell who they are."

Here, scrambling over the heads of the crowd, he managed to get to the wall; when, seizing a flambeau from one of the Caryaides, he returned, as he went, to the centre of the room—leaped, with the agility of a monkey, upon the king's head—and thence clambered a few feet up the chain—holding down the torch to examine the group of ourang-outangs, and still screaming, "*I* shall soon find out who they are!"

And now, while the whole assembly (the apes included) were convulsed with laughter, the jester suddenly uttered a shrill whistle; when the chain flew violently up for about thirty feet—dragging with it the dismayed and struggling ourang-outangs, and leaving them suspended in mid-air between the sky-light and the floor. Hop-Frog, clinging to the chain as it rose, still maintained his relative position in respect to the eight maskers, and still (as if nothing were the matter) continued to thrust his torch down towards them, as though endeavoring to discover who they were.

So thoroughly astonished were the whole company at this ascent, that a dead silence, of about a minute's duration, ensued. It was broken by just such a low, harsh, *grating* sound, as had before attracted the attention of the king and his councillors, when the former threw the wine in the face of Trippetta. But, on the present occasion, there could be no question as to *whence* the sound issued. It came from the fang-like teeth of the dwarf, who ground them and gnashed them as he foamed at the mouth, and glared, with an expression of maniacal rage, into the upturned countenances of the king and his seven companions.

"Ah, ha!" said at length the infuriated jester. "Ah, ha! I begin to see who these people *are*, now!" Here, pretending to scrutinize the king more closely, he held the flambeau to the flaxen coat which enveloped him, and which instantly burst into a sheet of vivid flame. In less than half a minute the whole eight ourang-outangs were blazing fiercely, amid the shrieks of the multitude who gazed at them from below, horror-stricken, and without the power to render them the slightest assistance.

At length the flames, suddenly increasing in virulence, forced the jester to climb higher up the chain, to be out of their reach; and, as he made this movement, the crowd again sank, for a brief instant, into silence. The dwarf seized his opportunity, and once more spoke:

"I now see *distinctly*," he said, "what manner of people these maskers are. They are a great king and his seven privy-council-lors—a king who does not scruple to strike a defenceless girl, and his seven councillors who abet him in the outrage. As for my-self, I am simply Hop-Frog, the jester—and *this is my last jest*."

Owing to the high combustibility of both the flax and the tar to which it adhered, the dwarf had scarcely made an end of his brief speech before the work of vengeance was complete. The eight corpses swung in their chains, a fetid, blackened, hideous, and indistinguishable mass. The cripple hurled his torch at them, clambered leisurely to the ceiling, and disappeared through the sky-light.

It is supposed that Trippetta, stationed on the roof of the sa-loon, had been the accomplice of her friend in his fiery revenge, and that, together, they effected their escape to their own country: for neither was seen again.

FOUR BEASTS IN ONE;

THE HOMO-CAMELEOPARD.

Chacun a ses vertus.

Crébillon's Xerxes.

ANTIOCHUS EPIPHANES is very generally looked upon as the Gog of the prophet Ezekiel. This honor is, however, more properly attributable to Cambyses, the son of Cyrus. And, indeed, the character of the Syrian monarch does by no means stand in need of any adventitious embellishment. His accession to the throne, or rather his usurpation of the sovereignty, a hundred and seventy-one years before the coming of Christ; his attempt to plunder the temple of Diana at Ephesus; his implacable hostility to the Jews; his pollution of the Holy of Holies; and his miserable death at Taba, after a tumultuous reign of eleven years, are circumstances of a prominent kind, and therefore more generally noticed by the historians of his time, than the impious, dastardly, cruel, silly and whimsical achievements which make up the sum total of his private life and reputation.

*   *   *   *   *   *   *   *   *

Let us suppose, gentle reader, that it is now the year of the world three thousand eight hundred and thirty, and let us, for a few minutes, imagine ourselves at that most grotesque habitation of man, the remarkable city of Antioch. To be sure there were, in Syria and other countries, sixteen cities of that appellation, besides the one to which I more particularly allude. But *ours* is that which went by the name of Antiochia Epidaphne, from its vicinity to the little village of Daphne, where stood a temple to that divinity. It was built (although about this matter there is some dispute) by Seleucus Nicanor, the first king of the country after Alexander the Great, in memory of his father Antiochus, and became immediately the residence of the Syrian monarchy. In the flourishing times of the Roman Empire, it was the ordinary station of the prefect of the eastern provinces; and many of the emperors of the queen city, (among whom may be mentioned especially, Verus and Valens,) spent here the greater part of their time. But I perceive we have arrived at the city itself. Let us ascend this battlement, and throw our eyes upon the town and neighboring country.

"What broad and rapid river is that which forces its way, with innumerable falls, through the mountainous wilderness, and finally through the wilderness of buildings?"

That is the Orontes, and it is the only water in sight, with the exception of the Mediterranean, which stretches like a broad mirror, about twelve miles off to the southward. Every one has seen the Mediterranean; but let me tell you, there are few who have had a peep at Antioch. By few, I mean, few who, like you and me, have had, at the same time, the advantages of a modern education. Therefore cease to regard that sea, and give your whole attention to the mass of houses that lie beneath us. You will remember that it is now the year of the world three thousand eight hundred and thirty. Were it later—for example, were it the year of our Lord eighteen hundred and forty-five, we should be deprived of this extraordinary spectacle. In the nineteenth century Antioch is—that is to say, Antioch *will be*—in a lamentable state of decay. It will have been, by that time, totally destroyed, at three different periods, by three successive earthquakes. Indeed, to say the truth, what little of its former self may then remain, will be found in so desolate and ruinous a state that the patriarch shall have removed his residence to Damascus. This is well. I see you profit by my advice, and are making the most of your time in inspecting the premises—in

> ————satisfying your eyes
> With the memorials and the things of fame
> That most renown this city.————

I beg pardon; I had forgotten that Shakspeare will not flourish for seventeen hundred and fifty years to come. But does not the appearance of Epidaphne justify me in calling it *grotesque?*

"It is well fortified; and in this respect is as much indebted to nature as to art."

Very true.

"There are a prodigious number of stately palaces."

There are.

"And the numerous temples, sumptuous and magnificent, may bear comparison with the most lauded of antiquity."

All this I must acknowledge. Still there is an infinity of mud huts, and abominable hovels. We cannot help perceiving abundance of filth in every kennel, and, were it not for the overpowering fumes of idolatrous incense, I have no doubt we should find a most intolerable stench. Did you ever behold streets so insufferably narrow, or houses so miraculously tall? What a gloom their shadows cast upon the ground! It is well the swinging lamps in those endless colonnades are kept burning throughout the day; we should otherwise have the darkness of Egypt in the time of her desolation.

"It is certainly a strange place! What is the meaning of yonder singular building? See! it towers above all others, and lies to the eastward of what I take to be the royal palace!"

That is the new Temple of the Sun, who is adored in Syria under the title of Elah Gabalah. Hereafter a very notorious Roman Emperor will institute this worship in Rome, and thence derive a cognomen, Heliogabalus. I dare say you would like to take a peep at the divinity of the temple. You need not look up at the heavens; his Sunship is not there—at least not the Sunship adored by the Syrians. *That* deity will be found in the interior of yonder building. He is worshipped under the figure of a large stone pillar terminating at the summit in a cone or *pyramid,* whereby is denoted Fire.

"Hark!—behold!—who *can* those ridiculous beings be, half naked, with their faces painted, shouting and gesticulating to the rabble?"

Some few are mountebanks. Others more particularly belong to the race of philosophers. The greatest portion, however—those especially who belabor the populace with clubs—are the principal courtiers of the palace, executing, as in duty bound, some laudable comicality of the king's.

"But what have we here? Heavens! the town is swarming with wild beasts! How terrible a spectacle!—how dangerous a peculiarity!"

Terrible, if you please; but not in the least degree dangerous. Each animal, if you will take the pains to observe, is following, very quietly, in the wake of its master. Some few, to be sure, are led with a rope about the neck, but these are chiefly the lesser or timid species. The lion, the tiger, and the leopard are entirely without restraint. They have been trained without difficulty to their present profession, and attend upon their respective owners in the capacity of *valets-de-chambre*. It is true, there are occasions when Nature asserts her violated dominion;—but then the devouring of a man-at-arms, or the throttling of a consecrated bull, is a circumstance of too little moment to be more than hinted at in Epidaphne.

"But what extraordinary tumult do I hear? Surely this is a loud noise even for Antioch! It argues some commotion of unusual interest."

Yes—undoubtedly. The king has ordered some novel spectacle—some gladiatorial exhibition at the Hippodrome—or perhaps the massacre of the Scythian prisoners—or the conflagration of his new palace—or the tearing down of a handsome temple—or, indeed, a bonfire of a few Jews. The uproar increases. Shouts of laughter ascend the skies. The air becomes dissonant with wind instruments, and horrible with the clamor of a million throats. Let us descend, for the love of fun, and see what is going on! This way—be careful! Here we are in the principal street, which is called the street of Timarchus. The sea of people is coming this way, and we shall find a difficulty in stemming the tide. They are pouring through the alley of Heraclides, which leads directly from the palace—therefore the king is most probably among the rioters. Yes—I hear the shouts of the herald proclaiming his approach in the pompous phraseology of the East. We shall have a glimpse of his person as he passes by the temple of Ashimah. Let us ensconce ourselves in the vestibule of the sanctuary; he will be here anon. In the meantime let us survey this image.

What is it ?   Oh, it is the god Ashimah in proper person.   You
perceive, however, that he is neither a lamb, nor a goat, nor a
satyr ; neither has he much resemblance to the Pan of the Arca-
dians.   Yet all these appearances have been given—I beg pardon—*will* be given—by the learned of future ages, to the Ashimah
of the Syrians.   Put on your spectacles, and tell me what it is.
What is it ?

"Bless me ! it is an ape !"

True—a baboon ; but by no means the less a deity.   His name
is a derivation of the Greek *Simia*—what great fools are antiqua-
rians !   But see !—see !—yonder scampers a ragged little urchin.
Where is he going ?   What is he bawling about ?   What does
he say ?   Oh ! he says the king is coming in triumph ; that he is
dressed in state ; that he has just finished putting to death, with
his own hand, a thousand chained Israelitish prisoners !   For this
exploit the ragamuffin is lauding him to the skies !   Hark ! here
comes a troop of a similar description.   They have made a Latin
hymn upon the valor of the king, and are singing it as they go :

> Mille, mille, mille,
> Mille, mille, mille,
> Decollavimus, unus homo !
> Mille, mille, mille, mille, decollavimus !
> Mille, mille, mille !
> Vivat qui mille mille occidit !
> Tantum vini habet nemo
> Quantum sanguinis effudit !*

Which may be thus paraphrased :

> A thousand, a thousand, a thousand,
> A thousand, a thousand, a thousand,
> We, with one warrior, have slain !
> A thousand, a thousand, a thousand, a thousand,
> Sing a thousand over again !
> Soho !—let us sing
> Long life to our king,
> Who knocked over a thousand so fine !

* Flavius Vospicus says, that the hymn here introduced, was sung by
the rabble upon the occasion of Aurelian, in the Sarmatic war, having slain
with his own hand, nine hundred and fifty of the enemy.

Soho !—let us roar,
He has given us more
Red gallons of gore
Than all Syria can furnish o   wine!

" Do you hear that flourish of trumpets ?"

Yes—the king is coming ! See ! the people are aghast with admiration, and lift up their eyes to the heavens in reverence! He comes !—he is coming !—there he is !

" Who ?—where ?—the king ?—I do not behold him ;—cannot say that I perceive him."

Then you must be blind.

" Very possible. Still I see nothing but a tumultuous mob of idiots and madmen, who are busy in prostrating themselves before a gigantic cameleopard, and endeavoring to obtain a kiss of the animal's hoofs. See ! the beast has very justly kicked one of the rabble over—and another—and another—and another. Indeed, I cannot help admiring the animal for the excellent use he is making of his feet."

Rabble, indeed !—why these are the noble and free citizens of Epidaphne ! Beast, did you say ?—take care that you are not overheard. Do you not perceive that the animal has the visage of a man ? Why, my dear sir, that cameleopard is no other than Antiochus Epiphanes—Antiochus the Illustrious, King of Syria, and the most potent of all the autocrats of the East ! It is true, that he is entitled, at times, Antiochus Epimanes—Antiochus the madman—but that is because all people have not the capacity to appreciate his merits. It is also certain that he is at present ensconced in the hide of a beast, and is doing his best to play the part of a cameleopard ; but this is done for the better sustaining his dignity as king. Besides, the monarch is of gigantic stature, and the dress is therefore neither unbecoming nor over large. We may, however, presume he would not have adopted it but for some occasion of especial state. Such, you will allow, is the massacre of a thousand Jews. With how superior a dignity the monarch perambulates on all fours ! His tail, you perceive, is held aloft by his two principal concubines, Elline and Argelais ; and his whole appearance would be infinitely prepossessing, were it not for the protruberance of his eyes, which will certainly start out of his head, and the queer color of his face, which has become non-descript from the quantity of wine he has swallowed. Let us follow him to the hippodrome, whither he is proceeding, and listen to the song of triumph which he is commencing:

> Who is king but Epiphanes!
> Say—do you know!
> Who is king but Epiphanes!
> Bravo!—bravo!
> There is none but Epiphanes,
> No—there is none:
> So tear down the temples,
> And put out the sun!

Well and strenuously sung! The populace are hailing him "Prince of Poets," as well as "Glory of the East," "Delight of the Universe," and "most remarkable of Cameleopards." They have *encored* his effusion, and—do you hear?—he is singing it over again. When he arrives at the hippodrome, he will be crowned with the poetic wreath, in anticipation of his victory at the approaching Olympics.

"But, good Jupiter! what is the matter in the crowd behind us?"

Behind us, did you say?—oh! ah!—I perceive. My friend, it is well that you spoke in time. Let us get into a place of safety as soon as possible. Here!—let us conceal ourselves in the arch of this aqueduct, and I will inform you presently of the origin of the commotion. It has turned out as I have been anticipating. The singular appearance of the cameleopard with the head of a man, has, it seems, given offence to the notions of propriety entertained in general, by the wild animals domesticated in the city. A mutiny has been the result; and, as is usual upon such occasions, all human efforts will be of no avail in quelling the mob. Several of the Syrians have already been devoured; but the general voice of the four-footed patriots seems to be for eating up the cameleopard. "The Prince of Poets," therefore, is upon his hinder .gs, running for his life. His courtiers have have left him in the urch, and his concubines have followed so excellent an example. "Delight of the Universe," thou art in a sad predicament! "Glory of the East," thou art in danger of mastication! There-

21*

fore never regard so piteously thy tail; it will undoubtedly be
draggled in the mud, and for this there is no help. Look not
behind thee, then, at its unavoidable degradation; but take
courage, ply thy legs with vigor, and scud for the hippodrome!
Remember that thou art Antiochus Epiphanes. Antiochus the
Illustrious!—also "Prince of Poets," "Glory of the East," "Delight of the Universe," and "most Remarkable of Cameleopards!"
Heavens! what a power of speed thou art displaying! What a
capacity for leg-bail thou art developing! Run, Prince!—Bravo,
Epiphanes!—Well done, Cameleopard!—Glorious Antiochus!
He runs!—he leaps!—he flies! Like an arrow from a catapult
he approaches the hippodrome! He leaps!—he shrieks!—he is
there! This is well; for hadst thou, "Glory of the East," been
half a second longer in reaching the gates of the Amphitheatre,
there is not a bear's cub in Epidaphne that would not have had a
nibble at thy carcass. Let us be off—let us take our departure!—
for we shall find our delicate modern ears unable to endure the
vast uproar which is about to commence in celebration of the
king's escape! Listen! it has already commenced. See!—the
whole town is topsy-turvy.

"Surely this is the most populous city of the East! What a
wilderness of people! what a jumble of all ranks and ages! what
a multiplicity of sects and nations! what a variety of costumes!
what a Babel of languages! what a screaming of beasts! what a
tinkling of instruments! what a parcel of philosophers!"

Come let us be off!

"Stay a moment! I see a vast hubbub in the hippodrome;
what is the meaning of it I beseech you!"

"That?—oh nothing! The noble and free citizens of Epidaphne being, as they declare, well satisfied of the faith, valor,
wisdom, and divinity of their king, and having, moreover, been
eye-witnesses of his late superhuman agility, do think it no more
than their duty to invest his brows (in addition to the poetic
crown) with the wreath of victory in the foot-race—a wreath which
it is evident he *must* obtain at the celebration of the next Olympiad, and which, therefore, they now give him in advance.

WHY THE LITTLE FRENCHMAN

WEARS HIS HAND IN A SLING.

IT's on my wisiting cards sure enough (and it's them that's all o' pink satin paper) that inny gintleman that plases may behould the intheristhin words, " Sir Pathrick O'Grandison, Barronitt, 39 Southampton Row, Russell Square, Parrish o' Bloomsbury." And shud ye be wantin to diskiver who is the pink of purliteness quite, and the laider of the hot tun in the houl city o' Lonon—why it's jist mesilf. And fait that same is no wonder at all at all, (so be plased to stop curlin your nose,) for every inch o' the six wakes that I've been a gintleman, and left aff wid the bog-throthing to take up wid the Barronissy, i'ts Pathrick that's been living like a houly imperor, and gitting the iddication and the graces. Och ! and would'nt it be a blessed thing for your sperrits if ye cud lay your two peepers jist, upon Sir Pathrick O'Grandison, Barronitt, when he is all riddy drissed for the hopperer, or stipping into the Brisky for the drive into the Hyde Park.—But it's the iligant big figgur that I ave, for the rason o' which all the ladies fall in love wid me. Isn't it my own swate silf now that'll missure the six fut, and the three inches more nor that, in me stockings, and that am excadingly will proportioned all over to match? And is it ralelly more than the three fut and a bit that there is, inny how, of the little ould furrener Frinchman that lives jist over the way, and that's a oggling and a goggling the houl day, (and bad luck to him,) at the purty widdy Misthress Tracle that's my own nixt do r neighbor, (God bliss her) and a most particuller frind and acquaintance! You percave the little spalpeen is summat down in the mouth, and wears his lift hand in a sling; and it's for that same thing, by yur lave, that I'm going to give you the good rason.

The truth of the houl matter is jist simple enough; for the very first day that I com'd from Connaught, and showd my swate little silf in the strait to the widdy, who was looking through the windy, it was a gone case althegither wid the heart o' the purty Misthress Tracle. I percaved it, ye see, all at once, and no mistake, and that's God's thruth. First of all it was up wid the windy in a jiffy, and thin she threw open her two peepers to the itmost, and thin it was a little gould spy-glass that she clapped tight to one o' them, and divil may burn me if it did'nt spake to me as plain as a peeper cud spake, and says it, through the spy-glass, "Och! the tip o' the mornin to ye, Sir Pathrick O'Grandison, Barronitt, mavourneen; and it's a nate gintleman that ye are, sure enough, and it's mesilf and me forten jist that'll be at yur sarvice, dear, inny time o' day at all at all for the asking." And it's not mesilf ye wud have to be bate in the purliteness; so I made her a bow that wud ha broken yur heart althegither to behould, and thin I pulled aff me hat with a flourish, and thin I winked at her hard wid both eyes, as much as to say, "Thrue for you, yer a swate little crature, Mrs. Tracle, me darlint, and I wish I may be drownthed dead in a bog, if it's not mesilf, Sir Pathrick O'Grandison, Barronitt, that'll make a houl bushel o' love to yur leddy-ship, in the twinkling o' the eye of a Londonderry purraty."

And it was the nixt mornin, sure, jist as I was making up me mind whither it wouldn't be the purlite thing to sind a bit o' writin to the widdy by way of a love-litter, when up cum'd the delivery sarvant wid an illigant card, and he tould me that the name on it (for I niver cud rade the copper-plate printin on account of being lift handed) was all about Mounseer, the Count, A Goose, Look-aisy, Maiter-di-dauns, and that the houl of the divilish lingo was the spalpeeny long name of the little ould furrener Frinchman as lived over the way.

And jist wid that in cum'd the little willian himself, and thin he made me a broth of a bow, and thin he said he had ounly taken the liberty of doing me the honor of the giving me a call, and thin he went on to palaver at a great rate, and divil the bit did I comprehind what he wud be afther the tilling me at all at all, excipting and saving that he said "pully wou, woolly wou," and tould me, among a bushel o' lies, bad luck to him, that he was mad for the love o' my widdy Misthress Tracle, and that my widdy Mrs. Tracle had a puncheon for *him*.

At the hearin of this, ye may swear, though, 1 was as mad as a grasshopper, but I remimbered that I was Sir Pathrick O'Grandison, Barronitt, and that it wasn't althegither gentaal to lit the anger git the upper hand o' the purliteness, so I made light o' the matter and kipt dark, and got quite sociable wid the little chap, and afther a while what did he do but ask me to go wid him to the widdy's, saying he wud give me the feshionable inthroduction to her leddyship.

"Is it there ye are?" said I thin to mesilf, "and it's thrue for you, Pathrick, that ye're the fortunnittest mortal in life. We'll soon see now whither its your swate silf, or whither its little Mounseer Maiter-di-dauns, that Misthress Tracle is head and ears in the love wid."

Wid that we wint aff to the widdy's, next door, and ye may well say it was an illigant place; so it was. There was a carpet all over the floor, and in one corner there was a forty-pinny and a jews-harp and the divil knows what ilse, and in another corner was a sofy, the beautifullest thing in all natur, and sitting on the sofy, sure enough, there was the swate little angel, Misthress Tracle.

"The tip o' the morning to ye," says I, "Mrs. Tracle," and thin I made sich an iligant obaysance that it wud ha quite althegither bewildered the brain o' ye.

"Wully woo, pully woo, plump in the mud," says the little furrenner Frinchman, "and sure Mrs. Tracle," says he, that he did, "isn't this gintleman here jist his reverence Sir Pathrick O'Grandison, Barronitt, and isn't he althegither and entirely the most purticular frind and acquintance that I have in the houl world?"

And wid that the widdy, she gits up from the sofy, and makes the swatest curtchy nor iver was seen; and thin down she sits like an angel; and thin, by the powers, it was that little spalpeen Mounseer Maiter-di-dauns that plumped his silf right down by the

right side of her. Och hon! I ixpicted the two eyes o' me wud
ha cum'd out of my head on the spot, I was so dispirate mad!
Howiver, "Bait who!" says I, after a while. "Is it there ye are,
Mounseer Maiter-di-dauns?" and so down I plumped on the lift
side of her leddyship, to be aven wid the willain. Botheration! it
wud ha done your heart good to percave the illigant double wink
that I gived her jist thin right in the face wid both eyes.

But the little ould Frinchman he niver beginned to suspict me
at all at all, and disperate hard it was he made the love to her
leddyship. "Wouily wou," says he, "Pully wou," says he,
"Plump in the mud," says he.

"That's all to no use, Mounseer Frog, mavourneen," thinks I;
and I talked as hard and as fast as I could all the while, and throth
it was mesilf jist that divarted her leddyship complately and intirely, by rason of the illigant conversation that I kipt up wid her
all about the dear bogs of Connaught. And by and by she gived
me such a swate smile, from one ind of her mouth to the ither,
that it made me as bould as a pig, and I jist took hould of the ind
of her little finger in the most dillikittest manner in natur, looking
at her all the while out o' the whites of my eyes.

And then ounly percave the cuteness of the swate angel, for no
sooner did she obsarve that I was afther the squazing of her flipper,
than she up wid it in a jiffy, and put it away behind her back, jist
as much as to say, "Now thin, Sir Pathrick O'Grandison, there's
a bitther chance for ye, mavourneen, for its not altogether the gentaal thing to be afther the squazing of my flipper right full in the
sight of that little furrenner Frinchman, Mounseer Maiter-di-dauns."

Wid that I giv'd her a big wink jist to say, "lit Sir Pathrick
alone for the likes o' them thricks," and thin I wint aisy to work,
and you'd have died wid the divarsion to behould how cliverly I
slipped my right arm betwane the back o' the sofy, and the back
of her leddyship, and there, sure enough, I found a swate little
flipper all a waiting to say, "the tip o' the mornin to ye, Sir Pathrick O'Grandison, Barronitt." And wasn't it mesilf, sure, that jist
giv'd it the laste little bit of a squaze in the world, all in the way
of a commincement, and not to be too rough wid her leddyship?
and och, botheration, wasn't it the gentaalest and dilikittest of all
the little squazes that I got in return? "Blood and thunder, Sir

Pathrick, mavoureen," thinks I to myself, " fait it's jist the mother's son of you, and nobody else at all at all, that's the handsomest and the fortunittest young bogthrotter that ever cum'd out of Connaught !" And wid that I giv'd the flipper a big squaze, and a big squaze it was, by the powers, that her leddyship giv'd to me back. But it would ha split the seven sides of you wid the laffin to behould, jist then all at once, the consated behavior of Mounseer Maiter-di-dauns. The likes o' sich a jabbering, and a smirking, and a parly-wouing as he begin'd wid her leddyship, niver was known before upon arth ; and divil may burn me if it wasn't me own very two peepers that cotch'd him tipping her the wink out of one eye. Och hon ? if it wasn't mesilf thin that was mad as a Kilkenny cat I shud like to be tould who it was !

"Let me infarm you, Mounseer Maiter-di-dauns," said I, as purlite as iver ye seed, "that it's not the gintaal thing at all at all, and not for the likes o' you inny how, to be afther the oggling and a goggling at her leddyship in that fashion," and jist wid that such another squaze as it was I giv'd her flipper, all as much as to say, "isn't it Sir Pathrick now, my jewel, that'll be able to the protecting o' you, my darlint?" and then there cum'd another squaze back, all by way of the answer. "Thrue for you, Sir Pathrick," it said as plain as iver a squaze said in the world, "Thrue for you, Sir Pathrick, mavourneen, and it's a proper nate gintleman ye are—that God's truth," and wid that she opened her two beautiful peepers till I belaved they wud ha com'd out of her hid althegither and intirely, and she looked first as mad as a cat at Mounseer Frog, and thin as smiling as all out o' doors at mesilf.

"Thin," says he, the willian, "Och hon ! and a wolly-wou, pully-wou," and then wid that he shoved up his two shoulders till the divil the bit of his hid was to be diskivered, and then he let down the two corners of his purraty-trap, and thin not a haporth more of the satisfaction could I git out o' the spalpeen.

Belave me, my jewel, it was Sir Pathrick that was unrasonable mad thin, and the more by token that the Frinchman kept an wid his winking at the widdy ; and the widdy she kipt an wid the squazing of my flipper, as much as to say, "At him again Sir Pathrick O'Grandison, mavourneen ;" so I just ripped out wid a big oath, and says I,

"Ye little spalpeeny frog of a bog-throtting son of a bloody-noun!"—and jist thin what d'ye think it was that her leddyship did? Troth she jumped up from the sofy as if she was bit, and made off through the door, while I turned my head round afther her, in a complete bewilderment and botheration, and followed her wid me two peepers. You percave I had a reason of my own for knowing that she could'nt git down the stares althegither and entirely; for I knew very well that I had hould of her hand, for divil the bit had I iver lit it go. And says I,

"Isn't it the laste little bit of a mistake in the world that ye've been afther the making, yer leddyship? Come back now, that's a darlint, and I'll give ye yur flipper." But aff she wint down the stairs like a shot, and then I turned round to the little Frinch furrenner. Och hon! if it wasn't his spalpeeny little paw that I had hould of in my own—why thin—thin it was'nt—that's all.

"And maybe it wasn't mesilf that jist died then outright wid the laffin, to behould the little chap when he found out that it wasn't the widdy at all at all that he had hould of all the time, but only Sir Pathrick O'Grandison. The ould divil himself niver behild sich a long face as he pet an! As for Sir Pathrick O'Grandison, Barronitt, it wasn't for the likes of his riverence to be afther the minding of a thrifle of a mistake. Ye may jist say, though (for it's God's thruth) that afore I lift hould of the flipper of the spalpeen, (which was not till afther her leddyship's futmen had kicked us both down the stairs,) I gived it such a nate little broth of a squaze, as made it all up into raspberry jam.

"Wouly-wou," says he, "pully-wou," says he —Cot tam!"

And that's jist the thruth of the rason why he wears his left hand in a sling.

BON·BON.

Quand un bon vin meuble mon estomac,
Je suis plus savant que Balzac—
Plus sage que Pibrac;
Mon bras seul faisant l'attaque
De la nation Cossaque,
La mettroit au sac;
De Charon Je passerois le lac
En dormant dans son bac;
J'irois au fier Eac,
Sans que mon cœur fit tic ni tac,
Presenter du tabac.

French Vaudeville.

THAT Pierre Bon-Bon was a *restaurateur* of uncommon quali-
fications, no man who, during the reign of ——, frequented the
little Câfé in the cul-de-sac Le Febvre at Rouen, will, I imagine,
feel himself at liberty to dispute. That Pierre Bon-Bon was, in
an equal degree, skilled in the philosophy of that period is, I presume, still more especially undeniable. His *patés à la fois* were
beyond doubt immaculate; but what pen can do justice to his
essays *sur la Nature*—his thoughts *sur l'Ame*—his observations
sur l'Esprit? If his *omelettes*—if his *fricandeaux* were inestimable, what *littérateur* of that day would not have given twice as
much for an *Idée de Bon-Bon*" as for all the trash of all the
"*Idées*" of all the rest of the *savants?* Bon-Bon had ransacked
libraries which no other man had ransacked—had read more than
any other would have entertained a notion of reading—had understood more than any other would have conceived the possibility
of understanding; and although, while he flourished, there were

not wanting some authors at Rouen to assert "that his *dicta*
evinced neither the purity of the Academy, nor the depth of the
Lyceum"—although, mark me, his doctrines were by no means
very generally comprehended, still it did not follow that they were
difficult of comprehension.   It was, I think, on account of their
self-evidency that many persons were led to consider them abstruse.   It is to Bon-Bon—but let this go no farther—it is to
Bon-Bon that Kant himself is mainly indebted for his metaphysics.
The former was indeed not a Platonist, nor strictly speaking an
Aristotelian—nor did he, like the modern Leibnitz, waste those
precious hours which might be employed in the invention of a
fricasée, or, *facili gradú*, the analysis of a sensation, in frivolous
attempts at reconciling the obstinate oils and waters of ethical discussion.   Not at all.   Bon-Bon was Ionic—Bon-Bon was equally
Italic.   He reasoned *à priori*—He reasoned also *à posteriori.*
His ideas were innate—or otherwise.   He believed in George of
Trebizond—He believed in Bossarion.   Bon-Bon was emphatically a—Bon-Bonist.

I have spoken of the philosopher in his capacity of *restaurateur.*   I would not, however, have any friend of mine imagine
that, in fulfilling his hereditary duties in that line, our hero wanted
a proper estimation of their dignity and importance.   Far from it.
It was impossible to say in which branch of his profession he took
the greater pride.   In his opinion the powers of the intellect held
intimate connection with the capabilities of the stomach.   I am
not sure, indeed, that he greatly disagreed with the Chinese, who
hold that the soul lies in the abdomen.   The Greeks at all events
were right, he thought, who employed the same word for the mind
and the diaphragm.*   By this I do not mean to insinuate a charge
of gluttony, or indeed any other serious charge to the prejudice
of the metaphysician.   If Pierre Bon-Bon had his failings—and
what great man has not a thousand?—if Pierre Bon-Bon, I say,
had his failings, they were failings of very little importance—faults
indeed which, in other tempers, have often been looked upon rather
in the light of virtues.   As regards one of these foibles, I should
not even have mentioned it in this history but for the remarkable

* φρενίς.

prominency—the extreme *alto relievo*—in which it jutted out from the plane of his general disposition.—He could never let slip an opportunity of making a bargain.

Not that he was avaricious—no. It was by no means necessary to the satisfaction of the philosopher, that the bargain should be to his own proper advantage. Provided a trade could be effected—a trade of any kind, upon any terms, or under any circumstances—a triumphant smile was seen for many days thereafter to enlighten his countenance, and a knowing wink of the eye to give evidence of his sagacity.

At any epoch it would not be very wonderful if a humor so peculiar as the one I have just mentioned, should elicit attention and remark. At the epoch of our narrative, had this peculiarity *not* attracted observation, there would have been room for wonder indeed. It was soon reported that, upon all occasions of the kind, the smile of Bon-Bon was wont to differ widely from the downright grin with which he would laugh at his own jokes, or welcome an acquaintance. Hints were thrown out of an exciting nature; stories were told of perilous bargains made in a hurry and repented of at leisure; and instances were adduced of unaccountable capacities, vague longings, and unnatural inclinations implanted by the author of all evil for wise purposes of his own.

The philosopher had other weaknesses—but they are scarcely worthy our serious examination. For example, there are few men of extraordinary profundity who are found wanting in an inclination for the bottle. Whether this inclination be an exciting cause, or rather a valid proof, of such profundity, it is a nice thing to say. Bon-Bon, as far as I can learn, did not think the subject adapted to minute investigation;—nor do I. Yet in the indulgence of a propensity so truly classical, it is not to be supposed that the *restaurateur* would lose sight of that intuitive discrimination which was wont to characterize, at one and the same time, his *essais* and his *omelettes*. In his seclusions the Vin de Bourgogne had its allotted hour, and there were appropriate moments for the Côtes du Rhone. With him Sauterne was to Medoc what Catullus was to Homer. He would sport with a syllogism in sipping St. Peray, but unravel an argument over Clos de Vougeot, and upset a theory in a torrent of Chambertin. Well had it been if the same quick sense of propriety had attended him in the peddling propensity to which I have formerly alluded—but this was by no means the case. Indeed, to say the truth, *that* trait of mind in the philosophic Bon-Bon *did* begin at length to assume a character of strange intensity and mysticism, and appeared deeply tinctured with the *diablerie* of his favorite German studies.

To enter the little *Café* in the *Cul-de-Sac* Le Febre was, at the period of our tale, to enter the *sanctum* of a man of genius. Bon-Bon was a man of genius. There was not a *sous-cuisinier* in Rouen, who could not have told you that Bon-Bon was a man of genius. His very cat knew it, and forebore to whisk her tail in the presence of the man of genius. His large water-dog was acquainted with the fact, and upon the approach of his master, betrayed his sense of inferiority by a sanctity of deportment, a debasement of the ears, and a dropping of the lower jaw not altogether unworthy of a dog. It is, however, true that much of this habitual respect might have been attributed to the personal appearance of the metaphysician. A distinguished exterior will, I am constrained to say, have its weight even with a beast; and I am willing to allow much in the outward man of the *restaurateur* calculated to impress the imagination of the quadruped. There is a peculiar majesty about the atmosphere of the little great—if I may be permitted so equivocal an expression—which mere physical bulk alone will be found at all times inefficient in creating. If, however, Bon-Bon was barely three feet in height, and if his head was diminutively small, still it was impossible to behold the rotundity of his stomach without a sense of magnificence nearly bordering upon the sublime. In its size both dogs and men must have seen a type of his acquirements—in its immensity a fitting habitation for his immortal soul.

I might here—if it so pleased me—dilate upon the matter of habiliment, and other mere circumstances of the external metaphysician. I might hint that the hair of our hero was worn short, combed smoothly over his forehead, and surmounted by a conical-shaped white flannel cap and tassels—that his pea-green jerkin was not after the fashion of those worn by the common class of *restaurateurs* at that day—that the sleeves were something fuller than the reigning costume permitted—that the cuffs were turned up, not as usual in that barbarous peri. .1, with cloth of the same quality and color as the garment, but faced in a more fanciful manner with the particolored velvet of Genoa—that his slippers were of a bright purple, curiously filagreed, and might have been manufactured in Japan, but for the exquisite pointing of the toes, and the brilliant tints of the binding and embroidery—that his breeches were of the yellow satin-like material called *aimable*—that his sky-blue cloak, resembling in form a dressing-wrapper, and richly bestudded all over with crimson devices, floated cavalierly upon his shoulders like a mist of the morning—and that his *tout ensemble* gave rise to the remarkable words of Benevenuta, the Improvisatrice of Florence, " that it was difficult to say whether Pierre Bon-Bon was indeed a bird of Paradise, or the rather a very Paradise of perfection."—I might, I say, expatiate upon all these points if I pleased ;—but I forbear:—merely personal details may be left to historical novelists ;—they are beneath the moral dignity of matter-of-fact.

I have said that " to enter the *Côfé* in the *Cul-de-Sac* Le Febvre was to enter the *sanctum* of a man of genius"—but then it was only the man of genius who could duly estimate the merits of the *sanctum*. A sign, consisting of a vast folio, swung before the entrance. On one side of the volume was painted a bottle; on the reverse a *pate.* On the back were visible in large letters *Œuvres de Bon-Bon.* Thus was delicately shadowed forth the two-fold occupation of the proprietor.

Upon stepping over the threshold, the whole interior of the building presented itself to view. A long, low-pitched room, of antique construction, was indeed all the accommodation afforded by the *Cafe.* In a corner of the apartment stood the bed of the metaphysician. An array of curtains, together with a canopy *à la Greque*, gave it an air at once classic and comfortable. In the corner diagonally opposite, appeared, in direct family communion, the properties of the kitchen and the *bibliotheque.* A dish of polemics stood peacefully upon the dresser. Here lay an oven-full of the latest ethics—there a kettle of duodecimo *melanges.* Volumes of German morality were hand and glove with the gridiron—a toasting fork might be discovered by the side of Eusebius—Plato reclined at his ease in the frying pan—and contemporary manuscripts were filed away upon the spit.

In other respects the *Càfe de Bon-Bon* might be said to differ little from the usual *restaurants* of the period. A large fire-place yawned opposite the door. On the right of the fire-place an open cupboard displayed a formidable array of labelled bottles.

It was here, about twelve o'clock one night, during the severe winter of ——, that Pierre Bon-Bon, after having listened for some time to the comments of his neighbors upon his singular propensity—that Pierre Bon-Bon, I say, having turned them all out of his house, locked the door upon them with an oath, and betook himself in no very pacific mood to the comforts of a leather-bottomed arm-chair, and a fire of blazing faggots.

It was one of those terrific nights which are only met with once or twice during a century. It snowed fiercely, and the house tottered to its centre with the floods of wind that, rushing through the crannies of the wall, and pouring impetuously down the chimney, shook awfully the curtains of the philosopher's bed, and disorganized the economy of his patépans and papers. The huge folio sign that swung without, exposed to the fury of the tempest, creaked ominously, and gave out a moaning sound from its stanchions of solid oak.

It was in no placid temper, I say, that the metaphysician drew up his chair to its customary station by the hearth. Many circumstances of a perplexing nature had occurred during the day, to disturb the serenity of his meditations. In attempting *des œufs à la Princesse*, he had unfortunately perpetrated an *omelete à la Reine ;* the discovery of a principle in ethics had been frustrated by the overturning of a stew ; and last, not least, he had been thwarted in one of those admirable bargains which he at all times took such especial delight in bringing to a successful termination. But in the chafing of his mind at these unaccountable vicissitudes, there did not fail to be mingled some degree of that nervous anxiety which the fury of a boisterous night is so well calculated to produce. Whistling to his more immediate vicinity the large black water-dog we have spoken of before, and settling himself uneasily in his chair, he could not help casting a wary and unquiet eye towards those distant recesses of the apartment whose inexorable shadows not even the red fire-light itself could more than partially succeed in overcoming. Having completed a scrutiny whose exact purpose was perhaps unintelligible to himself, he drew close to his seat a small table covered with books and papers, and soon became absorbed in the task of re-touching a voluminous manuscript, intended for publication on the morrow.

He had been thus occupied for some minutes, when "I am in no hurry, Monsieur Bon-Bon," suddenly whispered a whining voice in the apartment.

"The devil !" ejaculated our hero, starting to his feet, overturning the table at his side, and staring around him in astonishment.

"Very true," calmly replied the voice.

"Very true !—what is very true ?—how came you here ?" vociferated the metaphysician, as his eye fell upon something which lay stretched at full-length upon the bed.

"I was saying," said the intruder, without attending to the interrogatories, " I was saying, that I am not at all pushed for time— that the business upon which I took the liberty of calling, is of no pressing importance—in short, that I can very well wait until you have finished your Exposition."

"My Exposition !—there now !—how do *you* know !—how came *you* to understand that I was writing an Exposition—good God !"

"Hush !" replied the figure, in a shrill under tone ; and, arising quickly from the bed, he made a single step towards our hero, while an iron lamp that depended overhead swung convulsively back from his approach.

The philosopher's amazement did not prevent a narrow scrutiny of the stranger's dress and appearance. The outlines of his figure, exceedingly lean, but much above the common height, were rendered minutely distinct by means of a faded suit of black cloth which fitted tight to the skin, but was otherwise cut very much in the style of a century ago. These garments had evidently been intended for a much shorter person than their present owner. His ankles and wrists were left naked for several inches. In his shoes, however, a pair of very brilliant buckles gave the lie to the extreme poverty implied by the other portions of his dress. His head was bare, and entirely bald, with the exception of the hinder-part, from which depended a *queue* of considerable length. A pair of green spectacles, with side glasses, protected his eyes from the influence of the light, and at the same time prevented our hero from ascertaining either their color or their conformation. About the entire person there was no evidence of a shirt; but a white cravat, of filthy appearance, was tied with extreme precision around the throat, and the ends, hanging down formally side by side, gave (although I dare say unintentionally) the idea of an ecclesiastic. Indeed, many other points both in his appearance and demeanor might have very well sustained a conception of that nature. Over his left ear, he carried, after the fashion of a modern clerk, an instrument resembling the *stylus* of the ancients. In a breast-pocket of his coat appeared conspicuously a small black volume fastened with clasps of steel. This book, whether accidentally or not, was so turned outwardly from the person as to discover the words "*Rituel Catholique*" in white letters upon the back. His entire physiognomy was interestingly saturnine—even cadaverously pale. The forehead was lofty, and deeply furrowed with the ridges of contemplation. The corners of the mouth were drawn down into an expression of the most submissive humility. There was also a clasping of the hands, as he stepped towards our hero— a deep sigh—and altogether a look of such utter sanctity as could not have failed to be unequivocally prepossessing. Every shadow of anger faded from the countenance of the metaphysician, as, having completed a satisfactory survey of his visiter's person, he shook him cordially by the hand, and conducted him to a seat.

There would however be a radical error in attributing this instantaneous transition of feeling in the philosopher, to any one of those causes which might naturally be supposed to have had an influence. Indeed, Pierre Bon-Bon, from what I have been able to understand of his disposition, was of all men the least likely to be imposed upon by any speciousness of exterior deportment. It was impossible that so accurate an observer of men and things should have failed to discover, upon the moment, the real character of the personage who had thus intruded upon his hospitality. To say no more, the conformation of his visiter's feet was sufficiently remarkable—he maintained lightly upon his head an inordinately

tall hat—there was a tremulous swelling about the hinder part
of his breeches—and the vibration of his coat tail was a palpable
fact.   Judge, then, with what feelings of satisfaction our hero found
himself thrown thus at once into the society of a person for whom
he had at all times entertained the most unqualified respect.   He
was, however, too much of the diplomatist to let escape him any
intimation of his suspicions in regard to the true state of affairs.
It was not his cue to appear at all conscious of the high honor
he thus unexpectedly enjoyed ; but, by leading his guest into conversation, to elicit some important ethical ideas, which might, in
obtaining a place in his contemplated publication, enlighten the
human race, and at the same time immortalize himself—ideas
which, I should have added, his visiter's great age, and well-known
proficiency in the science of morals, might very well have enabled
him to afford.

Actuated by these enlightened views, our hero bade the gentleman sit down, while he himself took occasion to throw some faggots upon the fire, and place upon the now re-established table
some bottles of *Mousseux.*   Having quickly completed these operations, he drew his chair *vis-à-vis* to his companion's, and waited
until the latter should open the conversation.   But, plans even the
most skilfully matured, are often thwarted in the outset of their
application—and the *restaurateur* found himself *nonplussed* by the
very first words of his visiter's speech.

"I see you know me, Bon-Bon," said he : "ha! ha! ha!—
he! he! he!—hi! hi! hi!—ho! ho! ho!—hu! hu! hu!"—and the
devil, dropping at once the sanctity of his demeanor, opened to
its fullest extent a mouth from ear to ear, so as to display a set of
jagged and fang-like teeth, and throwing back his head, laughed
long, loudly, wickedly, and uproariously, while the black dog,
crouching down upon his haunches, joined lustily in the chorus,
and the tabby cat, flying off at a tangent, stood up on end, and
shrieked in the farthest corner of the apartment.

Not so the philosopher : he was too much a man of the world
either to laugh like the dog, or by shrieks to betray the indecorous
trepidation of the cat.   It must be confessed, he felt a little astou-
ishment to see the white letters which formed the words *"Rituel
Catholique"* on the book in his guest's pocket, momently chang-

ing both their color and their import, and in a few seconds, in place of the original title, the words "*Régitre des Condamnés*" blaze forth in characters of red. This startling circumstance, when Bon-Bon replied to his visiter's remark, imparted to his manner an air of embarrassment which probably might not otherwise have been observed.

"Why, sir," said the philosopher, "why, sir, to speak sincere-ly—I believe you are—upon my word—the d——dest—that is to say, I think—I imagine—I *have* some faint—some *very* faint idea—of the remarkable honor——"

"Oh!—ah!—yes!—very well!" interrupted his Majesty; "say no more—I see how it is." And hereupon, taking off his green spectacles, he wiped the glasses carefully with the sleeve of his coat, and deposited them in his pocket.

If Bon-Bon had been astonished at the incident of the book, his amazement was now much increased by the spectacle which here presented itself to view. In raising his eyes, with a strong feeling of curiosity to ascertain the color of his guest's, he found them by no means black, as he had anticipated—nor gray, as might have been imagined—nor yet hazel nor blue—nor indeed yellow nor red—nor purple—nor white—nor green—nor any other color in the heavens above, or in the earth beneath, or in the waters under the earth. In short, Pierre Bon-Bon not only saw plainly that his Majesty had no eyes whatsoever, but could dis-cover no indications of their having existed at any previous pe-riod—for the space where eyes should naturally have been, was, I am constrained to say, simply a dead level of flesh.

It was not in the nature of the metaphysician to forbear ma-king some inquiry into the sources of so strange a phenomenon; and the reply of his Majesty was at once prompt, dignified, and satisfactory.

"Eyes! my dear Bon-Bon—eyes! did you say?—oh!—ah!—I perceive! The ridiculous prints, eh, which are in circulation, have given you a false idea of my personal appearance! Eyes!—true. Eyes, Pierre Bon-Bon, are very well in their proper place—*that*, you would say, is the head?—right—the head of a worm. To *you* likewise these optics are indispensable—yet I will con-vince *you* that my visier is more penetrating than your own.

There is a cat I see in the corner—a pretty cat—look at her—
observe her well. Now, Bon-Bon, do you behold the thoughts—
the thoughts, I say—the ideas—the reflections—which are being
engendered in her pericranium? There it is, now—you do not!
She is thinking we admire the length of her tail and the profundity of her mind. She has just concluded that I am the most distinguished of ecclesiastics, and that you are the most superficial
of metaphysicians. Thus you see I am not altogether blind; but
to one of my profession, the eyes you speak of would be merely
an incumbrance, liable at any time to be put out by a toasting-
ron or a pitchfork. To you, I allow, these optical affairs are indispensable. Endeavor, Bon-Bon, to use them well;—*my* vision
is the soul."

Hereupon the guest helped himself to the wine upon the table,
and pouring out a bumper for Bon-Bon, requested him to drink it
without scruple, and make himself perfectly at home.

"A clever book that of yours, Pierre," resumed his Majesty,
tapping our friend knowingly upon the shoulder, as the latter put
down his glass after a thorough compliance with his visiter's injunction. "A clever book that of yours, upon my honor. It's
a work after my own heart. Your arrangement of the matter,
I think, however, might be improved, and many of your notions
remind me of Aristotle. That philosopher was one of my most
intimate acquaintances. I liked him as much for his terrible ill
temper, as for his happy knack at making a blunder. There is
only one solid truth in all that he has written, and for that I gave
him the hint out of pure compassion for his absurdity. I suppose, Pierre Bon-Bon, you very well know to what divine moral
truth I am alluding?"

"Cannot say that I——"

"Indeed!—why it was I who told Aristotle, that, by sneezing,
men expelled superfluous ideas through the proboscis."

"Which is—hiccup!—undoubtedly the case," said the metaphysician, while he poured out for himself another bumper of Mousseux, and offered his snuff-box to the fingers of his visiter.

"There was Plato, too," continued his Majesty, modestly declining the snuff-box and the compliment it implied—"there was
Plato, too, for whom I, at one time, felt all the affection of a friend

You knew Plato, Bon-Bon ?—ah, no, I beg a thousand pardons.
He met me at Athens, one day, in the Parthenon, and told me
he was distressed for an idea.   I bade him write down that ο νους
εστιν αυλος.   He said that he would do so, and went home, while
I stepped over to the pyramids.   But my conscience smote me
for having uttered a truth, even to aid a friend, and hastening
back to Athens, I arrived behind the philosopher's chair as he was
inditing the 'αυλος.'   Giving the lamma a fillip with my finger,
I turned it upside down.   So the sentence now reads 'ο νους εστιν
αυγος,' and is, you perceive, the fundamental doctrine in his metaphysics."

"Were you ever at Rome ?" asked the *restaurateur*, as he finished his second bottle of Mousseux, and drew from the closet
a larger supply of Chambertin.

"But once, Monsieur Bon-Bon, but once.   There was a time,"
said the devil, as if reciting some passage from a book—"there
was a time when occurred an anarchy of five years, during which
the republic, bereft of all its officers, had no magistracy besides
the tribunes of the people, and these were not legally vested with
any degree of executive power—at that time, Monsieur Bon-Bon—
at that time *only* I was in Rome, and I have no earthly acquaintance, consequently, with any of its philosophy." *

"What do you think of—what do you think of—hiccup !—
Epicurus ?"

"What do I think of *whom ?*" said the devil, in astonishment;
"you cannot surely mean to find any fault with Epicurus !   What
do I think of Epicurus !   Do you mean me, sir ?—*I* am Epicurus !
I am the same philosopher who wrote each of the three hundred
treatises commemorated by Diogenes Laertes."

"That's a lie !" said the metaphysician, for the wine had gotten
a little into his head.

"Very well !—very well, sir !—very well, indeed, sir !" said his
Majesty, apparently much flattered.

"That's a lie !" repeated the *restaurateur*, dogmatically, "that's
a—hiccup !— a lie !"

* Ils écrivaient sur la Philosophie, (*Cicero, Lucretius, Seneca*) mais c'était
la Philosophie Grecque.—*Condorcet.*

" Well, well, have it your own way !" said the devil, pacifically
and Bon-Bon, having beaten his Majesty at an argument, though
it his duty to conclude a second bottle of Chambertin.

"As I was saying," resumed the visiter, " as I was observing a
little while ago, there are some very *outre* notions in that book of
yours, Monsieur Bon-Bon.   What, for instance, do you mean by
all that humbug about the soul?   Pray, sir, what *is* the soul?"

"The—hiccup!—soul," replied the metaphysician, referring to
his MS., " is undoubtedly——."

" No, sir !"

" Indubitably——"

" No, sir !"

" Indisputably——"

" No, sir !"

" Evidently——"

" No, sir !"

" Incontrovertibly——"

" No, sir !"

" Hiccup !——"

" No, sir !"

"And beyond all question, a——."

" No, sir, the soul is no such thing !"   (Here, the philosopher
looking daggers, took occasion to make an end, upon the spot,
of his third bottle of Chambertin.)

" Then—hiccup !—pray, sir—what—what is it ?"

" That is neither here nor there, Monsieur Bon-Bon," replied
his Majesty, musingly.   " I have tasted—that is to say, I have
known some very bad souls, and some too—pretty good ones."
Here he smacked his lips, and, having unconsciously let fall his
hand upon the volume in his pocket, was seized with a violent fit
of sneezing.

He continued :

"There was the soul of Cratinus—passable : Aristophanes—
racy : Plato—exquisite—not *your* Plato, but Plato the comic
poet : your Plato would have turned the stomach of Cerberus—
faugh !   Then let me see ! there were Nœvius, and Andronicus,
and Plautus, and Terentius.   Then there were Lucilius, and Catullus, and Naso, and Quintius Flaccus,—dear Quinty ! as I called

him when he sung a *seculare* for my amusement, while I toasted
him, in pure good humor, on a fork. But they want *flavor* these
Romans One fat Greek is worth a dozen of them, and besides
will *keep*, which cannot be said of a Quirite.—Let us taste your
Sauterne."

Bon-Bon had by this time made up his mind to the *nil admi-
rari*, and endeavored to hand down the bottles in question. He
was, however, conscious of a strange sound in the room like the
wagging of a tail. Of this, although extremely indecent in his
Majesty, the philosopher took no notice :—simply kicking the dog,
and requesting him to be quiet. The visiter continued :

" I found that Horace tasted very much like Aristotle ;—you
know I am fond of variety. Terentius I could not have told from
Menander. Naso, to my astonishment, was Nicander in disguise.
Virgilius had a strong twang of Theocritus. Martial put me much
in mind of Archilochus—and Titus Livius was positively Polybius
and none other."

" Hiccup !" here replied Bon-Bon, and his Majesty proceeded :

" But if I *have* a *penchant*, Monsieur Bon-Bon—if I *have* a *penchant*, it is for a philosopher. Yet, let me tell you, sir, it is not
every dev—I mean it is not every gentleman, who knows how to
choose a philosopher. Long ones are *not* good ; and the best, if
not carefully shelled, are apt to be a little rancid on account of
the gall."

" Shelled ! !"

" I mean, taken out of the carcass."

" What do you think of a—hiccup !—physician ?"

" *Don't* mention them !—ugh! ugh!" (Here his Majesty retch-
ed violently.) " I never tasted but one—that rascal Hippocrates !
—smelt of asafœtida—ugh! ugh! ugh!—caught a wretched cold
washing him in the Styx—and after all he gave me the cholera
morbus."

" The—hiccup ! — wretch !" ejaculated Bon-Bon, " the—hiccup!—abortion of a pill-box !"—and the philosopher dropped a
tear.

" After all," continued the visiter, " after all, if a dev—if a gentleman wishes to *live*, he must have more talents than one or two ;
and with us a fat face is an evidence of diplomacy."

" How so?"

" Why we are sometimes exceedingly pushed for provisions. You must know that in a climate so sultry as mine, it is frequently impossible to keep a spirit alive for more than two or three hours; and after death, unless pickled immediately, (and a pickled spirit is *not* good,) they will—smell—you understand, eh? Putrefaction is always to be apprehended when the souls are consigned to us in the usual way."

" Hiccup!—hiccup!—good God! how *do* you manage?"

Here the iron lamp commenced swinging with redoubled violence, and the devil half started from his seat;—however, with a slight sigh, he recovered his composure, merely saying to our hero in a low tone, " I tell you what, Pierre Bon-Bon, we *must* have no more swearing."

The host swallowed another bumper, by way of denoting thorough comprehension and acquiescence, and the visiter continued:

" Why, there are *several* ways of managing. The most of us starve: some put up with the pickle: for my part I purchase my spirits *vivente corpore*, in which case I find they keep very well."

" But the body!—hiccup!—the body!!!"

" The body, the body—well, what of the body?—oh! ah! I perceive. Why, sir, the body is not *at all* affected by the transaction. I have made innumerable purchases of the kind in my day, and the parties never experienced any inconvenience. There were Cain and Nimrod, and Nero, and Caligula, and Dionysius, and Pisistratus, and—and a thousand others, who never knew what it was to have a soul during the latter part of their lives; yet, sir, these men adorned society. Why is n't there A——, now, whom you know as well as I? Is *he* not in possession of all his faculties, mental and corporeal? Who writes a keener epigram? Who reasons more wittily? Who——but, stay! I have his agreement in my pocket-book."

Thus saying, he produced a red leather wallet, and took from it a number of papers. Upon some of these Bon-Bon caught a glimpse of the letters *Machi*—*Maza*—*Robesp*—with the words *Caligula, George, Elizabeth.* His Majesty selected a narrow slip of parchment, and from it read aloud the following words:

"In consideration of certain mental endowments which it is unnecessary to specify, and in farther consideration of one thousand louis d'or, I, being aged one year and one month, do hereby make over to the bearer of this agreement all my right, title, and appurtenance in the shadow called my soul." (Signed) A . . . . .*
(Here his Majesty repeated a name which I do not feel myself justified in indicating more unequivocally.)

"A clever fellow that," resumed he; "but like you, Monsieu Bon-Bon, he was mistaken about the soul. The soul a shadow, truly! The soul a shadow! Ha! ha! ha!—he! he! he!—hu! hu! hu! Only think of a fricasséed shadow!"

"Only think—hiccup!—of a fricasséed shadow!" exclaimed our hero, whose faculties were becoming much illuminated by the profundity of his Majesty's discourse.

"Only think of a—hiccup!—fricasséed shadow!! Now, damme!—hiccup!—humph! If I would have been such a—hiccup!—nincompoop. My soul, Mr.—humph!"

"Your soul, Monsieur Bon-Bon!"

"Yes, sir—hiccup!—my soul is"—

"What, sir?"

"No shadow, damme!"

"Did you mean to say"—

"Yes, sir, my soul 's—hiccup!—humph!—yes, sir."

"Did not intend to assert"—

"My soul is —hiccup! —peculiarly qualified for — hiccup! —a"—

"What, sir!"

"Stew."

"Ha!"

"Soufflée."

"Eh?"

"Fricassée."

"Indeed!"

"Ragout and fricandeau—and see here, my good fellow! I'll let you have it—hiccup!—a bargain." Here the philosopher slapped his Majesty upon the back.

* Quere—Arouet!

"Couldn't think of such a thing," said the latter calmly, at the same time rising from his seat. The metaphysician stared.

"Am supplied at present," said his Majesty.

"Hic-cup!—e-h?" said the philosopher.

"Have no funds on hand."

"What?"

"Besides, very unhandsome in me"—

"Sir!"

"To take advantage of"—

"Hic-cup!"

"Your present disgusting and ungentlemanly situation."

Here the visiter bowed and withdrew—in what manner could not precisely be ascertained—but in a well-concerted effort to discharge a bottle at "the villain," the slender chain was severed that depended from the ceiling, and the metaphysician prostrated by the downfall of the lamp.

THE END.

GS
SS
SM

Lightning Source UK Ltd.
Milton Keynes UK
UKHW010649040520
362748UK00010B/535